Praise *for* THE UNCONQUERED

"Wallace's foreboding is matched by his sense of wonder."
— *New York Times Book Review*

"Rousing." — *Time*

"Startlingly novelistic." — Salon.com

"[An] engaging adventure story . . . Wallace tells the story well, embellishing it with verbal snapshots and vivid portraits of his wilderness-wise companions." — *New York Review of Books*

"What a great book! An adventure story worthy of Joseph Conrad or Peter Matthiessen." — The *Oregonian*

"It's easy to picture *The Unconquered* being made into a movie."
— *Washington Post Express*

"Astonishing. . . . a real-life adventure story that had me both longing to be there and very glad I wasn't." — The *Sunday Times* (London)

"An eye-opening read . . . one of the most gripping pieces of nonfiction around. . . . You'll swear you are reading a thriller novel." — *Guernica*

"A blessing for readers . . . fascinating." — *Associated Press*

"Rife with poachers, drug smugglers, illegal gold miners, and violent tribes already acquainted with the dangers of modern life . . . Wallace describes the trek in vivid, if unsettling, terms." — *MacLean's*

"Masterful . . . positively cinematic." — *Yale Alumni Magazine*

"While it's hard to imagine that 'stone-age' tribes still persist in a world of cell phones, satellites, and social media, it's even harder to understand how difficult it is to police these isolated regions, to keep them free of outsiders who could endanger a way of life that has nearly disappeared . . . Wallace's narrative is apt and penetrating."
– *SE Journal*

"Wallace crafts a tale that is part gripping adventure story, part window into the unexpected complexities of a developing country where uncontacted tribes stand between a resource-hungry economy and an area abounding in natural wealth." — INDIAN COUNTRY TODAY

"An absolutely wonderful and gripping account of his journey into the Amazon." — DAVID GRANN, AUTHOR OF THE LOST CITY OF Z

"A search for a wild people in a last wilderness . . . a true adventure . . . exciting and authentic—a great pleasure to read." — PETER MATTHIESSEN, AUTHOR OF NATIONAL BOOK AWARD– WINNERS SHADOW COUNTRY AND THE SNOW LEOPARD

"As riveting as one of the old explorer's memoirs, The Unconquered left me with a sense of awe that we still share this world with people like the fleicheros—and profoundly moved by the inevitability of their extinction." — JON LEE ANDERSON, AUTHOR OF CHE GUEVERA: A REVOLUTIONARY LIFE

"May be the most engrossing and profound recounting of an Amazon adventure since that long-ago masterpiece Tristes Tropiques." — FRANCISCO GOLDMAN, AUTHOR OF SAY HER NAME

"Crowded with vivid detail and heart-stopping moments . . . Will keep you up at night." — CANDICE MILLARD, AUTHOR OF THE RIVER OF DOUBT AND DESTINY OF THE REPUBLIC

"Wallace writes with great verve about his extraordinary journey into the heart of the unconquered Amazon." — PETER BERGEN, AUTHOR OF MANHUNT AND HOLY WAR, INC.

"The Unconquered ranks among the very best of modern adventure stories, even more so for the profound questions about man and nature that it explores." — SCOTT ANDERSON, AUTHOR OF TRIAGE AND THE MAN WHO TRIED TO SAVE THE WORLD

"Set in the age of the World Wide Web, The Unconquered reads like the diary of a sixteenth-century conquistador venturing with wonder, dread, and half-mad tenacity into the implacable heart of the Amazon jungle." — JOHN CARLIN, AUTHOR OF PLAYING THE ENEMY

THE UNCONQUERED

THE

IN SEARCH OF THE AMAZON'S

Broadway Paperbacks New York

UNCONQUERED

LAST UNCONTACTED TRIBES

SCOTT WALLACE

BROADWAY

Copyright © 2011, 2012 by Scott Wallace

Published in the United States by Broadway Paperbacks, an imprint of the
Crown Publishing Group, a division of Random House, Inc., New York.

www.crownpublishing.com

BROADWAY PAPERBACKS and its logo, a letter B bisected on the diagonal,
are trademarks of Random House, Inc.

Originally published in slightly different form in hardcover in the United States
by Crown Publishers, an imprint of the Crown Publishing Group,
a division of Random House, Inc., New York, in 2011.

Library of Congress Cataloging-in-Publication Data
Wallace Scott.
The unconquered : in search of the Amazon's last uncontacted tribes / Scott Wallace.
p. cm.
Includes bibliographical references.
1. Indians of South America—Amazon River Region—Social life and customs. 2. Wallace,
Scott—Travel—Amazon River Region. 3. Amazon River Region—Description and
travel. I. Title.

F2519.1.A6W35 2011
981'.1—dc22
2011006717

ISBN 978-0-307-46297-8
eISBN 978-0-307-46298-5

Printed in the United States of America

Book design by Leonard Henderson
Photograph insert © 2011 by Scott Wallace
Photograph on pp. iv–v © 2011 by Scott Wallace
Cover design by Jennifer O'Connor
Cover photograph by Arctic-Images/Workbook Stock/Getty Images

3 5 7 9 10 8 6 4

First Paperback Edition

For Mackenzie, Aaron, and Ian,

and my parents,

Robert and Flora Wallace,

who would have been proud

to hold this in their hands

Poor Aruá, he had no way of knowing that the whites were not a tribe like ours or like others that occupy a single riverbank, or two at most. He didn't know that they were the first of a whole world of people, an inexhaustible anthill, occupying the entire earth, insatiably swarming over the globe. In the following years, more and more started arriving. They continue to surround us to this day. They have already taken possession of the side of sunrise; someday they will take the forests of the sunset. Then we will be reduced to an islet in a sea of whiteness.

—From *Maíra* by Darcy Ribeiro,
translated by E. H. Goodland and Thomas Colchie

Contents

Prologue

Deep In, Far Back

W E FOUND FRESH TRACKS in the morning, foot-prints in the soggy mud, adult size 8 or 9, and no more than a few hours old. They pointed in the same direction our column was headed, deep into the farthest reaches of the Amazon jungle.

We walked single file through dense foliage and lianas thick as anacondas that dangled 150 feet from the treetops to the jungle floor. Monkeys hooted and chattered somewhere above us, their calls punc-tuated by the four-note cry of a screaming piha bird in the canopy. I followed close on the heels of Sydney Possuelo, the expedition leader. "We're probably the only ones who have ever walked here—us and the Indians," he said. By Indians, he meant not the twenty men from three different tribes who formed the core of our expeditionary force, but rather the mysterious *flecheiros,* the People of the Arrow. *Índios bravos.* Wild Indians.

A day earlier our scouts had glimpsed a pair of naked Indians near the river, called out to them, then watched as they fled across a make-shift bridge and vanished into the forest. Now, the most visible evi-dence of the panic that must have been spreading through their realm lay right here before us—not so much in the footprints themselves as in the long spaces between them, which suggested the full stride of a runner bearing urgent news.

There was no way to know exactly how the tribe would react to our presence. They had little reason to view us as anything other than a hostile, invasive army. And not unreasonably, for despite our best in-tentions, any direct contact with the Arrow People could be disastrous. The tribe had no immunity to the germs we carried. We were not doctors and carried few medicines. We, too, were in danger; there was little chance for escape in the walled-in jungle, if their curare-tipped arrows began to fly.

Yet, who among us—yes, even the purist Possuelo—didn't secretly hope for a "first contact": that moment on the cutting edge of history when complete and utter strangers from separate universes stand face-to-face, look one another in the eye, and recognize their common humanity? That was how I liked to imagine it—smiles, handshakes, an exchange of gifts—a rewriting of the epochal encounters at Roanoke or Tenochtitlán. An experience for all time, a tale to recount to wide-eyed children and grandchildren: *Come on, Grandpa, tell us about the time you met the wild Indians in the jungle!* We'd bedazzle the world with images of the Stone Age savages, appear on the *Today* show, become celebrity journalists. Maybe I'd get a book contract.

Possuelo stopped dead in his tracks. A freshly hacked sapling, dangling by a shred of bark, hung across the path before us. The makeshift gate couldn't have halted a toddler, much less our contingent of nearly three dozen well-armed men. Yet, it bore a message—and a warning—that Possuelo instantly recognized and respected. "This is universal language in the jungle," he whispered. "It means: 'Stay out. Go no farther.'"

We were getting close to their village. Any encounter would mean an abrupt and definitive end to a way of life thousands of years old, which is exactly what we were there to prevent.

We had located the inner sanctum of the Arrow People. Now it was time to back off, if it wasn't already too late.

THE UNCONQUERED

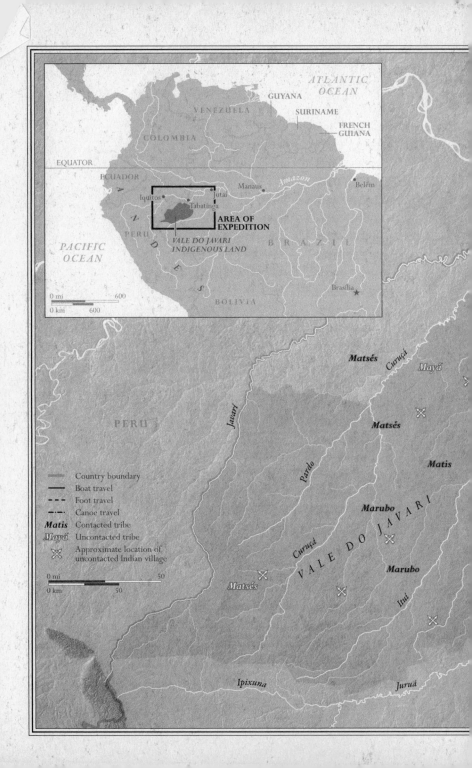

ATLANTIC OCEAN

VENEZUELA

GUYANA

SURINAME

FRENCH GUIANA

COLOMBIA

EQUATOR

ECUADOR

Manaus

Amazon

Belém

Iquitos

Jutaí

Tabatinga

AREA OF EXPEDITION

VALE DO JAVARI INDIGENOUS LAND

PACIFIC OCEAN

PERU

BRAZIL

Brasília

BOLIVIA

0 mi   600

0 km   600

Matsés

Curuçá

Mayá

PERU

Javari

Matsés

Matis

Pardo

Marubo

VALE DO JAVARI

Country boundary

Boat travel

Foot travel

Canoe travel

Matis Contacted tribe

Mayá Uncontacted tribe

Approximate location of uncontacted Indian village

0 mi   50

0 km   50

Curuçá

Matsés

Marubo

Iruí

Ipixuna

Juruá

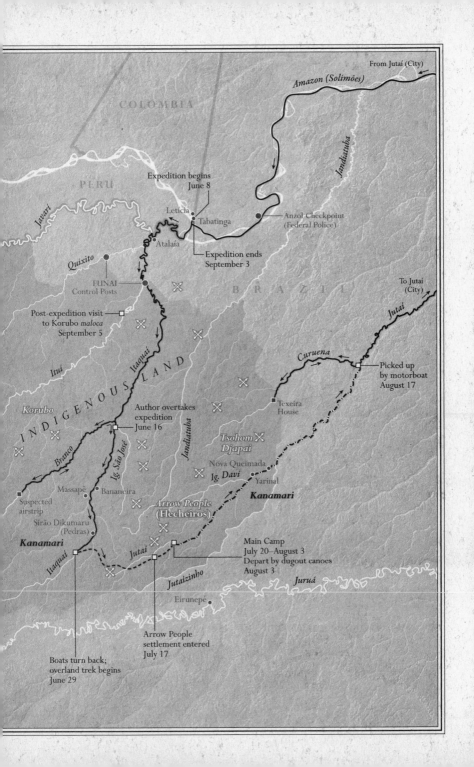

PART I

Into the Amazon

CHAPTER 1

A Rumor of Savages

THE CALL THAT LED ME from New York deep into the Amazon came one day in early June from Oliver Payne, a senior editor at *National Geographic*. I was settling into a summer sublet, a cavernous two-bedroom apartment on the ground floor of a gray granite building on the Upper West Side of Manhattan, having just returned from several months in Brazil, where I'd been reporting on environmental devastation in the Amazon. It was that idyllic time of year when winter is a dim memory and the sun glows benevolently before the blast-furnace heat of midsummer. I was looking forward to a summer to recoup—to solidify family ties and make life decisions about where I was going to sink roots after bouncing around for so many years. At forty-seven, I felt as rootless as I'd been as the newly minted college graduate who boarded a freighter bound for South America what seemed like several lifetimes ago. Since then, my career as a journalist had led me through wars and revolutions in Central America, the rise of criminal gangs in post-Soviet Russia, and most recently, the struggles of native tribes in places as far-flung as the Arctic, the Andes, and the Amazon, where indigenous people were manning the front lines against the advance of bulldozers and drill rigs that signaled the global economy's final offensive on the planet's shrinking pockets of primordial wilderness. It sounded incredibly romantic when I told people what I did for a living, especially since I usually glossed over the part about the failed marriage, the overdrawn checking account, and the guilt I felt about my three young boys, whom I didn't see nearly enough.

But this summer would be a time to reassess and make some changes. My father had just endured near-fatal open-heart surgery, and my mother was suffering from multiple ailments; it was a wonder she was still alive. I yearned for some kind of reconciliation, to tell them before it was too late that I loved them, and that I was sorry for all the things I'd done that must have broken their hearts a thousand times. I desperately wanted to see more of my boys. To do right by my ex-wife, a wonderful woman who juggled her own career and the demands of raising three sons during my long absences, but had ultimately decided she'd endured enough of my shortcomings. And then there was Sarah, in whom I'd discovered a blend of so many qualities that I admired: a quick mind and delightful laugh, a take-no-prisoners sense of humor, an utter irreverence for all pretentiousness. Our romance was passionate, but fragile. Perhaps it was time to lay aside the fleeting glories of the adventure journalist, at least for a while. Maybe it was past time to stop thinking about the next big story and to put my own tribe ahead of everyone else's.

But then there was that message from Oliver Payne. He and I had been bouncing around a story idea for *National Geographic* concerning the illegal timber trade, but when last we left off, Ollie had indicated that it still needed more work. So it was with more than mild surprise that I received his brief missive: "Scott, please call me ASAP."

His assistant put me through right away. "This isn't exactly about mahogany," Ollie began in his impeccable Oxford English, "but it may be something you'd be willing to take on." Was I familiar with a Brazilian Indian rights activist and wilderness scout named Sydney Possuelo? The magazine had decided to profile him for a forthcoming issue, and they were in need of a writer.

Sydney Possuelo was practically a household name across wide stretches of the Brazilian backwoods, a name murmured with reverence by the tribal populations he defended and with malice in equal measure by ranchers, loggers, and miners who sought to plunder the rainforest's riches. He was among the last great explorers of the Amazon, known to lose himself and his men for months at a time in its depths. "Sure," I said. "I know him."

I'd met Possuelo ten years before at the 1992 Earth Summit in Rio de Janeiro. At the time, he was president of Brazil's Indian affairs agency, the National Indian Foundation, known by its Portuguese acronym, FUNAI. He'd just presided over a monumental and herculean task: the expulsion of thousands of wildcat gold prospectors from the jungle homelands of the Yanomami, followed by the demarcation of a Maine-size reserve to protect the natives. It was the largest Indian reserve ever created in the history of Brazil, carried out despite howls of protest from powerful developers and enormous logistical challenges, the operation requiring surveyors to hack a physical boundary around the territory's entire perimeter. I couldn't dredge from memory the details of that distant conversation with Possuelo, but I did recall a hawklike beak, balding head, and thick auburn beard—and his uncanny resemblance to artistic depictions of Francisco Pizarro, the Spaniard who made South American rivers run red with Indian blood. His mission to save Brazil's Indians could not have been more diametrically opposed to Pizarro's. Yet, I recalled detecting a whiff of the same volcanic fury bubbling up through Possuelo's controlled discourse that had stirred the conquistador to sack the Incas' empire and put them to the sword.

Ollie explained that Possuelo was to lead an expedition into one of the least-explored redoubts of the Amazon, the rainforest homeland of a mysterious group known as the *flecheiros*, or "People of the Arrow," a tribe still uncontacted by the outside world. Few if any outsiders had ever traversed the heartland of the Arrow People and lived to tell the tale. Possuelo intended to. He needed to gather vital information about the tribe: the extent of its wanderings, the relative health of its communities, the abundance of game and fish in the deep forest where the people lived. Possuelo needed to demonstrate that the policies he'd fought so hard to enact were actually working, that tribes like the Arrow People were thriving in isolation and were far better off than they'd be under any scheme to integrate them into mainstream modern society. Positive results would bolster his support in the capital, Brasília, at a moment when pressure was building to roll back protection of Indian lands across the Amazon to generate jobs and profits. We'd be on the lookout for trespassers—loggers, poachers, even drug traffickers—profiteers large and small whose presence could pose a mortal threat to the tribe. Arrests were a possibility.

All of this was to be accomplished *without* making contact with the tribe. This, too, was part of Possuelo's singular vision. The Indians were to remain invisible, even to us, if things went according to plan. Possuelo had no interest in matters that anthropologists studying primitive societies care about: kinship, totems, or ethnicity. He sought "practical information"—the location of their villages, the breadth of their annual migrations—that could be gleaned from close proximity, but did not require direct contact. After all, the germs we would carry into the jungle were no more benevolent than those of any outlaw logger or poacher to immunologically defenseless Indians still as vulnerable to decimation by Western diseases as the very first natives encountered by Hernando de Soto or Jacques Cartier, early explorers of the hinterland who unwittingly spread contagion into the depths of the American continent, transforming it forever.

The chance to profile Sydney Possuelo, in itself, would not justify scuttling an entire summer resurrecting my personal life, especially the time with the boys and my parents on Lake George in the Adirondacks of upstate New York. It's a magical place where the Mohican, Algonquin, and Mohawk once prowled the woodlands and where eighteenth-century French and British colonial armies vied for global supremacy, largely at the Indians' expense. Even now, its crystalline waters and pine-shrouded slopes offer fertile terrain to arouse a child's imagination, and I looked forward to sharing that sense of wonder with my boys once more. After all, they wouldn't be kids forever. But it was impossible to miss in Ollie's offer the wider ramifications and potentially transcendent nature of the story he was proposing: the possibility of contact—and the certainty of near contact—with a tribe of indistinct origin that resisted all overtures from outsiders and still held forth in a kind of Parallel Realm in the deepest recesses of the jungle. It sounded almost too fantastical to be true, like a tale torn from the pages of Robert Louis Stevenson or H. Rider Haggard, harking back to a time when broad sweeps of the map remained uncharted and the world's tropical midsection teemed with "lost" indigenes awaiting discovery. Yet, if Ollie's words were to be believed, this was no extinct tribe that lived on only in history books or childhood fantasies. This was history unfolding in the present, in the now, no time travel—other than metaphorical—required.

As a journalist with extensive experience in the Amazon, I'd investigated allegations of malfeasance perpetrated by Western scientists among "Stone Age" Yanomami tribesmen in the Venezuelan jungle. I had uncovered evidence of a conspiracy to frame Kayapó chief and ecological crusader Paulinho Paiakan on charges of raping a non-Indian teenager—charges that effectively destroyed his image and inflicted lasting damage on the international movement to save the rainforest. I'd covered the simmering land war in central Brazil that pitted destitute squatters against powerful cliques of ranchers and timber bosses who maintained their grip through a system of threats and bribes and who dispatched their own brand of frontier justice, more often than not, through the barrel of a gun. Still the Amazon beckoned.

There was something about its towering forests, the silent sweep of its untamed rivers, the shrill cries and smoky fires announcing the approach to a native village, that seemed to awaken a dim sense of raw, primal existence, unfiltered by the trappings of "civilization" and the palisades it erects deep within us to suppress nature and wall off its wildest manifestations. Or so it was tempting to think. I was the product of New England's enlightened liberal academies during the waning years of the Vietnam War, when questioning authority emerged as the central paradigm in just about every field of inquiry. I'd studied philosophy at Yale, and on a year off in the mid-1970s, I'd worked as a literary instructor among Asháninka- and Quechua-speaking Indians in the Peruvian jungle, my first encounter with the utter strangeness of the Amazon. I went on to become a journalist covering the turmoil in Central America during the 1980s, and in later years I had come to be seen as something of an expert among magazine editors when it came to matters pertaining to the Amazon and its indigenous cultures. I was thus more inclined than most of my compatriots to embrace alternative viewpoints on questions surrounding aboriginal societies and their abysmal treatment at the hands of our forebears. Steeped in American pop culture from infancy, I was in many ways a product of the media I'd consumed. I'd played cowboys and Indians as a boy, and I'd watched *The Lone Ranger* and *Hopalong Cassidy*, only to have those early formulations challenged in later years by *Bury My Heart at Wounded Knee* and *Little Big Man*. Did that make me a citizen any more willing or able to right the injustices of the world, or simply a more avid consumer of mass-media portrayals of exotic cultures, having swapped the cultural clichés of one generation for those of the next?

But when it came to the prospect of venturing into the farthest reaches of the rainforest to write about uncontacted tribes, I felt as though I were teetering on the edge of a vast terra incognita, in both a literal and figurative sense, in everything from what kind of gear I should pack to what I should think about primitive tribes yet to be seen by the outside world. In the absence of visible signposts, it was tempting to fall back on some of the most deep-seated myths handed down through centuries of Western thought about the dark, dangerous forest and the presumed technological, if not moral, inferiority of such tribal polities. I was a purveyor of news and information traded to a public that spanned the globe, and it was perhaps impossible not to share with my editors and readers some presumption of our society's position at the pinnacle of human development, and perhaps even a twisted sense of voyeuristic titillation at the prospect of peeling back the rainforest to lay bare this tribe's crude and primitive existence for all the world to see. From the moment Columbus first splashed ashore in the Caribbean, Europeans perceived in America's naked aboriginals what they presumed to be a window into deep history. Whether we beheld a Noble Savage in that mirror or a beastly one, we still pictured the Indian to be inhabiting a place on the evolutionary scale we'd left behind aeons ago.

For nearly five hundred years, the Amazon has held a singular place in the Western imagination, at once fantastic and horrifying, an untouched Garden of Eden and an unmitigated Green Hell, a boundless wilderness where sojourners lose their way and lose their minds. For those of us raised in the temperate latitudes, it remains an alien land that crawls with strange, menacing life forms and harbors cultures of shocking habits, as radically distinct from our own as any on the planet.

Yet, as home to the largest tropical rainforest on Earth, the Amazon Basin was gaining recognition as one of the planet's critical battlegrounds in the fight to curb environmental devastation. Scientists were just beginning to unlock the secrets of its stabilizing influence on the global climate and to ponder the beguiling diversity of life forms sequestered in its forests, a differentiation of species unequaled anywhere, fed by rushing tributaries so wide they fenced off separate ecosystems, further fueling the frenzied speciation. At the same time, indigenous communities were just starting to be understood as key players in that larger equation. On satellite images never before available from outer space, their lands could be seen holding back a rising tide of rainforest destruction, and ethnobotanists were heralding the natives' prowess as knowledge keepers who had discovered the medicinal properties of hundreds of trees, plants, and lianas, and had safeguarded this vast repository, together with its potential for curing some of modern society's most vexing illnesses. At a glance, I could see how this story might yield important insights into that vortex of interlocking issues. The expedition would explore the depths of the enormous Javari Valley Indigenous Land, whose recent designation placed it off-limits to profit-taking enterprises, such as logging and gold prospecting, making the region a flash point of rising tension. It was an area fast on the border of Peru that neither Spaniards descending the Andes nor Portuguese sailing up the Amazon's maze of waterways had managed to subdue. Not even the Inca, whose last rulers vanished down its forested slopes, were able to conquer this land of permanent darkness they called the Antisuyu, the Eastern Quarter, with its implacable tribes and their deadly arrows. The Javari itself remained just beyond their farthest reach.

There was also the matter of the historical parallels between our own westward expansion and the present-day frontier advancing through the Amazon: land-hungry settlers looking to improve their lot, gold prospectors chasing dreams of grandeur, robber barons muscling in on the action, Indians clinging to age-old traditions in the face of an inexorable onslaught of strangers from afar, all playing out against the backdrop of a seemingly boundless wilderness. Except it turned out to be not so boundless after all. Within one hundred years of the establishment of the Jamestown colony in 1607, settlers were well on the way to eliminating the ancient eastern woodlands of North America in what was to become the largest and most rapid deforestation in human history, until the current industrial-scale assault on the world's tropical rainforests.

Nearly a century had now passed since Ishi, the last of the Yahi Indians, surrendered to a sheriff in central California, after forty-five years on the run from the cattlemen who had slaughtered his tribe. Ishi's appearance in 1911 electrified the country; "wild" Indians were presumed to have vanished from the West decades before, all either dead or corralled on reservations. Perhaps a similar shock awaited the present-day world. Even I, the so-called expert, had been unaware that uncontacted tribes still persisted in the Amazon, beyond the reach of modern society. I'd been in isolated tribal villages, but my very presence there presumed a certain level of previous contact. I knew Possuelo had been working with isolated tribes, but *uncontacted* tribes—that was news to me. That such indigenous communities continued to hold out in remote corners of the jungle, resisting all efforts to subdue them or even approach them, seemed to offer a chance to replay history, maybe even get it right this time.

At first glance, I figured my backcountry experiences would serve as adequate preparation for such a journey. But when I did a quick inventory of my earlier forays into the rainforest, a disquieting realization emerged: as deep into the forest as I might have ventured, I'd never actually been more than a few days' walk from the edge of a road, an airstrip, or a riverbank with a boat awaiting that could whisk me back to an Indian settlement by nightfall. Even embedded with troops in the deepest jungles of Central America, I was still with men linked by radio to a chain of command that could summon helicopters in a matter of hours to lift us out, drop us in, move us around the battlefield. This expedition would be far different, with Possuelo leading his team into a trackless wilderness. Scant would be the opportunities to communicate with the outside world.

It was both tempting and daunting. I'd be turning forty-eight somewhere out in the jungle. I'd let myself go to seed a bit in more recent years. I worked out daily, but at five feet eleven inches and weighing 205 pounds, I wondered about my capacity to endure months of deprivation in the wild. There would be all the dangers presented by the Amazon's highly refined repertoire of lethal creatures large and small, from man-eating jaguars to well-incubated microbes. Then there was the very real potential for attack by the tribesmen on whose land we trespassed. The journey promised to be especially arduous, for the planned route would take us far deeper into the jungle than most of Possuelo's expeditions, exposing the team to exceptional levels of privation and peril.

Perhaps even more disconcerting was the ridiculously short notice. Such a venture would normally require weeks, if not months, of preparation, but Ollie noted ruefully that I'd have to "get on it right away." In fact, I would have five days to get to Tabatinga, a sweltering outpost where the borders of Brazil, Peru, and Colombia converged. "The expedition's departure is imminent," Ollie informed me, no small measure of urgency in his voice. My life would be thrown into total disarray. I'd have to bail on the sublet and the rest of my summer plans. The fragile relationship on which I'd pinned hopes of future nappiness might not endure another long separation. And my boys—I wouldn't even have the chance to see them to say good-bye.

Yet, the journey offered an opportunity for exploration and adventure that had all but vanished from our planet by the dawn of the third millennium. It was, in fact, the chance of a lifetime.

CHAPTER 2

Scramble to the Amazon

I WAS JARRED AWAKE by an incessant pounding on the door. "Scott, Scott? Are you in there?" a baritone voice boomed from the hallway. I bolted upright. The room was dark, just a trace of light leaking from the edges of heavy curtains that extended from ceiling to floor. I looked over at the clock on the nightstand: 7:00 a.m.

Now it was coming back to me: the long succession of flights that culminated with the Varig Airbus that brought me from Caracas in over Manaus at two in the morning. The utter blackness outside as I pressed my nose to the cold window, the plane banking over the vast river. Then the bright beacons winking in the darkness that marked the Punta Negra, the prominent point on the north bank where the Rio Negro joined the Solimões to become the Amazon. Then came the geometric grid of the city's streets traced by the pale orange glow of the vapor lamps rising up to meet us, and the final jolt as our wheels hit the runway. It was well after 3 a.m. by the time the cab had wound its way past the crumbling pastel walls of seedy juke joints and tire-repair shops and pulled up in front of the Da Vinci, a glass-and-chrome boutique hotel on the outskirts of town that I'd made my home for two months earlier in the year. *"Ah, Senhor Wallace! Qué prazer!"* chimed the night clerk. "Great to have you with us again!" Rancid and fatigued, I left word before turning in: hold all calls until 9 a.m.

Evidently Nicolas Reynard had not gotten the message, or he'd chosen to ignore it. "So, are you ready to go?" He swept into the room like a storm trooper, a towering presence at six foot three. I closed the r behind him and scrambled to wrap a towel around my waist. His gray eyes looked down at me as if from a watchtower, through a pair of wire-rimmed glasses. He was in his mid-forties, I guessed, and his graying hair was clipped pageboy-style, with bangs and faux sideburns. It looked like a ten-buck hack job by an old-school barber. His face was thin, tapering to a long chin, squared off at the bottom, like the bucket of a small steam shovel. He sported the latest safari wear, as though he'd just stepped out of a Banana Republic catalog: quick-drying khaki shirt, cargo-style shorts, Teva sandals. "We should get going," he said, with a French accent that might have been pleasing to the ears if he were chatting to me in a Parisian sidewalk café rather than yanking open my curtains to flood my Brazilian hotel room with blinding light. "The plane leaves for Tabatinga at one, and we need to do a lot of things before."

"When did you get here?" I asked, my eyes still adjusting to the blast of tropical morning sunshine.

"Yesterday afternoon, on the flight from Miami. I left Paris two days ago." There was a certain *je ne sais quoi* about Nicolas, a blend of the self-satisfied and the gung ho that instantly aroused my suspicion. "Did you bring the money?" he asked.

"Yeah, here," I said, fumbling through my bag to find the envelope. Without a bank account of my own in New York, I'd had the *Geographic* wire our expense money—thousands of dollars in cash—through Sarah's account. It was one of the countless errands I'd run in the frantic days that followed the call from Ollie Payne. "So, you're French but you've lived in the States?" I ventured, picking up on the scant information Ollie had shared.

"My father is French, my mother American. We lived in New York together until I was eighteen. Then my parents got divorced, and I moved with my mother to Paris. I've lived in France ever since." He sat down on the bed, counting the brick of C-notes. "We looked you up on the Internet," he said. "Couldn't find very much."

I let the remark slide. His father had been a painter, Nicolas said, but since childhood he had pushed himself in another direction: to

be a photographer for *National Geographic.* Like me, he'd been nibbling around the edges, taking similar sorts of assignments with other
publications, rapping on the door, hoping to get noticed. It had finally opened, for both of us, at the same time. An odd coincidence. I
ducked into the bathroom.

"So, have you met Sydney?" Nicolas asked, shouting to be heard
above the rush of tap water. He pronounced it as though the *e* were an
a: "Syd-nay."

Sydney Possuelo was, of course, the reason we were both in Manaus.
He had come up through the ranks. He'd chosen to forgo university
studies as a young man for a life of adventure in the Brazilian jungles,
apprenticing himself in the late 1950s to Orlando and Claudio Villas
Boas, brothers who had acquired a reputation for fearless exploration
and ardent defense of the Indian tribes they encountered and pacified. Possuelo went on to pioneer Brazil's "no-contact" policy in the
late 1980s, when he pushed for the creation of the curiously named
Department of Isolated Indians, an elite unit within FUNAI. Both the
policy and the department represented a monumental shift in Brazil's
treatment of its *índios bravos*—"wild Indians." Since the late nineteenth
century, the succession of government scouts that preceded Possuelo
had been *agents of contact.* Known as *sertanistas,* they ventured deep
into the hinterlands and wooed Indians from the forest with gifts and
friendship. The idea was to assimilate the natives and move them out
of the way of the advancing frontier, to cushion the inevitable blow of
civilization's arrival.

The men (for they were almost always men) drawn to such difficult and dangerous work were idealistic adventurers, and they often
watched helplessly as Indians succumbed to disease, death, and despair
in the wake of the contact they initiated. In a very public resignation,
one *sertanista* lambasted the work of the agency, lamenting his role as a
"grave-digger of Indians." Having seen that same script repeatedly play
itself out with infuriating predictability, Possuelo experienced his own
change of heart in midcareer. But rather than resigning, he led a successful movement within FUNAI that advocated *avoiding* contact with

increasingly besieged isolated tribes. It was a tectonic change, ~~perhaps~~ the single greatest achievement in Possuelo's long and distinguished career. Starting in 1987 with Possuelo in charge, the newly created Isolated Indians unit investigated reports of fresh sightings of uncontacted Indians and took action to protect them. Measures included the creation of exclusion zones, known as Terras Indigenas, legally off-limits to outsiders, in those places where scouts confirmed the presence of such groups.

Once an Indigenous Land was established to protect an isolated tribe, Possuelo's unit would continue to monitor the group from a distance, often using aerial reconnaissance to check on their settlements of thatched huts, called *malocas*. These flyovers provided rudimentary information, such as rough population counts, based on the size and number of houses in a clearing. But the closed-canopy jungle yields precious few of its secrets from the air. Only an arduous trek of the sort Possuelo envisioned could produce the kind of information he sought. He was especially concerned about infiltration along the remote perimeters of the lands he was assigned to protect, and he saw the forthcoming expedition as a way of showing the flag, asserting government authority, and his own, over a vast region that was largely unknown to everyone other than the tribal people who lived there.

"Yeah, I met him a long time ago," I said, stuffing my toiletries into their ziplock bags. "But I don't know him the way you do." Nicolas looked up from the stack of bills with a wolfish grin. I'd said it to give him his due, but it was true. He had traveled with Possuelo before. They'd become close friends and stayed in regular touch, which is how he'd caught wind of the forthcoming expedition and convinced the *Geographic* to cover it.

"What do you think of him?" asked Nicolas. I sensed he was feeling me out, perhaps trying to gauge loyalties. Since that night ten years before at the Earth Summit in Rio de Janeiro, I'd followed Possuelo's career from afar, in occasional headlines, as he presided over FUNAI and resumed his role as head of the Isolated Indians Department. He'd gained renown over the years as a monomaniacal zealot who went to the ends of the Earth for Brazil's Indians and pursued his goals with frightening single-mindedness. Detractors within FUNAI called him a dictator—*o rei de tudo,* "the king of everything," as one put it. "A cross between Jesus Christ and Che Guevara," said another. In short, you either loved him or you hated him; there was no middle ground. Like Nicolas, I came down in the first camp, at least insofar as his policies were concerned. On a personal level, I had no way of knowing, not yet.

"Amazing guy," I said. "I'm looking forward to spending this time with him." I'd heard about Possuelo's adventures, and I'd long hoped, somewhere in the back of my mind, that I might get a chance to join one of his expeditions. That said, I really hadn't thought about what it would be like to spend months in the backwoods under the command of a man of such uncompromising repute, who had so brazenly shrugged off threats on his life and had engineered a sea change in the way Brazil dealt with its aboriginal peoples.

"I wouldn't want to get on his bad side," I said, laughing, with a quick snort. I crammed a bunch of dirty laundry into my backpack and laced it closed.

Expeditions like the one we'd be joining were not an everyday occurrence; owing to the sensitive nature of the mission and the extreme conditions that prevailed, journalists were usually barred from participating. Part of it was also a process of self-selection: who in his right mind would head off for months at a time into remote and inhospitable wilderness fraught with risk? The Indians were said to inhabit a rugged headwaters region within the Javari Valley Indigenous Land, an enormous wilderness reserve that harbored, I'd discovered in the quick research I'd done in the past few days, the largest concentration of uncontacted tribes anywhere on the face of the Earth.

Little was known about the *flecheiros,* other than their reputation as deft archers disposed to unleash poison-tipped darts against all intruders before melting back into the forest. Hence their name, the Arrow People, which was actually a contrivance pinned on them by others, like the Blackfoot or the Crow. Since there had never been peaceful contact, not even Possuelo knew what they actually called themselves.

Getting to and from their homeland would not be easy. The expedition would travel by boat up a tributary of a tributary of the Amazon called the Itaquaí River. Somewhere far up the Itaquaí, we'd leave the boats behind and commence what was bound to be a grueling overland trek through the jungles of the Arrow People, crossing into an adjacent watershed in the process. If we made it safely to the far side of their land, we'd eventually stop on the banks of another river, the Jandiatuba or the Jutaí, carve canoes from trees, and paddle downstream with the current for several weeks back to civilization.

Possuelo's expedition boats had already departed from the Amazonian port city of Tabatinga, six hundred miles west of Manaus. Nicolas and I would fly there and provision ourselves in the local markets before hopping a fast boat that Possuelo had left behind for us to catch up.

We made our way through the lobby and out to the street. It was only nine in the morning, but the heat was searing, the air heavy with moisture. "Oh, by the way, I need to buy some boots," I said as we climbed into a taxi. In the whirlwind that ensued following my acceptance of the assignment, I'd forgotten to pick up new boots back in the States, a glaring oversight that I was loath to disclose to Nicolas at this early stage in our acquaintance. But I had no choice. We'd be trekking hundreds of miles across rugged hills and pestilent swampland, and apart from my prescription glasses and maybe a good jungle hammock with built-in mosquito netting, there was no item more essential to survival.

"You don't keep a checklist?" I heard the thinly veiled reproach. Just as well he didn't know about how I'd left my cell phone in a New York cab right before the big conference call with *Geographic* execs to discuss, among other things, the expensive satellite phone they were placing in my care to take along on the journey. I'd had to call in to the conference rather than having them dial me in, inventing some elaborate excuse for the last-minute change.

We dashed into an army surplus shop while the driver waited at the curb. Even with the air-conditioning churning the soupy air full blast, there was no mistaking the scent of stale cardboard and mildewed can-vas, the hallmark of army-navy stores everywhere. "What about these?" Nicolas asked with an air of impatience, holding up a pair of shiny black leather lace-ups, standard Brazilian army issue. They were stiff as boards. I shoved my orthotic inserts in and tried them on. The beefy clerk, with bulbous nose and well-oiled hair, must have seen me wince. "They'll loosen up," he said with all the calming effect of a used-car salesman. "One week, two weeks, and no problem."

I was willing to bet the guy hadn't set a single toe in the jungle in all his fifty years. I tried on a pair of cloth jungle boots, but they didn't seem substantial enough to endure the anticipated rigors, so I settled on the leather boots, praying they'd stretch out. We grabbed a few more things—a machete and a buck knife each—and bolted back out into the liquid heat of midmorning.

"So what do you think of Sydney's no-contact policy?" Nicolas asked as the cab pulled out into traffic.

"Hard to argue with it," I said. "Unless you're a logger or a gold prospector."

Though not explicitly articulated at the time, Possuelo's new policy had the immediate effect of sequestering millions of acres of the most species-rich, biodiverse lands on the planet, placing them, at least the-oretically, beyond the reach of those looking to exploit their riches. The survival of isolated tribes depended, after all, on intact forests that could provide the Indians with all their necessities: food, water, shel-ter, security. As the policy's chief architect and enforcer, Possuelo was widely reviled in boomtowns across the Amazonian frontier, where the demarcation of indigenous lands had silenced sawmills, grounded in-dustrial fishing fleets, and shuttered the shops where gold bullion was bought and sold.

"Actually, there are a lot of missionaries who don't like Sydney very much either," said Nicolas as we pulled up in front of the airport. "And anthropologists. The missionaries don't get to save souls, and anthro-pologists don't get to study the strange habits of Stone Age tribes."

I took a window seat for the two-hour flight to Tabatinga. I always found it a treat to cross high over the Amazon during daylight hours, looking down through brilliant clouds at the quilt-work of light and shadow they cast on the bluish green jungle canopy far below. I'd watch the brown rivers snaking their way lazily through the forests, and wonder how they acquired the force to flow in a single direction, so expansive were the flatlands they traversed. It was easy to think of the wilds below as empty and uninhabited, save for the Amazon's staggering array of birds, beasts, and fish. But somewhere down there, primitive tribes stalked the woodlands, pursuing a way of life unchanged for hundreds, if not thousands, of years. Viewed from this safe distance, through double-paned glass and the climate-controlled comfort of the aircraft's cabin, the jungle seemed about as real as if I were watching it on television. Soon enough, we'd be down in the midst of it.

Nicolas had the aisle seat, his long legs sprawled out into the corridor, his face buried in a newspaper. "Listen to this!" he said suddenly, his face popping up over the opened pages. "'It's been eighteen years since FUNAI launched a major expedition in search of isolated Indians.' It's an article about the expedition! Then it goes on: 'In the Vale do Javari, there are at least six indigenous groups whose ethnicity and language are unknown. The area is legally protected, but loggers, miners and fishermen are taking resources, and drug trafficking routes cross the land.'" Nicolas flung down the paper.

"Can you imagine?" he stammered. "The article says there may be as many as forty-three groups in Brazil that don't have contact with the outside world. And what's the global population—six billion? One person stands between those six billion and the forty or so groups of uncontacted Indians. That one person is Sydney Possuelo!" He laughed, as if to say: *What could possibly be more important than this story? Where else could you possibly want to be, but on your way to cover it?* Though I hadn't warmed much to his style, he was right; it was going to be a remarkable adventure.

My thoughts shifted ahead to what life would be like—day in, day out—in the jungle. As we dropped through the clouds on our approach to Tabatinga, I suddenly realized that I'd failed to anticipate the need for some kind of pillow. A rolled-up shirt wedged beneath my head might work for a few nights, but not for entire months. I did a quick scan of the cabin. With no flight attendant in sight, I hastily stuffed the small airline pillow into my knapsack.

A middle-aged man with wiry hair, warm green eyes, and a firm handshake greeted us just outside the baggage claim area at the Tabatinga airport, an uninspired cement-block structure with buffed tiled floors and a men's room that reeked of piss and mothballs. The man's name was Siqueira, and he handled logistics for FUNAI's Tabatinga office. We filled the flatbed of the silver late-model Toyota with our stuff and climbed up after it. I'd managed to fit everything in three bags, including my trusty old backpack and a waterproof river bag. Nicolas seemed to be hauling just about everything he owned: two Pelican hard cases, three oversize waterproof duffels, a mammoth backpack, camera bags, a briefcase.

"Take us to the Anaconda in Leticia!" Nicolas shouted down into the cab window. Siqueira ground the gears and we lurched out into the dusty streets, holding tight on to the chrome roll bar. I loved the sensation of riding in the back of the open-air pickup truck, the wind rushing in my ears, drying the sweat on my brow, my knees slightly bent to absorb the shocks as we careened through a minefield of potholes. It was one of those simple pleasures of Third World living denied us in the litigious North, where spilling a cup of hot coffee could trigger an avalanche of court proceedings.

The dirt thoroughfare was crammed with bicyclists, pedestrians, porters pushing rickety carts with wooden wheels overloaded with bananas and pineapples, and vendors hawking wares of every description. The Amazon itself was several hundred yards off to the left, its waters lost from view behind shabby, wilted homes and shops interspersed among broad-leafed tropical trees. We passed an unmanned concrete blockhouse by the side of the road that marked the border with Colombia, the only evidence that we'd actually crossed an

international boundary. Evidently authorities thought it a wasted effort
to monitor land traffic between Leticia and Tabatinga. After all, there
were no roads of any significance into the interior of either country.
All travelers venturing beyond the border region would have to go
by boat or plane, which would presumably come under police scrutiny. But there were myriad ways to dodge the cops, whether through
stealth or the application of overwhelming force.

On the other side of the border, Leticia's clean-swept streets
teemed with purring motor scooters. Gleaming office buildings shot
up along the boulevards, a stark contrast to the run-down, unpaved un-
ruliness of Tabatinga. Narco-dollars, most likely. Bellmen in brocaded
coats offloaded our baggage beneath the marquee at the Anaconda,
an air-conditioned high-rise hotel with burbling fountains in the lobby.
"Let's meet down here in ten minutes, and we'll do our shopping,"
said Nicolas, pushing his glasses back up onto the bridge of his nose.
He vanished into the elevator with his bellman.

Soon after, we raced through the sweltering market stalls along the
banks of the muddy Amazon, snatching up bars of soap, fishhooks,
tackle, Bic lighters—anything that might be of use in the deep jungle. Bundles piled high on our shoulders, we were an easy mark for
shopkeepers, who beckoned with expansive waves and eager smiles.
"Something more for you, my friends? Where you from—Germany,
Italy, Spain?" At one establishment dedicated exclusively to the sale of
all things toxic—house paint, weed killer, turpentine—Nicolas swept
up an entire case of Repellex bug juice in pump-spray bottles.

"A whole case?" I asked.

"Everyone will want to use it. The insects are fierce out there!"

We bought shiny souvenir machetes with rawhide-fringed sheaths
for my kids. "These are great," Nicolas said, drawing one from its
leather scabbard. "Your boys will love them." I wasn't so sure, but they
weren't expensive. I took three.

The sky was already streaked with the first traces of morning light
when we checked out of the Anaconda the next morning. We loaded

our gear, along with two dozen boxes of supplies we'd bought on our shopping spree, into the pickup for the ride back through Leticia's manicured boulevards, back across the border to Tabatinga's warren of muddy backstreets, which led to the riverbank, where FUNAI's clapboard boathouse bobbed on giant balsawood floats.

Wishing us luck and crossing himself, Siqueira drove off with a screech of grinding gears and popping backfire. We picked our way gingerly down a steep, rain-slick stairway with the first of the heavy boxes. One at a time, Nicolas and I crossed a long, narrow plank that led across open water to the boathouse. As I bounced precariously to the plank's camber, I had the sense of crossing a threshold, the first of an infinite number that would eventually lead us into the depths of the wild.

A stocky man with an impish grin and close-cropped hair greeted us at the entrance with a vise grip of a handshake. Francisco wore a freshly laundered polo shirt, and a ball cap with a steeply rounded bill was pulled down tight above his eyes. Under his direction, we loaded everything into a twenty-foot boat powered by a Yamaha-85 outboard. Cushioned seats formed a long V leading back from bow to cockpit, where Francisco positioned himself behind the windshield. I stood next to him, and Nicolas stretched out in the bow as we backed out of the boathouse and entered the river. Up on the bank, a boy drove a goat through the trees. Someone shouted. A car horn honked. Francisco hit the throttle, and we plowed out into the mighty river, driven sideways by the current. Within minutes, Tabatinga was no more than an ill-defined, ashen scar spread along the green shoreline, rapidly receding from view at the edge of a vast sheet of water whose reflection mirrored back an enormous sky, mottled here and there with darkening clouds.

The main course of the Amazon River is called the Solimões along the six-hundred-mile stretch from Peru to Manaus. Soon we were cutting through it along a series of shortcuts, called *furos,* created by the seasonal floods. High walls of elephant grass whizzed past close on our flanks. A month from now, these channels would be dry land, but for now they shaved hours off travel time, cutting straight lines across the river's serpentine twists and turns. There was a drawback: the high grass and half-submerged trees provided perfect cover for would-be assailants. Navigating through them was a high-risk game. "Lots of bandits here!" shouted Francisco over the roar of the engine. From beneath the peaked visor of his cap, his sharp eyes darted warily from one side of the channel to the other. A week earlier, he said, gunmen had assaulted a family in the *furos*. The victims were returning from a fishing trip and lost everything to the *banditos*—their outboard motor, nets, clothing, their entire catch. They'd left the family bound and stripped naked in the bulrushes, where a passing boat found them as night closed in and the caimans began to stir.

"The guys spoke Spanish," Francisco said, arching an eyebrow with a conspiratorial air. "Colombians, for sure." That would have been the logical explanation, though not necessarily the correct one. A U.S.-financed offensive by the Colombian army was flushing leftist guerrillas and coca growers ever closer to the border region. Outlaws of all description were finding their way to the thinly patrolled "White Triangle," where the borders of Brazil, Peru, and Colombia converge. Brazilians were said to be getting in on the action as well, sometimes confounding witnesses by speaking Spanish in the commission of their crimes. The money was too good to pass up; the chance of prosecution, next to none. Local police were reluctant to investigate, but agents were said to be more inclined to take action after hours, for a hefty cut from victims seeking recompense and retribution.

I stood beside Francisco, the visor of my own cap pulled down tight against the wind, scanning for blind spots in the high grass. Between us, we had no more than the pair of machetes and knives we'd bought in Manaus, hardly a match for the AKs, AR-15s, and rocket launchers that seemed to be turning up with alarming frequency on the Upper Amazon. Nicolas slouched at the bow, the audio buds of my Walkman stuffed in his ears. He'd occasionally pull his camera from a pouch and point it toward shore, reeling off a series of shots. *Whirrr, click. Whirrr, click.* The other cameras, I guessed, were stowed away in one of his large Pelican cases.

Francisco gunned the engine as we broke free from the confined channels and entered the Javari, whose northward-flowing waters form much of the long, arch-shaped border between Brazil and Peru. We'd left the main branch of the Amazon behind. For the next hour or so, we passed through a series of intermittent showers, just enough to get a light dousing, punctuated by bursts of brilliant sunshine.

"Sydney chose this time of year, just at the end of the rainy season, to launch the expedition," Nicolas hollered from the bow. "The water is still high enough to get a long ways upriver in the boats, but it will be going down by the time we start hiking over land."

Francisco nodded. "The rains are much less frequent now. Winter is over." There are two seasons in the Amazon: the dry season, which people call "summer," even though it's technically winter in the Southern Hemisphere; and the rainy season, running from December to June, called "winter." Francisco cut the wheel hard to avoid a log floating in the current. It was exhilarating to be cruising all-out on the broad, watery sheet of the Javari, easy to forget the piranhas, electric eels, and stingrays that teemed beneath the surface.

Francisco throttled past a collection of rickety one-room shacks perched over the water on crooked stilts. "Contrabando!" Nicolas called out, pointing toward the shacks. It wasn't an accusation; it was actually the name of the place. "Can you believe it—a border town named *Contraband?*" Ladders dropped from doorways straight to the water, where dugout canoes bobbed in the current, outboard engines cocked in their sterns. Railed walkways and lines hung with colorful, freshly scrubbed clothes stretched between the houses. You could see straight through the open doorways and out the back of the stilted structures, but not a soul stirred as we passed. The locals had evidently chosen to make themselves scarce, probably suspecting the Yamaha's blare heralded an unwelcome visit from the authorities. In the diffuse light of late morning, with its weather-beaten pastel planks and the bright laundry rippling in the slight breeze, Contrabando offered a picturesque tableau that imparted a certain tattered appeal to the smuggler's life.

We soon cut to port and entered the mouth of the Itaquaí River. Along the inside of every bend rose a high white beach—vestiges from a distant era when the entire western Amazon was a vast inland sea that drained to the Pacific. The Andes rose up in a massive collision of tectonic plates some ten million to twelve million years ago, reversing the flow of the water, toward the Atlantic, and creating what biologists call a "species pump" of spectacularly differentiated biodiversity in microhabitats all along the mountain range's eastern rim, which plummets to the Amazon. The ancient sea and the relentless erosion from water cascading off the new mountains left behind sandy riverbanks, clay soils, and a near-total absence of surface rock—a geological oddity that has shaped in infinite ways the indigenous cultures that later arose along the jungle's waterways, confounding archaeologists in their attempts to reconstruct the cultural history of pre-Columbian western Amazonia. With little stone at their disposal for tools or building, the societies of the Upper Amazon have left scant evidence for the archaeological record. Even among isolated tribes today, arrow points— deadly as they may be—are fashioned from degradable bamboo.

Caimans as long as torpedoes slid from the beaches into the honey-colored shallows. One refused to budge as we passed, staring at us in perfect Lacoste-like repose, forepaws splayed in the sand, tail curled back, mouth agape in a hideous grin. The sun broke through the clouds and cast a strong yellow glow on the riverbank, turning the bark of the *imbauba* trees a pulsing white against the towering green wall of the jungle. Rounding a bend in the late afternoon, where the Itaquaí was joined from the west by the Ituí River, we approached a large complex of catwalk-linked buildings set on stilts atop a manicured hilltop, as unlikely a scene in the midst of the jungle as one could imagine. From a distance, the gleaming white compound could have been mistaken for the bucolic headquarters of a small pharmaceutical company in Delaware. This was, in fact, the FUNAI control post that commanded entry to the Terra Indigena Vale do Javari. Had we been travelers out on a casual cruise, this would have been the end of the line, beyond which we would not be allowed to pass. As it was, we were just at the beginning, the gateway to one of the largest tracts of unbroken tropical rainforest in the world.

CHAPTER 3

Through the Chokepoint

W E PULLED UP TO A FLOATING, two-story boat-house set on giant trunks of balsawood, where a small army of wiry young men dressed in ill-fitting T-shirts and Nike shorts greeted us on the landing. Their faces were streaked with tattooed lines, dowels pierced their noses, and mollusk shells sprouted from their earlobes like miniature saucers. *"Burrá?"* Nicolas called out to them. "They're Matis," he said of the Indians, turning back to me. The tribe's name was pronounced like the artist: Matisse. *"Burrá* is the basic greeting in Matis," Nicolas continued. "It means 'good,' but they use it for a lot of things." The Matis are one of at least five Panoan-speaking tribes in the Javari, first contacted by a FUNAI team in 1976. They still live in a pair of remote villages along the Ituí River, deep within the protected area, and despite the deadly epidemics that brought a monumental shift to their way of life in the wake of contact, they retain many of their traditions, including the elaborate facial ornamentation I was now trying to take in discreetly, doing my best not to stare.

A number of Matis had been with Nicolas six years earlier, on the expedition Possuelo had led to make contact with a splinter group of Korubo Indians. Like Lewis and Clark, and even earlier explorers of the New World, Possuelo and his Brazilian predecessors invariably recruited indigenous scouts such as the Matis to accompany their jungle sojourns. The Indians made skilled woodsmen and trackers, indefatigable porters and hunters. They could endure extreme hardship without complaint. And in case of possible contact with "wild Indians," their languages might bear sufficient resemblance to that of the isolated group to be understood. In rare instances, the isolated tribe might even be distant or long-lost relatives of the scouts, their families having scattered in separate directions generations before, when white intruders arrived in the backwoods and upended their world. On a FUNAI expedition such as the one we were about to undertake, such long-dormant ties, even just a series of mutually intelligible words, could mean the difference between peaceful contact and disaster.

The wooing of the Korubo splinter group was the last officially recorded "first contact" in Brazil, and the Matis had been instrumental interlocutors in that encounter. The entire Korubo tribe, believed to number roughly 220, relied exclusively on heavy clubs as instruments of war, and had thus come to be known as the *caceteiros,* or "Head-Bashers," as opposed to the *flecheiros,* who made use of bows and arrows to hunt and fight. Despite this difference, both the Head-Bashers and the Arrow People were widely feared for their violent treatment of outsiders.

The Korubo group contacted by Possuelo, about twenty people in all, had repeatedly clashed with loggers and fishermen along the boundary of the Javari territory, not far from the site of this very same outpost. Though Possuelo himself was the chief architect of FUNAI's no-contact policy, he'd made an exception in the case of the Korubo. When discussing why he'd contacted them, he usually cited the urgent need to shield the group from an escalating tit-for-tat war with loggers and poachers, which was undoubtedly true. But it was also true that the group's wanderings brought them very close to this strategic confluence, where Possuelo envisioned erecting this very same post, for the purpose of protecting not only the Korubo but also all the tribes of the Javari. It would have been too great a danger to undertake construction of the post with "untamed" Korubo lurking about; he had to "pacify" them first. He got an injunction against further logging in the region, banned entry to all outsiders, and launched a series of expeditions that eventually resulted in the Korubo contact. Those steps initiated a long chain of events that led to permanent protection for the entire Javari Valley Indigenous Land, an enormous exclusion zone for Indians only, half the size of Florida, in the very heart of the Amazon. The main body of the Korubo still lived beyond the reach of civilization—one of as many as eight uncontacted tribes still believed to persist in the Javari's deepest, most impenetrable recesses in what appeared to be a willful resistance to outside efforts to contact and pacify.

At any one time, a handful of Matis worked here at the base, on the FUNAI payroll. They rotated through in two-week shifts, an arrangement that provided families with currency to buy clothing, medicines, and shotgun shells. It was a crucial revenue stream, since the rules of the Terra Indigena banned them from selling timber, fish, or bush meat to outside traders. Until a manner was devised to produce a reliable stream of revenue from "sustainable" forms of rainforest exploitation, government patronage seemed to be the only alternative for a people now dependent on a cash-based economy for a host of goods they'd done without for thousands of years: guns, ammunition, axes, medicine.

Nicolas hopped onto the dock with his camera pouch on one arm and locked the eldest of the Matis in a bear hug with the other. The man was short and wiry, his thick black hair chopped in a bowl cut favored by many Amazonian tribes. "Scott, this is Biní." Biní's smile was framed by thin black stripes tattooed across his cheeks and forehead. A four-inch stick pierced his septum, but what impressed me most were the half dozen or so tiny shoots that protruded from the side of each nostril like the whiskers of a jaguar.

Two of the younger Matis hoisted our bulging backpacks and river bags and lithely bounded across the twenty-foot-long plank that led to shore without a second glance. My own crossing was far less graceful, but at least I made it without falling into the water. We followed a series of catwalks and continued on up a steep flight of stairs. By the time we reached the top, where the stairway gave out onto a long plank walkway, we stood fifty feet above the current level of the river. Beneath the platform, the sand was still soggy from the Itaquaí's floodwaters, now in full retreat.

"In a month or so, we'll be planting watermelons and beans on this ground," said a mixed-blooded Brazilian who introduced himself as Antonio Carlos, the man in charge while Possuelo's expedition was in the field. "You'll see when you come back, all of this will be about ready to harvest." He meant three or so months from now, when the expedition was expected to conclude. Considering where we'd be in the meantime, it seemed unimaginably far away, in another life after this one.

Antonio Carlos said he'd last heard from Possuelo three days ago, via radio. "They've been stopping at several communities to do medical checkups," he said. In our fast boat, Antonio Carlos figured, we'd be able to overtake Possuelo's flotilla by the next afternoon.

"They may be doing medical checks, but I know Sydney," Nicolas said to me in English. "This is Brazil. He can't come right out and say he's waiting for two foreign journalists, but that's what he's doing— going slow, giving us time to catch up."

We ducked into an immaculate open-air room commanded by a large desk, where the cleanliness departed so radically from the norm for government-run facilities in Brazil that I must have looked dumbfounded. "It's Sydney," Antonio Carlos said with a smile. "He likes to make sure things are kept a certain way." Evidently, they remained that way even when he was deep in the bush. I drifted over for a look at several index cards tacked to the walls.

"WHEN YOU SPEAK, MAKE SURE YOUR WORDS IMPROVE UPON THE SILENCE," directed one card written in meticulous block-letter script, citing an ancient Arab proverb. Another, attributed to the Portuguese poet Fernando Pessoa, read: "ALL IS WORTHWHILE IF THE SOUL IS NOT SMALL." There were more, equally somber and exacting, all executed in the same fastidious hand. "Sydney," Antonio Carlos explained with all the reverence of a caretaker at the Temple Mount. "These are quotes from his readings."

Above the desk hung an old sepia photograph of a gaunt, dashing man in full khaki field outfit. He sat on a tree stump, looking over one shoulder straight into the camera. A knotted kerchief flared at his neck; jackboots rose to his knees. A pith helmet rested on one leg, the butt of his shotgun on the other. Sunbeams pierced the jungle gloom beyond his shoulder like theatrical spotlights. It might well have been the image of Allan Quatermain himself, though in fact it was that of Colonel Cândido Rondon, the Brazilian army officer who'd accompanied Teddy Roosevelt on his harrowing journey down the River of Doubt and who figured among the greatest explorers of the Amazon.

At the dawn of the twentieth century, Rondon ventured deep into unmapped jungle to lay telegraph lines that would connect outposts in the interior to Brazil's metropolitan hubs on the Atlantic coast, and his expeditions produced scores of first contacts with Indian tribes. Half Indian himself, Rondon saw Brazil's natives as actual human beings, worthy of the same rights as everyone else, and he subscribed to the notion that, given an equal chance, Indians could flourish alongside their fellow citizens as full-fledged members of society. The problem was, the cards were stacked against the Indians; there was no such thing as an equal chance. In 1910, Rondon was tapped to assume command of a newly founded agency he'd lobbied hard to create: the Indian Protection Service, or SPI, the predecessor of FUNAI. Its mission was to contact and integrate Brazil's Indians into the national mainstream and to shield indigenous tribes from the wholesale death and dislocation that invariably accompanied the advance of white colonization of the Amazon. An ardent rationalist, Rondon believed in the ideals of progress and civilization. He had been the very first *sertanista*—or "man of the backwoods"—a uniquely Brazilian profession that enfolds all the skills and passion of a frontiersman, an ethnographer, an adventurer, and an Indian rights activist into a single, eclectic vocation. Rondon's somewhat antiquated and naive views notwithstanding, his example and the institutions he founded gave birth to the movement whose latest generation counted Possuelo among its most venerated. With the last uncontacted tribes confined to ever-shrinking pockets of virgin rainforest, the *sertanistas* themselves were now a dying breed, a relic from a vanishing era, as endangered as the untamed Indians they sought to defend. Following in Rondon's footsteps, later *sertanistas* had served as the spearhead of civilization's advance into the wilderness—sometimes in a benign role, at other times facilitating the wholesale theft of Indian land. But Possuelo had taken their entire mission and stood it on its head. Henceforth, the *sertanistas'* role was to halt the expansion of the frontier wherever it encroached upon indigenous territory, to stand up to powerful industrialists rather than pacify the "wild Indians" that stood in the way of their profits.

More of the Amazon Basin had been leveled and burned in the past fifty years than in the previous five centuries combined, as ranchers, growers, and timber barons threatened or bribed their way to industrial-scale devastation. Even as we stood before the photo of Rondon, chain saws and bulldozers were advancing through the heart of the Amazon. Thankfully, the Javari had mostly been spared the same fate; there were no penetration roads, and river access was blocked by FUNAI agents. That didn't mean there weren't still threats—threats to the reserve, threats to the security of those charged with protecting it. Loggers were eating around the edges, especially in far-flung stretches fast on the Peruvian border. There were reports of heavily armed lumberjacks operating with impunity in the remote reaches of Indian land, where Brazilian border guards dared not enter. Then there was the more immediate prospect of confrontation with agitated locals from downriver.

"There've been some scary moments here, not all that long ago," Antonio Carlos said. One afternoon two years before, a flotilla had come upriver from Atalaía, a sawmill town between the base and Tabatinga. There were dozens of boats, nearly three hundred men, liquored-up and aggressive, mostly unskilled laborers whose livelihoods depended on toppling the trees of the Javari and fishing out its rivers. They brandished shotguns and Molotov cocktails, spoiling for a fight.

"Good thing Sydney was here that day. He radioed to Tabatinga for a helicopter from the DPF." The DPF was the acronym for Brazil's

Federal Police, and luckily a helicopter from Brasília just happened to be in the area. The chopper swooped in over the treetops, agents clearly visible in the open doorways, training their weapons directly down on the boats below. The attackers backed off. It was a rare triumph of the rule of law, but at best a tenuous one. No one had any illusions about where the real nexus of power lay, nor did they forget that popular sentiment on the frontier ran decidedly against FUNAI, against Possuelo, and against anyone who defended the rainforest homelands of the Amazon's aboriginals.

Beneath Rondon's photograph, another of Possuelo's cards quoted the First Sertanista: "Die if you must, but never kill!" It was the very distillation of Rondon's creed, conveying to his followers the solemnity of their mission: not even in the face of death shall those charged with protecting Brazil's Indians fire upon them. "You won't find anyone who takes that command more seriously than Sydney," said Antonio Carlos.

Rondon himself had been caught in a hail of arrows while attempting a peaceful contact with Nambiquara Indians. One shot serendipitously deflected off his gun barrel, sparing his life. Other *sertanistas* had not been so lucky. No fewer than 120 FUNAI agents had perished in the line of duty since the 1970s. Among the most recent martyrs was Possuelo's friend Raimundo "Sobral" Magalhães, clubbed to death in 1997, just across the river from where we stood, by the same Korubo they'd contacted the year before. The motives remained unclear, but one of the Indians had recently died of malaria, and the group may have blamed the FUNAI agents for the death. True to Rondon's dictum, Possuelo never even considered retaliation, or prosecution. The Korubo were exempt anyway; they were considered "unacculturated" wards of the state, and the killing took place on their own land. "He bore them no resentment," Antonio Carlos said. "But it affected him for a long time. He kept to himself." Along the same stretch of beach a few years later, a young Korubo girl was hauled off by an anaconda as she waded into the water, never to be seen again.

Outside, the sun was falling fast, trees silhouetted against a bloodred sky on the opposite shore. Somewhere a generator sputtered to life, and a whiff of diesel fumes floated in on the air. A pair of bare electric bulbs dangling by wires from the rafters winked on in the dining room. After a dinner of wild boar stew and farinha—the gritty manioc flour that is the bedrock ingredient of Brazilian meals—Nicolas, Francisco, and I repaired to a spacious chamber that adjoined the dining room, where an ancient television in the far corner pulled in a fuzzy evening newscast. Police in Rio were investigating a gruesome double homicide; traffic in São Paulo was hopelessly snarled; lawmakers in Brasília were vowing to kill President Lula da Silva's free-lunch program for schools. The news hour concluded and segued, rather incongruously, to a series of rock videos. A scantily clad woman gyrated to the beat, leering into the camera, caressing her breasts. Four or five Matis sat bolt upright on high stools, riveted, their mollusk-shell earrings glowing in the dim light.

"Their first impressions of the outside world are formed by TV, and they get this," said Nicolas, pointing at the screen. "You wonder what they must think." He had accompanied ten Matis the year before on their first city visit to far-off Campo Grande, to attend the annual All-Indian Games, a national sporting event still in its infancy. On a break from the blowgun and archery competitions, he'd taken them to the city's new shopping mall. For an hour, they'd ridden nonstop up and down the escalators. "They loved it." The only other thing that interested them was a pet store whose window front was stacked with tanks of tropical fish. They plopped down on the floor by the aquariums, pointing and chattering excitedly. "I asked what was going on," Nicolas said, "and they told me how they liked the meat of one fish, that the meat of another was really tough. It was the only thing in the whole mall they could relate to."

By eight o'clock I was exhausted. I'd covered thousands of miles in the past forty-eight hours, each plane and boat taking me farther away from the ceaseless bustle of New York City. "The generator goes off in thirty minutes," said Antonio Carlos. I staked my claim to a sparsely furnished room off the dining area. There were screens on the windows, but I didn't trust them, so I passed on the coffin-size bed and slung my high-tech Hennessy hammock diagonally across the room, using hooks embedded in the concrete walls for the purpose. The hammock was light as a parachute, with a built-in mosquito net on top and underside fabric woven tight enough to thwart the ambitions of the most voracious malarial bloodsucker. I wriggled in through a slit near the bottom, lifted my legs inside, and closed the Velcro strip. Of all the shabby gear I'd hastily assembled, the hammock stood out as the one piece of equipment that could rival the quality of Nicolas's enviable array of accoutrements. There was just one thing about it that concerned me: the rope that secured it to posts or trees was no thicker than a parachute cord. But sleep beckoned. The generator sputtered out, ceding the night to the buzz-saw trill of cicadas and the hoot-hoot-hooting of some creature whose identity I could not even begin to divine.

CHAPTER 4

At a Bend in the River

W E PULLED AWAY FROM the boathouse the next morning at first light, bidding farewell to Antonio Carlos and the Matis. "See you in September!" Nicolas yelled. Just around the first bend, we passed beneath a brilliant orange billboard that read FIRST NATIONS in huge block letters. Beneath the lettering, the portraits of five Indian warriors stared out over the river, representing some of the tribes known to live in the Javari Valley. "From here on, we're in Indian country," Nicolas enthused, "like in the Western movies."

The sun seemed to shift in the sky as we followed the river's sinuous switchbacks. At times it was directly in front of us, at others nearly straight behind us, and then there were moments, cool and merciful, when it hid behind a screen of dull silver clouds. Nicolas had resumed his perch in the bow, earphones in his ears. I took my place alongside Francisco. I ducked behind the windshield to unfurl a country map of Brazil and saw that we were traveling south by southwest along a squiggly line that scarcely provided a hint of the river's true course. We pitched east, then due west, and back east again. The only constant was the Itaquaí's relentless current throwing itself against the Yamaha's 85 horses, threatening to sweep us back downriver. In most other countries on the planet, the Itaquaí would have been considered a waterway of significance—on the order of the Thames, the Tiber, or the Rappahannock. On my map of Brazil, it did not even merit a name.

We caught up with the expedition flotilla in midafternoon, four riverboats of varying sizes lashed together, side by side, just above the mouth of a tributary that entered the Itaquaí from the east. Though each vessel had its own distinctive features, they shared a vintage look, with wraparound wooden railings and tires slung over gunwales for bumpers. They rocked in unison beneath a wall of trees in a gently swirling eddy. Their names were hand-painted on their bows: *Etno*, a double-decked, steel-hulled hulk trimmed in blue; *Kukahá*, also of two decks, though constructed entirely of wood; *Waiká*, a medium-size boat with a single, open-air deck. The smallest of the four had a low-lying, single-story cabin painted pastel green, and it bore the name of Possuelo's old friend killed by the club-wielding Korubo Indians: *Sobral.*

A rotund man in shorts and a black T-shirt flashed a bright smile as he hauled me aboard the largest of the boats with a fleshy hand. "Danilo," he said, turning to face us. "Welcome aboard the *Etno*." The Ethnic. *Strange name for a boat*, I thought, but I was starting to get the idea that Possuelo missed no chance to remind everyone what the struggle was all about: the defense of Brazil's indigenous ethnicities and their rainforest homelands.

Danilo Rodrigues, captain of the *Etno*, was in his mid-thirties, a riverboat pilot and onetime mechanic reared on the banks of the Upper Amazon. His bronzed complexion, kinky black hair, and aquiline nose suggested the blending of Brazil's three main bloodlines: Portuguese, African, and Indian. He displayed his rank with a courtly flourish, waving us aboard with a deep bow and a jovial wink. "Senhor Sydney took almost everyone up to the headwaters of the Igarapé São José," he said, pointing up the tributary. *Igarapé.* Literally meaning "canoe path" in the Tupi language, the lyrical four-syllable word is a staple in the Amazonian lexicon, signifying something close to "creek"—usually one that's clear and amber-tinged, laced with tannic acid from decomposing vegetation. Depending on their length and the area they drain, *igarapés* can be narrow streams or major arteries. The São José was nearly as broad as the Itaquaí itself. "They're looking for vestiges of a group of Arrow People up there." Danilo expected them back tomorrow. "In the meantime, we'll get you set up."

He led us up a pair of steep, narrow stairways to the upper deck. "Your quarters," he said with mock formality, pushing open the door and bowing magnanimously. It was a shoebox of a cabin, with barely enough room to squeeze between a built-in desk on one side and a set of bunks on the other. But it was scrubbed spotless, and the linoleum floor was freshly waxed. Content with our murmurs of approval, Danilo hustled us down to the galley to meet the other two recruits who'd stayed behind to man the expedition's floating base camp.

Adelson Pereira Brás, pilot of the *Waiká,* was a gaunt scarecrow of a man in his fifties with strong Indian features—high cheekbones, eyes of black almond, a long beak of a nose—and a mischievous grin tugging at the corners of his small mouth, seeming to invite all comers to join him in a conspiracy of permanent amusement at the world. He wore an Australian bush hat tight on his head, the cord firmly knotted beneath his chin, where long strands of whiskers hung freely like the beard of Ho Chi Minh. His Brazilian name notwithstanding, Adelson was full-blooded Indian: half Tikuna, half Kokama. "My name got mixed up with whites because I was raised by them," he volunteered.

The third man, Paulo Souza, was a diminutive fellow in his late twenties with a wiry build and close-cropped, dirty-blond ringlets. He had a faux diamond stud in his left earlobe that, together with his thin mustache and low-brimmed hat, gave him the appearance of someone trying to affect the look of Clark Gable in the role of a tawdry riverboat gambler. He had an eager-to-please demeanor that spoke of military service—four years in jungle ops. He'd been out of the service without work for a year and a half before landing the gig as one of the expedition's two cooks. There was another Paulo as well, currently upstream with Possuelo, so everyone called Paulo Souza by both his first and last names, a habit I quickly fell into as well.

We formed a human chain to off-load our gear and provisions from the speedy little motorboat, stowing them aboard the *Etno.* Francisco snapped off a military-style salute as he backed his boat out into the current, pushed down the throttle, and started downriver, toward the FUNAI post. I watched him disappear around the bend, hoping he'd make it back by nightfall. It didn't seem all that safe to be out here alone once darkness fell.

In the tiny cabin, Nicolas and I began unpacking. His duffel bags were stuffed with photography books, magazines, even bottles of wine—stuff he couldn't have been planning to take into the jungle. "Presents," he said simply, "for Sydney." Syd-nay. He unloaded cases of film, batteries, medical supplies, and began arranging it all on the top bunk, as if it were his personal shelf. It was a bold landgrab, seizing control of the upper berth right before my eyes.

"Ah, I thought we were supposed to *share* this cabin," I said.

"There's a free bunk next door," he said. "Why don't you just move in there?"

Definitely an only child, I thought, *used to getting his way.* I took the bunk next door and left it at that.

Down in the galley, Danilo and Adelson stood leaning on the countertop, while Paulo, the youngest and slightest of the three, sat on a low stool peeling potatoes. "Have you met Sydney before?" Danilo asked, his belly hanging over the counter. I'd spoken to him once, I said, a long time ago. I couldn't really say that I knew him. "You're in for a treat," said Adelson. They all laughed, as if in possession of dark, forbidden knowledge.

"You should have seen him explode that day when the guy came back without the motor," said the captain of the *Etno,* contorting his face in pantomime rage.

"Poor guy looked like he'd been lashed fifty times." Adelson nodded, stroking his wispy beard. "One thing for sure, you don't want to get on his bad side."

Paulo Souza had finished peeling the potatoes. He grabbed a large pot, and went out through the back door to fetch water from the stern of the boat. Danilo grabbed my elbow and lowered his voice. "Don't misunderstand," said the captain with a confidential air. "Sydney is a

good man. He only wants his men to have the conditions and equipment they need to do their work." I might have believed what he said,
but I had the feeling Danilo had suddenly thought the better of sharing such gossip with a stranger, that he was hedging his bets.

*   *   *

Though we had made it to the expedition boats, there was still plenty
of work to be done before we'd be ready to head upriver to the land of
the Arrow People. Nicolas and I spent much of the next morning getting our gear sorted and repacked, filling our day packs with essentials
for quick forays into the bush: a change of clothes, a few energy bars,
a water bottle, a headlamp. Next, we broke out the satellite phone.
It was roughly the size of a laptop computer, with a detachable cover
that served as the unit's antenna. Pointed skyward at the proper angle,
it would latch on to a signal from the Inmarsat satellite in fixed orbit
over South America. "It seems to be working all right," said Nicolas,
watching the small LCD over the keypad for the series of asterisks that
indicated the phone had locked onto the signal and was ready to dial.
I hadn't spoken to anyone back home since arriving in Brazil. The
boys were in their last week of school. Sarah was looking for a job that
might take her just about anywhere, perhaps far from New York. Not
as far away as this place, of course, with its overwhelming silence, broken only by the lapping of water on our gunwales and the occasional
squawk of macaws winging their way upriver.

I'd brought along four cells for the phone, each the size and weight
of a laptop battery. We'd have to keep them wrapped in three layers of
plastic, tied with rubber bands, to protect them from the humidity. If
we were lucky, we'd have enough juice to stay in sporadic touch with
the outside world for the duration of the journey.

By late afternoon the sun was drenching the jungle in a mysterious golden glow. From somewhere far upriver came the faint but
unmistakable hum of an internal combustion engine—at least one,
perhaps more. "Here they come!" Danilo called out. We gathered on
the deck of the midsize *Waiká*, leaning our elbows on the railing, our

eyes locked on the point upstream where the São José vanished behind a wall of exuberant foliage. From around that distant bend, the
explorers now appeared through the haze, a single silhouette on the
glassy water that gradually resolved into three distinct vessels, long,
canoelike skiffs powered by small outboard engines, each skiff packed
with frontiersmen and Matis Indians like the ones back at the FUNAI
base. To a man, Indians and non-Indians alike, they were decked out
in camouflage fatigues.

As they drew closer, I could make out about two dozen expeditionaries slouched amid a thicket of flint-black shotgun barrels. Beneath
jungle hats, Indian faces were gilded with nose piercings and geometric streaks tattooed on cheeks. They wore white clamshell earrings and
the fine bamboo shoots that sprouted from the sides of nostrils like jaguar whiskers. The weary stares, the rifles, the jungle camouflage—all
infused the scene with a singular militarism that suggested a war party
returning from a raid: *Apocalypse Now* meets *The Last of the Mohicans.*

My eyes were drawn to the man who sat in the very center of the
middle boat, hands resting on his knees, staring off toward some ill-
defined point beyond the treetops. His beard, a blazing auburn when
last I saw him, was now a grizzled salt-and-pepper. Shocks of gray hair
protruded wildly from beneath his floppy camouflage bush hat, and
a spreading paunch tugged at the buttons of his black field shirt. But
despite the changes the years had wrought, there was no mistaking
Sydney Possuelo anywhere.

In a single stride, Possuelo bounded aboard the *Waiká.* Wildly
gesticulating, he ordered men to stow gear, clean rifles, and top off
fuel tanks from the large drums belowdecks. The sleepy tranquillity
that had reigned for the previous twenty-four hours vanished in an
instant. Matis hopped nimbly from skiff to skiff despite the heavy loads
they bore, balancing barefoot or in rubber flip-flops on the top of the
gunwales. The returning party included an equal number of Indians
and non-Indian Brazilians, whom Possuelo referred to interchangeably as *brancos,* whites, or *riberinhos,* literally "river dwellers," the rugged pioneers who eke out a living along the myriad waterways of the

Amazon. Other than the cooks and FUNAI agents, whites and Indians alike were also called *mateiros,* or backwoodsmen. In an earlier epoch, the term designated the mixed-blood men who were tasked with clearing trails between wild rubber trees—and clearing the forest of "wild" Indians. "Hey, *mateiros,* listen up!" Possuelo yelled. "I want someone to hose down the boats right away! They're filthy as hell and smell worse than the plague!"

He stopped abruptly, hunched over a malfunctioning pocket-size GPS. "Piece of junk hasn't worked for days," he said to no one in particular, scratching his beard with one hand, holding the device close to his eyes with the other.

"Let's see that, Sydney." Nicolas pushed his way through the clutch of scouts and extended his cranelike arm. Possuelo looked up in a daze, trying to focus, as if he couldn't quite place the face. Then his lips parted into a wide grin. He threw himself into Nicolas's arms and patted him on the back.

"Where have you been keeping yourself, old man?" he laughed. Then, remembering the ill-functioning device, he said: "*Os Americanos*— the Americans—are up to something, I'd be willing to bet." Maybe a joint operation with the Peruvians and Colombians against the narcos. It wouldn't have been the first time the gringos had jammed the Global Positioning System without telling anyone, he said, leaving not only the drug traffickers but "all of us poor underdeveloped people in the dark." He cocked his head to look up at Nicolas, seeming to feign a simpleton's confusion. The front visor of his jungle hat was folded back on his forehead, like the bugler in *F Troop,* adding to the comic effect. "Or maybe it's just shoddy merchandise. But who's this," he asked, turning to me, "another of your tribe?"

Nicolas waved me over and reintroduced us. Possuelo was shorter than I remembered, something like five seven, but he exuded the same vital energy and actor's repertoire of gestures and gesticulations—a sour grimace, an eyebrow raised in mock disbelief, a bug-eyed look of astonishment—that kept his face in a state of constant transfiguration, holding his audience spellbound. I reminded him of our meeting years before in Rio de Janeiro. He didn't remember, but I got a bear hug just the same.

We were meeting at a critical moment of his career. His efforts on behalf of Brazil's indigenous tribes were commanding more attention outside Brazil than inside. *TIME* hailed him as a "Hero of the Planet." Spain had recently awarded him the Bartolomé de las Casas human rights award. A grant from the European Union and another from the U.S.-based Moore Foundation had reinforced his surveillance and enforcement efforts in regions where isolated or uncontacted tribes were known to exist, including the Javari reserve. Possuelo was leveraging his renown into financial support that allowed him to operate base camps and control posts—even to launch major fact-finding expeditions like this one—while other FUNAI programs languished. Journalists with limited jungle experience, overloaded bags, and lousy boots might prove a liability, but he knew the trouble was worth it: we were megaphones who provided access to a global stage. The expedition, if successful, would consolidate his gains, vindicate his policies, attract more funding, strengthen his position within FUNAI, and allow him to launch further, more sustained efforts to locate and protect other isolated tribes elsewhere in the country. Their very survival, it seemed, hinged on his success.

Possuelo and Nicolas lapsed into small talk about women—wives, ex-wives, girlfriends. Possuelo noted their good fortune with women, how they'd both managed, even in divorce, to remain good friends with the mothers of their children. "In this kind of work, when you're gone for months at a time, you're bound to end up a cuckold." He shrugged and cast an eye about, as though daring someone to contradict him. "It's inevitable. Gone are the days when Penelope waits at home while her man is off saving the world." Women were no longer sitting home in wait, but all that was needed was a quick glance around to conclude that this was still very much a man's world, exclusively so in the case of this expedition.

I asked Sydney how many kids he had. He flashed six fingers. With how many women? *"Tres."* A bronzed and sculpted teenager with long,

sun-bleached tresses leaned against a nearby post and listened in, looking like a Greek god. I guessed this was Possuelo's son—Nicolas had
mentioned that he might be coming along—but he was so strikingly
beautiful that I wasn't entirely sure of my rush to judgment on the
absence of women, until Possuelo addressed him by name. "Orlando,"
he said, giving him a good-natured shove, "don't you have something
better to do?"

The teen flashed a dazzling smile, but he held his ground, arms
folded. Orlando was Possuelo's third son, a month shy of his eighteenth birthday. He'd grown up in Brasília with his mother, Possuelo's
second wife, a short drive from Possuelo's own apartment along the
wide boulevards of Brazil's weird, futuristic capital. But they didn't
see each other enough.

I felt a pang of jealousy. I had been pushed into signing divorce papers just before boarding the plane for Brazil. It would be years before
any of my boys would be old enough to bring along on a trip of this
sort, and I had no idea if I'd manage to remain a vital presence in their
lives. At least Possuelo and Orlando lived in the same city. And though
the expedition was expected to last well beyond the start of Orlando's
last year of high school, he had agreed to come along. School would
always be there; his father would not.

Possuelo was already sixty-two years old, and in the course of his
forty years in the jungle, he had endured three dozen bouts of malaria and received about as many death threats. By the start of the
third millennium, there was almost no one in FUNAI with more field
experience than Possuelo, a fact that conferred on him a moral authority and legitimacy virtually unmatched by his peers. He had been
pistol-whipped by white settlers invading Indian lands and had been
kidnapped by the same Kayapó warriors he was seeking to protect.
Steel plates held his head together after a near-fatal car wreck in Mali,
where he'd gone to visit Tuareg tribesmen. He still hobbled a bit, and
the wreck may have explained a slight wandering of his left eye that
gave him the quizzical look I'd noticed earlier. A pair of small metal
cylinders hung loosely on a chain about his neck. One contained

antimalarials, he said, the other nitroglycerin tablets, in case of a heart attack.

He'd been slowly grooming Orlando to succeed him as a jungle explorer and champion of the cause of besieged Indians. He'd taken him to visit remote indigenous villages, and he'd left him alone to live in the forest among the Zo'ê, a tribe previously contacted by American missionaries but now living once again in isolation, under the auspices of Possuelo's elite unit. Still, none of that could compare to a three-month sojourn together in the depths of the wilderness, during which he could impart countless lessons gleaned from a lifetime in the bush. The chance might not come again.

"Go on," he said to Orlando, now with more insistence. His son pushed the curls back off his forehead, rolled his eyes in playful exasperation, and glided off through the galley, shoulders thrown back in an Olympian posture.

Minutes later, the engines roared to life. Men swarmed the decks, moving up and down ladders, hauling backpacks and jerricans, as purposeful and sure as ants in a colony. Ropes were unbound and the boats pulled away from the bank, turning into the current one by one. The smaller skiffs had been tied to the sterns of the larger boats, two or three to a vessel, and they trailed in their wakes like minnows tagging after their parents. As quaint a picture as these diminutive craft presented, they would be our ticket to the upper reaches of the Itaquaí, taking us farther upriver and deeper into the jungle than the mother boats could possibly go. For now, there were more immediate challenges, not the least of which was getting an initial sense of the lay of the land and finding my way among thirty-some-odd men with whom I'd be journeying to the far corners of the Earth and on whom my life would almost certainly depend.

CHAPTER 5

A Topography of Strife

POSSUELO INVITED US to dine with him that night aboard the *Waiká*, which housed his quarters and from which he conducted the business of the expedition. "Danilo!" he barked across to the *Etno*. "Let's keep our boats tied together, so our guests can come and go as they wish." The *Waiká* and *Etno* plowed upriver, bound together side by side, so we could visit with Possuelo over plates of steaming piranha stew.

Though each vintage Amazonian riverboat has its unique peculiarities, all feature an ingenious blend of form and functionality that evokes a sense of Victorian-era exploration and Old-World charm. With open decks and wraparound railings, they feel roomy even when crammed. The gunwales taper in height from bow to stern, offering in the rear a kind of back porch to the galley, where fish can be cleaned, meat butchered, and laundry scrubbed.

As with all such vessels, the galley aboard the *Waiká*, a compact kitchen with stove, sink, and countertops, was positioned just ahead of the stern. Just fore of the galley was the common area of the main deck, perhaps fifteen feet from end to end, which would serve as our dining quarters, when its table, usually locked flush to the ceiling to conserve space, was lowered along two vertical posts. The common area was open to the air along both sides, with removable elbow-high railings to restrain passengers and tie off the tarps that would be rolled down from ceiling to deck in the event of one of the Amazon's frequent torrential cloudbursts. The open sides gave a light and airy feeling to the chamber and provided a view out onto the jungle as it slid past. That view was particularly inviting at this time of day, when the retreating sun cast long shadows across the river and splashed the upper stories of the trees with its rich yellow light.

The table was lowered into place for dinner, cheap plastic lawn chairs were drawn up, and Mauro, the expedition's second cook (in addition to Paulo Souza) began ladling aromatic dollops of stew into our bowls. Orlando and Possuelo sat on one side of the table, Nicolas and I on the other. There was still space for one or two more at the table, but none of the half dozen or so woodsmen approached, as if some unspoken signal warned them to keep their distance. They ate standing up, leaning against the railing, fixing us with unblinking stares and bemused smiles. Most had probably never met a journalist before, much less a pair of Americans. I dug into the stew. The fish was white and flaky, laced with bones, but otherwise tender and succulent, like halibut.

"Hey, Sydney, mind if I join you?" came a voice from over my shoulder. It was the expedition's number two, Paulo Welker, the other Paulo on board, whom Possuelo had tapped two years before to head the Javari Valley's Ethno-Environmental Protection Front. This was one of six special regions in the Amazon that fell under the authority of the Department of Isolated Indians, zones where FUNAI had operated so-called Attraction Fronts or Contact Fronts in earlier times, when the objective was still to lure the Indians from the jungle, make contact, and worry about protecting them later, as more of an afterthought. Now, the fronts existed to keep the forests, together with the tribes they harbored, intact and off-limits to outsiders. Paulo Welker was not a full-fledged *sertanista,* but rather an "indigenist," like an understudy. "Sure," Possuelo told him. "Get yourself a plate."

*   *   *

As head of the Department of Isolated Indians, Possuelo had devised the term "Ethno-Environmental Protection Front" to underscore what he considered to be the indelible link between the survival of isolated tribes and the preservation of their pristine habitat. "These people and their culture can only survive within an intact jungle environment," he said, spearing a piece of fish on his fork. "Within a living forest, the Indian has everything he needs to survive. The flora and fauna and land that we protect are for the nourishment and shelter of the indigenous groups who live here—period. In protecting the isolated Indian, you're also protecting millions of acres of biodiversity." It amounted to a clear expression of a new global movement called "socioenvironmentalism," which saw the protection of biodiversity as inseparable from safeguarding the cultural and territorial rights of indigenous peoples. All told, the territories under the protection of Possuelo's unit added up to fifty thousand square miles of virgin rainforest, an area larger than the entire state of New York. The term "ethno-environmental protection front" also highlighted the dramatic shift Possuelo had masterminded, moving FUNAI from a bureau that once tracked down wild Indians to contact and pacify them to an agency that now located isolated tribes and documented their presence in order to shield them from contact. In a heartbeat, the *sertanista*'s purpose was transformed—from "contact to save" to "save without contact."

It had been Possuelo's idea to cordon off areas where uncontacted tribes were known to exist and declare them off-limits to outsiders. Listening to Possuelo speak, I gathered that he saw himself as heir to a tradition of explorer-activists that began with Rondon and continued with the work of his early mentors, Orlando and Claudio Villas Boas. Starting in the mid-1940s, the Villas Boas brothers came to form the expeditionary core of the Central Brazil Foundation, a newly established agency tasked with hacking a series of airstrips from the jungle to open up the country's remote interior. Taking inspiration from Rondon, the Villas Boas brothers gained a reputation as intrepid adventurers and staunch defenders of the Indians they befriended while pushing deeper and deeper into the wilderness. At the start of the 1960s, around the time Possuelo first joined them as a young volunteer, the brothers won federal recognition for the enormous Xingu Indigenous Park, centered on the Xingu River in the central Amazon, nearly one thousand miles to the east of the Javari. Though the park was initially conceived as a homeland for tribes native to the Xingu basin, the Villas Boases came to see it also as a refuge where they resettled besieged natives from neighboring watersheds as the advancing frontier closed in.

By the mid-1960s, Brazil's military rulers had made colonization of the Amazon a national priority. Penetration roads were clawing their way into virgin rainforest, and the Villas Boases saw relocation to the park as the only alternative for many tribes to outright annihilation. It was a radical concept for its time—an enormous national park that would protect flora and fauna and allow indigenous people to carry on their traditional ways of life. Administering the park presented huge challenges: mediating disputes among various ethnicities, some in the initial stages of contact; fending off intrusions from white colonizers; rushing to inoculate villages from deadly epidemics. This was to become Possuelo's university. Within the Xingu's river-laced forests, under the tutelage of Orlando and Claudio Villas Boas, he learned the ways of an indigenist scout, coming in time to be recognized as a veteran *sertanista*. Possuelo earned the brothers' definitive approbation after he'd faced down an angry mob eager to invade Kayapó lands along the Xingu. He was knocked to his knees and had his arms pinned back by two men while a third shoved a loaded pistol in his mouth. He lost four teeth that night, but he stood his ground. From that moment on, the Villas Boases recognized in Possuelo a protégé of exceptional courage, to whom they could entrust the most exacting tasks.

For their dogged efforts on behalf of Brazil's indigenous peoples, the Villas Boas brothers were twice nominated for the Nobel Peace Prize, in 1971 and 1975. The Xingu Indigenous Park and a mosaic of adjacent Indian lands and protected reserves remain a formidable defensive corridor—five hundred miles in length and nearly two hundred wide—that has halted the advance of wanton rainforest destruction across the central Amazon.

Possuelo later named his son in honor of Orlando, the eldest of the Villas Boases. And he would venerate the brothers until their dying days for their extraordinary kindness and dedication, and for their unflagging love of the Indians. But he would by the late 1980s break with them on the issue of contact. "The paths that masters open for you aren't always the ones you agree with," he said.

Contacting untamed tribes had always seemed as inevitable as the weather. For Rondon, it was the first step on the road to integrating the Indians into the broader society. For the Villas Boas brothers, contact was a necessary evil, to move them out of the way of the advancing frontier and relocate them in safe havens where they could recoup strength and maintain their traditions. Whatever the ultimate purpose, contacting wild tribes had been the sine qua non of the profession for nearly a century. Which made it difficult for many of his contemporaries to embrace the new approach advocated by Possuelo. "For a *sertanista,* the glory was in the contact," he said. "They didn't want to lose the glory." In a way, the shift amounted to a resounding indictment of modern society, an acknowledgment of its boundless power to transform and obliterate, inimical to the survival and well-being of indigenous cultures: *We can't enter into contact with them without, in essence, destroying them.*

The point of departure for Possuelo, the primary raison d'être of the no-contact policy, was the Indians' extreme vulnerability to contagious disease. Not only had the Inca been vanquished by Pizarro's armor-clad horsemen; they'd dropped like flies in a smallpox epidemic that spread inland after the conquistador's initial exploration of South America's Pacific coast. Victims of the virus included the Inca emperor, whose death touched off a brutal war of succession that greatly facilitated the process of conquest. Deadly pathogens undoubtedly accompanied Francisco de Orellana's 1542 descent of the Amazon and subsequent forays by Europeans, bringing mass death to the Indians, emptying broad swaths of the rainforest of its native inhabitants. Having evolved in isolation from Eurasian diseases for thousands of years, the indigenous populations of the New World simply had no resistance to the germs. It was a story that continued to play itself out even now. Isolated tribes remained as vulnerable to illness as ever.

* * *

Paulo Welker plunked his steaming plate down on the table and pulled up a chair alongside me. He was tall and lanky, in his early thirties, with a golden ponytail that flowed halfway down his back. He hailed from a family of German farmers, but as a boy he'd seen *Dances with Wolves* and *The Mission,* he told me, and had decided to leave the rolling hills of southern Brazil to pursue a life of adventure as an *indigenista* fighting to protect the Indians of the Amazon. He'd previously been in Rondônia, trying to stave off an onslaught of loggers that had reduced several tribes to scattered bands of fugitives, on the run from encroaching chain saws. It was not only a futile exercise, but a dangerous one as well. "I was getting death threats—*ameaças,*" he told me, "so Sydney brought me here to the Javari." *Ameaças:* it was a word I was beginning to hear a lot from the lips of the defenders of Brazil's Indians.

In Mato Grosso, another Amazonian state besieged by loggers and prospectors, he'd witnessed the heartrending vestiges of a tribe uprooted by invasion. "They fled to the other side of the mountain to get away," he said. "They thought the chain saw was an animal they could outrun." They'd abandoned their village, their crops, the burial grounds of their ancestors. "How many of their dances were lost? How many of their memories were lost forever?"

Against the din of engines in full throttle, I strained my ears to keep up with the other conversations flying back and forth across the table. "That phone of yours probably won't work once we get into the jungle," I heard Possuelo bark to Nicolas as he shoved a spoonful of stew into his mouth. "You need to have a clear line of sight to the satellite." He swept his arm toward the ceiling and fixed his bulging eyes on the rafters, as though homing in on some imaginary speck in the sky. He'd brought his own Globalstar phone for dire emergencies. It would be no easier to use than ours, but it worked off a different satellite. He hadn't decided whether or not to bring it along on the overland trek, he said, but he thought he'd probably leave it on the *Waiká* when the boats eventually turned back downriver.

I learned that in addition to the lack of reliable phones, there were no doctors on the expedition. Medical evacuation would be difficult, if not impossible. The nearest helicopter was a thousand miles away in Brasília, probably too far to bother, especially since the chances of finding an adequate landing zone were even more minuscule than those of reaching the outside world by phone to request the chopper in the first place. Whether by phone or two-way radio, successful communication would depend on finding a large enough break in the jungle canopy. Such places, Possuelo explained, would be few and far between.

He must have read the anxiety in my questions about things like phones and doctors. "If you don't think you're up to it, you can turn around when the boats go back," he said. "You don't have to go with us into the jungle." His tone of voice was even-keeled, the rugged countenance beneath his scraggly beard revealing not the slightest trace of derision, as though he were merely offering some helpful advice. It may have been a well-disguised taunt, not a particularly mean-spirited one, but a taunt it was nonetheless. Dinner finished, we stepped out through the galley to the rear deck, where we swished our plates in the river while the minnow craft jerked on their tethers in the wake—scrambling, it seemed, to keep up.

The talk about phones only heightened my desire to call home. Darkness had fallen, and a pleasant breeze stirred as I climbed the steel stairway to the upper deck of the *Etno,* my footsteps clanking. I retrieved the Inmarsat phone and hopped back across to the *Waiká,* this time onto its roof, where I'd have privacy. Soon the phone at my old house in Utica, New York, was ringing. Mackenzie, the oldest of the boys at nearly twelve, answered. "Kenzie, it's Daddy! I'm calling from the jungle!" I began. I could hear him cup the phone and yell: "Aaron, Ian, come here, quick! Daddy's on the phone! He's calling from the Amazon!"

They bombarded me with questions: How hot was it, what animals had I seen so far, were there lots of bugs, what was I eating, were the Indians friendly? I looked out into the blackness of the jungle on our flanks as we plowed upriver, trying to picture them gathered at the kitchen table, wrestling over the receiver. Before we said good-bye, Ian, who had turned five a few months before, had some advice he needed to impart: "Watch out for the alligators, Daddy. They can bite your boat and eat the wood." Sure, I said, I'd keep an eye out. "Record the Indians talking," Mackenzie told me before hanging up. "I want to hear what their language sounds like." *That was an interesting request,* I thought. I was pleased he was curious enough to ask.

*   *   *

Later that night, Possuelo invited Nicolas and me into the cabin he shared with Orlando to discuss the expedition. "Watch your heads," he warned, his stooping figure silhouetted in the low doorway against a fluorescent lamp that burned inside. He stepped aside to let us into the cabin, which guaranteed more privacy than any other quarters on the flotilla. It was twice the size of the cabins on the *Etno*, though still tight, with built-in bunks, a desk, and a few chairs crammed in. Papers were neatly stacked atop the desk. Boots and sneakers lined the near wall, all arranged in pairs, heels first. A quick glance confirmed that the immaculate conditions that prevailed at the control post were also in effect here.

Possuelo invited us to sit on the lower bunk while he unfurled a large topographic map and spread it over his desk. Orlando drew up a chair. "This is the Javari Valley Indigenous Land," said Possuelo, tracing the oval-shaped boundaries of the exclusion zone with his finger, "the second biggest Indian territory in all of Brazil, after the Yanomami Park." Nicolas and I leaned in for a look. "We're about here, moving south by southwest up the Itaquaí." He pointed toward the center of the map. The Indigenous Land stretched over thirty-three thousand square miles of dense forest and steamy swampland. Not a single road, not even an airstrip. Huge as it was in its own right, the Javari sat

within the much larger Upper Amazon, a region of unbroken forest
and thousands of miles of waterways, encompassing much of western
Brazil and broad swaths of Bolivia, Peru, Ecuador, and Colombia. The
map was laced with tiny creeks and streams that drained the rugged
hills along the Javari's southern edge and led to a series of powerful
rivers, nearly all flowing north and east to the Solimões, the main
trunk of the Amazon. The uniformity of flow meant that any major
penetration into the depths of the territory would have to come from
downstream and could thus be controlled by positioning a handful of
strategic checkpoints along the main waterways.

In their totality, protected indigenous lands represented 11 percent of Brazil's national territory, more than 365,000 square miles, a
number that had doubled in the few short years that Possuelo served
as the president of FUNAI in the early 1990s. The Javari was the only
indigenous reserve in all of Brazil whose boundaries encircled a combination of both contacted and uncontacted communities. Some of
FUNAI's most dedicated scouts saw the presence of contacted tribes
within the reserve as an additional layer of protection for the more
vulnerable, isolated groups. In other parts of the Amazon, where the
pace of frontier expansion was particularly feverish, scattered bands of
uncontacted tribes were under unremitting pressure, even after their
lands had been declared off-limits to outsiders. Neither FUNAI nor the
police had the capability to enforce the boundaries. In some instances,
sertanistas found themselves navigating around recently toppled forest
giants, across ground still smoldering from recent burns, ducking gunmen in the pay of ranchers and land sharks, racing to contact besieged
tribes before the goons got to them first.

By comparison, since its designation just a few years before as a
protected area, the Javari was a bastion of tribal vitality. Eight different contacted groups found themselves in varying stages of adapta-
tion to, and interaction with, the outside world—a process called
"acculturation." Regardless of where they may have lived prior to
contact, those tribes now occupied hamlets along the region's main
rivers, where they could more readily receive health care and other

services, such as they were. The uncontacted Indians held to the rugged and heavily forested interfluvial zones between the rivers, in what appeared to be a determined effort to hide from the outside world. Their thatched *malocas* occupied tiny clearings nearly invisible in the undifferentiated sea of green that greeted the eyes of all but the most experienced aerial observers looking down on the forest canopy. Eighteen such sites had been observed by FUNAI overflights, making the Javari home to the largest concentration of uncontacted indigenous communities anywhere in the world, the Arrow People among them. Possuelo himself had made a detailed aerial survey over our anticipated route the previous month, marking with his GPS the coordinates of every clearing of *flecheiros* he could find while his aircraft swept back and forth over the forest. So little was known about the Arrow People, Possuelo said, that no one knew for certain if they represented a single ethnicity or more than one. In other words, the name signaled a technological attribute, the use of projectile-point weaponry, rather than an ethnic distinction. All told, Possuelo estimated the population of the Javari at 4,500 souls, less than the number of people living within a block of the sublet I'd left behind on Manhattan's Upper West Side.

"We'll continue upriver," Possuelo went on, finger drifting southward, tracing the contorted line of the Itaquaí against the north-flowing current, "until it gets too shallow for the large boats to go any farther. Then we'll keep going in the small skiffs with the *peci-pecis*." He was talking about the long-shafted putt-putt motors that powered the skiffs they'd taken up the São José while waiting for Nicolas and me to catch up to the expedition.

The idea was to stay aboard the four riverboats for as long as possible. They burned diesel, for one, which made them cheaper to operate, and the comforts were too obvious to ignore: the ability to stroll the decks, prepare mess in the galley, sleep under a roof. Originally Possuelo had envisioned it might take a full month to ascend the Itaquaí, but the rains were tapering off more quickly than usual, and the water level was dropping by several inches a day. Within two weeks, or perhaps even before that, we'd most likely reach the point where we'd have to leave even the shallow-draft skiffs behind.

"And that's when we'll begin our stroll," Possuelo said, with an ironic smile, "across this area." He pointed to the bottom of the map along the reserve's southern boundary, where the image rippled with tightly compressed contours and twisting blue capillaries hinting at a labyrinth of steep-walled ravines drained by rivulets of boot-sucking mud. "This is all *cabeceiras*," Possuelo said. "Headwaters—where the rivers are born."

This rugged bastion also harbored the disparate settlements of the Arrow People. We'd look for their tracks, fishing camps, discarded artifacts, anything that might provide clues to the tribe's numbers, habits, and well-being. Brazil's constitution guarantees permanent possession of a particular territory to the Indians who have traditionally occupied it. But landgrabs are routinely justified by claims that no one is there, and Possuelo and his teams of indigenous scouts found themselves under constant pressure to document with meticulous precision a tribe's ongoing existence and use of the forest. "We know where their *malocas* are. What we want to know now is the extent of their wanderings, how far they travel during their summer migrations." With a detailed picture of the "economic frontiers" of the Arrow People, Possuelo planned to spearhead an effort to create a kind of reserve inside a reserve, an exclusion zone particular to the *flecheiros,* to keep out everyone else, including the contacted tribes that provided an imperfect buffer between them and the outside world.

We would be vigilant for penetration by the usual suspects—loggers, poachers, or drug traffickers. Such intrusions are nearly impossible to detect by any means other than a grueling, boots-on-the-ground trek under the forest canopy. This was highest among his objectives, because an undetected invasion could quickly gather momentum, leading to an outbreak of a devastating illness or even to a genocidal raid on an unsuspecting *maloca*. So far removed were these woodlands, and so tenuous was the rule of law, that resentful loggers might be tempted

to give vent to murderous impulses. It had long been Possuelo's intention to explore this flank of the Javari to look for signs of trouble. Now,
he would have his chance.

Once we had gleaned whatever information about the Arrow
People we could, without actually meeting them, we'd build dugout
canoes and leave their territory by way of either the Jandiatuba or the
Jutaí River, "depending on where we find ourselves." Nicolas let out a
knowing laugh, as though he understood the potential perils implied
by such vagaries. It was hot and cramped in the cabin, but we were
equally spellbound. He flashed me a triumphant smile, as if to say:
I told you this was going to be the real deal.

The third phase of the expedition—canoeing back to civilization—would have its special challenges, Possuelo warned. "We'll all
be tired by then. We'll be rowing ten, twelve hours a day under the
sun, the rain." On that side of the protected area, a family of white
squatters had yet to get out, and Possuelo aimed to use the occasion
to expel them for good. And, he said, we might come face-to-face with
gold prospectors, a notoriously violent breed.

Possuelo rolled up the map and turned to Orlando. "My son,
where's the laptop?" Orlando handed him a sleek, brand-new HP,
and Possuelo powered up a slide show, a series of photographs taken
on a recent overflight of our anticipated route. Each image showed a
jungle clearing—a brownish splotch amid a sea of green—with a cluster of thatched huts in its center. I craned my neck and repositioned
my glasses to get a better view. Some of the *malocas* were peak-roofed,
others round and sloped like haystacks, hinting at the possibility of
distinct ethnicities building huts of different styles. In several of the
clearings, I could make out dark stick figures standing near the dwellings with their arms akimbo, hands on hips, heads thrown back, contemplating the enormous, droning bird as it passed overhead. No act
of the imagination seemed adequate to comprehend what they might
have been thinking.

What was evident to Possuelo was a desire among the Arrow People
to be left alone. He presumed the tribe had suffered the same fate as

others in this part of the Amazon one hundred years earlier, during the time of the Rubber Boom that gripped the region. A series of technological advances in Europe and North America during the nineteenth century—the vulcanization of rubber, and the invention of the inflatable tire tube for the bicycle and then the automobile—had sent the global demand for natural rubber soaring. The Amazon and the Congo were the two places on Earth where wild rubber grew in abundance. The revolution in transportation and the dizzying succession of technological breakthroughs not only fueled a growing appetite for rubber for consumer and industrial uses, ranging from hosing and gaskets to insulation for telegraph and electrical lines, but they also opened up the secluded hinterlands of both South America and Africa to the new, steam-powered boats of international traders who sought to secure larger and larger supplies of the vital raw material. While King Leopold II of Belgium established his notoriously brutal colonial regime late in the nineteenth century in the Congo, a system to extract rubber evolved in the farthest reaches of the Upper Amazon that was also based on terror, mass abduction, and forced labor.

Exploration of the Amazon by outsiders had been largely confined to the main rivers, until the price of rubber drove legions of men far up creeks and feeder streams in their quest to gather wild latex from the "trees that bleed." In some areas, freelance tappers worked independently or in small groups, selling their product to river traders. But elsewhere in the western Amazon, sprawling estates that encompassed entire river basins emerged as the central paradigm of rubber production. With labor in short supply, bosses imported destitute peasants from Brazil's drought-stricken northeast or turned to sources closer at hand, raiding Indian villages to swell the ranks of their workforce. The plantation lords became a law unto themselves, undisputed rulers over heavily armed private armies and thousands of laborers, their fiefdoms virtually sealed off from the outside world. Patrons struck deals with overlords: in exchange for permission to gather latex on their properties, they would hunt and exterminate "wild" Indians. Slaving expeditions trolled the rivers to round up indigenous recruits. Entire villages were kidnapped; those who tried to get away gunned down. On the Beni River in Bolivia, rubber boss Francisco Suárez was reported to hold sway over tens of thousands of Indians, and he stood accused of subjecting them to incremental torture and progressive amputations if they failed to meet his draconian production quotas.

Exports of Amazonian rubber quadrupled each decade from 1840 to 1900, with America's skyrocketing demand fueling the boom. During the final quarter of the nineteenth century, the United States imported half of the world's entire output, transforming the Amazon River ports of Belém, Manaus, and Iquitos from sleepy backwaters into thriving centers of culture and trade. The decade from 1897 to 1907 saw the value of rubber exports from Iquitos increase fourfold, a period coinciding with the emergence of Julio César Arana as the unrivaled kingpin of Peru's Putumayo River. Rubber exports from estates controlled by Arana jumped from 16,000 kilos in 1900 to 644,000 in just six years. By 1906, his company accounted for 30 percent of all rubber shipments leaving Iquitos for U.S. and European ports.

Profits came at the expense of his indigenous underlings. Witnesses at Arana outposts told of sadistic managers butchering Indian children with machetes to save on the cost of imported bullets. Henchmen inflicted excruciating punishment on Indian chiefs if they failed to persuade those who'd escaped to turn themselves in. Captives were worked to the bone; some were burned at the stake. Epidemics spread like wildfire, ghastly illnesses native healers did not recognize and could not cure. The Indian population under Arana's charge on the Putumayo soon suffered a catastrophic collapse, dropping from an estimated fifty thousand in 1906 to just eight thousand five years later.

Deliberately stoking internecine conflict, rubber bosses were known to advance rifles to tribesmen, to be paid off in slaves they captured from rival villages. With the express purpose of keeping native laborers and even bounty hunters steeped in debt bondage, self-destructing rifles, called "trade guns," were manufactured specifically for the rubber trade. The guns would fall apart after forty or fifty shots,

dooming owners to an endless cycle of indebtedness to gain possession of a new one. The stories of barbarity inflicted on the natives
that filtered out of the western Amazon prompted the British Foreign
Office to dispatch Sir Roger Casement, the diplomat who had earlier
exposed the horrors of Leopold's Congo, to investigate. Finding himself at a loss to describe the reign of terror he encountered on the Putumayo River, Casement coined a new term to do so: "a crime against
humanity."

*   *   *

Some Indians never did surrender. They scattered into the most impenetrable redoubts of the rainforest, moving into marginal regions
of difficult access, where their descendants continued to shun further
contact with the outside world right up to the present day. "The penetration of whites was so intense, the Indians were driven in all directions," Possuelo said. "They are not on their traditional lands."

It was incredible to ponder, as though ragtag remnants of the
Sioux or Cheyenne had escaped the U.S. Cavalry and retreated into
the deepest pockets of the Rockies—high in the Wind River Range or
the Bitterroots—where their successors endured even now, carrying
on their ancient hunting culture in a kind of Free Indian State.

Possuelo had personally seen the appalling conditions of the rubber camps and how easily natives were duped or strong-armed into a
system of indebtedness from which they were powerless to escape. On
one of his early expeditions, in 1972, he liberated forty Tupari and
Makurap Indians held against their will as indentured laborers on a
plantation far up the Guaporé River, along the border of Bolivia. "The
white man brings problems, never solutions," Possuelo said. "That's
why when you enter the forest, they greet you with bows drawn. It's a
simple reaction to a still-present history." A bug skittered across the
floor, and Possuelo's sandaled foot came down on it with a crunch.
He wadded a paper napkin, scooped up the goo, and tossed it in the
wastebasket. "It's not that they're savages," he said. "They once greeted

foreigners with gifts and hospitality. Read the early chroniclers, see what they say. They all remark on the kindness of the natives." But for all their kindness, the Indians were fleeced, bullied, massacred.

Some of the isolated groups—like the Korubo in the Javari, the Mashco-Piro in Peru, and the Tagaeri in Ecuador—were fragments or remnants of identifiable tribes. Others, like the Arrow People, remained obscure, almost entirely unknown. Tribes that had been reduced to a mere handful of survivors were doomed to extinction. Others had sufficient numbers to assure genetic viability into the future. For the most obscure groups, FUNAI had no names whatsoever, simply designating them by location: the "Isolated Group of the Envira River," for example, or the "Isolated Group of the Upper Tarauacá," nearly as vague a nomenclature as calling them Tribe X or Tribe Y. The Arrow People were also known, variously, as the "Isolated Group of the Upper São José" or the "Isolated Group of the Upper Jutaí."

Almost by definition, these groups were unstudied by anthropology. After all, they were as yet unpacified, and anthropologists generally were not in the business of beating the bush in search of hostile indigenes. Scientists typically entered well after first contact had been made, once a modicum of security had been established in which to conduct research. Lévi-Strauss famously joined a band of Nambiquara in the 1930s on the savannah of Mato Grosso, nine hundred miles southeast of here, after Rondon's earlier encounters with the tribe. Napoleon Chagnon set out in 1964 for the headwaters of the Orinoco River in southern Venezuela in search of "demographically pure" Yanomami communities for his doctoral research, but a smattering of intrepid Catholic missionaries and other adventurers had blazed the trail before him. The swashbuckling anthropologist claimed in later years to have made first contact with more remote villages high in the mountains. The Javari itself had drawn a number of anthropologists to study the contacted groups: the Matis, Kanamari, Matsés, and Marubo. There was a growing body of ethnographic literature about the small group of Korubo Possuelo had contacted in 1996. But the hostility of the tribes in the depths of the Javari—and the deadly illnesses the jungles were said to harbor—had put a brake on sustained exploration. As we moved farther south, farther up the Itaquaí into the far-western extremities of Brazil, we were moving into uncharted territory in every sense of the word, into woodlands and swamps that whites had never managed to subdue, where contact between outsiders and Indians had been sporadic, to say the least, and always fatal.

The head-bashing Korubo roamed the west bank of the Itaquaí, the *flecheiros* the east. One wielded war clubs, the other arrows. Most likely, they'd never met. But together, Possuelo said, they had managed to keep all but the most intrepid interlopers from venturing this far upriver. Of course, FUNAI now blocked the entry downriver at the strategic chokepoint, but the Indians' formidable reputation had served as a powerful deterrent for decades, perhaps even centuries. "Personally, I like them like this—violent," Possuelo said. In the low light, his hazel eyes seemed to pop from their sockets. "This river is one of the most preserved and intact in all of Brazil. Why? Because the Korubo are here, and they're fierce. And the Arrow People are over there."

In the years leading up to the reserve's creation, clashes between loggers and *flecheiros* on the upper reaches of the São José had become increasingly frequent. The timbermen had taken to traveling in packs, always heavily armed. There were rumors of massacres, the taking of trophy heads, lumberjacks shot through with arrows like pin cushions, reprisal raids that left no survivors. The body count among the whites was more easily verified; no one was keeping track of Indian casualties. "No one knows about the violence perpetrated against the Indians, because it has no echo here," Possuelo said. "Their screams are smothered by the jungle—and the huge distances." It must have been 100 degrees in the cabin and nearly just as humid, but I felt a sudden chill run down my spine. "It's rare that word of such massacres reaches the outside world. They happen, and nobody even knows." Nobody besides the perpetrators, that is. One encouraging sign: he had found fresh vestiges of the Indians far up the Igarapé São José, including trails and broken tree limbs. The Arrow People had returned, even seemed to be flourishing, now that the loggers were gone.

*   *   *

I ducked out into the night for a quick gulp of fresh air. The stars pulsed like fireflies. Voices sounded out fore and aft against the drone of the engines—a muffled command here, hoots of laughter there. The black wall of jungle rose high, pressing in on all sides. The loggers had been expelled before they'd gotten to these towering giants. But apparently, some intruders were still willing to take their chances for a shot at the Javari's riches.

Out on the deck earlier in the evening, I'd listened to a thin, sad-looking older backwoodsman I would come to know as Soldado—"the Soldier"—as he recounted a harrowing tale. It involved two poachers who'd recently slipped into the Terra Indígena to steal turtle eggs, eluding the checkpoint by portaging their canoe through the woods and emerging upriver from it. As they dug for eggs on a secluded beach, they were ambushed by a band of Korubo. The Indians clubbed one over the head and chased the other through the forest, until he flung himself into the river and escaped on a floating log, which carried him down to the FUNAI base, where he was detained. The agents later found his friend, unconscious but alive in shallow water, where piranhas had chewed off his fingers and toes. When he emerged from his delirium, he swore he'd never look upon the Itaquaí again.

Possuelo liked those stories; they had "educational value" for those tempted by visions of personal enrichment to breach the reserve's boundaries. Indians willing to resort to violence to defend their lands, or who had a reputation for doing so, made for the most tenacious guardians of the rainforest and provided another layer of deterrence beyond the FUNAI checkpoints. But the rights of indigenous people rarely got a sympathetic ear among power brokers in Brasília. They didn't vote, and their lands harbored precious resources that had already been picked clean elsewhere. Their traditional way of life required vast spaces for them to roam; less than 1 percent of the population on 11 percent of the national territory. "Our authorities are ashamed that so much of our forests are in the hands of naked people with bow and arrows," Possuelo said. "They think it's backward. I think it's beautiful."

In the suffocating cabin, I pondered the implications of Possuelo's words. The Arrow People would have no way of telling us apart from the aggressive loggers they'd clashed with in the past, and we would be penetrating to depths not even the lumberjacks had dared enter in their heyday. Not even Possuelo knew what language the Arrow People spoke, what gods they worshipped, what ethnic group they belonged to, or if they belonged to more than one. They had earned their name—and their fearsome reputation—for being implacable archers with zero tolerance for intruders. The only dialogue that had ever been sustained with them consisted of flying arrows in one direction and flying bullets in the other. To minimize the risk, we would give their settlements a wide berth, never venturing closer, if possible, than six kilometers. "Of course, it's within the logic of the situation that they could still attack us," Possuelo acknowledged.

Rondon's "die-if-you-must-but-never-kill" edict notwithstanding, Possuelo had recruited a large contingent, nearly thirty woodsmen and Indians, who would bear a formidable arsenal of 20-gauge shotguns and .22 rifles. I glanced over at Nicolas. Sweat plastered his graying bangs to his forehead, but he was hanging on Possuelo's every word. Of course, he and I would go unarmed. I never carried a weapon in the field; the tools of my trade were other. Though the guns were mostly for hunting, when it came to the Arrow People, they would also be for show. In Possuelo's calculus, an ostentatious display of weaponry, combined with our sheer numbers, would make the *flecheiros* think twice before attacking. Even if they fired upon us, no one would return the fire, in keeping with the Rondonian dictum. "Just warning shots—in the air," he said, pointing to the ceiling. Still, I couldn't help but wonder how many of the expeditioners—in the heat of the moment—would be willing to die rather than kill?

For Possuelo, the composition of the expedition was crucial; he wanted as many indigenous scouts as possible. He'd recruited a dozen Matis from the Ituí River and two Marubo Indians. Farther up the Itaquaí, he planned to take on five or six Kanamari tribesmen when we stopped at their settlements. We'd thus have a diversity of languages on hand to better be able to communicate our peaceful intentions, if it became necessary. The rest of the personnel included the cooks, hired in Tabatinga, and ten mixed-blood woodsmen, all considered "white" by Brazilian standards, more a cultural marker than a racial one that meant they were not full-blooded Indians.

"That's probably about as much as you can absorb for one night," said Possuelo, patting me amiably on the back on my way out. "But before any of this happens, there's a little problem we need to take care of. We'll discuss it tomorrow."

As I stretched out in the darkness in my tiny bunk, my mind raced with so many thoughts. And I kept flashing back to that moment earlier in the day, when I'd first laid eyes on Possuelo as he came downriver—the glint of the rifle barrels, the camouflaged Indians, his impassive stare—and I wondered if I hadn't delivered myself into the hands of some deranged Colonel Kurtz, in command of his own private army of indigenous warriors.

CHAPTER 6

White River, Black Night

"**D**O YOU KNOW WHAT *narcotraficantes* are?" The Matis and Marubo were pressed in around Possuelo at the table on the *Waiká*, which had been lowered to accommodate his map of the Javari. He spoke in deliberate, halting Portuguese, to make sure he was being understood. The Matis met his question with blank stares, the mollusk-shell earrings and jaguar whiskers seeming all the more otherworldly in the lengthening afternoon shadows. "They make a powder, white like sugar, that they sell to people in the city. People put it up their noses, and it makes them *doido*—stupid." The two Marubo stood amid the Matis, listening intently. It was easy to tell them apart; they had the same complexion, the same high cheekbones, but none of the facial adornments that made the Matis so striking. (The Marubo had been lured from the jungle decades before by American evangelical missionaries, who insinuated themselves into village life and discouraged such exuberant displays of native culture.) Possuelo cast his eyes about the circle, searching for confusion or discord. "These are dangerous people," he said, referring to the drug traffickers. "I've received word by radio they may be operating an airstrip up this river. But this is a fight between whites—*branco contra branco*." He knocked his fists together. "It doesn't concern you, so I'm not taking any of you with me. Are you all right with that?" The Indians nodded their consent.

These *narcotraficantes* and their airstrip on the far reaches of the Rio Branco—the White River—were the "little problem" Possuelo had mentioned the night before. We'd traveled an entire day back *down* the Itaquaí to reach the mouth of the Branco, where Possuelo now began loading the only skiff that had a 60-horsepower motor with what he thought he'd need to solve his little problem: food for two days, guns, ammo. He seemed oblivious of the preposterous figure he posed, clad only in his floppy hat and a skimpy Speedo, over which spilled his ample gut. Paulo Welker, balanced bare-chested on the gunwale of the skiff, blond ponytail flowing down his back, clipboard in hand, calculated how much gasoline they'd need. Toucans, shrill as wounded puppies, yelped from the treetops. Far beyond, high alabaster clouds rose into a sky on the cusp of nightfall.

Possuelo would set out at first light with three *riberinhos,* plus Paulo Welker and Nicolas, in search of the airstrip the narcos might be using. My initial dejection at not being included in the search party gave way to relief. Possuelo demanded a high level of performance from everyone around him at every moment, and I was already finding it exhausting. Then there was Nicolas's unremitting eagerness. I admired his upbeat spirit and even wished I had more of it myself, but I didn't entirely trust it. He seemed to need to prove constantly that he was the bravest man, the best photographer, the guy wringing the most out of every moment of life. I could do with a break from them both. Besides, I thought, it would give me a chance to get better acquainted with some of the other members of the expedition.

The airstrip, Possuelo told me, had previously been destroyed by his friends in the Federal Police, the DPF. I was familiar with the work of the DPF's demolition squad. There would have been no doubt that they'd done a thorough job, blasting craters at ten-yard intervals the entire length of the airfield. But the narcos were known to return in force to rehabilitate damaged landing surfaces, even floating earth compactors and bulldozers by barge to distant points to do the job. An airstrip provided an essential toehold for outlaw loggers, ranchers, gold prospectors, even missionaries seeking to convert souls in the remote jungle: once an advance team carved out a runway, the operation could move into overdrive, planes shuttling in foremen, crews, and supplies. Forests would be razed, gold plundered, precious hard-woods toppled—whatever the occasion called for. But drug traffickers were the worst, from Possuelo's perspective, first because of their lust for violence, and second because their operations placed Indians ipso facto on the wrong side of the law. Indians press-ganged into growing coca or marijuana often didn't even realize it was illegal until police commandos were rounding them up and torching their crops. "It's hard enough to be an Indian," he said. "Being an Indian with the po-lice on your trail is infinitely worse." It was therefore imperative to get to airstrips in their infancy, before they could flourish into full-blown enterprises with a life of their own.

In the fight to save the rainforest, the DPF'S demolition squad had emerged as a key player, but it was the only unit of its kind operating in Brazil, and its men were ridiculously overworked, continually on the move across vast stretches of wilderness from one assignment to the next. The unit could arrive at a job site in fixed-wing aircraft, but obviously its agents required other means to get out, once they'd blown the strip sky-high. That placed an undue burden on the DPF's beleaguered squadron of helicopters, a state of affairs—it occurred to me—that might further dim our own prospects for evacuation if the need arose. But the Federal Police were crucial allies to Possuelo and the entire Department of Isolated Indians. They'd driven off the lynch mob that came to firebomb the base. They'd provided muscle for FUNAI scouts on countless occasions. So when Possuelo's friends in the DPF asked if he'd check into rumors that *traficantes* had reacti-vated the Rio Branco airfield, he readily agreed, even if it meant losing valuable time.

Not that Possuelo had to punch any kind of time card; he was his own boss. Detractors within the agency even grumbled that he'd staked out his own private fiefdom, turning the Isolated Indians bureau into a "FUNAI within FUNAI," funded through his international contacts, answerable to no one. The clock was ticking, however, on the weather. River levels can fluctuate in western Amazonia by as much as fifty feet from their high-water mark to their summer lows, and they were dropping fast. Possuelo had timed the expedition to coincide with the tail end of the rainy season, to get as far upriver as possible while the water was deep enough to accommodate the large boats. We would then begin the overland trek, as solid ground reclaimed itself from the seasonal floods. But the rains were slacking off earlier than expected—perhaps the harbinger of a disturbing change in climatic patterns—and our window to get to the headwaters was rapidly closing. Nonetheless, drug trafficking posed too mortal and immediate a threat to the Indians' well-being to ignore. Even if the rumors proved groundless, they merited a detour.

I was just beginning to grasp how enormous a task it was to defend a territory of the Javari's dimensions. Its vastness did assure an unusual margin of protection for the tribes that lived there, especially those inhabiting its core. The control posts—the one downriver and another to the west on the Quixito River—had successfully stanched the bleeding of timber, fish, gold, and wildlife along its major arteries. But there was a constant thrum of low-level incursions nibbling at the edges: freelance loggers and poachers as noxious and numerous as the voracious insects that feasted on our exposed flesh at every opportunity. A single breach rarely posed a grave danger, but if such incursions were left unchallenged, they could add up to an eventual death by a thousand cuts. Then there were people with far more sinister designs, who operated well-financed syndicates and looked to carve out permanent enclaves in the most remote and difficult-to-reach areas, who managed to avoid detection for months, years even. These could be given no quarter. "You can never just say, 'Okay, we've done our job, we're finished here,'" Possuelo had told me the night before. "The vigilance must be constant." Of course, he lacked the means and know-how to blow up the airstrip if he found it. His mission was one of reconnaissance. Tilting at windmills perhaps, but Possuelo seemed to welcome a chance for confrontation, however uneven the battle might be.

"Father, let me come with you," Orlando pleaded. Possuelo gave him a pat on the shoulder. "I want you to stay aboard the *Waiká*," he

said. "You will be of much greater use here than if you come with us."
Possuelo's plan called for a backup team to follow his scouting party
up the Branco in the *Waiká*. This backup team consisted of five men:
me; Orlando; one of the *mateiros*, Soldado; the expedition's second
cook, Mauro Gomes; and the pilot of the *Waiká*, Adelson. Going half
the speed of Possuelo's fast skiff, we would be in position to relay a
distress signal if necessary and halve the distance they'd need to return
in their crammed little craft. The rest of the boats and expeditionaries
would wait at the mouth of the Branco. Possuelo gave Orlando a hug.
"Who knows—you might get all the way up there, only to find four
or five cadavers floating in the river." He chuckled at his own gallows
humor. "Or maybe we'll just disappear, like Fawcett, never to be heard
from again."

The reference was unsettling, to say the least. British colonel Percy
Harrison Fawcett had vanished in the Xingu River basin in 1925. Fawcett was a hard-bitten explorer with a reputation for brazen antics that
bordered on outright recklessness. He'd once waded across a river in
Bolivia into a cloud of incoming arrows to befriend a hostile tribe.
He was a man obsessed with visions of the exotic and the occult. But
he'd struck at least one note of reason when it came to his vision of
what pre-European Amazonia may have looked like. Victorian-era explorers had found only scattered settlements along the waterways of
the Amazon. They had dismissed as fanciful gibberish the accounts
of the early conquistadors, who wrote of dense populations lining the
riverbanks, gleaming white cities linked by broad highways, and advanced cultures with astonishing works of art. But Fawcett wasn't so
sure. Could the natives have suffered a demographic collapse, caused
by a smallpox epidemic brought by the first Europeans or by a natural disaster that wiped out millions, accounting for the stark discrep-
ancy between the accounts of the conquistadors and those of later
explorers? In a man otherwise possessed of a feverish imagination, his
suspicion that catastrophic disease could have decimated Amazonian
tribes amounted to a prescient insight, borne out by modern-day archaeologists and demographers.

But Fawcett was more interested in a corollary question: Did the jungle yet harbor that mythic city of gold, known to the Spaniards as El Dorado? He meant to find out, to etch his name forever in the pantheon of glory reserved for the world's greatest explorers. In May 1925, Fawcett set out into the rugged headwaters south of the Xingu River in the company of his son Jack and Jack's best friend, Raleigh Rimell. They were never seen again.

Several expeditions in subsequent years failed to locate the adventurers. In 1951, Orlando Villas Boas announced that members of the Kalapalo tribe had confessed to killing the trio, and his team exhumed a skeleton he believed to be that of Colonel Fawcett. But family members in London refused to accept the bones, and the fate of father and son remained wrapped in mystery. In all the confusion, one thing seemed clear: the long shadow Fawcett had cast over the Xingu had also touched something deep within Possuelo, and it continued to resonate even now, decades after his apprenticeship to the Villas Boas brothers.

"There's something about just disappearing that enhances one's mystique," Possuelo continued, his eyes bulging wide for dramatic effect. He seemed to be joking, but I wasn't sure. There was a wistfulness in his voice as he said, "You can never say for certain what happened. There's no gravestone, no marker that says, 'Here lies João Perez, born 1940, died 2002.' When you disappear, there's always a chance you could still be out there." I noticed he chose his own birth year for the imaginary epitaph. More disturbing was the date of death: 2002, the current year.

Orlando wasn't laughing. After all, like the Fawcett expedition, this, too, was an intergenerational quest of father and son. "What if you do stumble across *traficantes* armed with machine guns? They could just wipe you out."

"These are things a youngster would worry about," Possuelo said. "Leave this matter to your father." He turned to Nicolas and rolled his eyes in mock exasperation. "Children!" he huffed.

* * *

Mist was swirling on the White River early the next morning as the team prepared to depart. Standing at the stern of the small boat, the visor of his jungle hat folded back against his forehead, Possuelo shouted up to the Matis on the decks of the *Kukahá*. "There may be Korubo around here," he warned. "If you go out to hunt, go out in large groups—eight or nine Matis, all together, not two or three Matis. Understand?"

He gunned the Yamaha-60, and the party vanished into the fog. Soldado untied the *Waiká* from its moorings against the other boats, Adelson engaged the motor in a throaty rumble, and we turned up-river in the direction in which the skiff had just disappeared. One of two single-decked boats in the flotilla, the *Waiká* was about forty feet from the end of its sharply pointed bow to the washing platform at the stern. Just off the galley was a tiny toilet and shower stall, which used gravity-fed water from a rooftop tank, which in turn was replenished by pump straight from the river. The water in shower, toilet, and sink shared the same tannic brown tint as the river itself. It was the same water we drank, which was also used to prepare our morning coffee, such as the cup now proffered by the cook, Mauro, along with a plate of greasy, thoroughly incinerated fried eggs and a mound of beans and rice.

"G-g-good morning, Senhor Scotch!" Mauro said with good cheer. Like most Brazilians, he pronounced my name like the whiskey, seeming to take particular relish in the sound it made in his mouth. Mauro stood more than six feet tall, with a mane of unruly black hair and a thick mustache. At forty-nine, he retained traces of ruddy good looks, though he was missing all his front teeth. He'd traveled widely in South America, taking odd jobs here and there. He'd never married, and he had no kids. He had a slight stammer, as though in his excitement to get to the next word he couldn't get the present one out. "I di-di-didn't want to bother. You never have trouble finding women out there." The ease with which he shared such intimate details bespoke an utter lack of guile that won me over on the spot.

I took the cup of Mauro's syrupy sweet coffee and went fore to visit Adelson in the wheelhouse. Traveling on the river lent itself to lengthy chats; there wasn't a whole lot else to do. The cockpit was barely large enough for the pilot to squeeze behind the wheel, which was outfitted with round wooden spokes in the mariner style. But the doors were open and fastened back on both sides, effectively opening the space to conversation with those standing on the narrow decks to port and starboard. Beneath his wide-brimmed khaki bush hat, Adelson cut a classic Indian profile—the hawkish nose and wisp of a beard on his chin—as he guided the *Waiká* upriver, keeping to the middle of the channel, which seemed to be narrowing at every bend. "Are there *índios bravos* out there?" I asked, studying the riotous walls of palms and ferns on our flanks. Possuelo's words to the Matis rang in my ears: *Watch out for the Korubo.* "There could be," said Adelson, his eyes riveted on the river before us. "That's why I'm sticking to midchannel."

Recent reports warned that wild Indians were luring unsuspecting travelers to shore with gestures of goodwill, then clubbing them to death to take their belongings. Something like that had happened to Possuelo's friend Sobral, called to the far side of the Itaquaí, only to be bludgeoned. Neither whites nor Indians held an absolute monopoly when it came to the use of savagery along the Branco. Loggers had conducted extermination campaigns, hunting Indians with bloodhounds. Head-Bashers, in turn, brazenly attacked the camp of a FUNAI contact team in the early 1980s, before the no-contact policy was adopted, shattering the skulls of two *sertanistas*. Another FUNAI functionary, together with a geologist, had perished at the hands of the Korubo in 1984, when the state oil company, Petrobras, began seismic testing on the upper Rio Branco. After that, company employees traveled the forest with shotguns at the ready, and company roughnecks were rumored to have torched several Korubo *malocas*. The huts' charred remains were observed by FUNAI surveillance flights—blackened scars in an ocean of green—the following year, when oil exploration was banned outright. Petrobras pulled out from the Javari altogether in 1985, but not before another seismic crew, operating in the bastion of the Arrow People to the southeast, heaved dynamite to fend off a shower of arrows that wounded one worker.

We entered a sharp bend in the river where cecropia boughs heavy with fleshy leaves reached out toward the boat. Adelson braced his lean frame against the wheel and spun it to starboard. He was no stranger to the kind of frontier strife that racked the Branco, and the Javari in general. He'd been born into a Tikuna Indian village near the mouth of the Içá River that was in the grip of a brutal *patrão*—a plantation lord—who laid claim to every tree, every fish, and all the latex gathered up and down an entire *igarapé* and who exploited the natives as his personal labor force. "Quintino Mafra claimed to be the owner of everything," said Adelson as he brought the *Waiká* back toward midchannel. "If a Tikuna even sold a fish to someone besides him, he'd have him whipped." Witnesses watched in horror as Mafra hacked Indians to death by machete and left the body parts to cure in the sun like jerky. Things were so dismal that Adelson's father packed him off when he was only ten years old to live with friends in Tabatinga. Adelson was home visiting when Mafra's excesses finally led to his arrest many years later, and he witnessed the mayhem that ensued. "The Tikuna ransacked his house and set fire to all the buildings. They threw everything into the river. They killed all the animals—horses, pigs, cows," Adelson said. "They destroyed everything. It was a shame to see."

By then Adelson was already working for FUNAI, first as a boat pilot and later as chief of one of the agency's field posts in Yanomami lands near the Venezuelan border, where rumors of gold had sparked a tidal wave of *garimpeiros*—wildcat prospectors—that rivaled the rush on the Klondike. Yanomami communities with little or no exposure to the outside world were suddenly overwhelmed by the clatter of helicopters and the roar of low-flying aircraft as miners leapfrogged from one gold strike to the next, moving deeper and deeper into virgin forest. They slashed open airstrips and brought in laborers and equipment to gouge ore from the earth with high-pressure hoses, poisoning rivers with mercury to extract the gold. Adelson spent five years "pulling prospectors from Yanomami lands," once the government finally got around to ordering their expulsion. He barely escaped with his life when he ducked behind a tree as prospectors opened fire on a joint FUNAI-DPF patrol.

It was in the midst of that upheaval that Adelson first met Sydney Possuelo, who'd come to oversee the survey teams delimiting the boundaries of the newly created Yanomami Indigenous Park. Adelson was impressed that Possuelo, then president of FUNAI, made the effort to reach the remote site in a small, outboard-powered launch, ignoring the considerable personal risk posed by a series of treacherous rapids. The process of physically demarcating an indigenous territory is fraught with peril, requiring woodsmen to clear a ten-meter-wide swath of forest around the protected area's entire boundary, often in the midst of virgin wilderness. In the case of the Yanomami reserve, commandos rapelled down lines from helicopters straight into the jungle to carry out the work. More recently, Possuelo had called in helicopters to extract FUNAI agents from the Juruá headwaters after they were encircled by hostile Indians in the course of marking the boundary of a reserve set up to protect the very tribesmen who attacked them.

Another plus for Possuelo in Adelson's mind was the key role he'd played in pushing the government bureaucracy in Brasília to formally recognize Tikuna land rights. "I liked him because he worked for the Indian," Adelson said, using the singular to refer to Indians in general. I was getting the idea that Possuelo saw the subjugation of the Tikuna by the likes of Quintino Mafra and the invasion of Yanomami lands by violent desperados as part of a single continuum that also included the torching of Korubo villages on the Rio Branco and the hurling of live dynamite at Arrow People on the far reaches of the Jandiatuba River. A naturally peaceable people who inhabited lands of easy access along major rivers, the Tikuna had easily been overrun. The Yanomami had been spared a similar fate only by the massive, military-style operation to expel the prospectors and the formal demarcation of their lands. The Indians of the Javari had found similar respite, also thanks in large measure to Possuelo's efforts. Someone needed to stand up to the juggernaut; the Indians couldn't do it by themselves. In Possuelo's mind, that someone would be himself. It was a grandiose vision, seeming to require an extraordinary combination of altruistic impulse and an ego of Amazonian proportions.

We were joined at the cockpit by Valdeci Rios, known by all as "Soldado." He was a handsome dark-skinned man with sunken cheeks and a pencil-thin mustache who always seemed to have a hand-rolled cigarette pasted to his lower lip. Whether they called him Soldado because he'd been in the military or because he soldiered stoically through the most daunting tasks was unclear. His torso and shoulders rippled with muscles, but his brown eyes were soft, and they focused on whomever he was addressing with a directness that was both reassuring and slightly unsettling. At forty-three years old, Soldado was one of the oldest frontiersmen on the expedition and was certainly the most experienced. Like Adelson, he was very much the product of the frontier's turmoil. Though culturally "white," the blood that swelled the arteries in his sinewy forearms was half Marubo. "My father was kidnapped by whites from the edge of the river when he was nine," he said, reaching into his pocket and pulling out a small cloth bag of Fumo Coringa, the harsh, dark tobacco favored among Brazilian frontiersmen. He expertly pressed a wad into a leaf of rolling paper, licked its edge, and fashioned it into a crude cigarette. "They did that back then—just come along the river and grab anyone they happened to find."

Back then meant during the Second World War, when Amazonian rubber momentarily regained its turn-of-the-century prominence as a strategic resource, worth sending entire armies into the forest to collect it from wild trees. Many of the laborers were press-ganged into service, or soon found themselves steeped in debt to a rapacious *patrão* who supplied essentials at prices far too high for them to ever repay on their meager earnings.

"My father used to take me with him to tap latex," Soldado said, lighting the smoke and sucking it into his lungs. "He'd grab the bucket and stepladder, put the shotgun on his shoulder, and we'd go." Soon he was doing it by himself, still a boy, hiking along miles of trail to etch the neat diagonal grooves in the bark so the trees would ooze with white sap. The latex would drip into tin cups, which he retrieved on a second run-through in the afternoon. Soldado spoke softly, in a clipped frontier Portuguese that was hard to follow, but he didn't seem to mind when I asked him to repeat himself. There was an air of melancholic dignity about him. He would smile occasionally, but I got the feeling right away that he was a man who rarely allowed himself to laugh. He had a wife and twelve children waiting for him in one of the clusters of stilt homes Nicolas and I had passed on our way to join the expedition. Like Possuelo, he'd brought along one of his sons, a thin rail of a kid named Odair, whose woodcraft I'd already observed when he was standing barefoot atop a log, swinging his ax to bite just inches from his toes.

Tapping rubber was hazardous work, Soldado explained, rife with danger. There were *índios bravos* in the woods, not to mention aggressive, venomous snakes. And jaguars. One time he went to visit the station of a fellow rubber tapper and found it vacant. "His ladder was kicked over," Soldado said in his low, deadpan voice. "His bucket was turned over. Latex was splashed on the ground like spilled milk." Jaguar paw prints the size of a human hand led away into the forest, where he and his neighbors found the beast seated triumphantly on the body, the man's throat ripped open, head devoured, stomach spilling innards. The animal bolted, and when the men tracked it down and finally shot it, they found their friend's hair lodged in its teeth. "That jaguar came right up into the tree after him," Soldado said, dread seeming to strangle his voice, as though it'd happened only yesterday.

When Soldado was eleven, his parents got swept up in a messianic revival, he said, following a "Brother José" and his flotilla of devotees—hundreds of boats and canoes, thousands of people—down the Javari River to the Solimões. Soldado's family abandoned everything to join the crusade, eventually founding with the other faithful a community on the Içá River to await the End of Days. But Soldado couldn't make his own way as he grew older; there was no work. He returned to the Javari Valley before his twentieth birthday to resume a life of rubber tapping on the Ituí River. His father was dead now, he said, but his mother still lived on the Içá. Though it was no more than two or three days' journey downriver from Tabatinga, Soldado hadn't seen her in thirteen years.

Sometimes while out tapping rubber, he'd find evidence—a footprint, a twisted branch, a discarded piece of fruit—that signaled the proximity of untamed Indians. But Soldado persevered; he had no choice. He made money for his growing family any way he could. Besides bleeding the rubber trees, he would harpoon ancient pirarucu fish and sell the salted meat in the city, or he'd fell enormous cedar trees with no more than an ax for a dollar a day. But when the Indian Land was decreed, he and his family were expelled from the Javari, together with the rest of the white settlers. Despite yet another dislocation from house and home, he claimed to bear the government no resentment. He was an exception.

Once he'd moved his family downriver from the reserve, Soldado was soon back inside it, contracting with FUNAI as a *mateiro*—backwoodsman—blazing trails through virgin jungle, hunting down animals to feed scouting expeditions, building dugout canoes from scratch in the depths of the forest. He'd been on six expeditions with Possuelo over the years, including the mission that led to the contact with the splinter group of Korubo.

"So what's the most dangerous thing you've ever faced?" I asked. The fatuous question dangled there just long enough for Adelson, peeking out from the wheelhouse, to hear. Suddenly put on the spot, Soldado shrugged. "I've always managed . . . ," he said, his soft voice trailing off. He seemed to possess a rare combination of courage and humility so genuine it did not even recognize itself.

But Adelson wasn't having any of it. "The gravest danger this man ever faced," he said, grabbing Soldado by both shoulders, "is Sydney Possuelo!" We laughed, because we could: Possuelo wasn't around. Nor was Orlando, whom I'd last seen doing push-ups on the rear deck.

His fear of jaguars notwithstanding, Soldado's work for FUNAI may well have been the most dangerous of all. Other settlers viewed his willingness to work with the Indian affairs agency with undisguised contempt. "A lot of people don't like that I work with FUNAI, but one has to make a living," he said, the tar-stained cigarette burning low on his lip. "Besides, it's good they created the Indian Land. The animals and fish are coming back. The forest is still standing." That wasn't the kind of talk that earned you many friends in the redneck frontier towns downriver. Possuelo had said as much to me the other night over dinner. Nodding toward the white backwoodsmen he'd recruited for the expedition, he said: "Any of them could find themselves marked men when this is over and they go back home."

* * *

Adelson pulled the *Waiká* over to the riverbank late in the afternoon. "We'll put in here for the night," he said. The sun was starting to sink and thunderheads were building off to the east. It was the "magic hour"—when the harshest light of the day had passed, and the sun's slanting rays bathed the forest in a warm, mellow glow. The jungle seemed to let out a sigh as a breeze caressed the treetops and set the palms rustling. The water stirred nearby, as though flicked by a tail. The sound of sudden inhalation followed, like water being sucked down a drain. I caught a glimpse of a pinkish gray hump before it vanished beneath the murky surface. *"Boto,"* said Soldado as he tossed his cigarette butt over the railing. The legendary Amazonian river dolphin. It surfaced again, and this time the animal sprayed water ten feet into the air from its blowhole. A second dolphin blew its spout at the same time. They appeared to be feeding in the shallows, or maybe they were playing with us.

The dolphins had long since retreated from more heavily trafficked branches of the Amazon, and their presence here was a measure of how deep we'd already immersed ourselves in the jungle. Until recently, elaborate legends surrounding the pink river dolphin have served to protect the species from wholesale slaughter. Revered by locals, the dolphins are said to transform themselves into handsome studs and enter villages to seduce the most beautiful women. "They say the *boto* arrives at parties, all dressed up in a white suit," said Soldado. He spoke deadpan somber, as though reporting undisputed fact. "He wears a nice hat to hide his blowhole." He charms the ladies and bears them away to his underwater lair. Given its magical attributes, many considered it bad luck to kill the animal. But something had begun to change. Shocking reports were coming in from around the Amazon of dolphins poisoned or hacked to death, their pale and swollen carcasses left to drift in the current. Evidence pointed to commercial fishermen who blamed the dolphins for depleting fish stocks, or who sought to bait lines and traps with their meat, effectively killing two birds with one stone.

It would have been nice to kick back and watch the dolphins feed, but we needed to find food for ourselves. "Let's go fishing," Adelson suggested. Orlando and I agreed, and we hopped into a skiff, which Adelson guided around a bend in the river, then steered into the entrance of a small creek. We slid beneath a low trellis of barren branches that seemed to trap us underneath in a suffocating tunnel. We sputtered through the narrow passage, high banks on either side. No one spoke a word. A bird loosed an eerie cry from an invisible perch. Somewhere a branch snapped. Leaves rustled. The creek opened onto a lagoon of amber water.

Orlando had a fancy pole and tackle he'd brought from Brasília, while Adelson used a simple piece of cane with a hook-and-line tied to the end. "How are you going to catch anything without bait?" I asked. "Watch," Adelson said, bringing the pole straight back over his head and letting it fly. The bare hook hit the surface of the water twenty feet away. Nothing. Five attempts later, the line jerked, and Adelson hauled it in hand over hand. A small catfish wriggled on the hook. "Now we'll start fishing," he said and smiled, hacking the fish into bite-size chunks. He baited Orlando's hook, then his own, and tossed it out again. *Wham*—he had a strike. The cane bent to the breaking point, and Adelson whipped it back, propelling an orange-bellied piranha, thin but round as a pancake, straight at us through the air at the end of his line. The fish flopped around the boat with unnerving energy, baring its saber-sharp teeth. It let out a hideous croak. *"Puta!"* Orlando shouted. "Get that thing away from me!"

Adelson pried the blade of his machete into the mouth of the piranha, which clamped down on the steel edge with single-minded ferocity, its unblinking black eye staring up at us. He worked his machete like a sushi chef, excising the upper and lower jaws. The mouthless fish continued to flip-flop around the bottom of the boat, as though powered by some demonic force that refused to die. Adelson pulled in another piranha and repeated the ritual. He rinsed off a set of jawbones and handed it to me. "Here, for your boys," he said.

Orlando got the next strike, his slender pole doubling over, the tackle spooling out with a flash and whir. He landed a monstrous catfish—nearly four feet long—with a hard, flat head and olive green skin peppered with black dots. Its belly was a jaundiced yellow, the tail a blazing orange.

Mauro greeted our catch—four piranhas and Orlando's catfish—at the stern of the *Waiká* with a broad, toothless smile. "This will make a great dinner tonight." I followed him into the galley. "Did you enjoy the fishing, Senhor Scotch?" I claimed that I had indeed, skipping over the subliminal dread that attended the entire outing, the vague sense of being on the set of a bad horror movie—something like a cross between *Deliverance* and *Anaconda,* the hapless protagonists sliding inexorably toward their doom. I nodded enthusiastically in any case, happy to be back on board.

* * *

We gathered around the dinner table just as a bolt of lightning split the sky with a simultaneous crack of thunder. Rain lashed down in torrents, drops the size of marbles ricocheting off the river. The wind swept the downpour sideways through the boat, and we rushed to unfurl the tarp flaps from their mounts on the ceiling. Shielded from the elements, we sat down to Mauro's tasty catfish and piranha soup. Amid a chorus of pounding rain and eager slurps, Soldado turned the talk to the food we could expect in the jungle: tapir, boar, curassow turkey, and lots of monkey. "There's nothing I hate more than hunting monkey," he said, his soft eyes glittering in the lamplight. "It's horrible to watch them die." For a hardened backwoodsman, he seemed improbably sensitive.

Adelson nodded. "You shoot them, and they drop from the trees, still alive," he said, scratching his whiskers. "And when you come up to them to finish them off, they go like this." He scrunched himself into a ball, covering his head with his arms. "They cry, just like us." Orlando cracked a brilliant smile, the whites of eyes and teeth seeming to glow in the lamplight. "That reminds me of one time when I was with the Zo'ê," he said. "We were walking through the jungle when all the sudden, the Indians started to yell, '*Posi, posi!*' and took off running. I was like, what do they mean—*posi, posi*? And all the sudden, shit started falling from the trees. It hit me on the shoulders and right on top of my head! Man, it was disgusting! It was the monkeys up in the trees. They were throwing their shit on me!"

It seemed far-fetched, but howler monkeys were indeed known to hurl feces down on predators to drive them off, especially jaguars that prowled along the jungle floor, waiting for errant youngsters to fall from the trees. We laughed, a momentary respite from the macabre creepiness that seemed to have locked us in its grip. There was no denying our keen sense of vulnerability. The idea, after all, had been to stick together with a force large enough to deter an attack—from bandits, narcos, or Indians. Now, Possuelo was incommunicado somewhere upriver, the main core of the expedition was far downstream, and we were alone in a vast nowhere in the midst of an ink-black night. As Mauro got up to clear the plates, a rasping gurgle erupted from the bowels of the vessel, like a monster trying to clear a bone from its throat. "The bilge pump," Adelson said. "I'll fix it in the morning."

The tarp fluttered, reminding me that we were no longer in mid-channel, but lashed to an overhanging bough at the side of the river. The tarp drew slowly outward, then relaxed, like a large lung with a life of its own. I yanked it back and peered out into the darkness. The rain had stopped. Beyond the storm lamp's pallid reach, the forest was black and impenetrable. "Don't worry," Soldado said, reading my thoughts. "The Korubo don't move around at night." I wanted to believe him, but I was dimly aware of accounts of predawn raids that presumed a mastery among tribesmen of nighttime movement through the forest. Still, I took comfort in his words. After all, the jungle was vast, the Korubo were few, and the chance of an attack on our boat was probably minuscule. An uneasiness lingered nonetheless, undoubtedly the result of too many tales of man-eating cats and head-splitting clubs. The power of suggestion sets a sticky trap. Here we were, on a mission to defend the homelands and cultures of the Earth's last unassimilated indigenous tribes, and we still could not escape the fear that had marked the Indian in the white man's mind since the early days of conquest five centuries before.

The conversation shifted to death by other creatures, and I shared Ian's warning that a caiman might "bite your boat, Daddy." Orlando and Adelson smiled knowingly, but Soldado did not. "I've seen them six meters long," he said, "and they will attack canoes and bite into them. My uncle lost his leg that way." Maybe Ian knew more than I gave him credit for. Next time I called home, I'd have to give him his due. I pulled out my notebook and added to the list I'd begun to keep of the panoply of horrors that lurked in the jungle: anacondas, jaguars, bushmasters, stingrays, and of course, the *candirú* spine fish that lodged itself in the urethra and required surgery of unspeakable excruciation to remove. Orlando added packs of marauding wild boar, planting his forefingers on either side of his lower jaw to simulate tusks. "If they're coming at you, get up a tree!" he said. "*Puta!* Their teeth are razor sharp!" It was said they even turned on jaguars.

The bilge pump rasped. A cockroach the size of a small airplane buzzed the table. The radio crackled, and Orlando sprang from his chair. His father should have checked in hours ago. I'd noticed he'd been stealing glances at the radio.

"I know him," Orlando said. "If he says he'll make contact at six o'clock, he's on the radio at six on the nose. If he's in trouble, I'm going up there, even if I have to go alone." His concerns, which his father had so airily dismissed with a wave of the hand, suddenly did not seem so unreasonable. After all, the expedition's heaviest weapons were 20-bore single-shot rifles, quaint stuff for modern-day *traficantes*. "If we haven't heard anything by morning," Orlando huffed, "I'm going up there. I don't care what anyone says."

Perhaps we'd be spared after all. I suddenly recalled that I'd been issued the "Dazzler"—a letter of introduction from the National Geographic Society, embossed with golden seal and tricolor ribbons, meant to impress upon bumbling Third World bureaucrats the urgency and import of the bearer's mission. For an instant, I entertained the ludicrous notion that it might actually save us, or save me anyway, in the event of being overpowered by narcos.

I'd been completely on board when it came to Possuelo's quest, but now I was left wondering: What exactly were we doing here, five men surrounded by a boundless forest crisscrossed by drug traffickers and head-bashing tribesmen, another five even farther upriver, only static blasting on the two-way radio? If Possuelo was capable of a lapse of judgment when it came to the expedition's security, what did that say about his larger quest to save Brazil's Indians? Was he, as some critics alleged, attempting to play God with the indigenes, harboring them in a kind of exotic theme park for his own gratification while denying them the benefits of modern life? Was there any real point to this expedition or to his broader efforts to hold back the flood of progress? Wasn't he simply trying to plug a leaky dike with his finger? It was far too early to formulate any kind of authoritative answers. But one thing was certain: there was no way Possuelo would attempt any of it without an exceptionally powerful inner voice—some would say ego—that called him to the quest.

CHAPTER 7

A Government of One

I LAY IN THE CHILL dawn air wrapped in my poncho, looking up at the flaking paint on the ceiling through the gauze of my
hammock's mosquito netting. There were voices, pots clattering in
the galley, a hammer banging on something in the stern of the boat. I
looked at my watch. It was late by expedition standards: 7:15 a.m. Why
weren't we moving upriver? I crawled out to face the day.

Mauro was cleaning up in the galley, drying pots and putting them
in the cupboard. "Would you . . . li-like some coffee, Senhor Scotch?"
It had been only five days since Nicolas and I joined the expedition,
and I'd been aboard the *Waiká* only one night, but it already felt as if I
was among old friends. "Why are we still here?" I asked, holding out a
cup as Mauro poured my coffee. "What's going on?"

"Senhor Sydney entered into communication early this morning," Adelson interrupted, using the stiff, quasi-military jargon spoken by two-way radio operators the world over. His head, the bush hat
crammed down tight, popped up from the open hatch in the floor
that led to the hold. He clutched a wrench in his greasy hands. "They
found the airstrip, but he didn't say anything more about it. They're
heading back. Estimated arrival time: 1500 hours. We're to await them
here in our current location."

"Good thing," I said. "I thought Orlando was going to lead us all to
our deaths." Adelson and Mauro both laughed; evidently they'd been
thinking the same thing. The tarps had been drawn up, and a cool
breeze blew in from the forest. The light was soft; the day had yet

to relinquish its freshness to the white heat of midmorning. Adelson vanished belowdecks to resume work on the bilge pump. Mauro retreated into the galley alcove. Orlando appeared from the cabin wearing a radiant smile and climbed the ladder to the upper deck to do some push-ups and calisthenics. Soldado, barefoot and bare-chested, scrubbed the deck with a long-handled brush, a cigarette dangling precariously from his lips. I'd had a pretty decent night's sleep, but judging from his rather haggard look, Soldado had not.

"Muito carapanã," he complained. "Lots of mosquitoes." Not just any mosquitoes; *carapanã* meant the malaria-bearing anopheles strain. Whether he didn't have the money or just didn't think he needed to bother with it, Soldado had failed to pick up a mosquito net for himself before the expedition departed.

"At least the *vampiros* di-di . . . didn't get you," said Mauro, sounding upbeat. "Not last night, anyway." Little consolation for Soldado, who took a deep drag from his cigarette and went about his scrubbing. Reports of vampire attacks were on the rise across the Amazon, which scientists attributed to the rapid conversion of rainforest to pastureland and the explosive growth of cattle herds that were providing a feast for bloodthirsty bats. Both Mauro and Soldado claimed to have been bitten by vampire bats on multiple occasions, and I'd had a close encounter myself.

It happened a few months earlier on an open boat deck on the Rio Negro in northern Brazil. The boat was traveling through the night, and the breeze was sufficient to keep the mosquitoes off. I'd even considered sleeping in one of the boat's open hammocks, rather than the same enclosed one I had with me now. A young girl who had slept nearby in an uncovered hammock awoke in the morning to find a half dozen purplish puncture wounds, each the size of an oval on a standardized test form, on fingers and toes, even on the tip of her nose. I urged her parents to get her treated for rabies when they got off the boat at their tiny hamlet later that day, but I doubt they did, any more than Mauro or Soldado would have. On the far frontier, you took your chances. It wasn't just the Indians who were vulnerable; vaccines were a luxury few could afford. Rainforest destruction was invariably justified by those who profited as a necessary evil, an engine of wealth that would lift all boats. But what most people got instead was a host of other consequences—exploding vampire bat populations, poisoned rivers, the spread of rabies and malaria, and a deepening drought that was blistering the trees, frying the jungle. Wildfires never before seen had come to the Amazon.

*   *   *

I was sprawled in a chair on the deck late in the day, as the sun turned golden, when I looked out over the water and saw the skiff bearing the scouting party pulling abreast of us. They slouched in the boat, faces weary from the long hours beneath the pounding sun. "Nothing," said Possuelo as he clambered out of the small boat, his legs evidently stiff from the journey. Beneath the floppy hat, his hooked nose was burned crimson. "The strip was entirely overgrown. The narcos haven't been back there."

"We did find these," said Paulo Welker, holding up a pair of rusted motor-oil cans. They were from Colombia. Not exactly a smoking gun. I wondered why he'd bothered to bring them back. His blond hair was matted and unwashed, his cheeks covered in dark stubble. They'd also discovered a 50-volt battery, big enough to power a truck, discarded long ago. "Maybe they used it to light up the runway." It made sense. Clandestine flights often relied on the cover of darkness to avoid detection, but doing so also heightened the pilot's risk of losing his way.

"It was a lot of trouble," Possuelo said, mopping the sweat from his brow with a shirtsleeve. "But it's so rare for federal authority of any kind to pass through here, we couldn't just go by without taking a look."

Traffickers might not have reactivated the airstrip, but that did not mean they'd folded up operations. Western Brazil and the airspace above it had become a preferred route for smugglers moving semi-processed coca base from Peru to refineries in Colombia. Officials had just inaugurated a vast complex of mobile radar stations and AWACS

(Airborne Warning and Control System) flights to provide real-time, actionable intelligence on clandestine air traffic and illegal forest clearing. It was called the Amazon Surveillance System, known by its Portuguese acronym, SIVAM, but it had yet to be matched by actual enforcement capabilities. For the most part, all SIVAM technicians could do was sit in their air-conditioned consoles in Manaus and watch as crimes unfolded on radar screens right before their eyes.

*   *   *

Precious time had been lost, and Possuelo was anxious to resume the journey. There were a half dozen Kanamari villages strung out along the upper reaches of the Itaquaí where Possuelo hoped to gather information and recruit one last handful of men on our way to the river's headwaters, the jumping-off point for our overland march into the territory of the Arrow People. Judging from the high-water mark of dried mud that streaked the foliage in a ruler-straight line along the bank, the level of the river had already dropped by more than ten feet. We needed to move quickly if we were not to be stranded.

When we rejoined the expedition the following afternoon, Possuelo decided to press on right away, rather than wait out the night at the mouth of the White River.

With a throaty roar of the engines, the boats retreated from the bank, and once again, we started upriver, moving in single file. Possuelo was in the lead in the *Waiká*, somewhere out in front, hidden from view. Then came the *Kukahá*, vanishing around each turn and reappearing around the next, followed by the diminutive *Sobral* immediately in front of those of us who rode in the lumbering *Etno*. The way forward was strewn with floating logs and submerged trunks whose gnarled branches pierced the surface like ghostly fingers and slapped the water over and over to the rhythm of the current, like marionettes doomed to repeat the same action for an eternity by a diabolical puppet master.

The high forest walls that blocked the line of vision at every bend, the utter lack of human presence or habitation mile after mile, the seemingly endless river against which our engines whined and sputtered—all conspired to create the impression of a vast and powerful wilderness that was utterly indifferent, if not openly hostile, to our intrusion. The old-fashioned wooden boats with their wraparound decks and bright white railings looked as though they might have been bearing us into the depths of the Dark Continent at the dawn of an earlier century. The green-and-gold banners that snapped at their sterns aroused a similar sense of the heroic, which in this instance did not seem entirely misplaced, in their mission to show the flag in a place that rarely glimpsed one, where national boundaries meant little, where drug traffickers could conceal entire factories and airstrips from the prying eyes of aerial surveillance, and where thatched-hut villages teemed with aboriginals who had never heard uttered the names of Jesus Christ, Christopher Columbus, Osama bin Laden, or, for that matter, Brazil.

I scaled the steel ladder to the upper deck of the *Etno* and went fore to the cockpit, where I found Danilo at the helm, one beefy paw on the steering wheel, the other wrapped around the mike of the two-way radio. He was accompanied by one of the Matis, named Ivan Arapá, and they were carrying on a halting conversation amid intermittent blasts of static from the radio. *"Burrá?"* said Ivan, shaking my hand. He didn't know his exact age, but he must have been in his early forties, old enough to remember what life was like before 1975, when the Matis were first contacted by *sertanistas* from FUNAI. His hair was cut short, his cheeks tattooed with parallel lines from mouth to ears. He'd started calling me "Scotchie" from the moment he'd first heard my name, and a smirk seemed to curl the corners of his mouth whenever he said it: "Scotchie hunt monkey with us? Scotchie go to forest with us?" Like most of his fellow Matis, Ivan spoke in spare, stripped-down sentences, nearly always in the present tense. This was not because that was all he knew—*Me Tonto, you Kimosabe*—but rather because pidgin Portuguese was emerging as the lingua franca on this polyglot venture, and we were all beginning to parody ourselves, deliberately using mangled phrases in our discourse with a certain knowing irony.

His wry smile suggested a man of unflappable temperament who found humor in just about anything. I found myself returning his smile involuntarily, even when the topic at hand wasn't funny at all— like now, as he told Danilo and me about the long-ago events that led to his tribe's first contact with the white man and the lethal diseases that followed.

It began one day more than twenty-five years before, when Ivan and his fellow Matis were out hunting near their home in the headwaters of the Ituí River, about eighty miles west of our current location. They came across footprints like they'd never seen before, made by a waffle-soled boot. "We knew they were made by someone else," Ivan said. "They weren't Indian footprints." What Ivan didn't say, but what the Matis must have thought at the time, was that they weren't *human* footprints. Human beings didn't have feet with such bizarre soles.

Not long after that, he and his family saw strange, bearded men trudging past in the woods, clothed in brightly colored shirts and pants. They watched from behind a screen of foliage, careful not to reveal themselves. "When we first saw clothes," Ivan said, rubbing the lapel of my shirt between his fingers, "we wondered: How do they make that? How can we get that?" The Matis stole an ax around that time, when a logger left it propped against a tree and turned his back. "Matis were watching, take ax." Tensions began to mount. The loggers abducted two Matis children. Clashes seemed inevitable. It was around then that the FUNAI agents appeared on the scene.

"FUNAI made camp in the woods, and they put out many things for us: beads, fishhooks, pots, hoes, axes," Ivan said, recalling how the *sertanistas* carried out FUNAI's time-tested formula for seducing untamed Indians with gifts. "My grandfather said, 'They seem like good persons. They give us things. Let's go visit their *maloca*.'" The Matis knew where the FUNAI camp was; they had followed more of the strange footprints that led right to it. Ivan recalled how he trembled with fright when they'd first approached the *sertanistas*. "The man said, 'I am from FUNAI. Before, the white man killed you, but I am here to help you.'"

The top-heavy *Etno* pitched steeply as we entered a bend, forcing Ivan to grab the railing for balance. I shifted weight from one leg to another. "This boat is very dangerous," Danilo said. Possuelo had commissioned a shipyard in Manaus to build it a few years back, but he'd been disappointed with the results. He never even set foot on it, preferring to command his expeditions from the much older and smaller *Waiká.* "The *Etno* is good for two things," Danilo said, "the clinic and storage capacity. We've got nine thousand liters of diesel on board, enough to supply all the other boats." The clinic on the main deck boasted air-conditioning and bottled oxygen. He smiled and added: "Too bad there's no doctor."

Neither doctors nor FUNAI's best intentions could halt the pneumonia epidemic that ripped through the Matis in the wake of contact. The *sertanistas* should have known better. But back then, FUNAI field agents across the Amazon were under pressure to intervene without proper backup, to step in before a clash with whites could trigger wider bloodshed. They had meant to help the Indians, but in the end their own germs proved to be far more deadly than the most violent adversary. "Everyone was dying, everyone was very sad," Ivan Arapá said. "Everyone was coughing. Everyone was crying. Many, many Matis died. We didn't know why." The Indians were so enfeebled, they didn't have the strength to bury the dead. As many as two-thirds of the tribe may have perished, including most of the elders and shamans, the bearers of traditional knowledge and wisdom. The survivors were left to fend for themselves, like orphans in a terrifying new world.

Possuelo had recruited twelve Matis for the journey, Ivan said, making them the largest single ethnic group on the expedition. The oldest among them were in their late forties, early fifties, and spoke little Portuguese. The two youngest were in their early twenties, bilingual, and sported few of the traditional Matis adornments. Nonetheless, the Matis as a whole demonstrated an enviable cohesiveness. I had observed them on the decks, dispatching with efficiency whatever task Possuelo threw in their direction, all the while chattering and laughing among themselves, as if undaunted by their cataclysmic history. It

was easy to see why Possuelo opted to bring such a large contingent of
Matis. Minimizing discord was key on long expeditions, where hardship and deprivation could strain relationships to the breaking point.

*   *   *

By the time the boats were maneuvered into position and the floating base camp reassembled for the night, Possuelo announced that it
would not be safe for the *Etno,* which had the deepest draft of the riverboats, to proceed any farther. It had been in his plan from the beginning to send the larger boats back once the river became too shallow.
But he wanted to hang on to them for as long as he could. There was
no need to expose the men to merciless sun and lashing downpours
on the smaller boats before it was necessary; there would be plenty of
hardship farther on. Nonetheless, the time had come to send the *Etno*
back. "Let's move what we need off the *Etno* now!" Possuelo shouted.
"There will be no dinner until we finish!"

While a human chain formed to move drums of oil and sacks of
rice, beans, and sugar from the *Etno,* Nicolas and I went upstairs to
our cabins, our footsteps clanging on the metal rungs of the narrow
stairway, to perform a triage of our own stuff. We'd have to jettison
much of our bulk now; there would simply be no room on the *Waiká,*
where we'd be taking up quarters. "Can you imagine how happy we'll
be to see this stuff again?" Nicolas said, hoisting a pile of clothing into
a large, rubberized river bag. In the half-light of the cabin, I stuffed an
entire duffel bag with shirts, jeans, T-shirts, sneakers. All were clean,
barely touched. I packed the Discman CD player and the CDs. Music
was a luxury I'd have to do without. Nicolas was right; it was comforting
to think that all these nice things, products of our industrial world,
would be waiting for us at the end of our journey.

The next morning the engines aboard the *Etno* sputtered to
life, and in a throaty roar of diesel fumes with Danilo at the helm, it
turned and started downriver, drifting slowly away from us in the blinding sunlight, as definitively and irrevocably as the booster stage of a
rocket falls back toward Earth from a capsule bound for outer space.

To make room for our gear, Adelson climbed down through the hatch in the main deck of the *Waiká* and vanished into the hold. He reappeared moments later, head protruding from the hatchway, as he disgorged from the vessel's bowels wilted boxes of half-rotten potatoes, onions, and lemons, which Mauro promptly snatched up and piled on the galley countertop. From now on, we'd have to stow what was left of our gear in the hold and drop down into it to retrieve anything we might need, including our hammocks, which we'd sling from post to post across the width of the main deck.

In a matter of minutes, the same space that bustled with activity in daylight hours was transformed into the boat's general sleeping quarters. Timing was key to finding a choice spot, out of the way of the crowd, with sufficient distance between posts to ensure a taut sleeping surface. That evening, I staked out a position just above the portal to the ship's hold, where Adelson had been at work earlier. As I fastened the thin cord of the hammock to opposing posts, Soldado leaned in for a closer look. He'd been after me to change the cord since he first laid eyes on it. "This looks awfully weak," he said softly, tugging the line in his calloused hands. He blew a cloud of smoke into the muggy night. "You should let me change this. I could put real rope here instead."

"I'll be fine," I said. After all, the hammock was still pretty new, and the cord showed no sign of fraying. "Maybe you can do it tomorrow." Everyone had turned in by the time I brushed my teeth and picked my way through the maze of hammocks back to my own. Only then did I realize that the hatch cover had not been put back on the portal, over which my hammock dangled precariously. The cover was a fifty-pound monster, cumbersome and unwieldy, and it lay on the deck ten feet away. I stared down into the hold. It was a straight drop of six or seven feet to the bottom. The portal itself was only three feet wide, with a raised lip about two inches high. On the off chance that my hammock were to fail, the lip would likely act as a fulcrum, snapping my spine as I tumbled down into the hold.

I weighed this nasty, though seemingly remote, possibility against the unpleasant but very real prospect of having to fetch the hatch cover by myself. It would be a mildly hazardous task, considering its weight and bulk—and the fact that I was barefoot. Moving the thing was really a two-man operation, but I was loath to roust anyone from sleep. Lethargy was about to get the better of me, when I mustered the ambition to drag the cover over and seal the hatch.

Good thing I did. I awoke with a thud in the middle of the night. Pain shot through my elbows and knees. The hammock cord had snapped, and I'd landed directly on top of the hatch cover. At first light, while I nursed my bruises, Soldado changed the cord, skillfully wrapping the points of the hammock with sturdy clothesline. He could have said, "I told you so," but he said nothing. Perhaps he sensed in my own silence the tangle of thoughts that left me wondering how I'd managed to so narrowly escape near-certain paralysis—if it had been dumb luck, or a simple matter of taking commonsense precautions, or if some Larger Agency had intervened on my behalf.

During daylight hours, as we plowed upriver, the choicest spot aboard the *Waiká* was the bow, which provided a refreshing breeze and a respite from the ubiquitous clouds of voracious, gnat-size *piums* that left constellations of bleeding, itchy welts on any exposed patch of skin. The bow also afforded some peace from the din of the engine, which made it the best location for dialing up the outside world on the satellite phone. It was late afternoon, and Nicolas had already made a call to Lily Fleur, his nine-year-old daughter, in Paris. My French wasn't good enough to understand much, nor did I wish to eavesdrop, but I couldn't help noticing the tenderness and excitement in his voice when he spoke to her. *"Je t'aime beaucoup!"* he told her, hanging up. A broad smile lit up his face as he handed me the receiver. "Didn't you say you wanted to call your parents?" I was just punching the number in, when a squadron of blue macaws crossed the river in front of us, fifteen of them in a lopsided V formation, streamlined like thunderbirds. The slanted shafts of sunlight seemed to set their golden bellies aglow from the inside out as they passed, wings pumping in unison.

Their raucous shrieks spoke of a primordial sense of exuberance and celebration of life in the fullness of all its untamed creation that otherwise defied articulation. We were reduced to a reverent silence.

"Now *this* is adventure!" Nicolas said after the birds had disappeared beyond the trees. It was the kind of obvious statement that would have educed embarrassed winces in another context. But I nodded, allowing the moment to settle within me, like a photograph does in a tray of fixing solution.

I pressed the Call button on the phone, waited for the connection, and shared the moment with Mom and Dad, whom I pictured in their wingback chairs in front of the living room window, their backs to the neatly manicured lawn. It seemed so distant from the raw energy of the jungle, they might as well have been on another planet. The description of the macaws seemed to have brought a quick jolt to their lives, out of the blue, a missive from a lost world. "Be careful now," said my father, signing off. "Will do," I said. "Love you."

* * *

We traveled into the night without stopping to assemble the floating encampment. I stood at the bow, transfixed, as the moon rose over the trees to our left, brilliant white against a darkening sky, its liquid reflection an ever-changing kaleidoscope of mesmerizing distortions. Mauro's call to dinner brought me back along the main deck, where the table had been dropped for the evening's repast. Possuelo, Nicolas, and Orlando had already tucked into pan-fried fillets of *tucunaré*—a delicious fish, moist and tender, with only a few small bones. "One of the great delicacies of the Amazon," declared Possuelo, licking his fingers with gusto. I anticipated further commentary, but he simply scratched his beard and sank back into his thoughts. I was coming to see that education—perhaps *reeducation* was a better word for it—was part of the daily fare at Possuelo's table. Last night, a stew of wild turkey had prompted commentary about the egregious nature of Thanksgiving celebrations in the States. "Almost no one remembers the real origins

of Thanksgiving," Possuelo had said. "The Indians saved the white settlers from starvation. It should be a day of giving thanks to indigenous
peoples." One thing was beyond dispute: so far, the Javari was providing us with a rich bounty of fish, fowl, and meat.

This abundance was the result of tight enforcement, Possuelo
claimed, the control post downriver "100 percent" responsible for
the rebound of the region's fauna. It not only barred unauthorized
outsiders from entering, but it also choked off the flow of outbound
contraband. Not even the Indians who lived within the Indigenous
Land were permitted to take resources from the reserve. They could
hunt and fish as much as they could eat, but they could not sell any
of it on the outside. Of course, there were still occasional attempts
to make an end-run around the checkpoint. Sometimes the would-be
smugglers were government functionaries.

Mauro was clearing the plates when Nicolas said: "Sydney, tell Scott
about the time the health workers tried to get past the vigilance post."
Possuelo shrugged like it was no big deal. Two years earlier, he began,
public health officials were returning from a vaccination campaign
upriver when they tried to sail past the control post without stopping.
"They went by in the middle of the river, playing dumb, smiling and
waving." Possuelo mimicked the gestures, warming to the story. When
the health workers refused to heed orders to pull to shore, FUNAI
agents hopped in a motorboat, pursued the vessel, and boarded it.
They asked to inspect the cargo hold, but a medic who claimed to be
sick was sprawled across the hatch. "The agents said: *We don't care if
you're dying—move!*'" Possuelo chuckled. "They dragged the guy aside
and opened the cover." Inside the hold they found piles of illegally
hunted bush meat. Everyone was arrested, the meat confiscated. Two
of the health workers were later fired. "Mauro, do you have any coffee
back there?" he said. "Bring it out!"

I was getting the feeling that if Possuelo had his way, the only
outsiders allowed into the Javari would have to answer directly to him.
He seemed to harbor suspicions even of the small nongovernmental

organizations that were trying to promote a sense of empowerment among the contacted tribes. Some of their "sustainable development" projects, Possuelo said, had encouraged communities to expand beyond their traditional bounds, straying dangerously close to un-contacted nomads wandering the forest. While the assimilated tribes served as a buffer that helped shield the isolated Indians from contact with whites, Possuelo believed they posed a danger in their own right. There were rumors that Kanamari villagers on the upper Jutaí had enslaved a group of previously uncontacted Tsohom Djapá Indians. If we ended up descending the Jutaí, Possuelo intended to investigate and intervene. He'd previously tasked another *sertanista* with keeping acculturated Asháninka Indians from launching a punitive raid on isolated tribesmen in the headwaters of the Envira River, in the state of Acre. NGOs (non-governmental organizations) were another prob-lem. They were always talking about "*projecto* this and *projecto* that," he complained. "They think they're the big guys here—the owners of everything." But only the government had the authority to speak for the isolated groups, Possuelo made clear. "And the government here," he said, slamming his fist on the table, "is me."

* * *

Forward in the tiny wheelhouse, Adelson stood at the helm, staring into the night. His hawkish nose and bewhiskered chin were dimly silhouetted in the ghostly light of a moon veiled by a sheen of high clouds. The boats advanced single file. Their spotlights probed the darkness like the beams from a watchtower, skittering across the sur-face of the narrowing channel, on the lookout for logs or stranded treetops, anything that could bash open a rotting hull or bend an old propeller. The jerky circles of light did more to accentuate the dark-ness than to dispel it, a reminder of the impermanence of our pres-ence in this vast and wild domain, where not even our position at the top of the food chain was guaranteed. I stood silent alongside Adelson watching the night and the river.

Sometime close to midnight we slowed to a crawl, and then amid shouts and sputtering engines, the boats nudged alongside an enormous tree at the edge of the river. There were stirrings in its branches. Suddenly a pair of flashlight beams swept the deck. A half dozen men appeared on the log, barely discernible in the pale light. They climbed aboard, whooping excitedly. *"Seu Sydney taquí!"* they shouted. "Sir Sydney is here!" We'd made it to the first Kanamari settlement of Bananeira—the Banana Grove.

Of all the tribes of the Javari, the Kanamari had the longest-standing contact with the outside world. They once inhabited the *igarapés* of the upper Juruá, about fifty miles through dense jungle to the south, in what is now the Brazilian state of Acre. They'd lived in elaborately designed longhouses, grown a rich variety of crops, feasted on an abundance of fish and game. The Kanamari had managed to avoid some of the more punishing aspects of the upheaval the Rubber Boom brought to the western Amazon during the last half of the nineteenth century. They were seen by white rubber tappers as the "friendly Indians," as opposed to the "hostiles" upriver. Eventually, though, the Kanamari found themselves nudged out by settlers amid violent clashes. They drifted to the Itaquaí, which saw a mass exodus of white rubber tappers beginning with the drop in the price of wild latex in the apex year of 1910, when rubber fetched 40 percent of Brazil's export earnings. Other Kanamari found their way to the far reaches of the Jutaí, an adjacent watershed that Possuelo was weighing as a possible route for our egress from the jungle. It was also from the Jutaí that word was emanating of Kanamari contact with, and possible enslavement of, the isolated Tsohom Djapá tribe.

Nonetheless, the Kanamari's age-old hospitality was very much in evidence as the welcoming party pranced in the shadows of the *Waikã*'s deck, the smiles of our hosts glowing in the silvery light of the moon. "Let's go visit the community!" Possuelo shouted.

We climbed out onto the massive tree trunk that led up the bank and ended with a ten-foot jump down into the blackness of the thicket.

Dressed only in shorts and rubber flip-flops and without a flashlight, I scrambled to stay within sight of the sole lantern, which advanced dimly through the woods far ahead. A ten-minute walk brought us to an opening in the forest. The dark outline of a thatched hut perched on stilts loomed in the clearing opposite three fallen tree trunks arranged in a semicircle, evidently the community's gathering place. We took seats on the logs, and in groups of twos and threes, ghostly figures began to materialize from the forest gloom, their figures dimly silhouetted against the night sky. I couldn't manage to get a clear look at anyone: everything seemed to reverberate in the faint light, which strained retinal synapses to the limit, creating the effect of a very dim, low-level strobe.

"What do you need here?" Possuelo asked the assembled group. As the Kanamari inhabited the very last outposts of the civilized world on the boundaries of the Arrow People, Possuelo knew their support was critical to his project. It was a foregone conclusion that he would come bearing gifts.

"Medicine and gasoline," came a disembodied voice from the darkness.

"Especially medicine," another said. "There's malaria here. And diarrhea. Amoebas."

"Do you have any medicines? Let me see."

The silhouette of a man climbed a notched log that served as the stairway up into the nearby hut. He came back down clutching a plastic bag. Possuelo pointed his flashlight beam into the bundle. It was stuffed with vials, bottles, rolls of gauze, and a first-aid kit. The supplies had been left by public health workers on their last visit here, several months ago, the man said. Possuelo pulled out a random bottle and inspected the label: tetracycline. He looked for its expiration date: 1999. Three years before. He fished around in the bag and produced another, with the same result.

"These medicines are all expired," he said in disgust, flinging the bag aside. For Possuelo, the government's failure to provide Brazil's

Indians with adequate health care was a source of never-ending out-
rage. To begin with, there were the massive die-offs that inevitably
followed exposure to the white man's pathogens. That was the most
important reason for his no-contact policy. But even after decades of
"acculturation" and accommodation to Brazilian society, the Kanamari
still found themselves on the bottom of the heap, dispossessed of their
original lands and much of their culture, surviving on the very margins
of civilization. They did not even rate medicines with expiration dates
that pertained to the same decade as the actual calendar.

A man took a seat beside me on the log bench. His face was cast
in deep shadow beneath the visor of a baseball cap. I could barely discern the whites of his eyes. "We lived in the *igarapé*," he told me. "But
then the whites came, and they started killing Indians. They killed
a thousand Indians." It was difficult to pin down when and where any
of this had happened. It could have been a century ago. But one thing
was certain: the tribes of the Upper Amazon had been decimated, in
some cases suffering up to 90 percent mortality. They were, in effect,
refugees from the violence of the global economy. With their universe
turned upside down, there was little chance for a thorough accounting of who went where, of who survived and who did not. And those
who fled deep into the bush—whatever became of them? Did they
perish in the harsh wilds, far from the gardens and trading routes that
had sustained their way of life since time immemorial? Or had they
endured the dislocation and reconstituted their way of life, their descendants still holding forth in the jungle's deepest redoubts? Could
they in fact be the People of the Arrow, among the last unconquered
Indians of the Amazon?

Until this moment, we'd been surrounded by only men and
children. Now the village women entered the clearing, their arrival
announced by a high-pitched song. "Their way of welcoming us," Possuelo said. "They're bringing *caisuma* for us to drink." It was the near-
beer of practically all Amazonian tribes, made by fermenting the mix
of chewed cassava root and human saliva. Its sour reek wafted in the
humid air. Possuelo rose and approached the vat. Behind him the

Matis and Marubo lined up to drink amid excited babble and laughter. It was considered bad form to refuse such hospitality. I'd tasted variations of *caisuma* among various tribes, and I'd never managed to swallow it without a strong sense of revulsion. In the darkness, I managed to duck out of the line.

The last of the villagers now straggled in from the disparate gaps in the forest, dressed in threadbare clothing. As my eyes adjusted to the darkness, I could see the women were clutching babies; the men, machetes. All told, there were about thirty people, nearly all barefoot. The moon was now straight overhead, providing just enough of its pale light to illuminate my notebook as I held it close to my nose and scribbled.

"Let's see that *facão*," Possuelo said, reaching for one of the machetes. He pulled its blade into the glow of his flashlight and ran his finger along its edge. Now everyone wanted Senhor Sydney to have a look at his machete. A man broke into the circle with an ax head for Possuelo to inspect.

"Hmmm," Possuelo said. "This ax is old but good—like me. I'm old, but I'm still good." The crowd laughed.

Possuelo turned to Paulo Welker. "Can we tend to our friends' request? How much gasoline can we spare?" Welker rounded up a handful of men and vanished into the shadows down the path that led back toward the boat.

"What do you know about the *flecheiros*?" Possuelo called out to the circle of faces pressing in around him. "Has anyone seen them lately?"

An older man with a wrinkled face spoke up first. "We've seen *rastros*—signs—but no one has seen them."

"They've killed monkeys," another man said. "We've seen the bones."

"A guy from Pedras was killed by the Arrow People, but that was a long time ago."

"A logger named Flavio killed many of them, but that, too, was a long time ago."

"That's why we've closed off the entrance to this area," Possuelo said. "So loggers can't go up there."

"We don't see Brazilians around much anymore," the older man agreed. I noted his use of the term "Brazilian," as though his people were not. "We're all satisfied without the white man around here," he continued. "Before, when whites were coming here, there were no fish left in the rivers. The loggers put the Kanamari to work, but then they cheated us." Possuelo nodded. I couldn't tell if the Indians were just saying what they thought Possuelo wanted to hear, or if they were telling the truth. Perhaps it was both.

"Does anyone here still hunt with arrows?" he asked.

Someone said: "We use *espingarda*—shotgun. But cartridges are scarce."

A man tromped off into the night, returning minutes later with a bow and three ancient arrows. Possuelo turned on his flashlight for a closer look. The cane shafts were battered, the tail feathers mangy and exhausted. In this settlement, anyway, the bow and arrow were clearly a dying technology. Possuelo fit an arrow into the bow and drew it back, then spun and pointed it at the Matis, who were seated on a log off to the side. *"Eu sou flecheiro!"* he grunted with mock ferocity. The Kanamari laughed and hooted. At first I wondered why Possuelo would choose to ridicule the Arrow People. But I was probably just reading too much into a moment of frivolity he'd seized to bring some laughter into the lives of a largely forsaken people.

Paulo Welker came back up the path with gifts for the community: two ax heads, six machetes, a whetstone, a bolt of cloth, and sewing needles. Most treasured of all were two 25-liter containers brimming with gasoline. It would take nearly that much fuel and an entire week just to reach the nearest filling dock in Benjamin Constant. The return trip, against the current, would take even more time and more fuel. Up here, every drop of gasoline was precious. As far as medications were concerned, Paulo Welker said, there were none to spare. "I will make a report," Possuelo promised. "They need to come back with medicines—ones that aren't old and useless! I'm old but still good. These *medicamentos* are old but no good."

We bid farewell and picked our way in darkness back to the boats. There would be other settlements to visit in the days to come, more opportunities to exchange gifts and to inquire about the Arrow People as we moved farther upriver, deeper into the forest, drawing ever closer to their domain.

CHAPTER 8

Between Two Worlds

ANOTHER HALF DOZEN Kanamari settlements lay farther upriver, and despite the urgency imposed by the slackening of rains and dropping water levels, diplomacy demanded that we make at least a cursory stop at each hamlet. Possuelo could ill afford to alienate the tribe that lived closest to the *flecheiros*. Especially in light of rumors that Kanamari on the Jutaí River had been making contact with *índios bravos,* he needed to impress upon their brethren here on the Itaquaí the dangers of attempting such contact with the Arrow People—for themselves and for the isolated tribe. Important intelligence—the suspicious appearance of outsiders, the opening of new trails—could be gleaned from the Kanamari villagers as well, and he still needed to draw a number of recruits from among them for the expedition. Both Nicolas and I needed porters—Nicolas thought he'd need two to haul all his gear and extra film—and we'd begun to quietly agitate with Possuelo to hire them on our way upriver.

After traveling through the night, we arrived at the village of Aremací early the next morning. Its thatched huts, tired looking and jaundiced yellow, appeared suddenly as if out of nowhere through swirls of gray mist rising off the river. Just the three expedition boats remained now—the *Waiká, Kukahá,* and *Sobral*—and we trundled down their gangplanks into a small throng of shouting children. Men scrambled from the huts and sidestepped down the steep embankment, dressed in ragged cutoffs and grimy T-shirts. The community was clearly larger than Bananeira, with at least a dozen houses spread out along the top of the bank, decrepit structures made of weather-beaten planks topped with shaggy mats of straw. The women appeared from between the huts, threadbare gingham skirts swishing at their calves, faces smeared with crimson bands of *urucum* dye. Their high-pitched ululations sounded more like a funeral dirge than a welcoming song, but there was no mistaking the ritual vat of fermented *caisuma* brew they beckoned us to drink. Possuelo went to the head of the line, and I fell in behind him. I hoisted the ladle to my lips and took a gulp of the frothy concoction, suppressing a gag to get it down. I followed on Possuelo's heels as he stiffly scaled the bank. He'd donned a black expedition T-shirt for the occasion, with the logo of the Department of Isolated Indians on its breast pocket, together with his camouflage shorts and signature floppy jungle hat. The crowd reconvened around him at the top of the bank, where he stooped to scratch a crude map in the sand with his finger.

"The Itaquaí is here," he said, tracing a squiggly line in the dust. His finger halted. "This is Aremaci, right here." Everyone leaned in to look. Unlike the Matis, the men here had facial hair—beards, goatees, mustaches—which made many of them virtually indistinguishable from mixed-blooded Brazilian mestizos. Possuelo gazed up into the ring of faces surrounding him. "We're going over here, where the *fle-cheiros* are," he said, drawing a second squiggle line to signify another river to the east. "Do any of you dare come with us?"

"The ones you call the Arrow People are known to us as the Capy-baras," said a man with red smudges on his cheeks. The capybara, of course, was the pig-size rodent native to the Amazon. A tattoo stretched down the length of the man's right forearm, bearing the Portuguese word MATEMATICA in big block letters. His left bicep was adorned with a much smaller tattoo, of a primitive stick figure that resembled an ancient petroglyph of a horned bipedal creature. I thought it might be a denigrating term, *capybara*, not unlike calling someone a *savage*, except that the Kanamari had similar names for other isolated clans that surrounded them who spoke a similar Katukinan dialect, and who may even have been distantly related—the King Vulture People, the

Squirrel Monkey People, the People of the Wild Pig. In any case, such deprecating terminology would more likely have been reserved for old enemies, like the Panoan-speaking Kaxinawá from the upper Juruá. The Kaxinawá historically preyed on Kanamari settlements, kidnapping their women and children, but had themselves been forcibly relocated by a rubber boss named Felizardo Cerqueira and hired to do his dirty work, not only gathering latex but also rubbing out recalcitrant tribes that refused to be "tamed."

"What do you know about them—the Arrow People?" Possuelo said. He wasn't asking about clan affiliation or kinship. He didn't care about their fetishes or totems. Those questions fell within the purview of anthropology, a discipline for which Possuelo had little use. Rather, he sought "practical information"—recent sightings, footprints, possible attacks. "Have you seen them?" he wanted to know. In remote places like this, where all information begins with rumor or word of mouth, questioning the locals marks an early step in a process that might eventually lead to definitive proof of the presence of an isolated tribe and the installation of the legal framework to protect it. Flimsy leads are discarded, credible tips pursued, followed by reconnaissance flights and possibly field expeditions to document the tribe's existence and map its territory. Here, the presence of the Arrow People was not in doubt; their relative safety and well-being were. "We haven't seen signs of them in a long time," said the man with the Mathematics tattoo. "We're afraid of them here." Possuelo nodded with grim satisfaction.

Despite the fear, four young men rose to the challenge and decided to come with us. Whatever the possible dangers, the trip promised an escape from the tedium of the village and a chance for adventure that might never come again in their lifetime. They went off to pack and say their good-byes. We now had three native languages represented in our ranks, heightening the prospects, Possuelo hoped, for a peaceful outcome in the event of an encounter with the Arrow People. He didn't say it at the time, but Possuelo was also assembling a core of young men whom he could inculcate in the course of the journey with a new kind of pan-Indian consciousness. It was critical to involve the Indians in the protection of the reserve, to raise their awareness beyond the near horizon of tribal self-interest toward collective defense of their land and cultures in the face of the common enemy: the white man. That Possuelo was himself full-blooded Caucasian did not strike him as the least bit odd; it only seemed to call him more urgently to the mission. "I may be white," he said, "but I have the soul of an Indian."

Within fifteen minutes, the four new recruits returned with gunny-sacks slung over their shoulders. As we pushed off, Possuelo stood at the bank, reassuring their teary-eyed mothers, girlfriends, and wives that he'd return with them safely in three months' time. "Which one is my porter?" I inquired in a low voice to Possuelo's frosty stare. "None of them," he said, and walked off, leaving me to think I'd probably end up having to haul my own load after all.

My anxiety over such loose ends heightened with each mile of jungle-choked riverbank we passed. There was also the matter of the boots I'd bought in Manaus. I'd oiled them, walked the decks in them, stuffed them with newspaper. Nothing seemed to work. It was torture just shuffling from one end of the *Waiká* to the other with the boots on, the stiff leather raking across the tops of my toes, gouging into my heels. In desperation, I turned to Paulo Souza, hoping his military experience might have taught him a thing or two. "No problema, Scott," he said with the breezy air of a confident man, his zirconia earring catching a golden ray of sunlight. "Bring them to me." In the galley minutes later, he filled each boot with dried black beans. "Let me show you how this is done in the army," he said. The next thing I knew, he was pouring water into them.

"What the fuck are you doing?" I said. "Those are *my boots!*"

"We'll leave them like this overnight," he said as he laced them tight at the ankles. "The beans will expand and stretch them out. By tomorrow, your boots will fit."

The next day, I found the boots in the galley cupboard where Paulo had secreted them. I went out on deck and turned the boots upside down over the railing, the soggy mass of beans hitting the water with a plop. I anxiously slipped them on, my toes wriggling into the depths of the clammy chambers. It was all for naught; they were actually tighter and stiffer than before, like some especially cruel instrument of torture.

Our upriver journey took us through five Kanamari hamlets in as many days. They were wretched collections of sagging thatched huts perched precariously on stilts at the river's edge, places forgotten by time and ignored by the government, where the arrival of our flotilla was greeted with such wide-eyed astonishment that we might as well have been disembarking from flying saucers. The initial decorum of our hosts soon devolved into a frenzy of flailing arms and elbows as Possuelo began dispensing gifts—fishhooks and tackle, bolts of cloth, bars of detergent soap, machetes. He would invariably steer the talk toward queries about the Arrow People. We heard vague, contradictory tales, third- or fourth-hand accounts, translated into halting Portuguese, of sightings of the Indians or their footprints, and of clashes between them and white intruders. Some said the *flecheiros* were tall and muscular, with long, flowing hair. Others told of painted faces and bodies red with *urucum* dye and hair clipped in the classic bowl shape common to many Amazonian tribes. But all agreed on this: the Arrow People were dangerous, "untamed," and villagers carefully avoided their lands upriver. "We don't go up there," said a man paddling by in a small dugout, pointing upstream to the Itaquaí's headwaters. "There are *índios bravos* up there. That's their territory."

* * *

A Kanamari Indian stood before us at rigid attention in the sun-drenched plaza of Massapê, a dreary, treeless village two days upriver from Aremací. His head was bowed, and he clutched an ancient breech-loading shotgun before him in both hands. "This is Alfredo," Possuelo said to me. "He is to be your porter." The display of deference gave me an uneasy feeling, but I didn't know quite how to break through the formality. He wore a navy blue T-shirt and Nike shorts over a robust frame, and the strap of a canvas pouch was slung bandolier-style across his well-muscled chest. There was something almost Prussian about his appearance—his pencil-thin mustache, square jaw, and close-cropped hair—that suggested the mixing of bloodlines. A tattoo bearing his name ran along the inside of his left forearm, scrawled in crude uppercase letters as if by a second-grader: ALFREDO. The other arm bore the letters FUNAI in similarly hackneyed script, not unlike brands used by bosses at rubber-gathering stations a hundred years before to mark their human chattel. The markings not only discouraged them from running off but also kept Indians from being commandeered by rival rubber tappers, known as *caucheros*. In Alfredo's case, the tattoos appeared to serve a more decorative function.

"You will carry his backpack," Possuelo told Alfredo, who remained bolt upright and expressionless in the center of a patch of sun-drenched sand. "You will set up his camp every afternoon and help him take it down in the morning. He will pay you at the end of the expedition, when everything is finished. Same as what FUNAI pays everyone else. What I pay to other Kanamari, he pays you." That was roughly $3 a day—a pittance by our standards, but a small fortune for anyone living here on the edge of the world in the far reaches of Amazonia. Alfredo nodded his assent but otherwise said nothing. The 500 to 600 Brazilian *reais*, around $300, I'd give him at journey's end would likely amount to the largest sum he'd ever hold in his hands in his life.

Part of me winced at this stilted arrangement. Still, it was a huge relief to know I'd have someone to haul the bulk of my gear. Fearing the worst—that I would have to manage by myself—I'd been ditching stuff left and right, not just the things I was sending back downriver, but items I'd brought along to make the trek more bearable: chewing gum, packets of instant Gatorade, candy bars. At least I'd been endearing myself to fellow expeditionaries in the process. Nonetheless, Possuelo warned, I would need to pare down my gear to a bare minimum. "He's going to have to carry his own stuff and his share of expedition provisions besides your bag," he said. "Don't overload him with a lot of needless weight."

I sensed it was going to be an uncomfortable relationship. No matter how good a guy I might try to be, we were locked in roles that would be difficult to transcend: me the neocolonial master, Alfredo the aboriginal serf. My Portuguese was good enough to work my way around and through most situations. What I lacked in vocabulary or syntax I could usually make up with extroverted smiles and excessive gesticulation. But such was not the case with Alfredo. We'd only gotten as far as introductions, but I hadn't gotten him to speak more than two words; he simply stared into empty space. I couldn't tell if he didn't understand what I said, if he just didn't want to bother, or if something else was going on. It portended a tortured interaction, a mutual lack of comprehension.

By the time we left Massapê, Possuelo had assembled his full team. Twenty Indians now formed the core of our expedition: twelve Matis, two Marubo, and six Kanamari. There were ten Amazonian frontiersmen who, notwithstanding their mixed-blooded heritage, were considered culturally white—*brancos*. Possuelo, Orlando, and Paulo Welker rounded out the roster, along with me and Nicolas. Aboard the *Kukahá*, Paulo Welker called the Kanamari together to issue them the standard gear other expedition members had already received: camouflage pants, shirts, and hats; T-shirts bearing the Department of Isolated Indians logo; rucksacks; and a bright blue six-foot-by-six-foot plastic tarp that, when stretched between a pair of trees and tied off at the corners, would serve as roofing over their hammocks. Everyone also got an enamel cup, a bowl, and a spoon, together with a forest green souvenir canvas pouch to store them in. Each received a pair of canvas jungle boots, and a pair of Kachutes—low-cut walking shoes with a distinctive rubber tread. Finally, rifles of differing calibers were handed out, together with ammunition. Some received the 20-bore shotguns; others got the quieter .22s.

The mix of weaponry, Possuelo said, was tailored to meet a range of possible exigencies. The shotguns were most effective for hunting; a single blast could drop a fleeing boar, even stop a good-size tapir if the aim was true. But once we entered the sensitive zone proximate to the Arrow People, their ringing reports would resound through the forest, carrying the attendant risk of rousing the tribesmen. In such instances, .22s would be preferable, the dull spank of their discharge quickly smothered by the jungle's luxuriant foliage. If, on the other hand, the Arrow People were to ambush us, then the shotguns would be the instruments of choice, for the same reason their use would be circumscribed in the first place: to produce earsplitting shots, meant to drive off attackers without inflicting casualties. What all the guns had in common was the high visibility of their long barrels. That alone might be sufficient to dissuade the Indians from ever loosing an arrow in our direction; even the most isolated tribesmen of the Amazon seemed to have more than a passing acquaintance with firearms, having been targets of gunfire.

With the six Kanamari swelling our ranks to thirty-four men, Possuelo now had what he considered to be a contingent of sufficient size and firepower. The Arrow People would have to think twice before launching an attack on such a numerous and well-armed contingent. Possuelo had devised something of a variation on the doctrine of overwhelming force; in this instance, there was no intention whatsoever to use it. He had been coached in the school of the Villas Boas brothers, who recruited large numbers to their expeditions and provisioned them with copious quantities of glass beads, knives, and other trade goods, to be bartered or gifted to the Indians in their path. Generosity showed a sound grasp of native sensibilities, and it was understood to be fundamental to securing their cooperation. Such thinking stood in strong contrast to that of the unfortunate Colonel Fawcett, who advocated stripping down to the bare essentials in personnel and supplies. It made for a less intrusive presence, Fawcett believed, and thus enhanced an expedition's security in the midst of potentially hostile tribes. Whether the Fawcetts were murdered by Indians, devoured by jaguars, or simply left to starve to death in the trackless wilderness, they had clearly failed to enlist the cooperation of natives in their quest to locate the fabled Lost City. Their definitive disappearance, it could be said, offered a resounding rebuttal to Fawcett's minimalist approach.

Perhaps because our own enterprise would have the rigor and feel of a bygone era of exploration and discovery, and perhaps also to confer a sense of historic resonance on the expedition, Possuelo somewhat grandiosely bestowed on it a name: Captain Alípio Bandeira, in honor of an early-twentieth-century Amazon scout and cofounder, with Cândido Rondon, of the Indian Protection Service, or SPI. In naming the expedition for Bandeira, Possuelo was affirming the core values of the SPI, even though the agency eventually crumbled amid allegations of corruption and abuse. He was also creating, it seemed, yet another opportunity to impart lessons of Brazilian frontier history and the struggle for indigenous rights to his underlings—Indian and non-Indian alike. The most immediate effect, however, was to be seen in the way everyone went about attempting to imitate the commemorative inscription Possuelo had drawn on the flap of his canvas pouch. With borrowed Sharpies and Magic Markers, the men took turns scrawling their names on their own shoulder bags, followed in block letters by EXPEDIÇÃO ALÍPIO BANDEIRA, Vale do Javari, 2002.

*   *   *

About four hours after our departure from Massapê, I was suddenly thrown to the deck. A low, sickly groan issued from the depths of the vessel. The *Waiká* had ground to a halt. "Sandbar," said Soldado, holding tight to a post. He took a drag from his tar-blackened cigarette. "We've hit bottom. We'll have to abandon the boats soon." It turned out that we'd have to leave them right then and there.

"The rudder cable broke!" Adelson shouted from the wheelhouse. "We're finished!" In twos and threes, men plunged from the decks of the *Sobral* and *Kukahá* into the waist-deep water and rocked the *Waiká* back and forth until we drifted free. "Let's pull off over there!" Possuelo shouted as he pointed across the river to a beach shaded by lofty palms. The time had come to off-load the *Waiká* and *Kukahá* and send them back. Of the original four expedition boats, only the tug-size *Sobral* had a shallow enough draft to proceed. Possuelo probably would have sent it back from here if he could have, but it was now hauling the drums of fuel that would power us the rest of the way in the skiffs with their long-shafted putt-putt engines.

Muscles straining beneath enormous sacks of rice, coffee, and beans, the men bounded barefoot down the gangplanks, like steve-dores unloading a pair of tramp steamers in some Conradian tropi-cal backwater. Paulo Welker stood off to the side, blond hair in its tight ponytail, taking inventory. Soggy cardboard boxes tumbled to the beach, where they were stacked and sorted: powdered milk, cooking oil, crackers, flashlight batteries. Items deemed a luxury and too heavy to carry, like canned tuna and guava jam, were set aside to be loaded back onto the boats going downriver.

The imminent departure of the *Waiká* also meant the loss of Pos-suelo's mobile communications center. His laptop, connected to his Globalstar phone, had enabled us to send and receive the occasional e-mail. Trying to send a message, or download one, was an exercise in frustration for the most part, requiring extraordinary patience, as we wound our way through the twists and turns of the river, the signal dropping each time the boat repositioned itself. Still, it represented an important link to the outside world. The only one left to us from here on would be the Inmarsat phone I'd brought from the States.

The operation to reshuffle the cargo and repack the boats came off without a hitch, at least until one of the whites, a guy named Fran-cisco, balked when Possuelo commanded him to outfit the smaller skiffs with paddles in case of engine trouble. When he rolled his eyes in response, Possuelo exploded.

"What are you pissed off about?" he demanded. "The only one who has the right to be pissed off here is me! Wipe that look off your face, or I'll wipe it off for you!" The rage unleashed in Possuelo's out-burst left everyone frozen in a stunned silence. Even as its echo con-tinued to reverberate through the forest, Possuelo ordered a bulky frontiersman named Raimundo to take charge of preparing the boats. Raimundo was in his early thirties. He wore close-cropped hair on his large square head, and he had the steroid-inflated biceps of a weight lifter. His black eyes peered out from beneath an overhanging ledge of heavy eyebrows, giving him a perpetually sullen appearance. He'd come from a large family that once lived along this same river, until the fish and game turned scarce about ten years earlier, when they moved down to Benjamin Constant, a border town named for an eighteenth-century Brazilian general. He was the kind of guy you'd want on your side in a barroom fight, and he looked like he'd been in many.

That night on the upper deck of the *Kukahá,* one of the older Matis set up an impromptu barbershop beneath the glare of a portable spotlight. With an electric clipper powered by the boat's generator, he buzzed the heads of successive expedition members like he was mowing grass. In a matter of minutes, Orlando's spectacular tresses gave way to a military-style buzz cut. The change was dramatic, but there was still the vague suggestion of Mediterranean divinity in his olive skin, full lips, and chiseled cheekbones.

We bade farewell the next morning to Adelson, his Tikuna face framed by the roughrider hat. He waved from the wheelhouse as he threw the *Waiká* into reverse and drifted backward into the current, motor gurgling. The boat slowly came around and started downriver, followed by the *Kukahá.* We shoehorned ourselves into the small skiffs, taking whatever space we could find alongside stacks of rifles, sloshing jerricans, and piles of overstuffed backpacks, and set off in the opposite direction, upriver, to the unmuffled blare of the *peci-peci* motors. When the *Waiká* and *Kukahá* turned back, the eye-rolling Francisco went with them. We never saw him again.

*   *   *

I sat alongside Nicolas toward the stern of the skiff piloted by Soldado, an ever-present cigarette pasted to his lower lip. We proceeded upriver at a much slower pace now, three overloaded skiffs in single file followed by the *Sobral,* which hauled most of the expedition's provisions. It didn't take long for the monotonous din aboard the skiff to begin playing tricks with my sun-broiled brain; I was seized by the unshakable certainty that just beneath the racket, ten thousand parakeets were shrieking at us from the surrounding forests. Finally yielding to curiosity, I yelled to Nicolas: "Do you hear all those parakeets?" He gave me a funny look and shook his head. When Soldado cut the motor, all I could hear was the swish of the current sliding inexorably beneath our hull and the baseline trill of a million cicadas, along with the blaring engine still reverberating inside my brain.

The sun reached its midday apogee, relentless and blistering. As we passed a low sandbar to our right, a creek joined the Itaquaí in a rush of crosscurrents. To the left, the bank rose straight up, exposed tree roots protruding hideously from its sandy declivity like the ganglia of some huge terrestrial jellyfish. A shiny black vulture studied us from his perch high up in a tree. *"Urubú,"* Soldado instructed, watching as I scribbled the word in my notes.

In the early afternoon we came upon a Kanamari village, where a huge dugout canoe carved from a kapok trunk was pulled up to the beach. The canoe was a good sixty feet long, with a thatched canopy over the midsection to provide shelter from sun and rain, and a small *peci-peci* motor was propped at its stern. Possuelo evidently had an idea, for he stood up in the bow of his skiff, shielding his eyes with his hand, and yelled out: "Where's the owner of this canoe?" Soon the silhouette of a rotund man appeared from behind a distant hut. He approached lazily, barefoot, a baseball cap pulled down backward over unshorn locks. Gray stubble dotted his chin. From the looks of it, he'd just woken from a nap. His unbuttoned plaid shirt was parted by an enormous gut that spilled over the waist of his faded cutoffs.

He introduced himself as Puruya, the village headman. I went to shake his hand and stifled my surprise at finding he had no thumb. Even as his eyes squinted in the blinding light, a smile stretched across his face like a permanent feature on a rugged landscape. You could tell right away that Puruya was not a man who considered himself poor. And by Itaquaí standards he wasn't. The canoe and motor were proof enough. And they'd given Possuelo an idea for relieving some of the overcrowding in the skiffs. Would he be willing to transport our cargo to the upper reaches of the Itaquaí, Possuelo wanted to know, in exchange for two hundred liters of gasoline, payable upon reaching our objective? "Two hundred liters total, or two hundred liters plus the gasoline it will take me to get there?" Puruya asked. The latter, Possuelo assured him. They had a deal. Two hundred liters represented no small fortune this far upriver. *"Ótimo negócio,"* Puruya said with a smile, repositioning the backward ball cap on the top of his head as though it were a crown. An excellent deal.

We were ready to shove off within a half hour. Sizing up the shade afforded by the canoe's shaggy thatched canopy, I staked out a space and climbed aboard. Puruya took a seat in the back, manning the motor, alongside his thirty-three-year-old son, Luciano. He had raised four sons, he said, but the others had died of illness. He'd recently fathered a baby girl with a sixteen-year-old mistress from another village. So Puruya now had a daughter who was younger than his grandson, Araruyo, who now rode in the stern on Luciano's lap. Hiding the affair from his wife took some doing, Puruya said, clearly relishing his tale of sexual prowess and derring-do. He couldn't marry the girl outright, as her father demanded; he would have risked losing his wife. So he built her a house instead, on the sly. The thatched hut set him back $150, but he wasn't complaining. "Good investment," he said with a wink. "Women don't want to go with kids their own age anymore. They like older men, because they know we have money."

The casual machismo sounded familiar. Maybe it was a measure of the deep inroads Brazilian frontier values had made in Kanamari culture. When I asked a Kanamari elder in one village to tell me about the origins of his people, he recited a creation story that was part Christian, part animist. It began with Adam and Eve, then moved on to Noah, who at God's command had built a huge canoe from a towering *itaúba* tree, loaded it with animals, and set out on the river as the deluge began. But God did not allow the Kanamari on board. Instead, they fled to higher ground, atop the riverbanks, where their settlements remained to this day. In a way, the hybrid legend seemed to capture the Kanamari's larger quandary, caught in a kind of nether zone between two worlds, belonging to neither. They'd been evicted

from their Eden and banished as well to the margins of the whites'
civilized universe. The part about God not allowing them on the boat
seemed particularly fitting.

* * *

We were the first to arrive two days later at the last Kanamari village on
the river called Sirão Dikumaru. Indeed, it was the very last outpost of
the global society we know as "civilization," beyond which the Brazilian state effectively ceased to function. The villagers told me as much
when I disembarked from Puruya's canoe and scaled to the top of the
slick embankment and stood before the first house I came to. It was
an open-air hut raised on stilts, topped with palm thatching. Several
more huts, perhaps fifteen in all, stretched away along the crest of the
bank, hemmed in by the high green wall of the jungle. A handful of
men sat side by side on the elevated platform of the first house, their
bare legs dangling off the edge. They were a disheveled lot, outfitted
in grimy shorts and ill-fitting T-shirts. One was wearing a necklace of
jaguar teeth. My attempt to pronounce the name of their hamlet was
greeted with howls of laughter.

"This is the last village—*a última aldea*," one of them said in Portuguese. "That's all you need to know." He pointed upriver. "Up there is
nothing."

"The Brazilians call it Pedras," said another. "That might be easier
for you." His bare chest featured a crude tattoo scrawled across its entire width. It read DEMARC in large block letters on one side of his
breastbone and TER on the other. It took me a second to grasp the
meaning: *DEMARCAÇÃO DA TERRA,* or "Land Demarcation." It seemed he'd
either run out of room on his chest for the entire phrase, or run out
of ink. Maybe the tattoo artist simply didn't know how to spell. It could
have been all of the above, but then again, maybe he wanted it that way
for reasons I couldn't fathom.

The body art was crude, but it no doubt sprang from the same urge
that spurs people everywhere to emblazon their flesh with depictions

and inscriptions of pivotal events and people in their lives: the names of lovers, buddies killed in action, gang affiliations. The range of experience may have been more circumscribed here, the art a bit archaic. But to the Kanamari it was no less meaningful: the arrival of FUNAI, the demarcation of the Javari reserve, the opening of a school that offered classes in mathematics.

The men looked me up and down. I was a sight to behold: pasty white skin, cheeks covered with five days' growth, a mat of graying hair caked to a sweaty forehead. I could barely stand how I smelled, my clothes rank with the odor of sour sweat. I respectfully kept my distance. "Where is the *senhor* from?" Land Demarcation asked at length, addressing me in the third person.

"The United States," I said. "New York."

"Nova Iorke," he repeated. "That's near Brasília, right?"

I understood why he thought so. For a Kanamari Indian on the upper Itaquaí, there was virtually no distinction between a Brazilian from Brasília and an American from New York: we were all *kariwa*—whites—who seemed to possess infinite wealth and moved with impossible ease through an outside world that for them remained opaque, largely forbidden, but a source of fascination nonetheless. It was perhaps no accident that their perch atop the platform looked out in that direction, back down the river, toward the sweeping S-turn we'd just navigated and through which they received all the news and every emissary from that great world beyond. It was from around that bend that the rest of our flotilla now appeared.

Dogs barked, the men hooted. Women grabbed their babies and headed for the beach with their pots of *caisuma.* I followed them, reaching the bottom of the embankment as our men leapt from the boats and lined up for a gulp of the welcoming beverage. Possuelo and Welker brought forth gifts and dispensed them on the beach. When the crowd had dispersed, Possuelo scratched his beard thoughtfully, looked upriver, and said: "Perhaps we should keep going." It was still morning, with most of the day before us. But the rotund Puruya gently grabbed Possuelo's elbow and steered him aside.

"Sir Sydney," he implored. "Let us spend the night. I have family here. Besides, the village would like to honor you, and you will honor them by staying." Possuelo was without a doubt the highest-ranking federal official to show his face this far upriver, at least in a generation. His position as head of the Department of Isolated Indians trumped all other FUNAI functionaries who worked in the region. He answered only to the agency's president in Brasília, a rank he himself had once held. In every hamlet, along the shoreline, and from the small dugouts they paddled in the current, the Indians had called and waved with undisguised adulation: "Senhor Sydney! Senhor Sydney!" They adored him, plain and simple, and it was easy to see why. He listened to them, made them feel important, and inspired their confidence. They had a friend in faraway centers of power that they would never come to know. Just as he was an ambassador from that forbidden realm, so too was he their envoy to it. So when the villagers asked Possuelo for a bit of his time, it was a request he could not reasonably refuse.

"Paulo!" he barked. "We're going to stay here till tomorrow. Send men out to hunt, and have others prepare a site here on the beach." He clambered up the bank to the first house, where the small group of men still sat, their bare legs still hanging off the platform.

"This is the last village," repeated Land Demarcation. To be the last place on Earth, the final outpost on the very edge of the known world, was clearly a matter of some pride among its denizens. As he'd done with me, he pointed upriver. "No one lives up there."

"What about the *flecheiros*?" Possuelo ventured.

"I've been up there," Land Demarcation said, "and I didn't see any Indians. Just jaguar." Possuelo sank into a crouching position, contorted his face in a pose of deranged fury, and sprang up, swiping the air with his fingers, like a wild cat baring its claws. "I want to meet three jaguars!" he snorted. "I'll take them on all at once—bare-handed! I have no fear! *Eu sou valiente!*" The men howled with delight. Possuelo's rapport with the Indians was extraordinary. He seemed to grasp intuitively what pleased them and what made them angry, what made them feel respected and what did not. It was almost as though he were another person entirely when he was dealing with natives. With whites, he could be surly, contemptuous, explosive. With Indians, he was possessed of charm, patience, and good humor.

It hadn't always been this way for Possuelo. Dealing with Indians was something of an acquired taste. He'd fared especially poorly in his first outing more than forty years before, when he'd arrived by bush plane at a jungle outpost on the Xingu to join the Villas Boas brothers, the men who were to become his lifelong mentors. The plane slid off the runway upon landing, burying him beneath an avalanche of cargo. As he picked his way out of the aircraft, someone brought a winch to pull the plane back onto the airstrip. But the cable slipped and yanked off the finger of an army sergeant who'd shared the flight with Possuelo. He rushed to get help, but his feet went out from under him, and he went over backward in a spectacular fall that brought fits of hysteria to a group of bystanding Indians. "Cretins," Possuelo recalled thinking. "I was seething. Here I was all banged up, a guy had just lost his finger, and all they could do was laugh." At the time, Possuelo wasn't even all that interested in Indians. What drew him to the jungle was the romance of exploration and adventure. He'd decided to skip university and go straight to the bush. The "indigenous question" came later, he said, after he'd lived among the Indians, shared their food, and begun to understand what he called the "drama" of their existence.

The men at the house on the top of the bank said there was an elderly gentleman in the hamlet who'd once met the Arrow People. They sent a kid off to find him. Soon a large hulk of a man appeared at the far end of the path, hobbling toward us. He introduced himself as "Wura." From his graying hair and arthritic limp, I judged him to be in his sixties.

"The *flecheiros* had killed three Brazilians," he began, speaking in Kanamari as Puruya translated to Portuguese. When the whites had failed to return from a latex-collecting foray up an *igarapé* across the river, a search party was dispatched. They were found far upriver,

shot through with arrows. The whites blamed the Kanamari and promised to exact revenge. "We denied it," said Wura. "But they didn't
believe us."

In an attempt to prove their innocence, he set off with a handful
of neighbors into the forest to seek out the Arrow People and demand
that they halt the killings. They came upon their vestiges—footprints,
snapped twigs, masticated fruit. They came to a trail and followed it.
Early in the morning of the eighth day, they reached the Arrow People's village—several palm-thatched buildings set in a large clearing.
They watched silently from the forest before summoning the courage
to enter. Many Indians were there, Wura recounted, all naked, the men
armed with long arrows, which they nervously pointed at the chests of
the interlopers. "I entered the clearing with my hands raised to show I
was unarmed. My heart was pounding in my chest." As he advanced, he
kept his eyes locked on the man he guessed to be their leader. When
they saw the visitors meant no harm, they lowered their arrows.

His eyes drank in the scene. The men were tall, the sides of their
heads shaved, and each had a long tuft of hair hanging loose at the
crown. They spoke a language he could not understand, but Wura
was astonished when an old woman beseeched them in a Katukinan
dialect similar to Kanamari: *My brothers! My brothers!* She had been
kidnapped as a child by the Arrow People, she told them, never to
see her native village again. Wura and his friends sang an old song
for her, and she wept with nostalgia. With the woman translating, the
flecheiros admitted to killing the whites to avenge the deaths of their
own people. "They said they wanted no more killing; they had taken
their revenge." The woman offered them a peach-palm drink. Fearing it might be poisoned, Wura and his companions refrained until
their hosts drank first. They were invited to spend the night, but the
Kanamari suspected treachery and chose to depart. As darkness fell,
they could hear the Arrow People following close behind, chanting
war songs. The Kanamari didn't stop until they reached their village.
When Wura recounted his extraordinary tale to the rubber gather-

ers, they refused to believe him. "They said there were no wild Indians up there." They grabbed Wura's brother and threw him in jail. Fortunately, agents of the newly constituted FUNAI appeared shortly afterward. The rubber tappers were expelled, never to be seen again. It was also the last time anyone caught more than a fleeting glimpse of the People of the Arrow, the only known instance of peaceful contact anyone had ever sustained with them. Though it all seemed like only yesterday, the events Wura recounted had transpired a distant thirty years before.

Possuelo politely thanked Wura for the tale and promptly ended the meeting, turning to leave. It was a story he didn't want to give too much credence to, not because he doubted it, but rather because it might have undercut the image of the Arrow People he was seeking to nourish, as fierce tribesmen to be avoided. Granted, Wura's account did impart a sense that the *flecheiros* were dangerous, volatile. But Possuelo didn't want anyone to get any fresh ideas about seeking them out. "We don't need the Kanamari going out there and trying to contact them," he told me as we ambled down to the boats. Contacted Indians were every bit as capable of spreading deadly epidemics as white intruders; they carried the same pathogens. The buffer that the Kanamari and other contacted tribes afforded the uncontacted ones was a double-edged sword. Even if their intentions were peaceful, any overtures to the Arrow People could pose a mortal danger.

Late in the afternoon, the Matis and Kanamari returned in the skiffs from their hunting foray. The boat bottoms were awash in animal blood. They stacked the carcasses of nine wild boars on the beach, along with several game birds and five dozen fish. Using an overturned canoe as a butcher block, they set to skinning the peccaries and hacking them apart with machetes. Alfredo was joined by Wilson, who'd been recruited from Massapê to serve as Nicolas's porter. His dark eyes sparkled beneath a single brow with the casual insouciance of a man who'd never heard an order he saw fit to obey. The two companions had been inseparable since we'd left Massapê. Soon they were up to their elbows in blood, and the water that lapped at their feet on the edge of the shore had turned a bright crimson.

We still had a generator and a string of electric lights aboard the *Sobral*, and to lend a festive air to the occasion, they were hauled out and stretched halfway up the bank between high poles hacked from the jungle for the purpose. Bonfires were lit on the beach; the pork was set to boil in large cauldrons. Several fires soon blazed in the gathering darkness: one for the meat, one to smoke the fish, yet another for drying clothes. The stars came out with startling intensity. The Milky Way flowed across the top of the sky like a magical river, the one believed by many tribes to bear the souls of the departed back to their Creator. I took a stroll down the beach, away from the lights and the bonfires. We were in the center of one of the darkest places on Earth, a huge black void on the World at Night maps stitched together from composite images taken from orbiting satellites. It was rivaled in size and darkness only by a few even more remote and less inhabited places: Tibet, Greenland, Siberia, and the far-flung stretches of the southern Sahara. In those images captured from outer space, the entire eastern half of North America appeared as one gigantic parking lot drenched in artificial light, stretching all the way to the Mississippi. The West wasn't far behind. But the rush to electrify the planet had so far bypassed western Amazonia. Our tiny string of lights notwithstanding, the night here was safe, for now at least, the sky overhead a wonderland of glowing jewels on a backdrop of black velvet. Even the nearest pinpricks of wildfire, which on those same maps lapped in ominous abundance along the Amazon's eastern and southern frontiers, were hundreds of miles away. Here, the stars flooded the nocturnal sky by the tens of thousands, pulsating with the same savage intensity that seemed to govern this entire realm of unvanquished wilderness.

It was the river that afforded this unimpeded view of the heavens. Once we entered the jungle, we might not see the sky again for weeks, except as tiny patches leaking down through the latticework of foliage. The tilted mast of the Southern Cross loomed over the water, beckoning toward mysterious austral lands. Behind me, the familiar shape of the Big Dipper tipped at a distinctly unfamiliar angle, only the last few stars at the end of its handle visible above the silhouetted line of treetops. Shortly after our dinner of boar stew, Possuelo sent word to join him back at the first house on the top of the bank. When I got there, he had his map sprawled out on the open-air platform. Villagers gathered around in the glow of a storm lamp as Possuelo traced the route we'd covered so far with his finger. We were 150 miles south of Tabatinga as the crow flies, but we had actually traveled more than 300 miles, factoring in the Itaquaí's twists and turns. "Do you know what's here?" Possuelo asked the assembled villagers. He was pointing to the bottom of the map, the southern flank of the reserve, an area rippled with tightly packed contours. "This is the divide: on one side, the water goes to the Jutaí, on the other to the Itaquaí. And right here"—he tapped twice with his finger—"there's a *maloca* of wild Indians." It was a big one, he said, with fourteen separate houses. (Because Indians often reside in large communal huts, and because an entire community may dwell within a single structure, the word *maloca* is often used interchangeably, sometimes to designate a native settlement, sometimes a house.) There were other villages as well, and Possuelo said he intended to maintain a six-kilometer cushion between the expedition and any settlement he knew about.

But avoiding the *flecheiros* would be complicated by the dry season, which was just beginning. It was the time of year Brazilians call "summer," when the floods pulled back from the forest floor, and living creatures of every description would be on the move in a primordial quest for food and water. "It's the best time of year for mobility—for them and for us," Possuelo said. The spawning season for the *tracajá*, the yellow-spotted Amazonian turtle, was also about to begin. Untold thousands, perhaps hundreds of thousands, of mature turtles would return home to the high white beaches throughout western Amazonia, excavating nests to disgorge their nutrient-rich eggs. The *desovo*, as the spawning season is called, sends a yearly shock wave through the entire food chain, setting in motion a seasonal migration of predators large and small through the most distant corners of the forest, from birds and rodents to jaguars, crocs, and human beings.

"They move along the edges of the *igarapés* hunting for *tracajá* eggs," said Possuelo, referring to forest people in general, his experience telling him it would also apply to the Arrow People. "They cover lots and lots of ground." His eyes flashed in the glow of the kerosene lamp. Families or clans develop proprietary claims to several beaches over the years, and for strangers to dig for eggs there is tantamount to stealing. That would explain why the Korubo reacted with such ferocity to the poachers they caught on that beach downriver. A single beach could have scores of nests, thousands of eggs, a bonanza worth defending tooth-and-nail from rivals. "The Indians will cover lots of ground, from one creek to another," he added. Clearly his plan to skirt the *flecheiros'* settlements wasn't exactly a foolproof method for avoiding contact in this season of heightened locomotion.

I strolled out into the night, down the single lane of the settlement, and pulled up outside a wilted shack set three feet off the ground on posts, the very last building at the edge of the forest. The orange flicker of a kerosene lamp seeped out through the gaps between the boards. Laughter spilled into the night, and the entire structure seemed to bounce up and down to the jerky rhythm of a Brazilian *forró*. At least one boom box had found its way here, with enough juice in its batteries to power a send-off party at the end of the world.

The fires flared up on the beach below us, and a human silhouette occasionally passed in front of the flames. A full moon rose high overhead, bathing the scene in its mysterious silver glow: the jagged outline of the jungle on the far side of the river, the thatched huts, the boats tethered to trees along the shore. However basic the comforts here were, they were comforts nonetheless. We balanced on the cusp of the civilized world, but we were still a part of it; on the rim of the forest, but not yet *in* it. This was our last night on the edge of the known world. Tomorrow, we'd plunge into terra incognita. It was a long time before I could tear myself away from this scene of tranquillity and find my way back to that first house, where we'd been offered a place to sleep on the split-palm floor.

*   *   *

We awoke to a gray drizzly morning. Close by, someone cleared his chest. A dog snapped at a pestering fly. Pigs snorted. Down on the beach, the men were readying the boats. This was the end of the line for the *Sobral.* It would wait here for our smaller skiffs to return, then turn back with all of them in tow. The river was now no more than four or five feet at its deepest pockets. In some places, where the amber current washed across rippled sand, it was no more than inches deep.

The rain had left the path down the bank a slick mess. As I made my way gingerly down the hill, both feet slid out from under me, sending all my gear—hammock, camera bag, day pack—flying in every direction. As I sprawled there in the mud, the Indians howling, I was tempted to glare daggers at them, though it would have served only to compound the absurd figure I cut. Possuelo's own misfortune from years ago came to mind, and I laughed, too, hoping to salvage a shred of dignity. "The first fall of hundreds that await me," I announced, though I had no way of knowing just how true those words would turn out to be. Soldado was the only one who offered me a hand. As he helped round up my stuff, he quietly said, "That was quite a tumble, Scott." It was a disarming gesture of kindness, a rarity in the relentlessly macho culture that seemed to be embedded in the very grain of expeditionary life.

Out by the boats, Possuelo was barking into his handheld Globalstar, relaying details we'd heard from the Kanamari to the Federal Police of a suspect plantation along the Juruá. Unidentified "foreigners" were clearing a wide swath of jungle, the villagers had told Possuelo. He wondered why such a large operation hadn't been spotted from the air. Whoever was responsible may have retained the larger trees to conceal their activities from aerial reconnaissance. "Intriguing," I heard him say. "Maybe some kind of ayahuasca cult." Ayahuasca was

the most renowned hallucinogenic plant of the Amazon, regarded by
Indians as a magic elixir that freed the soul from the confines of ordinary reality and opened the doors to mystical encounters with animal spirits and the dead. In recent years, ayahuasca-drinking cults had
gained momentum across Brazil and neighboring countries, along
with a new kind of exotic tourism that featured mind-bending jungle
retreats directed by Indian shamans. Taking ayahuasca wasn't against
the law per se, but whatever was happening on the Juruá, the police
would check into it. Possuelo was sending his Globalstar phone back
with the *Sobral*. After speaking with the DPF, he made one last call
to FUNAI in Tabatinga. He advised that we might require an airdrop
at some unspecified date and indeterminate location, depending on
"how plentiful the game is, how difficult the terrain." He'd be in touch
by radio when the time came.

A few minutes later, the villagers all huddled around Possuelo in
rapt attention as he bade farewell in true Sydney Possuelo fashion. He
was putting on a mock newscast from some future date, clutching an
imaginary microphone, spoofing the caged, earnest tone of a broad-
caster. "The bearded man was last sighted in the jungle three years
ago, accompanied by a band of armed Indians," said Possuelo, raising
an eyebrow. He paused for rhetorical flourish. "The people call them
os cavernosos—the men of the caves." The Kanamari laughed. It was a
fitting, though somewhat unsettling, departure, bound as we were for
parts unknown.

CHAPTER 9

The Point of No Return

A THRESHOLD HAD BEEN BREACHED. With the last of the Kanamari villages behind us, we set our sights on reaching the upper extremities of the Itaquaí, where we would abandon the boats and begin our trek into the land of the Arrow People. We had traversed the buffer zone between civilization and the completely wild Amazon, and we now entered a place rarely glimpsed by outsiders, a primordial forest of staggering size and terrifying possibilities that has remained virtually untouched by industrial society. Caiman eyed us with calm malevolence from the beaches, not even bothering to stir. Enormous kapoks and *sapopemas* lined the banks, dripping with vines and lianas that screened all but the slightest peek into the forest shadows, where jaguars, anacondas, and highly venomous pit vipers slithered. The *Sobral* had stayed behind in Sirão Dikumaru, and we proceeded upriver in the three long skiffs, together with Puruya's thatch-covered canoe, the only vessel to offer any respite from the merciless sun. The boats strained against the current, sometimes in single file, sometimes two abreast, but nearly always close enough to maintain visual contact with the other craft and even to shout back and forth above the blare of the *peci-pecis*. The sensation of the ten thousand shrieking parakeets continued to reverberate within the vault of my cranium, leading me to wonder if this wasn't some kind of wishful thinking on my part, as though I expected untrammeled nature to be a happy-go-lucky Eden, brimming with life, where birds chirped giddily to their hearts' content and monkeys swung freely through the trees.

Recent floods had triggered landslides all along the upper Itaquaí, sweeping enormous *jatobá* and *samaúma* trunks off the banks in a wild tangle of branches and upended root systems. Early in the day, we encountered the first in a maze of trees that lay across the entire width of the river. The crooked gray trunk dipped below the surface, only to reappear above the water farther on, stretching across the river like a cartoon sea serpent. There was no going around it, over it, or under it. The only way forward was through it. The boats pulled abreast of the behemoth and cut their motors. Cottony clouds drifted lazily across a baby blue sky. In the respite from the engines' blare, the air filled with a cacophony of languages—Matis coming from one boat, Kanamari from another, Portuguese from the third. "Raimundo!" called Possuelo from the bow of the lead skiff. "Bring the chain saw!"

Machete in hand, and hand-rolled cigarette pasted to his lip, Soldado led a handful of men from his skiff up onto the log, where they commenced a spirited assault, clearing away branches with deft swipes of their blades to make room for Raimundo's chain saw. As he picked his way forward through the seated men, Raimundo looked every bit the weight lifter, with his pumped-up pecs and rippling biceps, his deep-set eyes lost in the shadow of his overhanging brow. He planted his bare feet on the slippery trunk, fired up the saw, and laid its teeth into the tree's flesh. With an earsplitting whine and a spray of water and flying wood chips, Raimundo brought the saw's full force down on the trunk. When he couldn't penetrate any farther, he broke off, then buried the blade backhanded into the tree's submerged underside, just inches from his exposed feet. It was probably the first time the growl of a chain saw had split the silence of this remote jungle since loggers were definitively expelled from the Javari reserve six years earlier.

When he'd completed his first cut through the trunk, Raimundo moved to another position some fifteen feet farther along the log. Here, the tree peered out above the water just high enough to wedge the bow of the skiff beneath it. From this platform, Raimundo again started the chain saw with two quick tugs on the cord. It sputtered, then sprang to life with an angry snarl. He resumed the task as Possuelo observed, arms folded across his chest, stripped naked save for his floppy camouflage hat folded comically across his forehead and the skimpy navy-blue Speedo.

A full hour after we'd first encountered the tree, we slid through the passageway opened by Raimundo's handiwork. The freshly dissected cross sections revealed several dozen concentric rings, hinting at a long life cut short by the torrent that had swept the embankment weeks before. It seemed odd that the motorized chain saw, the quintessential instrument of rainforest destruction, the very distillation of Western society's long and unrelenting quest to dominate nature and subdue its forests, now served our own, very contrary purpose—to establish unequivocally the presence of the Arrow People in these lands and bolster protection for both.

No sooner had we cleared this obstacle than we came upon another. Again, Raimundo came forward with the chain saw. Muscles flexing, he braced the saw against his hip and opened a deep gash in the tree's midsection. Two-thirds of the way through the tree, the machine came to an abrupt halt. The diameter was too wide; the blade had sunk in so deep that Raimundo was unable to extract it. Amarildo, a nineteen-year-old *riberinho* and one of the youngest members of the expedition, bounded onto the log and freed the chain saw's blade with a few deft chops of his long-handled ax. With the rest of the log too far under water to safely use the chain saw, Amarildo continued on, raising the ax high overhead and bringing it down with mind-boggling precision, delivering blow upon blow within a hair's width of his bare feet.

It was horrifying to consider the consequences had he slipped just once, given the vast distance that separated us from anything that resembled a proper medical facility. It was a distance that would only grow longer and more difficult to surmount in the weeks ahead. Despite the accoutrements of industrial society that eased our passage into the untamed wilderness, despite our firearms and the survival skills accrued by so many frontiersmen among us, we were still beholden to forces much larger than ourselves: providence, fate, the whims and mercies of the jungle, which could conspire at any moment to sabotage our mission.

We hadn't gone another fifteen minutes before the motor on Raimundo's boat wheezed, spat, and conked out. While Raimundo removed the engine cover and began tinkering, several of us vaulted overboard into the water. It was thigh-deep, a khaki color that could match the color of my shirt, and clear enough to see through to the sandy bottom. The current tugged at my legs, whirlpools ripping around them with surprising force.

Nicolas, Possuelo, and Orlando waded over to a long white beach, exactly the kind of place a yellow-spotted *tracajá* might want to deposit a load of eggs. Soldado and I followed. A bird screeched from a concealed position on the far side of the river. A similar cry came back from somewhere overhead.

"Eagles," said Soldado, shading his eyes and scanning the treetops. "They like to eat the eggs of *tracajá*. They're just waiting." They'd gotten here first, but with the eggs in high demand and so many predators on the loose, they were by no means guaranteed a share of the booty.

We pulled off for the night at a sandy beach as the sun dipped below the treetops and cast long shadows across the river. In a single day, we'd hacked and sawed our way through a dozen trees blocking the channel. Some had been brought down by recent flooding, but others were a weather-beaten silvery gray that attested to long prostration beneath the withering sun, offering a clear signal that we were the first to penetrate this sanctum from the outside world in several years. No longer restrained by the light breeze the forward movement of the boats had sustained, swarms of vicious *piums* now commenced their assault, inflicting maddeningly itchy, bloody welts everywhere they alighted. There was virtually no repellent among us to deter them; it had fallen by the wayside in the radical triage we'd performed. Almost the entire case of Nicolas's Repellex pump-spray bottles had been sent back aboard the *Waiká*, deemed a luxury that could not be justified when weighed against the priorities of food, medicine, and axes. I had secreted a single bottle for my private stash, which I intended to deploy only in strict emergencies. What such an emergency might look like, I did not yet know. Under the circumstances, the *piums* had to be regarded as a mere nuisance, unworthy of a dab of the precious liquid.

"Scotchie!" called Ivan Arapá. "Come! Look!" He stood on the far side of a sand dune, only the upper half of his body visible. He wore his usual bemused smirk as I plodded barefoot over the top of the dune. He crouched low over a set of paw prints, each larger than the size of a human palm. They meandered across a stretch of mudflats and vanished behind a screen of sawgrass that fringed the green shadows of the forest. "Jaguar," he said, raising his eyebrows with mock apprehension. "Maybe jaguar comes to visit Scotchie tonight?"

I set about smoothing a patch of sand to prepare my camp, figuring the beach to be the logical location for our first bivouac. "Senhor Scotch, up h-here," stammered Mauro from the top of a steep embankment on the other side of the river. "Not on the beach. T-t-too many bugs." I waded across the river. It was just knee-deep, no more than thirty feet wide. I picked my way on all fours up the bank and stood on the edge of the forest. Huge trunks of kapok, cedar, and several species I'd never seen before—all dusted with electric green moss—rocketed straight up toward the canopy high above. Vines, creepers, and philodendrons dangled like stalactites from the ceiling of an enormous emerald cavern. The understory was dark and gloomy, but diffused light leaked down from overhead, scattering into soft shades of green, yellow, and brown. The ground featured almost no undergrowth, just a carpeting of dry, brittle leaves. I had been in the Amazon many times, but this was qualitatively distinct. This was ancient, old-growth forest such as I'd never seen before, virtually unaltered by the hand of humankind.

To my astonishment, an entire village was taking shape amid the trees. I'd been too caught up with the jaguar tracks on the beach to notice everyone disembarking and vanishing into the forest. The jungle now reverberated with the zing of machetes and the dull *thwop* of axes biting into wood. I caught sight of Soldado as he brought down a three-inch-thick sapling with two quick chops of his machete. He hacked off the crown, then cleaved away the remaining limbs. In a matter of seconds, he had appropriated from the forest a perfectly straight, seven-foot-long pole, which he hauled off toward his nascent camp-site. Everywhere men were putting steel to wood, dragging long poles through the clearing and fashioning the simple structures that would shelter them for the coming night. They worked in pairs, positioning a single pole between two trees, binding it with long vines to the trunks, then stretching a tarp over the top to create a peaked-roof cover, tying off the grommeted corners with thin creepers they yanked from random trees. The men called these shelters "tents"—*barracas*—but they were really open-air canopies, each just large enough to provide cover for a single hammock stretched beneath it. In fact, real tents would have been far less suited to conditions on the damp forest floor—and far more vulnerable to the ants, snakes, and spiders that crawled and slithered along it. The idea was to get yourself off the ground.

The campsite's main entrance was marked by the stairway that frontiersmen Raimundo and Amarildo were etching into the embankment—complete with log steps and long handrails—to facilitate access to and from the boats. Possuelo, Orlando, and Nicolas were setting up their positions close to the head of the stairway, on the bluff overlooking the river. Cooks Mauro and Paulo Souza had set up the kitchen hearth nearby, where a blaze was already crackling beneath a cauldron suspended between a pair of forked stakes. A number of other *mateiros* were building a series of benches—poles set on stakes, lashed together with creepers—around the fire, soon to become the encampment's central plaza and dining area. A network of freshly trod footpaths snaked back into the forest shadows, leading to clusters of blue-tarped bungalows set amid the foliage. Separate neighborhoods emerged with unique styles. The Matis favored low-hanging shelters, the peak of their roofs no more than four feet off the ground, sloping to a mere two feet, so that you had to practically crawl on hands and knees to enter. The whites seemed to prefer headroom beneath their roofs, and positioned their crossbeam poles as high as they could reach. The Kanamari got by with the least effort, simply tying off their tarps from the corners without bothering to erect crossbeams—a risky design that was bound to collect water and collapse in the event of a downpour. They had set up their own little subdivision in a pocket at the rear of the campsite, beyond Soldado and his fellow white frontiersmen.

The two Marubo—Adelino and Alcino—stuck close to Possuelo. They erected their shelters alongside his bivouac, near the top of the stairway. They may well have felt outnumbered by the other tribesmen, not entirely comfortable sleeping among them. It would have been understandable. After all, the Kanamari had long suspected the Marubo were kinsmen of their old foes, the Kaxinawá. Some thought they were even the same tribe, hiding behind a different name. Adelino and Alcino may have been aware of this simmering enmity and decided to keep some distance. Their forebears had endured a demographic collapse as dramatic as any in the region, with upwards of 90 percent mortality in the twenty years that marked the height of the Rubber Boom, from 1890 to 1910. Entire villages were wiped out, others reduced to a handful of survivors. The scattered remnants of various communities, no more than fifty people in all, found their way back into deep jungle at the headwaters of the Ituí and Curuçá rivers. Though all Panoan-speaking, the disparate villages had never thought of themselves as belonging to a single tribe. But over the ensuing years, they reconstituted themselves under one roof, as a tribe that did not exist before, called the Marubo. They remained in the forest for the next fifty years, rebuilding their society in seclusion, undergoing a miraculous cultural revival in the process. Only in the 1960s did they accept contact with the white man once again. Their numbers had rebounded in the interlude. With renewed contact, leaders of various longhouses took their people in different directions. Some followed FUNAI to an outpost on the Curuçá, among them young braves who would later serve as scouts and interpreters for the Matis Contact Front in the 1970s. Others were drawn to a mission village founded by Americans on the Ituí, called Vida Nova, or "New Life," where Alcino and Adelino were from. In all, there were now eight Marubo villages, with a total population nearing one thousand. It didn't seem altogether impossible that the Arrow People might be experiencing a similar process in the wake of their own cataclysmic experience, reconstituting themselves in isolation from the rest of the world as a hybrid, amalgamated tribe, distinct from the separate bloodlines that predated the White Invasion.

* * *

Feeling rather helpless before the prospect of setting up my own *barraca*, I went looking for Alfredo, picking my way along the path that led toward the Kanamari tents. I found him swinging in his hammock, sharing laughs with his comrades. "Alfredo," I said. "Please." I considered myself to be an enlightened citizen when it came to matters pertaining to indigenous rights, colonial exploitation, and so forth, so I was surprised to find myself irked by Alfredo's apparent lassitude. I led him back to the spot I'd staked out between a pair of strong trees, close to the top of the stairway. "Machete," he said, somewhere between a request and a command. I figured he'd bring his own machete, but he hadn't. I pulled mine from its leather sheath and felt its heft. It was a substantial piece of equipment: somewhere between two and three feet long, weighing about two pounds. In the few times I'd used it, I'd begun to appreciate its elegant simplicity. In the hands of an experienced woodsman, it could bring down a decent-size tree in short order. While it lacked the precision of a butcher's knife, it could still be used to field-dress an animal with reasonable results. Its tip resembled a parrot's beak, curved and pointed, perfect for prying open a can of evaporated milk. Second to a rifle, there was no piece of gear more valuable to a jungle explorer. I ran my thumb lightly along the blade, still factory fresh.

Alfredo took hold of it, bent into a crouch, and began to rake the leaf litter off the forest floor between my trees. I wanted to cry out: *"You're going to ruin the blade!"* But I held my tongue. The exposed black soil exhaled a powerful scent of fungi and decay. Alfredo got up and vanished into the woods, returning with a ten-foot pole and a few coils of vine. Together we hoisted the pole between the trees, and Alfredo lashed it fast with the vines, first to one trunk, then to the other. Next we draped my tarp over the crossbeam and tied off the corners. In the time it took to hang my hammock, my shelter for the night was complete. I thanked Alfredo. He nodded stiffly and wandered back through the woods to rejoin his mates. Not once did his black eyes make contact with mine.

I changed into nylon shorts, grabbed a towel and soap, and made my way to the newly constructed stairway down to the shore. It was an unexpected luxury, having a flight of stairs and a banister to ease the descent. I shuffled into the river, flip-flops on, kicking sand before me as I went. Stingrays abounded on the sandy river bottoms of the western Amazon. A jab from a stingray tail was about the last thing I needed this far from medical care. The water was cool and refreshing. I lathered up, keeping a careful grip on the soap. I had just two bars to last the entire journey.

The cauldron was bubbling with a pungent-smelling soup of wild boar and rice by the time I changed clothes and joined the others at the hearth. Three log benches fronted the fire pit in a semicircle, each long enough to accommodate five or six men. Those who hadn't found seats were standing around in groups of two and three, making small talk or staring into the flames.

Possuelo was uncustomarily quiet as he ate, which meant everyone else was quiet, too, the silence punctuated only by the slurping of broth and a few hushed whispers here and there. Afterward, I joined the line of men trundling down the stairway to wash off plates and silverware at the edge of the river. A greasy sheen floated atop the water. I dunked my plate in the water and watched as a few morsels of rice were snatched from the surface in a roiling vortex of ravenous piranhas. As I passed Possuelo's hammock on my way back to mine, he called from the shadows. The jungle pulsed with the chirring of insects.

"Tomorrow will be our last day on the boats," he told me, pulling aside his mosquito net. "After that, they will go back, and we will go into the jungle. If you have any doubts, you can still go home. No one will think any less of you for making that decision." I stood there, listening to the cicadas.

Possuelo was offering me a graceful exit. It was tempting, no question. But I was in too deep to back out now. Besides, I couldn't imagine writing a story that concluded: *And with that, Sydney Possuelo disappeared into the jungle, and* National Geographic *went home.* "I appreciate your concern," I said. "But I'm in on this for the entire ride." I folded myself into my hammock a short time later, snapping off my headlamp and, with it, any thoughts of returning downriver with the boats.

*   *   *

Everywhere guys were rolling up hammocks, folding tarps, tying up backpacks. My chest tightened. *Fuck, I need to get moving!* I crawled out of my hammock to face the morning. The faintest traces of gray light announced the start of the day. Ghostly wisps of mist swept along the river below. The Matis had already packed up their entire neighborhood. They huddled around a crackling blaze in the chilly half-light, looking calm and elegant with their palm-shoot whiskers and clamshell earrings.

Mauro came up the stairway clutching a pair of lifeless pacas by their scruffs. "Good morning, Senhor Scotch," he said with his toothless smile. "Do you kn-kn-know the paca? Very good meat. Very tasty." Their fur was rich brown, and with round faces and tiny ears, they looked like oversize hamsters, cute and cuddly. Except they were dead. As I scrambled to take down my hammock and get packed, Mauro skinned them down to their bare purplish pink loins and set a large pot of water to boil. The Matis silently folded the animals' severed heads into palm fronds and disappeared down the stairway to the shore. Nicolas saw me watching. He was all packed up, waiting by the fire. "They use the paca incisors to make the sights for their blowguns," he said, coming over. He took my notebook and roughed out a sketch of the cross section of a blowgun tube. The *zarabatanas* are up to eight feet long, he said, the tube made from hollowed-out shafts of cane.

"The sight looks like this," he said, filling in two tooth-shaped peaks on the top of the barrel. "The dart is a razor-sharp bamboo point that you pack in the tube with a wad of wild cotton." He dashed off a separate sketch of the dart. "You'd think it would be really clumsy for them to run through the forest with these long blowguns. But they do. And you wouldn't believe how accurate they are! I've seen the Matis shoot a monkey that's one hundred feet up in the trees!"

The Matis may have been taking the teeth for their blowguns, but I was pretty sure they had other reasons to make off with the paca heads. They were the most delectable part of the animal, any animal, and odds were ten to one they'd be roasting them later on for an evening appetizer.

With Mauro setting the rodents to simmer over the fire, I breathed easier, figuring I had plenty of time. But Possuelo popped his head up over the top of the bank. "What are you doing?" he groused, bug-eyed. "Don't cook those now! Bring them along and cook them later. We've got to go, man!"

The adrenaline kicked in. I stripped off my sleeping clothes and stuffed them in a plastic bag. I was beginning to develop a system, based largely on the use of ziplock bags, to impose order within the modest confines of my day pack. It was the only space, in the midst of this unruly wilderness, over which I exercised some control. Maintaining a change of dry, clean clothes for sleeping had become a top priority, together with protecting my film, notebooks, and cameras from the saturating moisture. But for now, all care went out the window. I dashed down to the river to look for Alfredo, needing help to break down my site and stow the gear.

I caught sight of him at the far end of the beach, with Wilson and the other Kanamari, standing over something dark and inert sprawled at their feet. A caiman. *"Bak!"* they shouted, smiling as I approached. *Bak* was the Kanamari equivalent of the Matis's *burrá*—a catchall for everything good. They'd gotten hungry in the middle of the night and decided to go hunting, said Márcio, the youngest of the Kanamari.

The quarry: the two rodents and a croc. "Here, you want?" he said with a broad smile. He was handsome, about twenty years old, with a jarhead-style haircut, a broad nose, and high, ruddy cheeks. He held out a hunk of what looked like forearm, its salmon-colored flesh still clinging to charred, scaly hide. I declined. Alfredo followed me back along the beach. I strode past Possuelo, a profile of impatience with hands on hips, kicking at the sand. I ducked eye contact, but I still felt his eyes bore into me as I made for the stairs. Just then a rifle shot resounded from the thicket above us. Not the thunderous boom from a shotgun, more like the flat spit of a .22. "What was that?" Possuelo yelled, raising his gaze.

"Accidental discharge," came Welker's voice from the bush.

"Who was it?" Possuelo demanded. "Take the gun away from him! We can't have clowns firing off their weapons in camp!"

"Adelino Marubo," replied Welker.

Possuelo's posture softened even before he spoke.

"The .22s are a bit more difficult to use," he allowed, lowering his voice. "The Indians have more experience with the shotgun. Let's see if we can change firearms for him—later. Now we need to get moving!"

Ten minutes later, Alfredo and I were bounding down the steps, still stuffing gear into my bags. The boats were waiting, engines idling. Possuelo stood in the middle section of his skiff, glowering. Out of breath, I heaved myself over the gunwale and into Puruya's battleship of a canoe. As we drifted out onto the river, I took a long look back at our campsite: the crossbar still lashed to the trees where I'd hung my hammock, the stairway, the eddy where I'd bathed last evening. I felt an uneasy stirring, a sense of loss. It didn't seem right somehow, abandoning things so soon after we'd labored so hard to construct them. Yet, here we were, leaving all of it behind forever: the shelters, the benches, the tables erected no more than twelve hours earlier. But we were leaving nothing that hadn't already been there. All the building materials came straight out of the forest, the alterations the men had performed completely ephemeral. The forest would reclaim it all soon enough. A bleary-eyed Puruya, his cap screwed backward atop his unruly graying hair, engaged the three horses of his *peci-peci* and pointed our canoe into the current.

It was a long and monotonous day of blinding sun and blaring engines, nodding in and out of sleep. More trees lay across the river, old and twisted, desiccated and forlorn. They'd fallen at odd angles, sometimes taking down several others in a jumbled mess. Flotsam had snagged in their gnarled limbs, complicating Raimundo's work. The chain saw's screech must have resounded for miles, and I wondered if its vituperations might reach the ears of the Arrow People, and if they might interpret them as an early warning, like an air-raid siren, of our imminent arrival.

We pulled off the river late in the afternoon at a high bank on the left-hand side. Like the evening before, the village materialized as if by magic in the green shadows of the forest. Again, the Matis took the lead in creating their own subdivision. The other groups followed suit, with the whites on one flank and the Kanamari deepest in the forest, farthest from the river. As before, the Marubo stuck close to Possuelo and Orlando, as did Nicolas and I, erecting our shelters with the help of our porters Alfredo and Wilson, just a stone's throw from the main campfire and the stairway down to the boats. Once we'd gotten settled in, Possuelo called me over.

"This is where the trek begins," he said.

"So the boats go back tomorrow?" I asked, doing my best to conceal any trace of anxiety. From snippets of Possuelo's conversations I'd overheard and put together over the past two weeks, I now knew for sure that staying with the expedition would mean kissing good-bye to any hope of seeing the boys before the end of summer, or even seeing Sarah by Labor Day. She'd be looking for a job over the summer. I didn't even know where she'd be by then. But I'd made up my mind.

"From our current location, we're only six kilometers from a settlement of the *flecheiros*," said Possuelo. "We're going to bypass it. That means the terrain will be difficult—steep and hilly. You'd better get some rest."

Nicolas and I took the phone down to the beach to make a few quick calls to the Northern Hemisphere. It might be a long time before we would again find a gap in the forest that would allow a clear line of sight to the Inmarsat satellite orbiting somewhere up there in the darkening sky. Nicolas spoke with his girlfriend in Paris, but it was already too late in Europe to speak with Lily Fleur. He retreated up the embankment, leaving me alone.

I called the boys. I told them about the jaguar prints Ivan had shown me in the sand below our campsite and the croc the Kanamari had munched on for breakfast. "Be careful, Daddy," warned Ian, the youngest, sounding very much like an adult. "I love you, Daddy," Mackenzie and Aaron piped up. I didn't know when I would talk to them again. Lastly I called Sarah. "This is what you've always wanted to do," she said. "Don't worry about what's going to happen between you and me. I'll see you when you get back. Go for it."

*　*　*

Several paces away I could hear the breaking of twigs and the muted whispers of cooks Mauro and Paulo Souza, then the *whoosh, whoosh* as they fanned the breakfast fire into a full-blown, crackling blaze. I crawled out into the morning chill.

Everyone went about packing up in silence. Paulo Welker supervised the final distribution of provisions for the overland trek. Personal gear counted for less than half the load each man had to carry; the rest was matériel essential to the expedition's survival: foodstuffs, ax heads, ammunition. "Everyone, make sure you have a flashlight!" Welker shouted. His blond hair was pulled into a tight ponytail. His camouflage shirt was unbuttoned. A dark stubble dotted his chin. He laid out the flashlights on a makeshift table, along with a few pairs of unclaimed canvas jungle boots. I saw a pair of 44s, roughly the equivalent of a 10½, and tried them on. They were a loose fit, the same size and the same boot I'd turned down at the store in Manaus two weeks earlier. I made a snap decision, ditching the stiff leather boots for this flimsy but far more comfortable canvas pair. The dark eyes above Márcio Kanamari's high cheekbones lit up at the sight of those shiny black leather boots being abandoned. I felt a slight twinge of regret when I saw them on his feet, but the die had been cast. I'd thrown my lot in with the Brazilian canvas.

What wasn't going with us into the jungle would be sent back with the skiffs. The chain saw, so vital to our upriver quest, was going back. It was simply too cumbersome to take with us. Not just because of the weight, but because Possuelo deemed it far too loud and offensive an instrument for the sacred stillness of the wilderness we were about to enter. From here on out, we'd have only machetes and axes to clear our way through virgin forest. There were also a few peculiar steel tools that looked like a cross between ax and hoe, with the cutting blade perpendicular to the handle. These were adzes, scooping tools especially useful in the construction of dugout canoes, and hence to us, since the plan for our escape from the wilds envisioned building canoes in the depths of the jungle and paddling them down one of two possible rivers, back to civilization.

Meanwhile, Nicolas was directing the Kanamari in a photo shoot around a separate fire set back from the rest of the campsite. The Indians were wearing little crowns made of strips of palm leaves, and they were singing a traditional incantation to mark the departure of loved ones. A few of them were naked; the others had stripped down to nylon shorts. Nicolas was crouching and shooting, then circling around to get a fresh angle.

He was trying to get a "candid" shot of the Indians as they might look at the outset of a ritual trek if there were no outsiders, no *kariwa*, around. Márcio and Remi, the two youngest Kanamari, exchanged embarrassed smiles, not entirely comfortable with the camera's presence. Neither was I, but this was Nicolas's business, not mine. Perhaps his sensibilities were more finely attuned to the market's appetite for images of exotic, naked tribesmen that suggested a connection to the deep, mysterious prehistory of our species.

Possuelo was the first to move out on foot into the jungle, and he did so quietly, without announcement. Nicolas was on his heels, tucking his camera into a waterproof pouch strapped to his chest. With them went Soldado and Raimundo, their machetes unsheathed and at the ready, followed by Orlando. Together, they vanished through a gash in the foliage at the rear of the encampment. I was still trying to decide what I should take and what I should leave behind, finally settling on carrying just a camera bag and my day pack stuffed with tarp, hammock, flip-flops, and the clean sleeping clothes. I placed them inside a large plastic bag and bound it shut, hoping it would somehow manage to keep dry. The rest would go with Alfredo.

All morning it had looked as though it was going to rain, and now it did: heavy, steady, pouring rain, drip-dropping down through the canopy, pattering and hammering on the leaves as it made its way down to the forest floor. There was no point in even putting on a poncho; you'd have gotten just as wet from your own sweat in the vaporous air. I folded my reporter's notebook sideways into a ziplock bag and prepared to march.

Paulo Welker stood at the top of the riverbank, the boats on the river below. Puruya and a crew of Kanamari hired to take the skiffs downriver descended the slick slope, bearing sacks and boxes with the leftover goods we could not carry. All around, men were making final adjustments to their packs, tying boots to the outside of their frames, stuffing tarps under their straps. The Matis shouldered their enormous loads, teetering under their packs as they found their balance. They moved out altogether, leaving behind the Kanamari and the white *mateiros*. I didn't yet understand the mechanics that governed how a thirty-four-man column would move through virgin jungle, but it didn't seem like the stragglers still in camp were in any rush to catch up.

"Hey, listen up!" Welker shouted. "We're going in the jungle for three months. Make your stuff last. There might be an airdrop later on, but it's not for sure, and anyway, when it drops, stuff falls all over the place—high up in the trees, in the river, everywhere." This last bit of information seemed odd and extraneous, given the fact that we were weeks away from this phantom event that might not even happen. Now that Possuelo was gone, Welker appeared intent on assert-ing his authority, but there was something about him no one could take seriously. He wanted too much to be one of the guys, and the men took liberties they wouldn't have dared take in Possuelo's pres-ence. Amid grunts and smacking lips, undeterred by the rain that beat down through the canopy, they began to gorge on smoked boar left over from the hunt three days ago. They tore greedily at the greasy meat and scooped farinha barehanded from a gunnysack, stuffing their mouths like a plague of locusts. By the time they were done, the burlap bag lay limp on the ground, tiny pools of rainwater collecting in its folds. The boar's shank, stripped to the bone all the way down to its cloven hoof, buzzed with flies. As nice a guy as he was, Welker would have been hard-pressed to maintain control of this group in the depths of the jungle for a day, let alone weeks or months.

Alfredo hoisted my heavy backpack onto his shoulders. I was sur-prised to see he wasn't bothering to use the manufacturer's padded shoulder straps. Rather, he'd fashioned his own from long strands of envira bark he affixed himself, and he'd lashed a gunnysack stuffed with his own belongings on top of the backpack. The others retrieved their rifles, shouldered their loads, and one by one disappeared into the forest through the gap that had swallowed Possuelo and the others a half hour before.

"Hey!" Welker cried out. "We need someone to carry these *pan-ela*s!" He held up a stack of shiny aluminum pots, the kind designed for field use, lightweight and potbellied, with a swinging handle like a bucket's that allowed for easy suspension over a cooking fire. There were about a dozen of them, all told. "If we meet the Arrow People, we'll have some presents to give them." That he even felt the need to say this was a measure of the inexperience among some of the younger whites and the Kanamari. Most of them had never been involved in a traditional FUNAI attraction campaign to woo wild Indians from the bush, nor in this kind of effort to track an uncontacted tribe.

Among the woodsmen were two brothers, Chico and José Bezerra, from the same riparian hamlet where Soldado made his home. The elder of the two, José, was married to Soldado's daughter. They were burly and cheerful, always eager to lend a hand. Both stepped forward to volunteer. Each ran a length of cord through the handles of a stack of pots and bound them tightly to the outside of his backpack. Now hoisted onto the brothers' shoulders, the pots were right in my line of vision. They were eye-catching: brand-new, brilliant and buffed, straight from the factory. And they were cheap, no more than a few bucks apiece. The abstract possibility of an encounter with the *flecheiros* suddenly assumed more concrete form in my mind as I inspected these potential instruments of pacification. They were as time-tested as the trinkets the Dutch traded to the Mannahattas for use of their island paradise. Here we were, some four centuries later and four thousand miles to the south, white men with Indian accomplices, once again knocking on the door, though for an altogether different purpose. We weren't here to trade with or swindle the natives, but rather to ally ourselves with them, without their even knowing it. A more paradoxical quest could hardly be imagined. Yet, while Possuelo's interests and Nicolas's and mine overlapped, they were not identical. We were also here because exotic tribes still held a particular fascination for the rest of the world, much as they did when Columbus hauled six Indians bedecked in feathers back to Spain and paraded them, together with gold nuggets and parrots, before the court of Ferdinand and Isabella at the conclusion of his first voyage, in 1493. The point, from Possuelo's perspective, was to leverage the magazine's reach—and the growing sympathy in the world's metropolises for the plight of besieged tribes and their rainforest homelands—into concrete protections that would buy more time, fend off the onslaught, and guarantee their survival for another generation. It would have been fair to describe us as willing accomplices in that venture.

I turned to see Welker sitting on a stump, scribbling in a cloth-bound book, attempting to shield the pages from the rain with the back of his left hand. "The expedition's logbook," he said. "The historical record. If the expedition disappears, then somewhere, someday, maybe this will turn up." Or maybe not. Fawcett's never did.

On the river below, the boat motors sputtered to life. I watched from the top of the bank as the pilots steered the skiffs out onto the silver river, its surface piqued and mottled by the endless beating of raindrops. Puruya's large canoe was last. He waved to me from the stern with his thumbless hand. Then one by one, the vessels started downriver, disappearing in succession behind a veil of overhanging branches. The final bridge had been burned. I cinched my waist pack closed, slung on my pack, and looped the strap of my camera bag over my shoulder. I tugged my floppy camouflage hat snugly onto my head and followed the others into the jungle. There was no way back now but forward.

PART II

In the Land of the Arrow People

CHAPTER 10

A Forest Dark

NOW THAT WE WERE traveling on foot, a whole new world of hazards opened up all around us. Snakes topped the list—corals, bushmasters, fer-de-lance—but there also were the ubiquitous creepers ready to snag an ankle and send you tumbling headlong. A rodent's burrow could swallow your foot whole and inflict a debilitating sprain or cartilage tear. Rivers of ants crisscrossed the jungle floor, and it was best to step over them if you didn't want to be set upon by these single-minded Lilliputians with their viselike mandibles and toxic stingers.

My clothes were thoroughly drenched. Sweat flowed in torrents from my forehead, and it required constant mopping with a bandanna to keep my glasses from steaming up to the point where I couldn't see anything. I quickly learned to execute this maneuver in full stride; I'd fall too far behind if I stopped to do it. Still, sometimes there was simply no choice but to remove my glasses and clean the lenses. It was too risky to take more than a step without the benefit of corrected vision.

It wasn't enough to keep your eyes riveted to the ground, because there was plenty to watch out for overhead, too. Vines yanked my hat off. Thorns ripped at my sleeves. Stands of bamboo encased in three-inch spikes threatened to impale an eyeball in a moment of carelessness. Snakes also lurked in the trees, deadly *papagalho* vipers, camouflaged bright green. Soldado cautioned me to watch out for them. "They jump from the branches," he said, cupping his fingers and imitating the motion of a snake going for his jugular. "You get bitten, blood starts coming out through your pores, all over your body." The same branches swarmed with fire ants as vicious as their brethren on the forest floor, and they had a way of dropping down your shirt to stab the flesh wherever they alighted, usually someplace in the midsection of your back where you could not reach. I took to buttoning my shirt all the way up to the neck and all the way down to the wrists. There were nasty black wasps with stingers big as darts said to attack in swarms at the slightest sound, and when we passed a nest in the trees, warning was relayed in pantomime from man to man along the length of our single-file column, pointing up at the hive, then pressing finger to lips without uttering a word.

*   *   *

We picked our way through muddy ravines and scrambled over rotting, moss-draped logs. The rain had stopped, but water continued to collect on large, fleshy leaves overhead and pelted us in huge drops from the exuberant foliage. The sky was barely visible through the high trellis of the canopy, but light seeped down, showing signs of clearing weather. The trailblazers slashed open the jungle with their machetes, but the column snaked so far back into the forest that only a single man was visible at any moment in the blur of electric greens and muted browns. I guessed myself to be somewhere in the middle of the formation, following Tepi Matis.

I kept my eyes riveted on Tepi, or rather, on his back and the overloaded rucksack piled high above his head. He'd momentarily vanish from view, and I'd accelerate to get him within sight. It was too freaky out here to risk going astray, even for a minute. Tepi was about five foot five, not a scrap of fat on his body. He couldn't have weighed more than 120 pounds. Like most of the other men, Tepi was hauling his load with a tumpline—or forehead strap—he'd fashioned from a wide strip of shaggy envira bark. It draped across the top of his forehead and fastened to the corners of his backpack, shifting much of the weight to head and neck. The simple contrivance had a long history in South America, where large pack animals did not exist before the Conquest, and Inca caravans traversing the Andes relied not only on llamas as beasts of burden, but on humans as well. With his bark tumpline snugly in place across the crown of his head, Tepi was hauling somewhere close to 80 percent of his own weight. Most impressively, he'd forgone the FUNAI-issued boots and the Kachute tennis shoes, seeming to gain added traction on the slick forest floor with the splayed toes of his bare feet.

Within two hours of leaving the boats, we ascended a small ridge and followed its gently curving crest. Through a screen of foliage off to the left, I was able to make out the silver band of a broad *igarapé* some twenty or thirty feet below. I followed Tepi's footsteps along the high ground parallel to the river. Soon we caught up with the others, everyone from Possuelo on back. The men were sprawled on the ground, having plopped straight down in the trammeled underbrush. Possuelo stalked with stiff gait around the men's sprawled limbs, like a peg-legged Ahab strutting his debris-strewn quarterdeck. He said nothing, and the silence seemed charged with the aftershock of some kind of altercation. He wore a wide-eyed look beneath his floppy hat that seemed to return the gaze of everyone and no one at the same time. A pair of baggy camouflage shorts left his pale calves at the mercy of lacerating thorns and bloodthirsty insects, but he didn't seem to notice. Raimundo stood facing him alongside a fresh tree stump about three feet high and nearly as thick. His chest was heaving, and sweat ran down his face. He leaned heavily on a long-handled ax, having just dropped the tree neatly over the river, its crown landing atop the far bank, a good twenty feet above the surface of the stream. Nicolas fired off a few shots of Raimundo, bare-chested, ax in hand, the toppled tree and the wide stream over his shoulder.

"From now on, you have something to say, you say it to me," said Possuelo through clenched teeth, stepping in front of Nicolas to address Raimundo, who stood there motionless, save for the narrow black eyes that darted beneath the overhanging ledge of his brow. "Now let's get moving!" shouted Possuelo, turning back to the men scattered along the sides of the path.

"What was that about?" I asked Nicolas.

."Nothing really." He shrugged. "Raimundo was saying something about how hard the trek is, and Sydney got pissed at him."

I looked across the log that Raimundo had toppled, more than one hundred feet to the far side. "We're going to cross the river on *that*?" I said to Nicolas, lowering my voice to a whisper. In the stillness that carried the reverberations of Possuelo's tirade, I didn't want to be seen—or rather heard—as the hapless chump.

"Yeah," Nicolas chortled. "Just like Indiana Jones."

Through a spray of overhanging branches I could make out Kwini Marubo crouched on top of the log with his machete, scraping away moss and cutting notches into the tree's bark, the better to keep our footing. The tree was about three feet in diameter, though its rounded surface provided a walking area no more than fifteen inches wide. Despite his name, Kwini was actually Matis, and he was the most hand-somely adorned of all the Indians on the expedition. It was evident he went to great lengths to preen, even here in the wilderness. He maintained the rim of a mollusk shell in the bore of his nose, and the simulated jaguar whiskers that radiated from the sides of his nostrils were the best groomed of all the Matis's, shining with a convincing vitality that made them seem real, as though he were indeed half cat.

Soldado scampered across the trunk and vanished into the jungle on the far side. Moments later, he came back along the log with a long pole he'd just cut from the forest. When he was about a third of the way across from the far side, he hurled it straight down like a javelin into the streambed below, then wriggled it back and forth to burrow the tip deep into the ooze of the river bottom. Txema, the eldest of the Matis, did the same from the near side. A pair of thinner poles were quickly bound horizontally with creepers to the vertical uprights to fashion a handrail. Within ten minutes, the bridge was ready for us to cross. The Army Corps of Engineers could not have done a better job.

Half the expedition had already made it to the far side—dashing across without the slightest hesitation, all bearing loads upward of eighty pounds—when it came to my turn. Txema Matis had positioned himself at the head of the bridge, one foot on the stump and another on the log, and hoisted me up. He had a kindly round face, decorated in the traditional Matis style, and incredible strength in his arms. I clung to his hand for support while my feet felt around beneath me for balance. I raised my gaze. The railing was on my right, so I shifted my camera bag to the opposite shoulder. I double-checked the ziplocks and waterproof bags protecting my notes and cameras. "Don't think," Txema said. "Just do." Heart pounding, I set out for the other side.

It was hard to gauge what the consequences of a fall might be. Perhaps nothing more than a good drenching and merciless ribbing for the rest of the journey. The Indians were still joking about the spill I'd taken back at the last Kanamari village. "Scotchie fall, go *whoooo!*" Ivan Arapá would laugh. But a more debilitating injury here would be serious business. "The injured person delays the entire expedition," Possuelo had told me one night when we were back on the river. He recounted an incident from the early 1980s, while attempting to contact scattered bands of the Parakanã tribe, far to the east in the state of Pará. One of his scouts broke an ankle, forcing a ten-day halt until the man could hobble on his own. As the expedition hunted the same forests day after day, game dwindled. Tedium set in, restlessness.

That might have been bad enough, but out here, a prolonged stop was out of the question. It would give the Arrow People both the reason to think we'd come to take their land and the time to mass forces to defend it. On the other hand, a quick evacuation would be next to impossible; there was no place to land a helicopter, even on the slim chance one could be summoned. I'd taken Possuelo's words as a not-so-subtle warning: avoid injury at all costs. I took a deep breath and brought all my power of concentration to bear, knowing a slip would mean plunging into murky waters of shallow depth with a host of possible outcomes, few of them happy ones. Step by step, my jungle-booted feet negotiated the slippery surface of the log. Halfway across, I reached for the railing, but quickly realized it wasn't substantial enough to provide any real support; the benefit was mostly psychological.

"Bravo, Scott!" Possuelo exclaimed, grabbing my hand as I reached

the far side. "You did it!" I felt the exhilaration of a young initiate
who's just gained the threshold of a secret order. When everyone had
crossed the bridge and reassembled on the opposite side of the waterway, Possuelo consulted his compass and pointed the way for Soldado
and Raimundo. Once again, machetes flailing, they laid into the overhanging vines and dense undergrowth. There was no path to follow,
just the way forward hacked from the jungle.

"When we speak of expeditions, we're not talking about a casual stroll to a
village whose location is known in advance, along a clear, well-marked trail,"
Possuelo wrote in an internal memorandum in 1981 that laid out the
essentials of how to penetrate the land of an isolated tribe. "We're talking about breaking open dense and closed jungle, using the needle of a compass
to indicate the general direction." We were following his prescription to
a T, even this curiously poetic detail from the memo, describing the
emotional strain of the trek: "With each step, we feel evermore distanced
from that which is known and familiar, our hearts heavy with longing for those
we love."

As we slogged uphill away from the bridge crossing, I fell in behind
Orlando, toward the front of the column. Now bereft of his flowing
locks, he'd taken to wearing a weird-looking desert fatigue hat with
high crown and short brim, like an officer's cap from Rommel's Afrika
Korps, turned backward on his head. His bronzed biceps burst from
a tight, short-sleeved khaki shirt, and he toted a full load in his knapsack, as well as a .22.

It didn't take long before our path was blocked by another river.
We followed the bank, our column strung along in single file, looking
for a way across. The water's pale band of silvery light shimmered up
from the left through overhanging boughs and dangling creepers. I
was now just behind Nicolas, the sixth or seventh man back from the
very front of the column, where Soldado and Raimundo slashed away
at the jungle. Suddenly, muffled shouts reached us from up ahead,
followed by the resounding blast of a shotgun. We rushed forward,
not knowing what to expect. We came upon Soldado, Possuelo, and
Raimundo at the top of the bank, overlooking an enormous tree that

had fallen of its own accord across the river, creating a natural bridge
to the other side. Soldado was inhaling deeply from a cigarette, hand
trembling. His warning had been prophetic; he'd just managed to
dodge a deadly *jaracuçu*. The snake had lunged at him as he was dropping down the slope to scout the bridge. It had barely missed striking
him in the face. As it scooted away, Possuelo had taken a crack at it with
Raimundo's shotgun, and missed. He was just handing the rifle back to
Raimundo when we pulled up.

"That was close," Soldado said in his deadpan mumble. "The
venom kills. I've known people who died from its bite." We were carrying a general antivenin in the expedition's medical kit. But it would
have been little use had the snake struck Soldado in the jugular. "It
could have been bad," Possuelo said with a nod. The effectiveness of
the antivenin depended on how much venom the snake injected, but
even a juvenile would have packed enough toxin to kill a grown man.
The *jaracuçu* is a near relative of the fer-de-lance, known for its hyper-
aggressiveness, responsible for more human deaths in South America
than any other snake. It was as close a call as Soldado had ever experienced in his forty-three years in the backwoods, he said. He shrugged
it off and joined Raimundo on the log, clearing away branches with
deft swipes of his machete. Then we started across, one by one. The
tree had fallen from low on the bank, but its trunk had landed on top
of the opposite bank, so that crossing was like ascending a long, gentle
ramp, sixty feet to the other side. There was no railing. I was just getting my bearings atop the trunk when shouts erupted from the far side
of the stream: *"Kill the motherfucker!"* Again, a shot rang out.

I picked my way across the bridge, anxious to find out what was
going on. When I reached the other side, yet another snake lay in a
heap in the grass at Possuelo's feet, blood oozing from its head. Its
yellow and brown length continued to twitch with the last vestiges of
life. It had risen up just as Possuelo cleared the bridge. Txema Matis
had seen it poised to strike and delivered a marksman's shot, just wide
enough to avoid hitting Possuelo's legs with the shotgun's blast, close
enough to keep the snake in its kill zone. It had been incredibly quick

thinking, deftly executed. "*Muito obrigado*—many thanks," Possuelo panted, wiping the sweat off his brow and stuffing the hat back down on his head. I assumed they were separate vipers, the one that attacked Soldado and this one, and I made a dark quip about them being the "Guardians of the Bridge." But Orlando said: "It was the same snake, I tell you. I saw it swim across the river and come up here after us."

Researchers have uncovered preliminary evidence suggesting an evolutionary link between snakes and some of our more advanced cognitive abilities. Our keen eyesight, our ability to distinguish primary colors, and the human brain's capacity for fear may have evolved together over the course of millions of years to counter increasingly deadly snakes, they say, in a kind of "biological arms race" between primates and vipers. I was inclined to believe it, judging from the instinctive jolt of adrenaline that kicked in at the sight of any shape that remotely resembled a serpent coiled on the forest floor. When it came to the part about vision, I was probably more an exhibit of a species on life support, so far removed from our origins in the forest that I wouldn't have survived here for an hour without my glasses.

After the snake episode, I resolved to stay close to the head of the column. I needed to keep Possuelo under constant scrutiny, to catch his running commentary, and to witness his reactions to the jungle in all its full-blown unpredictability. When the trek resumed on the other side of the river, I inserted myself in the column just behind Possuelo. We wound through claustrophobic tunnels of high sawgrass, low-hanging boughs, and dangling creepers. Nicolas used my slightest lapse to scoot ahead of me. We traded places back and forth in a kind of uneasy truce. He needed to be alongside Possuelo, too, he insisted, especially in the event of a sudden and inadvertent contact with the Arrow People in the middle of the forest. He'd need to capture that historic instant on film: Possuelo's tentative, outstretched hand, the wide-eyed Indians, the tension of contact.

A chance encounter would have been unlikely, but not entirely without precedent. One of Possuelo's earliest "first contacts" unfolded in such a way more than a quarter century before. He was leading an

exploratory team with fellow *sertanista* Wellington Gomes Figueiredo
to investigate reports of "wild Indians" on the upper Quixito River,
in the northwest corner of the Javari. The Indians had been slipping
undetected into logging camps and stripping buttons off the lumberjacks' clothing, apparently to use as ornaments. This was back in the
days when FUNAI's directive was to make contact, when loggers and
other deep-jungle entrepreneurs still had a strong incentive to report
such encounters to the agency: *sertanistas* would then be dispatched
to clear the woods of *índios bravos* and make them safe for their operations. The FUNAI team went out for a look. They came across footprints in the jungle and followed them. "Up ahead, we found a guy
leaning against a tree, holding a long blowgun," Possuelo told me as
we walked. "We approached very slowly. You don't know what's going
to happen—if you're about to get a dart in the chest." There were
about fifteen Indians in the group, all entirely naked except for raf-
fia armbands and penis sheaths, traditional jungle garb for men to
protect their intimate parts as they run through the jungle. Possuelo's
team advanced with hands held high, smiling and singing; in the forest, only enemies approach in silence. The man slowly lowered his
blowgun. They tried to communicate, but despite having Indians from
three different tribes in the contact team, they could not make themselves understood. The one thing they did ascertain was that this was
indeed the same group of Indians the loggers called the Mayá.

The contact was peaceful, but it differed markedly from a classic
attraction campaign, designed to slowly woo Indians to a FUNAI post.
The *sertanistas* were in the middle of wild forest, and both sides were
wary. Fearing treachery, the Mayá insisted on sleeping on top of Possuelo and Figueiredo when night fell, pinning their arms and legs to
the ground. The *sertanistas* found it impossible to get much of the Indians' story—if they had relatives elsewhere, if they were part of a larger,
extant tribe, or if they were its lone survivors. As they parted ways two
days later, the *sertanistas* gave them presents: a machete, a knife, some
axes, a handful of buttons. The Mayá seemed to have some familiarity
with the tools, which Possuelo understood to mean they'd lifted more

than just buttons from the loggers over the years. He hoped the encounter would mark the beginning of an ongoing relationship. "When we said good-bye, I pointed at the sky and explained that I would be back after the sun rose and fell thirty times and the moon changed once." But in the interim, Possuelo clashed with his commander, a man who "stuck his nose in everything," and he was transferred from the Javari. The Mayá were never seen again, though unconfirmed rumors spoke of a massacre that may have wiped them out. Possuelo did remember there being a young boy among the Indians who was missing an eye. So when vague reports surfaced decades later about a band of nomads wandering the upper Quixito, among them a man with a wounded eye, it set Possuelo to wondering. "Could it have been the same person, now all grown up?" he asked. "I think about that sometimes."

* * *

It was getting on midafternoon, and I began to ponder how much longer we had until Possuelo called it quits for the day. I was exhausted, soaked through from head to foot with rain, sweat, and swamp. We slogged through shallow knee-deep *igarapés* and plunged back into shadowy forest. The terrain was getting progressively more difficult: steeper inclines, more precipitous descents, more mud, more tumbles.

And then, in a most unexpected and understated manner, we discovered we had entered the land of the Arrow People. In a small clearing, several palm fronds were spread out on the ground beneath a large tree, some parallel to one another, others perpendicular, done with an intentionality that bespoke the hands of human beings. The leaves were brown, though not yet brittle, and they were indented lengthwise in the way a body leaves its mark in the mattress of a cheap motel.

"They slept here," Possuelo said, pointing to the palm leaves.

"How long ago?" I asked.

"Not very long. Several days, probably. This season, for sure."

As we stood there examining this place where strangers had slept, it felt as though we were cops intruding on a scene where no crime had been committed. Not far away, we found scraps of a purplish black palm fruit, called *patuá*, scattered amid the leaf litter. They were small, with fleshy white meat surrounding a dark pit the size of an olive. Several had been half chewed, then spit out.

"They must have brought them here from somewhere else," said Soldado, his brown eyes probing the branches overhead. He quickly rolled a cigarette and jammed it in his mouth. "No *patuá* trees around here." From somewhere in the canopy, a screaming piha let loose its shrill four-note cry. It ricocheted through the trees against the low thrum of crickets and cicadas. *"O capitão do mato,"* Soldado said: the jungle captain. It rang out again, and from the distance came an identical response, fainter and overlapping, like a forlorn echo through a long canyon.

"Hey, check this out!" Ivan Arapá called in a whispered shout from thirty feet away. He was standing over what looked like a crude, conical-shaped birdcage, fashioned from a dozen three-foot-high sticks gouged into the moist earth, then bound together at the top with vine. "For *jabuti*," Ivan suggested. "To keep tortoise."

"Or for any kind of creature"—Possuelo nodded—"agouti, maybe, or small birds they'll take home and raise." Sun had broken through the clouds, and a soft yellow light streamed down in broken shafts. He surveyed the scene around him, scratching his beard. Most likely, he surmised, this was an overnight bivouac for a family on its way to a more permanent fishing camp. Possuelo peered out beyond the trees that encircled us, as though directing his gaze into a looking glass focused across a great distance, aeons away. "These Indians are very close to the way Vespucci would have found them," he pronounced, his voice rapt with marvel and admiration. "They live from hunting, fishing, and gathering."

Encountering such *vestigios*—the vestiges of isolated tribes—was the lifeblood of Possuelo's work, and it was hard not to share his enthusiasm. If there was any such thing as time travel, this was about as close to it as you could get. Five hundred years of world history hadn't touched these people. Or if so, barely. Here we were at the dawn of the third millennium, the world more interconnected by the day. Instant communications, bar codes, and keystrokes tracking individuals from birth to death, surveillance cameras and satellite dishes sprouting from every rooftop. Yet here in this forest, nomads were afoot, drawing their daily sustenance entirely from its land, trees, and rivers, as their forebears had done for a thousand years, their names unknown to us, even the name of their tribe unknown to us.

"Are they Arrow People?" I asked.

"It's an indigenous group you can presume to be the *flecheiros*," Possuelo affirmed. "We're in their territory now." Or we were on the very edge of it anyway, at the limits of their "zone of perambulation," the forest realm they regarded as theirs and through which they wandered during the summer months. "As you walk toward a *maloca* previously marked by GPS," Possuelo explained, "you know you've reached the periphery of their territory at the point where you encounter the first vestiges of their presence." Rather than proceed in the direction of their village, we would now begin to skirt to the south and east, hoping to trace their boundaries as we went.

We resumed the march, me following on Possuelo's heels, more alert than I'd been all day. We were no longer tromping through a *terra de ninquem*, as he called it, a no-man's-land. We'd entered a forest that belonged to someone else. Along with a heightened sense of excitement came a feeling that we were intruders whose trespasses put us at risk of serious, perhaps fatal, consequences. Within a few minutes, Possuelo stopped and took hold of a scrawny limb that had been snapped, but not entirely broken off, about three feet off the ground, roughly at the level where a person's hands would hang while he or she walked. The once-straight branch was cocked at nearly a right angle, like an elbow, but I never would have noticed if Possuelo hadn't called it to my attention. "It's a *quebrada,*" he said. A break. He brought his face down to examine the mangled limb with his bug eyes. It was young and tender, more like a twig. The *quebrada* was the point where a human being had casually but deliberately bent the green wood back between thumb and finger, causing it to fracture.

"The Indians create them as they walk through the forest," Possuelo explained, "as a point of reference, so they know where they've been." He mimicked the action, swinging his arms as he walked and snapping a pair of branches on low-hanging trees. Suddenly it made a lot more sense. In fact, Raimundo and Soldado were doing something similar to mark our own path. They weren't snapping off twigs, but they were swiping the trunks of young saplings that sprouted from the forest floor with their machetes, cleaving them off at steep, razor-sharp angles. They did this even while tracking through relatively unobstructed stretches across level ground. It was part reflex—when you've got a machete in your hand, your instinct tells you to use it—but it was also to provide a clear marker to the left and right of the trail they were blazing, so that even those in the rear of our long column, which stretched as far back as a kilometer or two, could stay on course. In the process, they were sowing a trail of knee-high punji sticks as they went, but that was beside the point.

Though I would have missed nearly every *quebrada* we passed in the undifferentiated tangle of foliage, experienced trackers like Possuelo could not only spot them but also determine with surprising precision—from the color of the wood, its dryness, the degree to which bark had grown back over the wound—how long ago the fractures had been inflicted. Possuelo figured the breaks to be a few months old. "Not the same Indians who slept back there. A different group, a different time." So far, none of the markings were fresh enough to indicate the Arrow People's immediate presence. We proceeded without alarm.

As the day grew long, we crossed a third major *igarapé*, but this time the log bridge started out more than thirty feet off the water and twisted downward as it went, so we were ankle-deep in the current before we were two-thirds of the way across. It was a relatively easy go, compared with the earlier ordeals, but once across, we faced a messy scramble up a near-vertical thirty-foot embankment of slick mud. I must have been a sight to behold, for there was plenty of laughter when I finally found my way to the top, boosted up with a hand from Soldado.

"Escop!" someone shouted, another common variation of my name among the expeditioners. *"O homen da selva!* The man of the jungle!" There was no small amount of irony in those words, but I had made it over three rivers and arrived safely at the end of our first day's march through the jungle. I strode forward into the imaginary spotlight to receive the accolades and took a deep bow to hoots of delight.

Even up at the top of the bank, the ground squished under our boots. "All of this land was underwater just a short time ago," Possuelo said. It was hard to imagine. I looked down on the creek thirty feet below. That meant that huge stretches of the forest all around us, including the ground we were standing on, had been covered by a vast sheet of water only a few weeks before. Though it was still soggy, Possuelo deemed the ground sufficiently dry and free from insect plagues to make it our home for the night. It was nearing 4:00 p.m. The sunlight was just catching the upper story of the trees, still two hours away from fading definitively into twilight.

The forest soon resounded with the dull thud of axes and the zing of machetes as the men cleared away brush, hoisted tarps, and hung their hammocks. A campfire sprang to life, the damp wood snapping and popping, its pungent smoke curling up through overhanging branches. Brothers José and Chico, together with Raimundo and the rail-thin and ever-ebullient Amarildo, formed a team to build benches around the fire, using poles pounded into the ground as vertical uprights, then lashing horizontal struts to them with vines. Split logs were then laid in place, providing a somewhat smooth surface for sitting.

But it was a full hour before Alfredo and Wilson wandered in from the bush with our bags, the last stragglers to arrive from the day's march. Nicolas and I had been hanging out, slapping mosquitoes, unable to set up our *barracas* without our stuff. Possuelo, who was just hanging his mosquito netting when the pair sauntered into the clearing, glowered but otherwise said nothing. They wore blank expressions that seemed to border on the defiant.

"Alfredo, I need you to be here when I arrive, not an hour later," I said. His eyes shifted from left to right, barely making contact with mine. He dropped the backpack, unsheathed his machete, and set to work. With Alfredo's help I finally got my own site straightened out, then went down to bathe. A stairway had already been installed down to the water, which was clear and sepia in color, rich in tannic acid from decomposing vegetation. My skin glowed with an orange tint as I slipped naked beneath the surface. The current was surprisingly swift. I soaked off the sweat and the filth, ruminating on the extraordinary events of the day: the high jinks of the bridge crossings, the snakes, the wasps, the mud. And most important, the first signals that we'd entered the land of the Arrow People.

But the sense of accomplishment was tempered with ominous forebodings. There'd been the grueling march itself and the hardships it portended. There'd been the sparring between Possuelo and Raimundo. I couldn't help but wonder where that might lead. No place good, that much I knew. And the dawdling of our porters. True, they were bearing heavy loads. But so was everyone else. It wasn't only an inconvenience; a larger security issue loomed. Two stragglers could make easy pickings for *indios bravos* unhappy with this invasion of their sanctuary.

CHAPTER 11

The Headwaters

No matter how early I awoke, it didn't seem to be early enough. The men were already breaking camp by the time I emerged from my hammock. I felt tightness clench my chest, gnawing away like some kind of flesh-eating disease. Mauro and Paulo Souza had put out the call for breakfast, and a line had formed for a ladleful of sweetened coffee and a hunk of corn bread. Possuelo was fully dressed and had nearly finished packing. Every morning, he went about his preparations with a quiet and steady deliberateness, folding his tarp into his backpack with an extra flourish, as though someone might be watching. He looked over and caught my eye, raised his brow in a kind of greeting, but otherwise said nothing.

Alfredo appeared through the trees to untie my tarp and haul it down. We worked without speaking, and as we finished folding it up, Possuelo called Alfredo over. I went about packing, ears tuned to Possuelo's words. "It's dangerous to lag behind," I could hear him say. He pretended to draw an arrow back from a bow, and he pointed it at Alfredo. "The Arrow People could kill you! From now on, you guys need to keep up! Do you understand?"

It was impossible to tell if it registered. Alfredo nodded, his Prussian face inscrutable, his eyes never meeting Possuelo's. He sauntered off, his steps rustling the carpet of dry leaves. Possuelo shouldered his pack.

"Paulo!" he called to Welker. "Let's get the people moving! Make sure everything's cleaned up around here! And secure the rear of the column! Keep the Kanamari ahead of you!" We were now following an east-by-northeasterly course, and, after double-checking his compass, he pointed the way for Soldado and Raimundo. They plunged into the jungle, machetes flashing, with me trailing right behind.

I'd swished my shirt and mud-caked pants around in the water with some soap the night before, then spent the better part of two hours drying them and my boots over the fire. They were drenched with sweat again within five minutes of departing camp. So were my feet, soaked in a brook too wide to lunge across. We started up a steep incline. The carpet of leaves that covered the ground was quickly kicked aside by the first few travelers, exposing a treacherous path of slick red earth. It was impossible to get any footing whatsoever. Handholds were equally sparse. Toiling on all fours, I reached for a tree to hoist myself up, only to realize it was covered in spikes.

It took a half hour to gain the crest of the hill, the forest thinning as we reached the top. The sun came out, sending brilliant shafts of golden light scattering down to the forest floor. We caught our breath and started down the backside, along an equally precipitous slope, with a 60-degree drop-off. One by one, we negotiated the descent, breaking our momentum from tree to tree, from sapling to dangling liana to overhanging branch, reaching for anything that could break our fall, praying it would also hold our weight and not bristle with flesh-piercing thorns. Too late one time, I grabbed for a tree, and a spike three inches long shot straight through the webbing between my thumb and forefinger and out the other side. I cursed the day Oliver Payne had called, throwing my life into disarray and leading me to this place so remote and inhospitable that only those desperate enough and determined enough to resist a five-hundred-year-long conquest would even consider making it their home.

We collapsed at the bottom of the hill along a gently flowing creek of black water. It was clear along the shallow edges, where the sandy bottom shone orange in the rippling current and gradually faded beneath its cloudy depths. The air was thick with the smell of fungi and decay. The ground was spongy wet, but we collapsed just the same. As they'd done at innumerable streams already, the men dipped their cups straight into the creek and guzzled. I sloshed the warm, halazone-tinged water around in my bottle and unscrewed the lid. A chemical odor—part swimming pool, part waste-treatment plant—wafted out.

"Is the water safe to drink here?" I asked Possuelo.

"We're in *as cabeceiras*—the headwaters of the rivers," he said. "If there's one place on Earth where it's safe to drink the water, it's here. You won't find cleaner water anywhere." We were at the point where four rivers began—the Itaquaí, Jutaí, Jutaizinho, and Jandiatuba. They all eventually joined the main trunk of the Amazon, each taking a twisting, serpentine course in varying degrees to the north or north-east to get there. The divide that separated each watershed from the others, like interlocking pieces of a mind-boggling puzzle, ran along the ridgelines and through the labyrinth of hollows we were traversing.

The headwaters. Birthplace of rivers. Givers of life. Shrouded in mystery. Sacred. Remote places of near-impossible access. The quest to find the ultimate source of any river always seems to lead away from the lowlands and their madding crowds, traveling back in time, toward wild, primordial beginnings and mist-shrouded heights. Yet here, the waters were not borne on glacial runoff, a trickle sliding through lichen-painted boulders on a wind-tossed alpine meadow. Here, the water seeped out of the ground all around us, collecting in pools amid the brown leaf litter. It ran over sand in tiny rivulets and collected in larger pools, which in turn fed meandering streams that drained into the creek from which I now withdrew a cupful and raised it to my lips. The water was cool and sweet.

"Forget those pills," Possuelo went on. "They're a waste of time. In the Amazon, you drink straight from the rivers." He didn't bother telling me until later, when it was far too late to matter, that he suffered from an incurable gastric condition.

A brilliant iridescent blue butterfly lilted past, the size of my out-stretched hand, the largest butterfly I'd ever seen in my life. It drifted through the air, pumped its wings in short jerks, drifted again. It went down the creek, flashing its eye-catching wings every two or three seconds, then turned and came back, as if playing with us. We watched, spellbound. So astonishing was its presence here, this beautiful and fragile creature, it seemed as though it must have been an emissary from another world.

"It's a Morpho," said Nicolas, holding his camera to his eye in a futile effort to nail a shot. He'd taken to wearing a yellow baseball cap since we left the boats, the visor turned backward so he could work the camera without obstruction. "In New York, collectors pay up to $100 for specimens." It wasn't only Indians who had found safe harbor in these woods; countless other threatened species had as well. What could the Arrow People possibly stand to gain from us, I thought, a civilization that desecrates the sacred, mows down the forest, and commodifies even these fleeting, delicate works of beauty?

* * *

We encountered further evidence of the Arrow People later that afternoon, just as we were crossing another log bridge. Ivan Arapá and Tepi Matis had decided to slog straight through the water, rather than cross the bridge, when they came upon tracks on the beach. "Look!" they called from down on the shore, pointing to the footprints that led to a series of excavated pits, each with sand piled along its lip. The beach looked as though a rambunctious dog had been turned loose on it to dig for buried bones.

"They're looking for the *ovos de tracajá*—the turtle eggs," Possuelo said. "It's the time of year. Looks like they've already gotten here. Let's hope we don't cross paths with them."

The concern was real. They must have unearthed the turtle nests very recently, within the past week at the most. We were, in essence, transecting their domain, cutting through the land of the Arrow People in as close to a series of straight lines as the terrain would permit, from Point A to Point B, and on to Point C, each point representing one of our evening bivouacs. In so doing, we were intersecting the earlier wanderings of the *flecheiros* at random junctures. We could have been intercepting the tracks of the same party at various intervals or witnessing traces of entirely distinct groups that had moved through the jungle at different times in the past, or both. The trick, as Possuelo said, was to avoid an intersection both spatial and temporal—in other words, contact.

I suspected that everyone on the expedition had his own notion of what that contact might look like, were it to occur. But for now, even the darkest thoughts about the Arrow People took a backseat to the punishing terrain, our growing misery, and the imperative to survive. Men were slipping and sliding, tumbling into jabbing thorns, bleeding, cursing as they regained their footing, teetering beneath their top-heavy loads. Our course took us up and down countless rain-slick hills, each man clawing his way to the top, inch by inch, crawling on all fours, desperate for footing, reaching for anything that might support his weight—a protruding root, a young sapling—or at least support it long enough to gain the next step before it gave way. A misstep or miscalculation could unravel in seconds what had taken fifteen or twenty minutes to attain, gravity dragging you back to where you began, leaving rich deposits of muck caked down your entire front side. It was as if we were clawing our way through a huge, vaporous terrarium, an enormous laboratory where the process of evolution continued to unfold by the minute, spawning a mind-boggling array of deadly creatures and toxic plants, all locked in a terrifying contest of survival.

Even Possuelo was surprised by the ferocity of the terrain. "The worst I've ever seen," he acknowledged as he gasped for breath after a half-hour battle to gain the crest of a hill. What made it so torturous, he said, was the fact that we were traversing the *divisor das aguas*—the divide separating the four different river systems.

He pulled out his map to get his bearings. Straight as our course might have appeared when plotted between nightly bivouac points, the reality was far different. He mopped his brow with a shirtsleeve and peered out into the forest, as though attempting to fathom the secrets it concealed behind the foliage that pressed in from every direction.

"I'd rather be working off a better map, like a 1:100,000." That way, he said, he might have been able to chart a course that skirted the most grueling inclines and some of the more treacherous descents. As it was, his 1:250,000-scale map provided just enough detail to make an educated guess, not an informed decision, about which way we should go. "We could escape all this if we could see what the contours looked like."

It may have been a mere bureaucratic snafu. Then again it may have been a measure of the contempt that many in the federal government, particularly among budget planners, had for FUNAI and its mission to protect the country's indigenous peoples. But in the end, it boiled down to the same thing: there weren't sufficient funds in the agency's coffers to provide its most dedicated scouts with much of the gear they needed to traverse the continent's wildest, least explored dominions.

Even Possuelo's GPS, a vital tool for navigation in the wilderness, had been paid for with funds from the European Union, not the Brazilian taxpayers. The fact that it happened to work only when we encountered a crack in the jungle canopy wide enough for it to hit the high-orbiting geospatial satellites did not diminish its value. Other than a two-way radio and the satellite phone, both of which were also useless under the tree cover, it was about the only piece of equipment in our possession that marked a significant advance over the technology available to Lewis and Clark. In the business of protecting remote Indians, the GPS was an indispensable tool; their *malocas* had to be pinpointed and their coordinates assigned before establishing a buffer zone off-limits to outsiders. It was equally important in Possuelo's current mission to track the extent of their wanderings. The fact that funding for such vital instruments was coming from foreign sources was both a measure of the growing commitment of the international community to protect standing tropical forests in cash-strapped countries, as well as a sign of the deep ambivalence that divided Brazil on the question of preservation versus exploitation of her natural resources. It also left Possuelo and his cadre of *sertanistas* vulnerable to charges from business interests and right-wing zealots who portrayed them as stooges of nefarious foreign interests seeking to keep Brazil mired in the Dark Ages.

Whatever the sources of funding for the GPS, it could do nothing to ease the burden of the trek. The whites seemed to be taking it especially hard, starting to exchange dark, sidelong glances, grumbling under their breath.

"It's not fair," Raimundo said, "that I'm hauling this heavy fucking load *and* opening the trail, too." He was half whispering, as though he hadn't decided if he was just talking to himself or if he wanted someone to hear. Possuelo stopped in his tracks, his eyes wide with rage.

"It's a bit too late to return to Tabatinga at this point, don't you think?" he sneered. "If you don't want to be out in front, move to the back! Trade places with someone who's carrying one of the *really* heavy loads. You think you're carrying too much weight? You'll find out what a heavy load really is, I promise!" Raimundo held his tongue, but his pinched brow and downcast stare said it all: *I'd kill this motherfucker if I could get away with it.*

* * *

As the second day wore on, desperation grew. We needed to stop. We'd eaten all the peccary the night before, leaving nothing for tonight, so the men needed time to hunt before sundown. What we required— relatively dry, level ground with a water source nearby—was proving maddeningly elusive. It was looking increasingly grim, when we staggered down a last hill and came upon a burbling brook, clear as crystal, that wound its way through a cool green glade. A dead tree had fallen across the narrow ravine, providing a quaint footbridge.

"It's been made for us!" said Possuelo. Indeed, a more perfect location could not have been conjured by fairies. Here and there, enormous moss-flecked trunks soared like Gothic columns toward the canopy high above. A soft yellowish green light danced on the forest floor. We followed the stream another twenty yards, coming to a natural pool where it veered sharply to the left. "We'll make camp here,"

Possuelo pronounced. The first men to arrive set to work clearing the campsite. Soldado and Raimundo shed their backpacks, grabbed their rifles, and vanished into the forest to look for our dinner.

The rest of the column was still arriving, the men staggering in under their loads, when the first muffled shot rolled in from the distance: *BOOM!* It was followed by another and another, resounding through the forest, gunshots overlapping with their echoes. In allowing Soldado and Raimundo to hunt with big rifles, Possuelo must have figured the *flecheiros* were still a long way off, too far away for the shotgun blasts to reach their ears. All isolated Indians, he said, understood the meaning of the sound of a gun: *Tem branco por aí.* Whites on the prowl. Either they knew from direct experience—having been shot at themselves—or they'd been told about it from others. Such were the subtle nuances of what it meant for a tribe to remain "uncontacted." It wasn't that the Indians had been hermetically sealed off from the rest of the world; it was that they had experienced its intrusions as a form of terror from which they fled.

I selected a site for my hammock between two stout trees just above the edge of the pool. Alfredo hadn't arrived yet, so without waiting to set up my *barraca*, I stripped and made my way down to bathe. The pool was a marvel of nature. A mesh of interwoven roots formed a vertical wall that dropped beneath the surface straight down to a hard-packed sandy bottom five feet below. I stood chest-deep in the current with soap and razor perched on the lip of the stream at the level of my eyes. The water was so clear I could see my feet on the bottom, tinged a pinkish orange by the tannin. Never in my life had a bath been so welcome. I shaved for the first time in days. I washed my shirt, my boots, both kerchiefs, even my hat and mud-caked pants, piling the clean garments atop my flip-flops on the edge of the stream.

The main campsite was taking shape on both sides of the brook, with the main hearth across the bridge from the spot I'd picked for my personal bivouac. Possuelo was nearby, hanging his hammock and mosquito netting, scatting cheerfully to himself. I recognized the tune: "New York, New York." *Start spreading the news.* If he was bothered by the day's events, he showed no sign of it. *I'm leaving today.* He seemed completely oblivious of the unease stirring in the expedition's midst. The uncompromising terrain, the jungle's insistent gloom, and his bizarre mood swings had conjoined to produce a collective angst among the whites, a sense of drifting terribly off course, toward a place they didn't want to go, led by someone they didn't want to go there with. Under the circumstances, it did not seem entirely unreasonable to ponder the prospects for desertion or outright rebellion.

The potential for violent removal at the hands of skulking malcontents is a reality that stalks all commanders who have ever led expeditions into the unknown. Sometimes, their leadership is weak, indulgent. At other times, their tyrannical abuse invites conspiracy. Additional factors enter the equation: the magnitude of the distance, the depths of deprivation and isolation, the hostility of the climate. All combine to loosen the constraints that bind men together in civil society. Like individuals, expeditions can crack under pressure and self-destruct.

I dried off, stepped into some shorts, and wandered over toward Possuelo's bivouac, thinking I might gain insight into his thinking on the question of mutiny—starting in the abstract and working toward the very specific and very pressing context of the lugubrious pall that had descended on the expedition. I found him sitting sideways in his hammock, jotting notes, shrouded in the gauze of his mosquito net. He seemed mildly surprised—and pleased—by my visit, looking up over the rims of his reading glasses. He pushed aside the mosquito net veil. "Scott! To what do I owe this honor?" We made small talk about the trek, the mud, his vague hope that conditions might lighten in the next day or so. He was so pleasant, I'd almost forgotten why I'd come over. Eventually I got around to the flagging morale among the whites, and I wondered aloud if a gentler approach might prove a more effective motivator.

A deep frown creased his face, as though he had never entertained a less welcome thought. "No," he said flatly, "this situation requires a firm hand." With the exception of Soldado, he said, these whites he'd recruited were a sorry collection of misfits and crybabies. He'd had no choice. Long gone were the days when he could count on a ready supply of experienced, toughened woodsmen to fill the ranks of his expeditions. In any case, it was only the whites who troubled him; the Indians were not a problem. They did as he asked and never griped. They had, he believed, a much higher threshold for discomfort.

"Remember that guy, the one I sent home when we were on the river?" he asked. He meant the eye-rolling Francisco, whom Possuelo had summarily dismissed and sent back with the *Waiká* and *Kukahá*. "Best thing I did," he said, like amputating a limb before it turned gangrenous and imperiled the entire expedition. "The most dangerous men are the ones who don't confront you directly. They talk behind your back and sow discontent." One time long ago, a trailblazer had deliberately led his expedition in circles after being rebuked for a minor offense. As soon as Possuelo figured out what was happening, he took the man's rifle away and moved him to the rear of the column for the remainder of the journey. "Once you call out a dissident, keep an eye on him," he said in a hush, as though wrapping me in a cloak of complicity. "He's the guy who will try to sabotage you." His eyes bore into mine like beacons plumbing a wreckage for possible snags. I knew what he was going to say next before he said it. "This guy Raimundo? You can bet I'm going to be watching him very closely."

He got up from his hammock and stretched. He looked out into the gathering shadows. I thought the conversation was over and turned to leave. He'd made it all sound so reasonable. "Being in the midst of the jungle is much like being out in the ocean," he said, his voice returning to normal decibel level, stopping me in my tracks. "Of course, there are differences. At sea, you can see for great distances. You have the horizon, stars, the sun." The sense of disorientation in the jungle was much worse, he said, since most of the time you couldn't see the sky at all. "One has a sense of being *abafado*—smothered, claustrophobic." That was the feeling, precisely. What I found particularly disorienting was Possuelo's own erratic behavior, how he could hold the entire expedition on edge with his scowl one moment, only to be humming "New York, New York" the next.

In the end, Possuelo thought it was probably worse at sea. Perhaps nothing could match the sheer terror of being tossed up and down hundred-foot swells, driven by hurricane-force winds in tiny lifeboats, as Sir Ernest Shackleton's men had been on the Southern Ocean. Still, tropical expeditions had produced their own share of horror stories, from Fawcett's mysterious disappearance to the mutiny staged by Lope "El Loco" de Aguirre four hundred years earlier, which devolved into an orgy of bloodletting. It was hard to imagine things going that far in our case. But all it would take was a split second of bloodlust for events to spin completely out of control. Once that threshold was breached, there would be no turning back, and who could say what might happen or where it would end?

Alfredo and Wilson finally straggled into camp. Possuelo's admonitions had gone unheeded yet again, but he said nothing. Alfredo dropped my pack and got to work. He prepared the pole, and we lashed it to the supporting trees. We tossed the tarp up over it, stretched it out, and tied it off. A few new touches were added this evening: palm leaves were spread beneath the hammock, a kind of throw rug, along with a simple platform contrived by laying a half dozen sticks together side by side on the damp ground, where I could set my camera bag. I thanked Alfredo. He nodded stiffly and wandered off to join his fellow Kanamari.

I'd just started drying my clothes over a small fire, when Nicolas called out: "Scott! You've got to see this!" I looked across the stream to the main campfire. Men were huddled around Soldado and Raimundo, and from the distance, they appeared to be wearing fur coats. "We're going to be having monkeys for dinner!" I grabbed my cameras and dashed after Nicolas, who was already snapping away by the time I reached the bridge.

There were seven monkeys, all told, larger than any other monkeys I'd seen before, each about four feet from head to foot. They had lustrous light brown fur that turned darker along the limbs and tail. Soldado and Raimundo cuddled them, almost as though they were children. Their long arms flopped limply at their sides, reminding me of a stuffed animal I'd once bought for Mackenzie. Their faces were stretched in grimaces filled with sharp, pointed teeth, and their brown eyes were wide open, seemingly fixed on some place far beyond the treetops.

The hunters had come upon an entire extended family, somewhere between forty and fifty, swinging through the branches. "They were high up there," said Soldado. "It took a few shots to bring them down." Even after they were shot, Raimundo added solemnly, two of the monkeys gripped the branches, refusing to fall. "They were screaming," he told me in a hushed aside. I wondered if there might be more to Raimundo than I'd thought, and if he might be a good bit more sensitive than his particular circumstances in the Amazon's macho frontier culture would ever allow him to safely express.

He handed the monkeys over to the Matis. Ivan Arapá and Tepi dropped the animals into large cauldrons of boiling water, fur and all. They boiled them for a while, yanked them out, and began scraping off the fur. Then they returned them to the pots, and repeated the process several times. At last, the bodies were stripped pink and naked. Mauro had an even more gruesome task. With his machete, he severed their hands, then artlessly hacked limbs and shanks into large chunks. "I never get used to this, Senhor Scotch," he said, twisting one animal's shoulder out of its socket. A cigarette dangled from his pressed lips, a cloud of smoke enveloping his face, as though he'd drawn a curtain about himself to unplug from the carnage he'd been called upon to perform. It was haunting, the sight of those monkeys piled one on top of the other, like a half dozen naked toddlers dismembered and set to boil. And we were going to eat them.

By the time dinner was served, it was past 9:30 p.m. Many had retreated to their hammocks. Now, calls went out through the encampment in Matis, Kanamari, and Portuguese, along with the banging of spoons on plates. Like zombies in a trance, the men slowly emerged from the darkness, faces sullen and weary in the pale orange glow of the fire. They lined up for a hunk of monkey meat, dished out by Mauro and Paulo Souza, served with rice and farinha, topped with a ladle of broth. We ate in silence. I plucked my fist-size piece of primate from the bowl with thumb and forefinger, ripping the flesh with my incisors. It was about the only way to eat it, as there was no place where you could set the bowl down and use your two hands to cut it properly. The meat was tough and rubbery. It had a strong, gamy flavor, and the smell was nauseating. But I'd eaten almost nothing else all day, it was sustenance, and we didn't know where our next meal might come from.

CHAPTER 12

Lessons in Biology

THE AFTERNOON SUN WAS dropping low, and once again, we struggled to find a suitable bivouac. Either the ground was too wet, or it wasn't sufficiently level. Or it wasn't close enough to a water source. It was our fourth day in the jungle since leaving the boats. We'd crossed more streams and scaled more hills. Mauro was keeping count: we were averaging sixteen hills a day. Sixteen punishing inclines, sixteen treacherous descents. We had seen more signs of the Arrow People, mostly in the form of the bent-back limbs, or *quebradas*, that signaled the movement of small groups through the forest. We hadn't seen the sun, except as a diffused luminescence that barely managed to penetrate to the forest floor. We were wet, filthy, exhausted, famished. Finally we broke through the underbrush into a broad clearing bisected by a meandering creek. It looked inviting enough, with ample water and relatively solid ground.

"We'll stop here," Possuelo announced with a decisiveness that seemed to foreclose discussion. The men dropped their backpacks, relieved at the prospect of another day's end. They drew their machetes and set to work. But something wasn't right. Tepi and Ivan Arapá had yet to unburden their loads. They chattered back and forth, pointing up into the trees. "*Isamarop*," they said in Matis. Then in Portuguese: "*Malo*." They were joined by the rest of the Matis, the collective judgment rising among them like a choir: *Isamarop. Isamarop.* No good.

"What's the problem?" I asked.

"*Tracuá*," said Tepi, still pointing toward the treetops.

"Tracuá," Ivan repeated.

I followed the pointed fingers with my line of sight up around seventy feet into the trees, where several trunks swelled into large, bulbous protrusions. These, I was given to understand, were home to the *tracuá,* a particularly nasty breed of carpenter ant. The ants have evolved a symbiotic relationship with several species of canopy plants—bromeliads, orchids, philodendrons—grooming bountiful gardens of them high up in the trees. With a kind of papery carton the *tracuá* produce from chewed wood and soil, they build nests suspended high up in the trees, embedding seeds in the carton, which in turn germinate and anchor the nests to trunks and high branches. The ants get secure shelter high above the forest floor. The plants get gardeners that tenaciously protect them from disturbance of any kind.

What we were about to get was a little piece of hell. Just tying a hammock cord to a trunk that hosted a *tracuá* nest in its upper story was an invitation to torment. From the looks of it, few trees in the glade appeared to be free from the pernicious pests.

Possuelo was undeterred. "Clear the brush," he ordered. "We're staying." I performed a quick inspection and selected a pair of solid trees that appeared to be free from infestation. I wrapped the hammock cords around them, as if they were posts on a dock, and tied them off. By the time I turned to retrieve the rest of my gear from the ground, my backpack was swarming with the large-headed black ants. I called Alfredo back and had him devise a wobbly table I could pile my bags on, hoping the ants would desist. But quickly they undertook a determined march up the table's legs. For the first time since the trek began, I broke into the precious supply of Repellex; the emergency I'd vaguely anticipated had arrived. I sprayed it around the table's legs. Just then an even more harrowing sight caught my eye: ants by the dozens swarming the cords of my hammock, advancing along it single file, like tightrope walkers, intent on invading the hammock itself. I hastened to apply the repellent, saturating a three-inch swath of the rope at either end of the hammock with the pump-action spray. The ants came to a halt, antennae twitching, held off, at least for the moment,

by the chemical barrier. Next I saw them flooding the crossbar, traversing the blue tarp until they reached the underside and started out over
the hammock. I quickly sprayed more Repellex around both ends of
the crossbeam. Alfredo placed a bundle of smoky, slow-burning wood
at the base of either tree. The rising smoke seemed to further stifle
their advance.

At the campfire where the men waited for dinner, all were seated
on the benches with legs retracted off the ground, heels pressed into
their buttocks. Space was in short supply on the benches, so I retreated
back to my hammock to await the call to dinner. When it came, I
lowered my feet into my flip-flops, which out of habit I'd left on the
ground directly beneath me. I was immediately set upon by dozens of
ants. They greeted my frantic efforts to brush them off with fresh assaults on hands and wrists. I hopped over to the three-legged table to
retrieve my plate and spoon, hands and ankles starting to swell.

Dinner was a grim affair: monkey yet again, boiled into toughened
balls of gray, gristly hide. Everyone ate and retreated to their hammocks. Even Possuelo called the place *um inferno* the next morning as
we made haste to pack up.

* * *

We slurped coffee and crammed our mouths with corn bread while
executing further evasive measures, shuffling and dancing to keep the
ants at bay. It reminded me of a story I'd read as a kid, I told Possuelo,
who sat near the fire, flicking *tracuá* off his bare legs with studied care,
their bodies catapulting willy-nilly across the clearing. It was entitled
"Leiningen Versus the Ants," and it was one of those early, formative
reading experiences that shaped my view of the Amazon as an alien,
terrifying place governed by inscrutable forces far greater than the
human mind could fathom. In the story, a foreign rancher in Brazil
faces a tidal wave of army ants closing in on his property. Livestock are
eaten whole, trees stripped naked. His panic-stricken serfs fall back
to Leiningen's mansion, where he orders them to dig in behind a
series of concentric, water-filled moats. The ants pause at the edge of

the first moat—an enormous, writhing mass. And then, as if possessed of a singular, demonic intelligence, they pitch themselves in, creating a living bridge with interlocking jaws and limbs so that the horde may pass. On they come. When all seems lost, the rancher floods the final moat with oil and sets it ablaze. The scourge is halted, disaster averted.

"It's true," said Possuelo, swatting an ant from the backside of his forearm. "They converge in a mass, like locusts, and start moving through the jungle. I once had to abandon a house on the Xingu because the ants were coming. They ate everything—cockroaches, frogs, plants—everything. They left behind only husks, the outer shells."

Possuelo was like that. There was almost nothing you could mention that he hadn't already experienced, or at least claimed to have experienced, at some point in his life. Jaguars, anacondas, pestilences of every description, Possuelo had ten stories for every one that might come up at night in the flickering glow of the campfire. Like a few nights before, when Orlando had called out to me across the encampment: "Scott, come here!" After nearly three weeks together, I knew that when Orlando summoned, it most likely portended some bizarre or disgusting oddity he wanted me to see: a freakishly oversize scorpion, stinger as big as a hypodermic needle, or a monkey the Indians had skinned from crown to toes, leaving eyeballs intact in their sockets.

As I came abreast, Orlando pointed down at an enormous black spider, hairy as a wolf. Its body alone was nearly three inches long, and even bent, its legs covered an area the size of a softball. With one whack of the machete, Orlando sliced it in two and flicked the halves into the fire. "You have to be careful with spiders like that," said Possuelo, who had been watching us from his hammock nearby. "They're called *carangejeira* spiders. Just touching their hair causes infections that are very ugly, very difficult to cure." One night during his pursuit of the Parakanã Indians twenty years before, on the same journey when the scout broke his ankle, Possuelo and his men were overrun by the "crab" spiders. Scattered bands of the Parakanã had fled con-

tact after the Trans-Amazonian Highway first pushed into their homeland, bringing a flood of ranchers and gold prospectors. More than
one-third succumbed to influenza and malaria. The survivors were divided. Some accepted contact with FUNAI and submitted to the white
man's medicines. But others suspected the injections were actually
the cause of, not the cure for, the spreading sickness. They fled but
found themselves increasingly squeezed from all sides, the advancing
frontier pushing them into the lands of their traditional enemies—the
Kayapó and the Araweté. Clashes ensued. By 1983, the situation was
dire. Over the decades, the Kayapó had acquired a formidable arsenal
of .44 Winchesters, and they were ready to use them. "The Parakanã
would have been annihilated—not by whites, but by other Indians,"
Possuelo said. "It was an emergency." He hastily conjoined a campaign
to contact the roving bands of Parakanã, before they provoked their
own destruction. The so-called Penetration Front pursued the Indians
deep into *varzia*—flooded forest—along the Iriri River. Lashing downpours had already kicked off the rainy season. Everywhere floodwaters
were on the rise.

One evening, they pitched camp on a small patch of high ground,
a shrinking island in the rising water. "It was a horrible spot," Possuelo
recalled. "You had every imaginable creature there, all trying to escape
the flood." They didn't realize until nightfall that among those creatures were legions of the hairy spiders. "At dusk, they started coming
down the trees, all over the place, crawling down the trunks. They
climbed along the cords of our hammocks. It was like a horror movie."
The men batted them off, but the spiders kept coming. Then they tied
rags soaked in gasoline around the tree trunks that supported their
hammocks. After a sleepless night keeping the spiders at bay, they
were relieved to move on at first light, much as we were now.

Possuelo hoisted his pack and departed, disappearing into the
gash in the foliage opened by Soldado and Raimundo on the far side
of the encampment. Orlando and Nicolas followed closely behind. I
was anxious to join them at the front of the column, but as I hastened
to leave, Paulo Welker stepped in front of me, his finger pressed to

his lips. "Shhhhh!" he whispered. "Listen!" At first I heard nothing above the baseline chorus of chirring insects. Then my ears detected the faintest hint of a melody, growing louder. It sounded like someone playing random notes on a flute, high ones interspersed with low. Except the randomness was repeated over and over until I discerned a recurring pattern. "It's the *uirapurú* bird," Welker said. "No one ever sees it. It's very rare even to hear it. The Indians say you'll receive a blessing on a day when you hear the *uirapurú* sing." To the haunting tune of the unseen bird, with a rich yellow light dappling the forest floor, we shouldered our loads and plunged into the thicket.

The grueling march uphill and down began anew. The upward slogs were exhausting, but there was little cheer in reaching the top. Graver perils awaited on the way down. By the time even five or six men had trudged along the path ahead of you, its leaf cover would be obliterated, leaving a treacherous soup of slippery red clay. As I started down the first slope of the day, both feet flew out from under me. My back came down on a sapling cleaved moments before to a fine point by either Soldado or Raimundo as they went about marking the trail. I felt the razor point slide up under my pack, ripping my shirt. It came to rest just beneath my shoulder blade. I lay there, stunned. Nicolas came scrambling back up the hill. "Sydney!" he yelled. "Scott's been hurt!!" My eyes were wide as plates, unblinking. "Are you all right?" He yanked my pack aside and tugged up on my shirt. "It looks all right," he said. Miraculously, the spike had barely pierced the skin. There was a nasty bruise, already turning purplish blue. By now, Possuelo was there, along with Orlando. Each took an arm and they helped me up. "Scott!" Sydney exclaimed. "We almost lost you! Can you walk?"

My back was beginning to lock up. But I was alive, and I was on my feet. I bent down to run my thumb along the edge of the sapling point. It was a killer—an inch in diameter, growing up from the ground to knee height, where it had been swiped clean by the machete, sharp as a saber. Had I fallen at a slightly different angle, a slight fraction of an inch more, I'd have been impaled straight through the back. I shuddered, then resolved to endure the filth, the sweat, the bugs. From then on, I'd take the hunger, exhaustion, and deprivation, grinding out the yardage on the uphill slogs, sliding on my butt down the long, steep descents. No complaints. Just get me home safely, I prayed. Spare me a debilitating injury. I'll do as You want, whatever You say. Promise.

I was surprised that my feet were doing as well as they were, under the circumstances. The canvas boots were way too big, but they were comfortable. The same could not be said for the leather ones I had dumped, as I found out when I passed Márcio Kanamari. He'd set his backpack down and had pulled off the boots, exposing nasty-looking blisters on both heels. He gave me a pained smile, and I shrugged apologetically. Still, I was grateful those things weren't on my feet. There were enough discomforts as it was.

We passed through a stretch of clear forest, devoid of undergrowth, just a thick carpet of desiccated leaves covering the ground. "Scott, look at this!" said Nicolas in a muted shout. Looking in the direction of his pointed finger, I saw nothing. Straining my eyes, I caught a sudden movement in the leaves. It was a toad the size of a fist, but its camouflage was remarkable: horned points jutting out over its shoulders and haunches, in the exact shape and color of the leaves on which it reposed. "If we had enough time we could study it and name it," Nicolas said with a laugh. He was probably right, but we didn't have the time. We moved on, scrambling to keep pace with the head of the column.

I followed Nicolas over a fallen tree blocking the path. He bounded over it, but his legs were longer, and I deemed the move too risky. Instead I performed a swivel-chair maneuver—sitting down on it, swinging both legs over, and continuing on without delay. I was just pushing off when I felt a jab at the base of my finger. Damn! Blood on my palm. Now another jab pricked the back of my hand. I looked down at the log. It was crawling with the most bizarre-looking ants I'd ever seen: ivory bodies, bright red heads with large white jaws that matched their thoraxes. Perhaps it was another species as yet undescribed by science. The Javari remains one of the largest, most species-rich, and least explored biological hot spots on Earth. I lamented the lack of a botanist or an entomologist who could have interpreted the biological wonders—and horrors—we were witnessing all around us. It was likely he could have made a number of fresh discoveries for science.

Such findings were apt to be a long time in coming, as long as Possuelo held sway in these parts. It would have pleased him, I thought, to place this entire territory beyond the bounds of scientific research in perpetuity. He seemed to possess an inherent distrust of science, or perhaps it would be more accurate to say that he placed little trust in its practitioners. All too often, scientific inquiry served to bolster the domination of the privileged few over the many. Anthropologists subjected traditional societies to denigrating studies of kinship and mating practices, as though they were laboratory mice whose behavior could be predicted, perhaps even controlled, once a baseline of empirical data was established and analyzed. Their work rarely, if ever, benefited the tribes they put under the microscope. Geologists probed the subsoil with acoustic devices in search of oil and mineral wealth that would ultimately be usurped from the Indians, despoiling their lands in the process. No doubt, there were plenty of scientists dedicated to the selfless pursuit of discovery for the sake of humankind. But how could you know who was friend and who was foe, who sought a cure for cancer to share with the entire world and who sought to pirate the jungle's biological secrets to patent them for private gain?

But there was something else, I sensed, a deeper, visceral suspicion at work in Possuelo's mind—one that shunned anyone who might possess deeper knowledge than he. Possuelo thrived on holding forth in the presence of underlings. I got the feeling he didn't want anyone around who might challenge him in any way: *Well, actually, Sydney, it's not quite like that.* He didn't want to hear it.

Despite all that, we were in truth in a biologist's paradise, or would have been, had one been along for the ride. There was such a juiced-up differentiation of species going on in every imaginable phylum on the ground beneath our feet, in the trees growing overhead, who among us could say what here was known to science and what was not? This was as true for the plant life as it was for insects and animals. Every acre of western Amazonian rainforest holds an average of 250 trees from at least eighty different species. By comparison, a typical forest in North America rarely contains even twenty species in a single acre. There were low understory trees with fleshy, palmated leaves that reached for us like outstretched hands, gigantic kapoks with enormous buttressed roots that could shelter entire families in their folds, and coiling vines that oozed toxins the natives knew to have psychotropic and medical properties. We weren't all that far from the Andean foothills, where evolutionary biologists believe the sudden upthrust of mountains powered a burst of species diversification unique to the natural history of the planet. Like the horn-pointed toad that resembled a dead leaf, many species have evolved elaborate camouflage that render them all but invisible. Others have developed toxic skins, together with ostentatious colors, to ward off predators. Yet other creatures present the coloration without the poison, a kind of deliberate mimicry of their flashy but deadly counterparts. Furry caterpillars with brilliant designs of black and white, yellow and red, inched their way along trunks and branches. "Don't touch!" Soldado warned. "Their hair is poisonous. There is no cure." A tiny fluorescent green tree frog gripped the edge of a leaf with huge, goofy-looking hands, its fingers tipped with what appeared to be miniature suction cups. "Be careful," Possuelo said. "You never know what could happen from touching one of those." A researcher he'd known had once handled a tree frog with his bare hands while exploring in the jungles in Pará. He came down with a crippling illness that ended in his eventual death.

Possuelo may have been wary of scientists, but there was an undeniable resemblance between his work and that of a wildlife biologist seeking to protect the threatened habitat of an endangered species. The conservation movement, most notably the renowned biologist George Schaller, had long used "charismatic megafauna"—high-profile mammals such as lions or pandas that capture the public imagination—to galvanize support for creating protective sanctuaries. Wasn't Possuelo using the Arrow People to similar effect, leveraging a particularly rare and exotic species for like purpose? I expected him to bridle at the question, but he seemed intrigued by the idea.

"We create national parks to save animals; why not do it for humans?" he said. But at its core, he added, this was a struggle not for animals but for the rights of human beings. "That's the fundament of my work," he said. "I fight for the human rights of those who do not even know that human rights exist."

In any case, the idea wasn't to cordon the Indians off forever from the outside world; it was to allow them to choose if and when they wanted contact. They could make contact any time they wanted, Possuelo said. All they had to do was head down any river and they'd find their way to civilization. The fact that the Arrow People and like tribes had not done so provided a sufficiently clear message: they wanted to be left alone.

*　*　*

The air was heavy with the scent of rot and decay. Just beneath the leaf cover, intricate masses of white threads laced the thin soil, everywhere interwoven with the rootlets of trees. The fungal mycelia, as they're called, provide a pipeline of crucial minerals to the trees that would otherwise be washed away by the rains. They're one of the reasons why the soils of these forests are so poor, completely unfit for large-scale agriculture, yet able to sustain the giant trees that dwarfed us as we stumbled on. On another fallen trunk, dozens of funnel-shaped mushrooms sprouted from the rotting wood, brimming with rainwater like delicate champagne flutes. It was as if a banquet table had been set for an elves' feast. Here and there, streams of light pierced the gloom like a projector in a darkened theater, and wherever the shafts penetrated, they illuminated swirls of motes suspended in the air. I wondered what I might be breathing, and if I might end up finding out someday far in the future, lying intubated on a hospital bed, flanked by teams of pulmonary specialists intrigued by my rare condition. Possuelo's own pronouncements did little to dispel my paranoid fantasies. "Lots of dangerous fungi out here," he said as a creeper yanked my hat off, unleashing a cloud of gray spores. I tried my best not to inhale until we cleared the zone. "People have gotten very sick. Almost nothing is known about them. They remain to be studied."

One thing was sure, the forest dwellers among us commanded extensive knowledge of the flora we encountered. A short way ahead, Soldado grabbed hold of a thick, bark-sheathed liana that dangled from above like an enormous python. This was the *titica* vine, he said, and it descended out of the canopy to sink its roots on the forest floor. "It's born when the *tucandeira* ant dies. Its front legs grow all the way down to the ground," he said with the conviction of absolute truth. An infusion made from the vine, he added, could cure most snakebites. "You count nine knots, cut it, and boil it in water. Drink it down. It takes the fever away."

The *tucandeira,* or bullet ant, is the nastiest of all, worse than the dreaded *tracuá.* An inch or more in length, the creature comes equipped not only with piercing, sicklelike jaws, but also with a rear-end stinger that injects a toxin capable of sending a full-grown human into fevered shock. The ants are used by several tribes in sacred rites of passage, with initiates exposed to dozens of stings to arms, chest, and face. The pincer jaws of the ant are also put to ingenious use as field sutures, lacerations stitched closed by a series of *tucandeira* bites. Once an ant locks its pincers on the wound, its head is torn from the thorax, leaving the suture in place.

It was probably no coincidence that the curative properties of the *titica* vine had come to be associated with the *tucandeira.* In preliterate societies rich in oral tradition, such as those inhabited by Indians and even some *riberinhos,* where knowledge is handed down from one generation to another encoded in fables, it would make sense that it would take the potent *tucandeira* to counter a serpent's deadly venom—and that such vital information would come wrapped in a graphic tale so readily available to recall.

Nearly all the Matis elders and shamans perished in the epidemics that followed contact, taking much of the tribe's storehouse of accumulated wisdom with them. Even so, the Matis had salvaged at least some knowledge of medical and psychotropic plants. "Ah, what the Matis are doing over there is worth observing," said Possuelo, when we took a break for a light lunch of smoked monkey and manioc flour at midday. "Let's take a look." In a clearing behind us, the Matis crouched in a circle around Kwini Marubo, who was grinding bark shavings over a green palm frond. With water, he then prepared a pliable mass, like dough. Rolling it up in the leaf, he added more water. The leaf was then folded and bound with a thin creeper. When he was finished, Kwini was holding a homespun eyedropper, loaded with an infusion that dripped from its pointed tip like an IV awaiting an open vein.

One by one, the Matis knelt before Kwini. He pulled back one eyelid, then the other, squeezing juice from the leaf a drop at a time into their rolled-back eyes. Each recipient of the treatment clutched his eyes and grimaced, alternately rubbing his thighs and chanting in clipped, rapid-fire bursts to the forest spirits: *Large deer running, quick ants crawling*. Tepi took over while Kwini knelt to receive the drops, and continued on, administering the potion to all the Kanamari, the Marubo, several of the whites, and even to Possuelo. As I watched the facial contortions and heard the agonized shouts resound through the forest, I dismissed any notion of taking part myself. It was an Indian thing, I figured, and it looked more painful than it was worth. I doubted that the linear passageways of this straitlaced Western mind could bend sufficiently to benefit from this ancient indigenous rite. Besides, these were *my eyes;* whatever these guys were doing, it looked too risky to consider. But the Matis wouldn't have it any other way. "Scotchie, come!" beckoned Tepi. "Scotchie, Scotchie!" echoed the other Matis, their eyes now wide open, tears streaming down their cheeks. I had no choice.

I prostrated myself before Tepi, gazing up into a face of complete serenity. The tattooed streaks, the simulated cat whiskers, and his tender brown eyes all faded from focus as the eyedropper appeared front and center, suspended like the sword of Damocles above my eye. The drops fell in like liquid fire. It felt like my eyes were scorched with sulfuric acid. I let out a roar. Everyone howled with laughter. It took several minutes for the burning to subside. I opened my eyes and looked around. Beyond the circle of faces beaming at me, I beheld a different forest from the one I'd been marching through for the past four days. It was no longer a two-dimensional, monochromatic screen of dull browns and greens. Everything stood out in sharp, almost psychedelic relief. I perceived depth where before there was none. The colors seemed to vibrate—the greens electric, the browns more differentiated. There were shades of gray, purple, amber that had previously escaped my notice. I wasn't hallucinating exactly; it was more like looking at the jungle through a 3-D View-Master.

"*Buchité,*" said Ivan Arapá, pointing at the eyedropper. "That's what we call it. Good for hunting. Matis see monkey, see tapir. Kill them. Good." He made a pantomime gesture of aiming a rifle into the treetops and pulling the trigger. It was also good for marching long distances, he said. "No get tired."

Indeed, as we resumed the march, I felt the bounce return to my spent quads and hamstrings. My steps were surer, my balance steady. I could bound over huge, prostrate trunks with astonishing agility. "What Merck would do to get their hands on this!" I yelled to Nicolas, who was just ahead of me. I was joking, but he said: "Merck has been involved in several cases of biopiracy in the Amazon." Most notable perhaps was the case involving an anticoagulant the Uru-Eu-Wau-Wau tribe in Rondônia extracted from the bark of the *tiki uba* tree. Painted on their arrow points, the extract could drop large quadrupeds with a single shot. Researchers at Merck were quick to see the anticoagulant's commercial promise after viewing images of a tapir bleeding to death from an arrow wound in a 1988 *National Geographic* story, "Last Days of Eden," a celebration of tribal knowledge and a lament for a rapidly vanishing way of life. "In addition to such deadly jungle lore," read one photo caption, "knowledge of potentially useful foods and drugs, accumulated over thousands of years, may be lost forever if the forest and its inhabitants disappear." After being contacted by the drugmaker, photographer Jesco von Puttkamer agreed to send *tiki uba* specimens to Merck, believing he might help salvage this potentially lifesaving know-how from oblivion. The company was thus positioned to exploit the Uru-Eu-Wau-Wau's ancient knowledge with no obligation to compensate the tribe. In the end, commercial development apparently fizzled after trials failed to find dosage levels safe for humans, though not before stoking an increasingly embittered tug-of-war over intellectual property rights, "bioprospecting," and the alleged pirating of traditional knowledge by transnational drug manufacturers.

I could think of many practical applications for the *buchité* potion, but I had no particular interest in facilitating access to it for a foreign biotech firm, and I certainly had no desire to land myself in a Brazilian jail on charges of biopiracy. I was content to experience a few hours of its vision-enhancing magic, bounding with sureness of foot through the myriad hazards of the jungle.

One-quarter of all prescription drugs have their origins in tropical rainforests, owing in large measure to the elaborate defenses their plants and animals (most notably frogs) have evolved to ward off a multitude of would-be predators. Scientists have no doubt that other important cures await discovery as well. What remains to be seen is if scientific research can progress in the overheated atmosphere of mutual suspicion among governments, indigenous communities, and pharmaceutical companies over how to share equitably in the costs and rewards of new product development.

* * *

We couldn't see much of the sky, but we could hear it. Thunder snarled overhead. The first raindrops pinged off the leaves. And suddenly the sky opened into a deluge. "Stop here!" yelled Possuelo, cupping his hands to be heard over the roar of rain beating down through the foliage. Here and there, woodsmen pulled tarps from their backpacks and huddled beneath them, shivering. The Matis fashioned umbrellas from wild banana fronds they hacked from a tree.

The *buchité* was wearing off. In the dull gray light, the two-dimensional monochrome of the forest reasserted control, choking off the visual passageways that had so briefly and vividly opened among the tree trunks and choking lianas that dangled from their branches. Nonetheless, that extra torque was still in my step a half hour later, when the rain's intensity eased and we resumed the march. We were thoroughly soaked. I could barely see through my fogged and rain-streaked glasses. The conditions were worse than miserable. I no longer cared. My life could have ended earlier in the day. But I was still intact, still putting one sodden foot in front of the other, still keeping pace with this unlikely entourage, still moving in the only direction that would ever get us home—forward.

As the day grew longer and the rain tapered off, we came to a halt alongside a swollen stream. "Look here," said Soldado, pointing along the forest floor above the stream. "A path!" said Tepi Matis. All I could see were leaves scattered over mud. "A path!" Tepi repeated. Possuelo stood there contemplating the scene, hands on hips. It was the first indication that we'd actually penetrated deep into the land of the Arrow People, along their very pathways. Still, I saw nothing but mud and leaves. "How do you know there's a path there?" I asked. "I don't see anything."

"I can't explain it to you," snapped Possuelo. "You either see it or you don't. If you're familiar with what you're looking for, you see it; if not, you don't." He regarded me with bug eyes and puckered mouth, as if he'd just eaten a lemon. I returned his gaze. His tone softened. "A lot of it depends on the conditions. When the leaves are dry, for instance, they break when someone steps on them. So you can observe that. But when the ground is wet, like now, they leave footprints and other impressions. There are trade-offs; one thing compensates for another."

I had to take his word for it; I still failed to discern the path that seemed so obvious to him and the Indians. Possuelo gave his compass a quick read. "I thought they would just go to the headwaters of the Jutaí to hunt," he said. "But now I see they range farther than I thought."

He slipped off his backpack and pulled out the map. From the scant vestiges we'd observed so far, he'd already pushed the boundaries of what was previously known about the Arrow People. "If you look here," he said, pointing between the Ituí and Itaquaí rivers, "you can see the Korubo are well protected from intruders, right in the center of the reserve." His finger wandered right and down, to the Javari's southeastern flank, where its border gave way to forests increasingly under siege by loggers. "Here, where we are now, is *terra dos flecheiros,* the Arrow People's territory. You can see they are much more vulnerable. To defend them, we need to protect these peripheries."

I stood there looking beyond his shoulder, to the muddy pathway that disappeared into a screen of rain-drenched thicket. With this most inconspicuous piece of evidence, Possuelo declared that we had arrived in the heartland of the Arrow People.

CHAPTER 13

A Guerrilla Army

WE TURNED IN HUNGRY, having arrived in camp with twilight already upon us. Too risky, Possuelo deemed, to send men out to hunt. A dull and constant ache knotted my stomach. The only game animals the hunters had managed to find in the past six days were the same woolly monkeys with the exceptionally beautiful coats of fur, which would then be so crudely hacked apart by Mauro's machete and tossed in chunks into a cauldron to boil. Whether it was the relentless pangs of hunger or the subliminal suggestion of cannibalism that attended our meager and monotonous diet, dinnertime had acquired a glum, utilitarian aspect. We came to the fire, ate in silence, and returned to our hammocks. But it was the affable Mauro who suffered the most unnerving effects of our cheerless repast.

In the middle of the night, we were awakened by his bloodcurdling shrieks. Daylight couldn't come soon enough after that—not for Mauro, not for anyone else, either. Bleary-eyed, his thick black hair a tangled mess, he greeted the jokes with his broad toothless smile as he ladled out coffee by the smoke of the morning fire. "Hey, Mauro, what happened last night—had a go with a pair of monkeys?" But as the others drifted away and we were left alone, he tugged on my sleeve and pulled me close. "It was a ni-ni-nightmare, Senhor Scotch," he whispered. "I was walking thr-through the forest, when suddenly I was surrounded by *macacos,* many monkeys. I was naked, and I tried to escape, but I couldn't." The monkeys hauled him off and bound his wrists to a tree. Then one of them pulled a knife and stepped forward. "They wanted to cut off my penis, Senhor Scotch. That's when I screamed." He looked at me with wild, supplicating eyes, as though he'd survived the horror of an actual event but wasn't so sure he would next time.

There seemed to be little relief in sight. By midmorning, Possuelo put out the word: be on the lookout for food. "You see monkeys in the treetops, shoot," he commanded. In normal conditions, the men would hunt once we'd found our evening bivouac; dead game added crushing weight to already excessive loads. But food was at a premium today, taking precedence over all else.

I followed on Possuelo's heels across a stretch of level ground. At least the terrain was beginning to relent. We were about five or ten minutes behind the front of the column, throwing one-line comments back and forth between steps, when we heard a gunshot ring out up ahead, followed by a cacophony of shouting. *"Cobra?"* I asked. A snake? I recalled the shot that heralded Soldado's run-in with the *jaracuçu* some days earlier. Possuelo didn't reply. We heard a second shot and quickened the pace. We followed a gentle incline to the top and started down into a broad depression free of undergrowth, where several men were clustered together, pointing up into treetops, their backpacks scattered on the ground behind them. Raimundo was there, along with several of the Matis. Orlando was in the middle of the group, his rifle drawn skyward, muscles taut, the weird Afrika Korps hat cocked sideways on his head.

"Scotchie, look up there!" said Tepi as I came abreast. He pointed up in the canopy, but all I saw was milky white seeping through the forest ceiling. "There!" he said, stabbing the air with his finger, as though it too were a weapon. My focus finally came to rest on the silhouette of a monkey moving along a branch, about sixty feet off the ground. She didn't appear to be in much of a rush, more like a leisurely climb through the trees. But as I looked more closely, I finally discerned what the other men apparently had seen all along: an infant clinging to the adult monkey's back.

My vision now broadened and I saw several more of them, perhaps a dozen in all, scattered about in the canopy. All except the mother and infant were beating a full retreat, graceful trapeze artists swinging by prehensile tails from tree to tree, climbing hand over hand from branch to branch, the rustling foliage marking their imminent departure.

Tepi leaned in. "Better *zarabatana* for hunting monkey," he whispered to me. In pantomime, he pursed his lips and pressed them to the barrel of an imaginary blowgun, puffing into it. His jaguar whiskers seemed to bristle in the mysterious ethereal light as he looked up into the trees. Blowguns were silent, he said, the best weapon for knocking prey out of the canopy. Several animals could be hit before the rest of a band caught on and took flight. The Matis had long since incorporated rifles into their hunting culture, but they continued to find ancient methods more effective for certain tasks, and always more affordable. Shotgun shells cost money; blowgun darts do not.

The other monkeys had moved on, but the mother was going nowhere. Soon it was just her and her baby, and the men on the ground sixty feet below. Orlando stood in their midst, drawing a bead, rifle braced to shoulder.

"Don't shoot!" I implored. "She's got a baby with her."

"You can't kill a mother carrying her *filoche*!" Raimundo echoed.

Orlando broke off his aim, seeming inclined to desist. But his father, who'd been watching in silence from the edge of the group, stepped forward, his eyes wide and wild.

"What is this—Disneyland?" he snarled. "Don't give me that sentimental crap! This is survival in the jungle! Shoot it! We'll eat the baby, too!" The effect on Raimundo was immediate. He grabbed his pack and bolted, brow knit tight over his eyes, seething like a soldier on the verge of fragging his CO.

KUFH! The shot lurched from Orlando's rifle with a hard spank. Now the mother began to move, loping along the branch on all fours, still at an excruciatingly glacial pace. I was praying she'd somehow get away. "That one hit the tree," Orlando said sheepishly, still keeping her in his sights. He fired again. "She doesn't want to die." You could see that his heart was no longer in it, but he couldn't back out now, not with his father watching, arms folded across his chest.

The drama unfolded with the horrific, slow-motion inexorability of a Greek tragedy, the players locked in roles they did not want and from which they could not escape. The mother let out an agonizing shriek, and as she did, I realized that she was already wounded and probably had been since Possuelo and I heard those first shots several minutes before. She emitted a succession of low, monosyllabic clucks and sauntered back and forth along the same branch, as though she couldn't decide which way to go. The noose was tightening, and it seemed as though she'd finally realized how much danger she was in.

The rest of the column was catching up, men shuffling downhill into the clearing, the brittle leaves swishing at their feet. Some glanced over and just kept going; others stopped to watch the heartrending spectacle. They flopped down on the ground, still strapped into their overloaded rucksacks, conversing among themselves in low voices.

The mother now made a last, desperate attempt to get away, lunging through the air and latching on to a branch from the next tree over, her baby hanging on to her back for dear life. Orlando gave chase along the forest floor, keeping his eyes locked on the canopy overhead as he ran. Tepi and Damã Matis followed, and I stumbled after them. We splashed through a stream, scrambled up a steep bank, and stopped beneath a towering tree.

Orlando took aim and fired again. The mother did not flinch, but he must have hit her: She began to droop, as though she'd ingested a fatal dose of poison. Slowly her grip on the branch loosened. She went into free fall, tumbling headlong from the heights, crashing into one branch, then another, finally plummeting to the ground twenty feet away with a terrible thud.

"Come on, Scott, let's go see!" Orlando shouted. As we came closer, he said: "Be careful. She might be alive." It was a woolly monkey, like all the others the hunters had killed, a bundle of rich brown fur sprawled on the ground. Remarkably, the baby still clung to her back. Damã grabbed a stick and poked her. *"Tá morta,"* he said. Dead.

But even as he spoke, the mother lifted her head and looked up. Damã jabbed again. She grabbed a pair of thin saplings with either hand and hoisted herself up to a sitting position. She bared her teeth, and saliva bubbled from her lips. She looked around, dazed.

"Kill her!" someone shouted from across the stream. Orlando raised a heavy stick high over his head. I winced and turned away. There was a sickening crunch. Tepi pried the baby off her back. It turned out to be a boy, and he was still alive, trembling. Blood trickled from a wound on the inside of his thigh. He let out a pitiful bleat. Tepi set him on a low branch, and he instinctively wrapped his tail around it, hanging there upside down. "You can't leave him alone out here," I said to Orlando. "He's completely defenseless. You should kill him."

"I'm not going to kill him," he said, with the tone of a schoolboy refusing to take a dare. "Will he live?" he asked, turning to Damã and Tepi. They shrugged.

"Don't Matis eat *filoche*?" Yes, they nodded. They did. "So why don't you kill it?" Orlando handed his club to Tepi. But they refused.

"Kill baby, no good," said Tepi.

"Fuck it," I snapped, and lunged for Orlando's .22. "I'll kill him." Orlando wrestled the gun back, which was probably just as well; I didn't need the murder of an infant on my conscience.

"Is there a chance he'll live?" Orlando repeated the question, fishing for an answer that would satisfy him. Tepi looked at the infant hanging from the branch at eye level, trembling. Maybe, he nodded hopefully.

"Maybe the others come back and get him?"

"*Sim, pegam,*" Tepi agreed. "Yes, they'll get him."

It seemed doubtful; the rest of the entourage was long gone. But perhaps he was right. After all, tribal hunters are experts at imitating the speech of birds and animals, and their mimicry of baby monkeys pleading for help is a tried and true method for luring adults from the treetops to their awaiting arrows. Maybe the others would come back and get him. In any case, that was all Orlando needed to hear to assuage his conscience. When we got back to our packs, his father was nowhere to be seen. Orlando didn't even want to take the dead monkey with him. He was feeling sick, he said, with fever, and he wasn't sure he could handle the extra load.

"You can't leave her here after all that," I said. Damã seemed to agree, for without speaking a word, he proceeded to lash the monkey to the top of Orlando's pack with strips of envira bark. We set out to catch up with the rest of the column. I followed close behind Orlando, mesmerized by the lustrous brown coat of the monkey perched on his back, still thinking of the baby boy who had ridden so happily atop hers until a half hour before, when we stole into their idyllic realm and shattered it forever.

* * *

As the ordeal with the monkeys played out, Soldado and Txema, who had taken over for Raimundo at the head of the column, discovered fresh footprints along the bank of an *igarapé* where we made camp a short time later. The prints belonged to a woman and a small child, Soldado and Txema reported, and they were no more than a few days old. Possuelo listened and nodded calmly. He dispatched a group of six Matis and some of the Kanamari to hunt. Orlando's monkey was merely a start. "We need to eat," he told the Indians as they grabbed their guns and filed out. "Find boar, monkeys, snakes, anything."

We stretched tarps and tied off hammocks, all the while fending off swarms of stingless bees drawn to the scent of sweat and the taste of salt. This was the first day we'd encountered them, an early indication that we were descending into lower elevations. I fought to drive them off as they brazenly invaded my open collar, swarmed my face, buzzed their way into my ears. I had to keep my mouth closed to keep from inhaling them. They clung like dull yellow burdocks to anything that bore the slightest whiff of sweat—backpacks, camera bags, shirts. Our hats, drenched from the long day's march, were a prime target. As we hung them in the branches to dry, the bees set upon them by the hundreds.

Meanwhile, the *riberinhos* set about installing the camp

infrastructure—digging the fire pit, setting up benches, pathways, a stairway down to the water. As he cleared the area around the main hearth, the rail-thin Amarildo laid his ax into the base of a half-rotten tree and unearthed a nest of honey bees. *"Mel!"* he shouted. Honey! Everyone stopped and looked. With a few quick chops, a panel of wood came flying loose. Raimundo reached in with his hand and brought out a dark brown nest dripping with honey. Paulo Souza dragged over a large pot. Raimundo wrung out the nest like a sponge, the honey gushing into the bucket like liquid amber, his hands and face black with angry, buzzing bees. But they had no stingers and could only swarm harmlessly while their nest was ransacked. The men converged in an excited mass on the pot, dipping in fingers and tin cups to get what they could, oblivious to the debris, chunks of nest and wax, and the twitching insects suspended in the nectar. It was the first treat we'd had in what seemed like weeks.

A shot rolled in from the distance. "Ha!" Possuelo enthused. "Dinner!" It was followed by a second shot minutes later. "Monkey," Soldado declaimed. He needed only to count the gunshots and the intervals between them to tell what was being hunted, even from a mile away. Nauseated at the prospect of enduring another supper of simians, I wondered if there might be wild pigs about, anything to spice up the menu a bit.

"Only farther down, toward the rivers," he said. "Now that summer is here, that's where they go to find food. They wouldn't be back this way until the floods force them back up into the forest, to the *igarapés.*"

"We'll have eaten so much monkey by then, we'll all have grown tails," Possuelo quipped. He was in a good mood, and when he was in a good mood, everyone else was too. Camping early with the sun still high overhead made it feel like a day off, like a Saturday. I was losing all sense of the days of the week; such distinctions out here were meaningless. I'd consult my Casio at the beginning of the day when I'd date a fresh leaf in my notebook, but I rarely thought about what it meant for it to be a Wednesday or a Monday. Such conventions had meaning

only back in that world I'd left behind, which seemed increasingly remote, another reality whose hold on me seemed more tenuous with
each passing day.

Of course, shooting monkeys—and many of the other birds and
animals we would end up eating—would have been completely beyond the bounds of legality, had this not been a government-run expedition that included Indians from the reserve. Legal or not, it was hard
to escape the impression—from the way we foraged for food and built
our bivouacs from materials yielded up by the forest, not to mention
our ragtag appearance in FUNAI-issued camouflage—that we were a
guerrilla army that had retreated into the deepest backwoods under
pressure from the authorities. We moved through the jungle in silence
and stealth, our single column like a military formation on the lookout
for ambush.

It called to mind times I'd been out in the Nicaraguan jungles with
the Sandinista Popular Army in the 1980s. Despite the fact that the
Sandinistas were actually in power in Nicaragua, their army operated
much like partisan irregulars defending their homeland from a foreign occupier, which, in a way, they were. There was a similar sort of es-
prit de corps and egalitarian spirit, with everything from candy bars to
cigarettes shared equally among the troops, much like the vile tobacco
we'd taken to rolling in pages from my notebook or the spoonfuls of
powdered milk we'd scarf on the sly when Possuelo wasn't looking.
Back then, when our Bulgarian C rations ran out, the Sandinistas took
to blasting game from the trees with their AKs, fishing the streams with
hand grenades. We were a scourge that no stretch of forest should
have to endure more than once in a generation.

Obviously, our thirty-four-man expedition exerted a lighter touch
than the impact of a battalion eight-hundred strong. But we were still
capable of inflicting significant losses on the local fauna. Luckily for
the animals, we were on the move every day, our single-night stopovers
culling relatively few specimens from any one locale. As with the Sandinistas, a similar sort of idealism also prevailed. At least in the case of
the leadership, if not the entire rank and file, there was a sense that

something transcendental was at stake, that those present were being summoned to a mission of far greater import than themselves. It was almost as though the socialist ideal that the United States had invested hundreds of millions of dollars to smother in Central America in the 1980s had resurfaced two decades later, far to the south. It may have been stripped of its strident anti-Yankeeism and the Cold War context, but it was no less opposed to the same concentration of wealth and power that had robbed Nicaraguan peasants of their dignity and Amazonian Indians of their land and culture.

* * *

"Hey, Scott, I've got an appetizer for you," Possuelo called from the hearth. He came toward me brandishing a barbecue skewer run through with twisted chunks of dark, sizzling meat. "A delicacy of the Amazon—liver of *jabuti*!" I'd seen the tortoise when it was still alive. One of the Indians carried it back from the hunting foray, its limbs and head retracted within a green and orange shell of beautiful geometric design. It was nearly two feet long. Now, that shell was a bloodied husk discarded near the fire. Had it not been for the knot of hunger in my gut and my weariness of monkey flesh, I might have refused. As it was, I slid a chunk off the skewer and devoured it greedily. It was one of the most delicious things I'd ever eaten: tender, rich, moist.

The tortoise liver was followed by another treat: *jacu*, a black-feathered guan about the size of a small turkey. Tufts of its plucked feathers blew about the campsite as Mauro boiled it up in a small pot. The aroma wafted in the air like a breeze blowing in from another world we could scarcely remember. It was as if the hunters had returned from a butcher shop with a Cornish game hen. Still, there were many mouths to feed, just one bird. I got a tiny piece of its juicy meat, just enough to whet the appetite for the main course: monkey.

I turned in just after dinner. Remarkably, as we traversed the rugged headwaters region, the tiny *piums* that made life so miserable out near the river had entirely disappeared. Nonetheless, there were mosquitoes and untold other flying pests, from which the hammock was the sole respite. It was remarkable that something so light and thin could provide such an effective membrane that protected against so many perils.

The one thing the hammock could not fend off was the nighttime chill, which was something I hadn't counted on. I'd forgotten how, like in a desert, temperatures in an upland rainforest could fluctuate wildly between day and night, by as much as thirty or even forty degrees. A thin layer of Capilene was no match for the damp cold of the Amazon night. I awoke with teeth chattering. The waterproof poncho I'd taken to using as a blanket had slid off. I checked the luminescent face of my Casio: 3:18 a.m. Raindrops tapped intermittently on the tarp overhead. Somewhere far beyond that, a jetliner cruised through the night, engines rasping with a faint but insistent reverberation, like a distant train of thunder that went on and on. It called me back again to the jungles of northern Jinotega, where aircraft also droned overhead in the dead of night. They were part of what was later revealed to be the CIA's clandestine air force: low-flying C-7 Caribou, bellies stuffed with freshly oiled AKs and ammo they would parachute to the Contras. Calls would go out in the darkness: *Flechero! Flechero!* the word being almost identical in Spanish. Funny, the connection between then and now. Back then, the *flechero* was a marksman of a different order, trained to deploy a heat-seeking antiaircraft missile: *la flecha,* or "arrow." With no interceptor jets, the Sandinistas had to rely on shoulder-mounted SAM-7s to bring down the aircraft that intruded on Nicaraguan airspace. Thus summoned, the bearer of the missile would attempt to get a clear shot off. Most of the time, the forest canopy was too thick to even bother.

Now, listening to the jet engines rasping high above the Amazon, I wondered whence the flight had departed, where it might be headed: Santiago, bound for Madrid? São Paulo to Mexico City? I pictured the passengers in their upholstered chairs, dozing in the dimmed light of the cabin, some wearing those silly-looking eye masks, legs stretching into the aisles, everyone entirely oblivious of the reality thirty thousand feet below on the jungle floor. I nestled my head on the small pillow I'd commandeered from the flight to Tabatinga, one of the most useful extralegal acquisitions I'd ever made. I recalled that daytime view out the window, down onto the broccoli-topped forest, bisected by snaking brown rivers. Now here I was, in the middle of it. *If I were on that plane,* I thought, *I could get up right this second, head to the galley, ask the flight attendant for anything I wanted, a drink maybe, any drink that struck my fancy.* That would be a Coca-Cola, with lots of ice. I might have been shivering, but after weeks of tepid river water, I'd begun dreaming of bottles of ice-cold Coke and the fleeting breath of vapor they exhaled when you popped the cap off on a hot summer's day. I'd liked to think that I was above such crass, consumerist cravings, but I was learning otherwise.

What did these *flecheiros,* the ones with the real arrows, make of these nighttime disturbances? Some kind of dark omen, a signal that all was not well in their world? Or perhaps the distant rumbles had come to signify something quite different, a comforting routine, maybe a kind of reassurance, like the ongoing blessing of a benign spirit.

It was my intention to ask Possuelo about it before we broke camp in the morning. But it would have to wait. As first light seeped down through the branches and dewdrops pattered on the leaves, Possuelo called out into the encampment: Meet by the campfire in five minutes. He had an urgent announcement, and he wanted to make sure everyone heard it.

CHAPTER 14

In the Footsteps of Rondon

SMOKE DRIFTED UP IN lazy ringlets as we gathered around the fire. It had been eight days since we'd left the boats behind and vanished into the jungle, eight days scaling up and down forested hillocks and steep ravines, through boot-sucking mud and thorny undergrowth. Most of the Indians looked none the worse for it, but the rest of us were haggard, gaunt, and spent, our faces long and peppered with stubble, our uniforms filthy, malodorous, and tattered. We shuffled into the clearing as the first rays of sun caressed the tops of the trees far overhead, scattering a diffuse yellow light down through the jungle.

"We saw fresh tracks yesterday," Possuelo began. He wore his signature camouflage shorts, and his khaki shirt, a snug fit just a week ago, now hung loose on his slumped frame. "We're now crossing through an area where the Arrow People move back and forth in the summer months. They must be out looking for eggs of the *tracajá.*" It was hard to believe a simple river turtle, with its seasonal migrations and reproductive habits, could dictate the wanderings of entire tribes. But the riverside nests, packed with dozens of leathery-shelled eggs, represented a virtual bonanza of protein and nutrition in the midst of scarcity. "Poachers and loggers come over from the Juruá and enter Indian land illegally," Possuelo continued. "They'll be looking for turtle eggs, too." While the Juruá's eastward-flowing waters provided no direct route into the reserve, intruders were opening footpaths across the ridgelines to penetrate the Javari. The eggs would serve as

their sustenance while they trolled for larger trophies—valuable hard-
woods, perhaps, or jaguar skins—that would earn them cash in the
frontier markets. "They see Indians, they shoot, no questions asked."

He paused, and repositioned his floppy hat. From beneath its visor
sprang shocks of his graying hair, which seemed to be growing longer
and wilder by the day, as though it were itself a small patch of the riotous jungle that enveloped us.

"The Indians, if they see us, will think we are just like the other
whites they've seen before," Possuelo continued. "The ones who have
shot at them." Again, he was speaking in slow, deliberate Portuguese,
making sure his words were hitting their mark. "We must be prepared
for an attack in the days ahead." The whispering and jostling ceded to
Possuelo's booming voice and the electric pulse of insects.

"If an arrow flies, don't panic," he said. "If we are attacked, no
one shoots back. We will only shoot in the air, to make a racket and
scare them off. That's how we will defend ourselves." It was a dubious
proposition; few among us had received any kind of military training.
Under the circumstances, such restraint seemed to presume a level
of discipline and a commitment to high-minded ideals that were not
altogether in evidence here. Still, these were the very same orders that
had been issued by Colonel Rondon to his men nearly one hundred
years before. "We're here to protect the Indians," Possuelo said, "not
to attack them."

* * *

By the time Cândido Rondon assumed leadership of the newly created
Indian Protection Service, or SPI, in 1910, he'd spent years exploring
Brazil's vast hinterlands to lay strategic telegraph lines through the
interior. His encounters with scores of tribes, some hostile and others
less so, led him to champion the Indians as the true owners of the
land and its most dedicated stewards, to whom Brazilians owed a "great
moral debt."

As Rondon conceived it, the SPI would safeguard the lives and
the rights of Brazil's natives, especially from the predations of rubber

bosses. They were to be gradually assimilated into the mainstream. Implementation was imperfect, to say the least. Early contact teams called out to wild tribes from the treetops by megaphone, quaintly naive perhaps in their faith that the Indians would heed the call of "civilization." But once tribes were subdued or seduced, officials who may have had the best of intentions often remained powerless to defend them from the landgrabs and massacres that followed, or were themselves complicit in the abuse. They failed miserably when it came to providing care in the face of the ensuing epidemics. *Assimilation* was itself a misleading term. The Indians weren't assimilated; they were segregated, relegated to the lowest rungs of society. Nevertheless, the principles stood in stark relief to the treatment meted out to Indians elsewhere in the Americas, most notably in the serial abrogation of treaties and scorched-earth policies visited on the natives during the westward expansion of the United States during the previous century.

Would that the Sioux or the Comanche, the Cheyenne or the Arapaho, have had a man of Rondon's stature and pugnacity in their corner. Instead, they got the likes of Colonel Ranald "Three Fingers" Mackenzie and General Philip Sheridan, brilliant but ruthless commanders who elevated to an art form the genocidal predawn raid on unsuspecting Indian villages. Their extermination campaigns extended even to the buffalo, slaughtering the herds deemed the "only way to bring lasting peace and allow civilization to advance." Which meant, in basic language, starving the Indians into submission.

The Rubber Boom had been to the western Amazon what the invasion of the U.S. Cavalry was to the High Plains and the Rockies. The fevered search for latex had led legions of invaders into the distant forests of the Upper Amazon to press-gang and pillage. By the time the rubber industry collapsed on the eve of the First World War, the entire western rim of the Amazon had been thoroughly upended— entire tribes gone, others barely clinging to existence. As the twentieth century progressed, dozens of tribes disappeared altogether around the Amazon, many before their existence was ever documented, victims of disease, massacres, or aggressive contacts by ranchers, loggers, oil companies, even missionaries who imperiled the lives of converts in order to "save" them.

But unlike the wide-open plains of the American West, the dense forests of the Amazon offered an unusual degree of protection for natives who managed to flee the ravages of the rubber industry. Those same jungles—with their thin, impoverished soils, vast distances, and multitude of perils—offered little incentive for white homesteaders to stick around. When the price of wild latex began to crash on global markets in 1910, thousands of outsiders who had sought their fortunes in the western Amazon packed up and left. The Indians gradually came to realize, like terrified home invasion robbery victims hiding in a closet long after the intruders have departed, that their tormentors were gone. The Rubber Boom was over. Little by little, they began to pick up the pieces of their shattered lives. It would be decades before the whites returned in large numbers. Next time, it would be with chain saws, in search of prime timber.

By the start of the third millennium, many indigenous groups were on the rebound. Nearly 400,000 Indians belonging to some 270 tribes occupied 11 percent of the national territory. Indian lands and indigenous reserves had emerged as a bulwark of ecological preservation that held back a five-hundred-mile-long "arc of fire" advancing across the eastern and southern Amazon to make way for crops and pastureland. In remote, mist-shrouded redoubts and in sweltering lowland bogs still beyond the reach of the chain saws and backloaders, if just barely, Possuelo's department had confirmed the existence of at least 17 uncontacted tribes within the boundaries of Brazil. Reports of several dozen other groups awaited investigation. Rondon's ideals had endured, continued to inspire, remained the law of the land. And the most incontrovertible evidence of that truth was our presence here, however tentative the inner convictions of each of us might have been, gathered around Sydney Possuelo, in the very heartland of the People of the Arrow.

*   *   *

"When we make camp from here on, be careful where you hang your hammock," Possuelo continued. "The *flecheiros* can observe how the hammocks are arranged, then come back at night to shoot arrows at them. And be careful using your flashlight. It could make you a target. Keep its use to a minimum." Now he held a shiny steel whistle above his head. "If I blow on this, that means the situation is grave. It means: Everyone stick together. Absolutely no one should run off into the jungle on his own."

His admonitions were greeted with smirks and guffaws among the whites hanging back in the rear of the assembly.

"Chico is *viado,* a queer," someone snickered. "Of course he'll turn tail and run."

"Fauk you," Chico said, using the one English expression I'd successfully imparted to my expedition mates, even if the pronunciation was a bit mangled.

"I can see it now, an arrow stuck in Chico's ass!"

"This is no joke," snapped Possuelo. "I've seen what these tribes can do! I've had companions killed and others wounded. It's not that the Indians are bad people; they're doing what they have to do to defend their land."

It was not out of the ordinary for expeditions to come under attack. Francisco Meirelles, a renowned SPI *sertanista* and one of Possuelo's early mentors, lost eleven men in three years of violent ambushes at the hands of a single tribe, the Pakaá Nova. Many more were wounded. True to Rondon's dictum, Meirelles never retaliated. Contact was finally achieved, after Meirelles left the same arrows the Indians had shot at his men, together with other gifts, out on the trail for the tribesmen to take.

Possuelo had his own experiences with indigenous violence. Back in 1980, Arara Indians unleashed a hail of arrows at the outpost he'd set up to draw the tribe out of seclusion. Two of Possuelo's men had been struck in the attack, adding to three others wounded the year before. The attempt to pacify the Arara was complicated by the unremitting pressure of a rapidly advancing frontier. When the Trans-Amazonian

Highway pushed into the central Amazon in the 1970s, the tribe splintered, some fleeing north of the road, others to the south. They took what they could carry on their backs, shifting overnight from a society of sedentary agriculturalists to a life on the run as nomadic hunters.

Their murderous disposition notwithstanding, the loggers and land-grabbers who followed the road into the Araras' forests differed little from us in their understanding of the Indians whose lands they usurped. Those who hadn't suffered their attacks called the fleeing Arara an "invention of FUNAI," concocted to halt development. Victims and nonvictims alike presumed the Indians to be "savages," primitive nomads low on an evolutionary scale that tended toward ever more complex social hierarchies and accumulation of material comforts. We peer into the shadows from the forest edge and see naked hunter-gatherers, still distant from the advent of crop domestication that ushered in the Neolithic Revolution a dozen millennia ago. Rarely does it occur to us that these primitive societies may already have been profoundly altered by our presence, even before we've actually laid our eyes upon them.

Such was the case with the Arara, the "Macaw People." Like the communities in flight Paulo Welker had described in Mato Grosso, like the Hi-Merimá in the state of Amazonas, and countless other tribes, the Arara ran from the chain saws, the bulldozers, and the men who operated them. To stay a step ahead of the invaders, they abandoned their crops and villages to forage in the forest. Unable to distinguish between the whites who wanted to help them and those who wanted them dead, the Arara fled from well-intentioned FUNAI scouts, sometimes turning on them to let their arrows fly. FUNAI's efforts to defang the Arara were foundering. In 1979, Possuelo was brought in to make something happen. He began by overflying the zone to pinpoint *malocas*, logging camps, clear-cuts. He interviewed settlers and local functionaries. He drew up a plan for a protracted attraction campaign with a methodology, an organization, and logistics. It was the time of the dictatorship, and he reported to an army commander. "Okay, now you're going to apply it," the general told him.

Possuelo's strategy borrowed heavily from the groundbreaking work of Curt Nimuendajú, a German-born ethnographer contracted by the SPI in 1922 to pacify the bellicose Parintintin in Mato Grosso. Possuelo expelled all intruders from Arara lands and called off FUNAI's aggressive pursuit of the Indians. He then erected a fortified Attraction Post deep inside Indian territory from which to wage his *namoro,* or "courtship," of the Arara. For the campaign to work, it was critical for the Indians to be able to differentiate the FUNAI personnel from the other whites with whom they'd been locked in long-standing hostilities. For starters, Possuelo dressed members of the Contact Front in uniforms emblazoned with a logo, which was also painted conspicuously on the wall of the outpost. Second, team members would refrain from any action the Indians might interpret as hostile. Not even when showered with arrows would the Contact Front return fire. At the same time, Possuelo erected a *tapiri de brindis,* or "offering hut," a thatched lean-to at the very edge of the clearing, where gifts were left out for the Arara to take: knives, machetes, bricks of brown sugar, even cane flutes. The courtship had begun.

Sixty years earlier, Nimuendajú came to realize his own strategy of nonaggression lacked a critical ingredient. The Parintintin had evidently mistaken his restraint for weakness and were mounting attacks on the outpost with escalating ferocity. A bloodbath—of whites, Indians, or both—seemed inevitable. He needed to make the Indians understand that his men could shoot them at will, but that they'd chosen not to, even in the face of their repeated provocations. Possuelo did likewise. He had the men take target practice, with gunshots resounding through the forest. They ported rifles at all times, so the Indians— spying from the thicket—could see them.

Like the Parintintin before them, the Arara eventually succumbed to the overtures—and to the irresistible allure of steel gifts. What other *sertanistas* failed to accomplish in years, Possuelo pulled off in nine months. Scouts from the first group of Arara then helped agents contact the other two bands. But once the Arara were tamed, the flow of gifts dried up. Ineffectual bureaucrats took over the FUNAI post, and a full-fledged invasion of Indian lands resumed, this time bringing in loggers lured by their rich stands of mahogany.

Possuelo was disgusted by the ultimate outcome. The once-proud warriors who had made the road builders quake now staggered drunk along the Trans-Amazonian Highway's dusty shoulders, begging for handouts. Old-school SPI agents believed that walling off the Indians from the rest of society was racist, not to mention impractical; the advance of civilization into native lands was inevitable. But the precipitous decline of the Arara served as a trumpet to arms for a new generation of field agents. In 1987, a FUNAI contact team pacified the last of the wild Arara. In June of that same year, amid contentious debate at FUNAI headquarters in Brasília, Possuelo rallied his colleagues to support a sea change in Brazil's policy toward the still-uncontacted tribes.

"We can never forget that in the process of attraction, we are in truth acting as the spearhead for a cold, complex, and determined society, one that has no forgiveness for technologically inferior adversaries," read the *sertanistas'* petition, which bore the unmistakable hand of Possuelo. *"We are invading their lands without their invitation. We are inculcating needs they never had before. We are wreaking havoc with extremely rich social organizations. . . . In many instances, we are taking them to their death."*

Then-president of FUNAI Romero Jucá, who was later implicated in a corruption scandal, signed the recommendations into law, simultaneously creating the Department of Isolated Indians to implement the changes. Henceforth, the government would ally itself with tribesmen it hoped it would never come to know, assuming a radical and unprecedented defense of their land and their way of life. The new unit was to be led by Sydney Possuelo.

*   *   *

A long silence followed Possuelo's rebuke. Thin smoke drifted lazily from the dying campfire. Slouching against trees and sprawled on the benches, the men hung their heads. We were already weary, and the day's march hadn't even begun. The sun broke through the overcast,

broadcasting powerful shafts of light down through the canopy. The cicadas built toward a pulsing buzz-saw crescendo, tapered off, then rose
again. Possuelo swept the circle with his eyes, on the lookout for dis-
sent or confusion. "From here on," he said, "we've got to be on guard."

We tromped through saturated mudflats, water oozing into our
boots. It didn't matter that you spent two or three hours every night
drying your clothes and boots over the fire; within minutes of breaking
camp, everything would be drenched and filthy all over again. Still, it
was worth it just to be able to slip into something dry and somewhat
clean before heading out in the morning.

We marched to the spooky, unremitting sound track of the screaming piha bird. There was an oddly ventriloquistic quality to the shrill
voice, as if it were coming from everywhere and nowhere—the sliding
two-note uptake, followed by the descending slide of equal measure.
It sounded like a demented come-on whistle to a passing woman in
a minor key, but its exact provenance could never be discerned. A
nearby call would elicit a distant, identical response from another bird
farther on, the cries at times overlapping. It was the same monotonous score that accompanied the doomed conquistadors in *Aguirre:
The Wrath of God,* and there were times when it felt like we were on
the film's real-life set, a half-unhinged Klaus Kinski at the helm. It was
uncanny how in turns Possuelo could radiate warmth and inspire absolute confidence, only to descend into the dark brooding and explosive
outbursts that imparted to the march the feel of a roving penal colony
from which there was no escape.

We clawed our way up a near-perpendicular bank and emerged on
squishy ground studded with scores of bizarre-looking *Socratea* trees,
also known as "walking palms." They were like something from a storybook tale, their bark covered with spikes and a luminescent, pastel
blue lichen that seemed to throb in the shadowy forest. Each trunk
balanced atop a dozen stiltlike roots that shot down from three or
four feet off the ground and vanished into the black soil. The roots
formed a domelike structure not unlike a large birdcage, an evolutionary strategy that allowed the trees to withstand months in knee-

deep water during the seasonal floods. In dry weather, the strange root system made an unlikely refuge for animals on the run from hungry predators.

"Tapirs hide in here when they're being chased by jaguars," said Soldado, pausing to light a cigarette. "The jaguar gets stuck between the bars here"—he tapped the roots with his machete—"and the tapir gets away." A specimen of health only a few weeks ago, Soldado now looked wasted. His skin had taken on a greenish pall; his eyes were sunk deep in their sockets. He was racked with fever and beginning to spit blood. Malaria, he was sure. So far, he'd said nothing of it to Possuelo.

We soldiered on through a silent world of preternaturally subdued light, along a broad stretch of level ground free of undergrowth, navigating past enormous trees that soared like Roman columns from the jungle floor. A vague, diffuse light filtered down in greens and yellows through the canopy. In the utter stillness of the midday forest, it felt as though we were walking on the bottom of the ocean.

As we approached a colossal mahogany tree with buttressed roots, our column split—some going right, others to the left. The sprawling roots make it possible for canopy giants to balance in the Amazon's thin soils as they reach for sunlight at heights that nearly rival those of urban skyscrapers. They also make ideal concealment for would-be ambushers, which is why we skirted it on both sides. But most of all, the mahogany's towering presence demanded respect. I craned my neck and gaped.

The trunk soared skyward, ramrod straight, and vanished into the canopy. Its rich red grain, the density of its wood, and its resistance to insect plagues have made mahogany one of the most coveted building materials on the planet, putting it in the crosshairs of loggers throughout the upland forests along the Amazon's western and southern rims. Shadowy criminal enterprises had built hundreds of miles of clandestine roads, virtually undetectable from the air, deep into the jungle to reach stands of the precious trees. Timber mafias had become the new spearhead of rainforest penetration, threatening uncontacted

tribes and opening up huge swaths of pristine forest to subsequent
waves of settlers, ranchers, and land-grabbers. Between 1982 and 1996,
Indian lands lost an average of 250 truckloads of mahogany a month,
with the connivance of corrupt tribal chiefs or through outright lar-
ceny. The environmental group Greenpeace had just led a successful
campaign to ban the logging of mahogany throughout Brazil. But to
the southwest, on the far side of the Peruvian frontier, heavily armed
gangs were cutting the trees in protected forests at the headwaters of
the Purus and Envira rivers, forcing isolated bands of Mashco-Piro,
Nahua, and Amahauka to take flight, with potentially catastrophic consequences for the Indians. Asháninka communities inside Brazil had
decried an ongoing invasion of Peruvian timber thugs in their lands,
and they were beseeching the police or the army to intervene. Under
such circumstances, it came as a relief to find this majestic tree still
standing tall, safe—at least for now—from the men with the guns and
the chain saws, whose contempt for life was rivaled only by their greed
for profit.

We came upon a series of freshly snapped *quebradas* in the understory. Paulo Welker turned to me without saying a word. He put his
finger to his eye: *Watch out!* We crossed a footpath. I couldn't tell if it
was a thoroughfare of the Arrow People, or if it had been opened by
infiltrators from the Juruá. Paulo put his finger to his lips: *Stay quiet!*
We advanced with caution, taking care to muffle our steps. We crossed
another path. Wait a second: Why wasn't Paulo bringing up the rear,
as Possuelo had ordered? That meant the end of the column could
be anywhere—no doubt wherever Wilson and Alfredo happened to
be wandering. But it was just a momentary flash, gone in an instant.
I was far more focused on right here, right now. Suddenly, a bloodcurdling scream rang out from somewhere behind us. It hung in the air,
wavering and changing pitch, as though someone was enduring unspeakable torture. We froze in our tracks. Another screech followed.
Possuelo shrugged and went on, as though nothing had happened. I
turned back to Tepi. "What was that?" I asked, my heart racing. "*Ma-
caco prieto,*" he said matter-of-factly. Black monkey. Objecting to our

intrusion perhaps, or maybe issuing a mating call. In any case, it was his good fortune we were passing through early, before the call went out to hunt for the evening dinner.

Blinding white light poured down through a huge gap in the forest, a few hundred yards across. It wasn't exactly a clearing; the entire space was piled high with the wreckage of toppled trees. I couldn't tell which of the trees precipitated the event, but it didn't matter; the result was the same. When one canopy tree weakens and dies in the jungle, it takes several others with it, so interwoven and bound together are their crowns with thick, tenacious vines. These spontaneous clearings are a dream for botanists and entomologists. Without having to climb to vertigo-inducing heights, they can examine insect colonies, flowering bromeliads, an entire spectrum of flora and fauna that have evolved in the microclimates of the canopy. The clearings also make great sites for primitive tribes who have no axes to plant gardens in open daylight. But for us, the jumbled heap presented an obstacle course rife with hazards—pitfalls and deep shadows where bushmasters could be lurking, overhanging boughs that swarmed with ants, nests of angry wasps. It took half an hour to pick our way along the haphazard ramparts of the fallen trees to gain the far side. With an odd sense of relief, I plunged back into the gloom of the jungle.

The terrain began to shift. Fearing that the rugged landscape was exacting too high a toll on the men, Possuelo had adjusted our route. We now followed a more easterly course, cutting sideways along the muddy slopes, rather than scaling straight up and down. Gradually, the ground began to level out, which presented a whole new set of challenges: more streams, more nail-biting crossings along slippery logs, more wading through fetid, knee-deep swamps that would have sucked the boots right off our feet had our laces not been double-wrapped and knotted about the ankles.

Possuelo paused at the top of an embankment and mopped his brow with a grimy shirtsleeve. In the bright sun of late morning, he held out his GPS with an extended arm, like a photographer reading his light meter.

"Hmmm," he said. "We're probably the only ones who have ever walked here, us and the Indians." By Indians, he meant the Arrow People. It was an amazing thing to consider. In fact, the terrain had been so inhospitable, damn near close to impenetrable, it would have been logical to conclude that no other humans had ever been here at all. Except for a fresh footprint we came upon a short while later.

The imprint was well defined, sunk into a patch of slick red earth otherwise carpeted in brittle leaves. I leaned down and measured it against my outstretched hand, from thumb to little finger. It was a bit longer, roughly a men's size 8. It was perhaps a day or two old, no more. Which meant the chances of a random encounter seemed to be gradually mounting. "We're only seven kilometers from their nearest village," said Possuelo, once again checking his GPS. By now, we'd skirted three, perhaps four of their settlements. Even so, he was certain the Arrow People remained unaware of our presence. "If they knew we were here, they would be on top of us, at the very least to keep us under observation."

When we stopped for lunch on a patch of high ground, I sprawled out on damp leaves, wedged between a pair of thin saplings. I unknotted my plastic bag of monkey-meat *farofa*—a blend of smoked flesh and coarse manioc flour. I dug into the greasy crumbs with my bare hand. My fingers were caked with filth, but normal standards of hygiene had long since gone out the window. Worm in the soup? No problem, flick it out and keep eating. A fly crawling on a piece of meat? No big deal.

A small avalanche of moist yellow crumbs tumbled off my lap, and in no time, a troupe of black ants appeared and began carting them off. I watched spellbound as they hauled their loads up and over leaves, over the skid marks in the mud from our errant footsteps, and most impressive of all, through the tangle of moss that covered the rotting log I leaned against. Like a fleet of tiny forklifts, they hoisted morsels nearly as large as themselves, seeming to defy the laws of strength and gravity. Indeed, their determination seemed to far exceed our own; it was simply a question of scale.

* * *

I lost sight of the trail more than once in the course of the afternoon's
march. Or rather, I lost sight of the guy immediately in front of me—
whether it was Possuelo, Orlando, or one of the Matis—for I could
rarely tell otherwise where the actual trail was. Now that the ground
had leveled out, the slick track created by the tramplings of the first
four or five men had mostly disappeared. Against the dizzying back-
ground blur of greens and grays, trying to pick out the trail-marker
saplings hacked off by the lead scouts was nearly impossible. When I
looked down to sidestep a rodent hole and looked back up again, the
column ahead of me had vanished. I continued on for a few strides,
confident I'd pick up the trail. But a few more steps and I found myself
encircled by an unbroken wall of foliage. I tried to retrace my steps
and quickly realized I had no idea which way I'd come from. I called
out: *"Onde estão?"* Where'd you go? I remembered Possuelo's words:
The jungle smothers the screams. I yelled louder, with more urgency. But in
a land of hostile tribesmen and hungry jaguars, shouting had its own
drawbacks. I felt panic begin to surge in my chest. Just then, Alcino
and Adelino Marubo appeared through a screen of dangling lianas,
bark tumplines strapped across their foreheads, shotguns in hand.
"Por aqui, Scotch." They pointed. "Follow us."

The day's march culminated in a perilous log crossing over a broad
igarapé that fed into an even wider one. By the time we pitched camp,
the waters of three major streams had joined to form a single waterway
perhaps fifty feet wide, affording a view into mid-distance such as we
hadn't seen in days. My eyes drank in the rich yellow light of late afternoon, the deepening blue of the sky, the puffy alabaster clouds.
The closed forest had imposed a kind of claustrophobia I'd been only
dimly aware of until now.

While the morale among the rest of us had drained away under
the weight of the march and the gloom, the Matis maintained a level
of good cheer that could at times make it all feel like a schoolboy outing. They quipped among themselves in high-pitched staccato bursts,

punctuated by laughter, and they were quick to shift into Portuguese for the outsider's benefit, even if they happened to be talking about him in less than flattering terms, which was often the case.

"*Scotchie Chui Wassá?*" said Ivan Arapá as I passed by the low-lying Matis shelters on my way to bathe. He was wearing his customary smirk, and the other Matis were laughing. "What's that?" I asked. "*Scotchie Chui Wassá,*" he repeated, this time not a question but an assertion. They had a new name for me, he said. Scotchie White Dick. It seemed my immodest habit of bathing without shorts—I didn't want to have to dry them over the fire—had made me an object of their curiosity and good-natured derision. I went back to my hammock and pulled on a pair of briefs.

The camaraderie, together with the daily rhythms and rituals, conspired to create a sense of domesticity in the midst of the wild, perhaps a false sense of security. In the course of this sustained encounter with the elements, I was beginning to see how the human mind—or my own at least—grappled at every moment to graft mental coordinates onto a geographic landscape without even realizing it, attempting to impose order out of chaos. That was what made getting lost in the forest such a terrifying prospect. You turned around in the undifferentiated thicket and found no way to get a fix on anything. In an instant, that sense of security was ripped away.

The threat of utter solitude always seemed to hum just beneath the surface, in the indifferent trilling of insects, the croaking of frogs, and it made the daily birth of a campsite, and the lilting laughter of the Matis, all the more comforting. By dint of the time of day and some particularly inviting qualities—dry ground, a clear creek nearby, plenty of sturdy trees—a patch of random wilderness would be deemed worthy of bivouac. Within minutes, the place would be transformed, as if by magic, into a recognizably human community, replete with small neighborhoods, winding footpaths, a bathing area, a refectory. The modifications were fleeting; time would begin to erase all evidence of our presence as soon as the last of us departed the next morning. But the alterations to the locale that occurred in the mind were more definitive, so that the memory strained to picture what it had looked like in its natural state only moments before, when we first arrived. Like the thin hammock membrane that shielded us from the elements and parasitic illness, the community itself provided a kind of invisible bubble that operated on a submerged, subconscious level to assure us that we were safe and sound. Whether we actually were was another matter.

A succession of gunshots rang out from the distance, the discharges rolling in one after another in the gathering twilight: *Boom. Boom. Boom.* Soldado lifted an ear. *"Porco,"* he declared. Pig. Wild boar. I was impressed by his uncanny ability to interpret the distant gunfire. The Matis and Marubo assigned to the hunt soon arrived in camp lugging nine white-lipped peccaries, bound at the hooves and slung upon their shoulders with long strips of bark. I had just finished bathing when Alcino Marubo staggered down the bank with bloody pork flanks draped on his back. I got out just before he plunged into the stream, sending a scarlet tide rippling through the water. By the campfire, large slabs of meat and pig livers were stacked high on palm leaves. Bees swarmed around the bloody flesh. I was drying off when Nicolas dashed over. "D-did you hear?" he stammered. "The Matis have found a camp of the Arrow People! Come on, let's go!"

"Hurry!" Txema shouted. There was no time to get dressed. I bounded after them into the underbrush, dressed only in wet underwear and flip-flops. Five minutes turned to ten, then fifteen. I was beginning to think I was absolutely out of my mind. Two or three weeks ago, I'd have sooner been dead than here, running nearly bareass naked through deep jungle. I found myself falling behind, my feet slipping sideways on the wet sandals. I pressed on, desperate to keep my companions in sight as they bounded into the closed thicket.

CHAPTER 15

The Meaning of Contact

A T LENGTH WE CAME TO A GIANT KAPOK, its buttressed roots shooting down from above, sprawling along the forest floor. Around the back side of the tree, decaying old palm fronds lay scattered on the ground between two of its buttresses. A primitive cage fashioned from sticks, much like the one we'd seen days before, stood nearby. Most strikingly, V-shaped grooves were hacked into two of the buttress roots, about four feet off the ground. The slots most likely supported a pole, though no longer in evidence, that would have held up a palm-leaf roof to cover the nook between the rocket-fin roots. The notches, each about four inches deep, could only have been made by a steel blade.

Sweeping aside the leaf cover with his foot, Paulo Welker uncovered a half dozen slender poles, none more than an inch in diameter. By all appearances, they'd also been cut with the steel tool. Judging by the feathered ends of the poles, the blade must have been very dull; multiple swipes had been required to cut through them. A freshly sharpened machete could have cut off any of them cleanly with a single blow.

"They used these to hang their hammocks," said Paulo as he held a pole in both hands. It was hard to believe the poles could have supported much weight; the people who used them must have been very lean, or very small. Welker judged the camp to be about two years old.

But it would have been a mistake to conclude that we were putting distance between ourselves and the Arrow People. In the excited babble that attended our return to camp, Alcino Marubo said he'd seen a severed boar's head while out hunting, just twenty minutes away. The head, he said, was no more than a few days old.

We dined on a delicious wild boar soup with noodles and gritty manioc flour. There were seconds—even thirds—for everyone. There was far more meat than Mauro and Paulo Souza could possibly cook. Additional fires sprang up around the encampment, straddled by wooden racks to smoke the pork. Soon the air was heavy with the thick aroma of barbecue.

Slurping on the tasty boar broth, I told Possuelo about the crude hackings evidently made by steel tools we'd seen at the Arrow People's camp. He wasn't the slightest bit surprised. "They steal axes and machetes from loggers and fishermen," he said, shrugging matter-of-factly. "That's what touches off many clashes. A logger realizes his ax is missing, and he chases after the Indians to get it back." It sounded strikingly similar to Ivan's tale of how the Matis acquired their first ax, in the days prior to contact. The dullness of the blade, evidenced by the repeated hackings, hinted at even more elaborate possibilities. It could have been traded through a succession of exchanges among several tribes over long stretches of time and distance, in which the Arrow People sustained no contact whatsoever with the original bearer. Or they could have snatched it from a logging camp, as Possuelo suggested. But he supposed they would have taken it long ago, given that the blade was as dull as I described, and most likely from someplace farther down toward the lowlands, along a navigable waterway used by lumberjacks and other invaders as routes of penetration into the jungle. Though we were beginning to enter those lowlands from higher ground, we'd still seen no signals—not a single tree stump—to indicate loggers had been in these parts in recent years.

* * *

What it means for a tribe to be "uncontacted"—and what it does not mean—has become a matter of heated debate among anthropologists, indigenous rights advocates, and even business interests who accuse their enemies of concocting the notion of pure, unadulterated Indians to stymie development. Some captains of industry have gone so far as to accuse certain *sertanistas* of "planting Indians" on their property, dressing them up with bows and arrows and macaw feathers in order to seize their land and sequester its timber for FUNAI's own profit. The possession of a steel blade would only serve to prove their point: how could you call a band of Indians "uncontacted" if they owned products of industrial society and put them to use in their daily lives?

Even many sympathetic to the plight of persecuted Indians view the term *uncontacted* as a misnomer that discredits their cause, conjuring images of Stone Age savages inhabiting a kind of fictional Lost World. They prefer "indigenous people living in voluntary isolation," to underscore the willful determination, or rather self-determination, that seems to attend all the isolated tribes still roaming the forests of the Amazon, be they in Brazil, Peru, Ecuador, or Bolivia. Indigenous groups living in isolation are isolated because they choose to be. It's not for complete lack of contact, but precisely because previous experiences of contact with the outside world proved so negative.

In Brazil, the term *índios isolados*—isolated Indians—constitutes a legal concept that defines those indigenous societies "about which little information is available," which avoid regular contact with the outside world, and which depend entirely on intact forest for survival.

The isolation, even from other tribes, appears to be a relatively recent phenomenon, born of the violent imposition of the White Intruder. Indigenous groups that scattered into remote headwater sanctuaries could no longer sustain intertribal trade relations that may have dated back centuries. In many cases, their trading partners disappeared altogether. In others, white colonization and dominance over major transportation corridors would have rendered contact between tribal entities too risky to sustain. Which is why, for example, the Arrow People would recognize the meaning of distant gunfire or why they might reasonably be expected to flee warning shots fired over their heads. This was not, in other words, like the interior of New Guinea,

circa 1930, which had been completely sealed off from the outside
world, and where highlanders refused to believe the "firespears" of
invading Australian prospectors could kill human beings until they
saw their fellow tribesmen sprawled dead on the ground. Nor was it
even like the western Amazon of 1892, when Mashco warriors at the
headwaters of Peru's Mother of God River sneered at the seemingly
harmless Winchester cartridges shown them by the notorious "King
of Rubber," Carlos Fermín Fitzcarrald, when they asked to see his arrows, only to be slaughtered with the very same bullets moments later.
By now, indigenous peoples everywhere, even in these deepest jungle
redoubts, had received a graduate-level education in the meaning of
gunfire. For many tribes, the fact that the white man possessed firearms was of far greater practical significance than the color of his skin.
Some indigenous languages even evolved names for whites that had
nothing to do with their pale faces, but were rather onomatopoeic
renderings that mimicked the crack of a fired gun. Amid the war
cries and arrows they showered down on Nimuendajú's outpost, the
fierce Parintintin shouted noises that imitated the blast of gunshots.
If the Indians whose vestiges we sought and scrutinized were known
to us as the Arrow People, then we rightly could have been called the
"People of the Gun."

Yet, did the mere fact of possessing a dull-edged machete or the
ability to recognize the sound of a gun qualify as "contact" with modern society in any meaningful sense? Even when tribesmen like the
Matis or Mayá steal buttons or pilfer axes from white frontiersmen,
does that bring them any closer to the full embrace of our global village? Maybe. Maybe not. It could mark the beginning of a gradual
seduction, a growing dependence on the manufactured goods that invariably bedazzle technologically primitive aboriginals. The allure of
our magical objects—mirrors, matches, phonographs, cameras—lay at
the strategic core of campaigns waged over decades to attract countless
tribes of *índios bravos* from the bush, not just by the SPI and FUNAI,
but also by missionaries, oil companies, road builders, adventurers.

The Huitoto Indians of the Putumayo River, who would suffer horrific abuse during the reign of latex baron Julio Arana, initially venerated steel axes as divine objects that conferred fertility and abundance, and they willingly swapped orphans or low-status members of their clans to obtain the goods from slave traders.

But most of the isolated tribes it was now Possuelo's duty to protect had engaged in far more perfunctory transactions: glancing encounters involving theft, accompanied perhaps by an exchange of flying bullets and arrows. That was why the Indians remained, in essence, uncontacted. The absence of peaceful contact meant they were still "virgin soil populations," as vulnerable to the communicable diseases that evolved over millennia on the Eurasian landmass—measles, flu, tuberculosis, pneumonia, even the common cold—as were the very first Taino encountered by Columbus on Hispaniola. Within sixty years of Columbus's landfall, the Taino were extinct, reduced to zero from a population that modern demographic studies indicate may have been as high as eight million. In that regard, *how* a tribe has come to possess a knife or a machete—or even a rifle—would reveal more about its degree of contact with the outside world than the mere fact of its possession. Where the Arrow People and other uncontacted tribes were concerned, those stories—the stories of *how*—would remain largely unknown to us, as long as Possuelo had his way.

Yet there were a few tantalizing clues. In the years 1980–84, heavily armed loggers made their way farther and farther up the São José Creek, occasioning repeated raids on their camps by *flecheiros*. Time and again, the Indians managed to make off with tools and other goods. Though the mouth of the São José was weeks behind us, we were in fact quite close to its headwaters, having traced a long, C-shaped arc to reach our current location. Granted, the terrain was extremely rugged, but the upper São José was probably less than a week off for light-trekking nomads. Could the blades evidenced by the crude hackings we'd seen in these woods be the very same ones lifted from the logging camps years ago? Perhaps so.

Though the Arrow People could be expected to recognize the

sound of the gun, that did not mean they could grasp the enormity of the world beyond their jungle homeland, or have an inkling that whites were a particularly numerous tribe that had spread across the entire Earth. As for their thoughts about things like rasping jetliners crossing their skies, who could say? I'd meant to ask Possuelo about it in the morning. Now I had the chance. At first he said nothing. He rose stiffly from his seat by the fire to stretch. Darkness was falling, and from the encroaching shadows came the high-pitched whir of insects, pulsing in unison. Most of the men had retreated to their shelters, though a few of the Matis—Tepi, Txema, Ivan Arapá—were still present. Possuelo tossed a fresh log on the fire, raising a shower of sparks that drifted up into the blackness and winked out like shooting stars. Muted laughter and belches came from the satellite fires set back in the woods, where pork loins sizzled and the Kanamari carried on with the feast. Possuelo returned to his seat on the bench. "I don't know," he said tentatively, staring into the fire as if lost in thought. "But it reminds me of something I once heard from a Txikão Indian."

The Txikão were a warrior tribe from Mato Grosso, contacted in a daring mission by Orlando and Claudio Villas Boas in the 1960s. The Txikão had long been locked in simmering, tit-for-tat warfare with neighboring tribes, but by the early sixties, previously unknown diseases had jumped ahead of the advancing frontier, heightening the imperative for tribes to kidnap women and children from rival villages to repopulate their ranks. Raids were followed by revenge killings. The Villas Boas brothers had attempted to contact the Txikão years earlier, when they learned through native informants that tribal enemies were planning an all-out assault on their village. The Txikão had survived that attack, but now they were dropping like flies from sickness, and they didn't know why. Enemy witchcraft was suspected. It was not unheard of in such situations for shamans who failed to expel the strange illnesses to be put to death by their own people.

"Orlando and Claudio decided to do something," said Possuelo. "They took an airplane over the village and dropped aluminum pots, soccer balls, photographs of themselves, bricks of brown sugar, and other gifts." There was no time for a protracted attraction campaign; the airdrop was meant to "soften up" the natives for the daring contact mission that would soon follow. At the roar of the flying monster swooping in over the village, the Indians scattered in panic. Women and children took shelter inside their huts. Men futilely launched arrows at the winged beast. Strange bundles tumbled from the rear of the aircraft, landing with a thud at the edge of the clearing. The braves approached cautiously, sniffing for a malevolent odor, poking the packages with long spears.

"They thought this large bird had taken a shit on their village," Possuelo said. "He told me this with a lot of shame, as though he should have known better at the time." The Txikão's curiosity soon got the better of them. They opened the packages. They tried the sugar and found it sweet. But they were bewildered by the photographs. Never having seen people represented two-dimensionally in such vivid detail, they kept turning the photos over, wondering where their backsides had gone.

American missionaries in Ecuador had tried a similar tactic as a prelude to contact with Waorani Indians in the late 1950s. The Waorani had been likewise baffled by the images, but they'd taken a far dimmer view of their significance. Believing the photos to be the calling cards of evil sorcerers, they speared the missionaries to death when they landed their plane on the remote river the following week. Half the Waorani tribe eventually accepted contact and were evangelized. The other half remain in the forest to this day, avoiding interaction with the outside world.

Only days after dropping their gifts to the Txikão, the Villas Boases touched down with their own Piper Cubs on the scrublands just beyond the village. They rushed from the planes to greet the Indians, holding machetes and mirrors aloft as tokens of peace. It was a lightning strike, fraught with the same risks the missionaries had taken, unlike anything previously attempted in Brazil. Perhaps owing to their vast experience and sensitivity to Indian ways honed through years of work, they succeeded where the Americans had failed. In the months that followed, the brothers convinced the Txikão to relocate within the bounds of the Xingu Indigenous Park farther east. It was one night many years later, in the Txikão's new village, that the man recounted to Possuelo the tale of the flying monster that had first cast its shadow on their *maloca*, changing their lives forever.

By the time Possuelo brought his story to a close, the circle around the campfire was nearly empty. But Ivan Arapá still sat gazing into its dying embers. "Before, Matis thought the big airplanes were our dead ancestors—*xokeke*," he said. He pointed straight up, indicating the space far beyond the treetops. "We saw them pass waaaaaaay overhead. And we said, 'There go our ancient ones.'" Like the Txikão, the Matis believed the ear-splitting Piper Cubs were some kind of large, scary birds. "We thought: It must be a powerful demon. Did we do something to provoke it?" He repeated the word in Matis: *binkeke*.

I could see why an isolated tribe would see high-flying jetliners as an utterly distinct phenomenon from the bush planes that might buzz their village. If they'd never seen either take off or land, how could they draw a connection? In midflight, a jumbo jet presents itself as a mere speck topping the sky, while a swooping Cessna can shake the Earth and blot out the sun. It was only years later, when Ivan traveled to the All-Indian Games in Campo Grande, that he learned commercial jets were in fact much larger than bush planes, not the other way around. The Matis imbued the high-altitude aircraft with supernatural powers: the reassuring, though distant, presence of their departed loved ones. But the Cessna, with its intrusive swoop and startling roar, was a creature of terrifying immediacy, much more of this world than the next.

Such was certainly the case for the Cinta Larga Indians in the state of Rondônia, who were bombed with sticks of dynamite tossed by prospectors from a low-flying bush plane in 1963. The plane reportedly made a first pass over the village, dumping packets of sugar to lure a crowd to the central plaza. Then it swooped in low on a second run, dropping TNT on the assembled Indians. No one knows how many Cinta Larga may have died that day. The bodies were buried in the riverbank, and the village was abandoned forever.

*   *   *

Back at ground level, I returned to my hammock to find I'd once again selected a site astride a thoroughfare of nasty black ants. I pranced about, flicking them off my feet and legs. As I climbed into bed, I knocked off my flip-flops and suspended them from the cord at the foot of the hammock. If I needed to get up in the night, I figured, I'd have ant-free sandals I could slip into with relative ease. When that time came, somewhere around 3:00 a.m., I groped my way down toward the foot of the hammock, trying to reach for the flip-flops. Retrieving them was turning out to be a more delicate operation than I'd antici-pated. I was in a contorted position, turned more than three-quarters the way around, my hand reaching for the flip-flops, when the ham-mock flipped completely over, leaving me dangling facedown, arms pinned back, nose and mouth pressed into the mesh of the mosquito net. I hesitated to call for help, especially since Possuelo's announce-ment at the start of the day. We were in the heart of *flecheiro* country; a shout in the night would amount to a blatant breach of security mea-sures. But the more I struggled to free myself, the more entangled I became. I was helpless as a fly in a spider's web. Finally, I screwed up my courage. "Orlando, Orlando!" I pleaded. "Help me!" He was sleep-ing only ten paces or so away, and I figured he was probably the only person within earshot who'd come to my rescue. At first, my entreat-ies went nowhere. I called out again, this time louder. Finally I heard Orlando stirring nearby.

"What the fuck, Scott," he said, his voice thick and drowsy. But once he caught sight of my ludicrous situation in the beam of his flash-light, he burst into hysterics. "How did you manage *that?*" He hoisted me up with one arm while he untangled the hammock with the other. My ineptitude did earn a rebuke at dawn—not from Possuelo, but from Nicolas. As I hurried to pack up, I saw him out of the corner of my eye, striding toward me with grim determination. He looked gaunt and ashen, and severe lines around his eyes and mouth were taut with pent-up anger. "We're in Indian country now," he chided. "It's dangerous out here! The *flecheiros* attack people! Would you have made that kind of noise in the jungle in Nicaragua with Contras all around?" He stalked off without awaiting an answer. I wasn't sure I had one.

Besides the imperative to defend their lands, some isolated tribesmen were also known to launch attacks to gain access to manufactured goods they may have developed a taste for but could acquire by no other means. The Kayapó raided settlers time and again during the 1950s with the express purpose of taking their guns and ammunition, which they used in turn to gain an upper hand on their traditional tribal enemies. The raids ceased only after the SPI *sertanista* Francisco Meirelles lavished the Kayapó with gifts of shotguns and cartridges, instead of the standard fare of machetes and knives. In taking goods from settlers or logging camps, the Indians would sometimes leave behind arrows or war clubs as payment, unwittingly sowing panic among those with whom they sought to trade: *Good God, wild Indians!* Across the border in Peru, Nahua warriors routinely raided loggers and the settlements of civilized Matsigenka Indians to get their hands on manufactured goods. When they ransacked the outpost of a Shell Oil seismic team in 1982, they departed with the workers' hard hats.

Discerning the general purpose of a construction helmet is about as simple as putting it on. But for tribesmen insulated from modern society, the uses and inner workings of most industrial commodities are far from obvious. When New Guinean highlanders first saw the glow of flashlights in the night, they thought the white men had bottled moonbeams. During the Arara contact, Possuelo mistakenly left his own flashlight one night out at the *tapiri de brindis,* where he'd just hung some axes and machetes—standard fare for an attraction campaign. In the morning, he found fresh footprints. The gifts were gone. So too was his flashlight. Years later, he heard that young braves had returned to their village that night with the machetes and something else they'd never seen before: a shiny metallic cylinder with a glass eye at one end. The man who'd taken the flashlight was fussing over it, shaking it, smacking it. Then, in the darkness of the *maloca,* the flashlight suddenly turned on, as if by its own accord. The startled Indians pounced on it, smashed it with clubs, and tossed the pieces into the fire. When the batteries exploded minutes later, they fled the communal house in a panic, convinced the lantern was a demonic creature still very much alive.

It was easy to make light of the Indians' bewilderment over things like airplanes and flashlights; indeed, with the benefit of hindsight, they were the first to laugh at themselves. But it was another matter to confuse the technological prowess of our society—or the fancy products I possessed as one of its privileged members—with some kind of moral or intellectual superiority. In the course of the eighteen days since we'd left the boats, I'd come to appreciate how utterly lost I would have been without my companions—ripped apart by a jaguar maybe, bitten by a bushmaster, bones picked clean by ants, or left to suffer slow starvation and derangement. They carried my stuff, picked me up when I fell, steered me away from imminent threats, hunted the food that I ate. I shared the evening campfire with men who in this lifetime had believed jet aircraft to be supernatural beings. But their forebears had evolved a way of life perfectly suited to this harsh realm. They'd known how to survive in it, even to thrive in it, with nothing of our complicated technology. Every one of them at one point or another had stood face-to-face with a jaguar in the forest, armed with only an arrow or a stick, and come out on top. Did the bearer of a SAM-7 missile, who with a squeeze of a finger could shoot one of those ancestral spirits out of the sky, possess any greater intelligence than a *flecheiro* who knew how to stalk prey silently in the forests and whose people had managed to arrive at the third millennium still free from civilization's relentless efforts to subjugate them, dispossess them, and have at their resources?

* * *

A dim whiteness seeped down through the foliage as I took the morning's first steps into the forest. As I'd started to do in recent days, I made the sign of the cross and launched into a silent recitation that had begun to take shape within me, as if of its own accord, from the extenuating circumstances of the trek. I hadn't prayed since early childhood, when I'd kneel at bedside to say the Lord's Prayer under my father's guiding eye. I wasn't even sure I knew how to anymore. But now each morning as the march got under way, the words came to me. The prayer seemed to be evolving daily, as I became more sensitized to the growing litany of perils that awaited us: *Protect me today, O Lord, from the dangers of the jungle. Protect me from the snakes, the spiders and scorpions, the jaguars and other predators of the forest. Protect my joints—my knees, my shoulders, my feet. Protect my eyes, my hands, my ankles.* I moved from the specific to a more scattershot approach, sparing no eventuality: *Protect my health, protect me from disfiguring injury, serious illness, or strange disease. Give me heightened powers of perception to make good, quick decisions, give me sureness of foot, give me strength and energy. Protect us all, dear Lord, from the arrows of those who know not that we come in peace. Deliver us safely to the end of this day.*

There was a decidedly superstitious bent to this newfound faith, which was probably why I sought to cover the most immediate perils first, and cover them fast. We were already on the move as I mouthed this incantation, and each step presented a fresh danger, some potential evil to be warded off. The Matis evoked their animal spirits; my god was far more free-floating and abstract. But we basically wanted the same thing: survival, some measure of security, well-being for our loved ones. With that in mind, my prayer continued: *Bless Mackenzie, Aaron, and Ian. Fill their day with love and happiness and challenges that make them grow. Bless their mother, Jennifer, and all her family. Bless Mom and Dad. Give them a day of health and small things to be grateful for. Please give them life, keep them until I get home safely to see them again.*

If there was also a tone of melodrama to this invocation, it no doubt had to do with a growing sense of isolation and foreboding. The jungle's closed canopy had rendered our Inmarsat phone useless for two solid weeks, and when we finally found a gap in the canopy at the previous night's bivouac, the phone wouldn't work, no matter which way we pointed its antenna. We'd been cut off, this time definitively. Had we known in advance that we'd be completely out of touch for weeks or months, we could have at least prepared ourselves and our families for the coming silence. Instead, we were left to wonder about them, they were left to wonder about us, and we were left to wonder about them wondering about us. It was into that void that I now dispatched my daily prayer, a message in a bottle.

Our route roughly paralleled the twisting stream. From time to time, it came into view as it snaked toward us through the trees, its silvery reflection like an oasis for our light-deprived eyes. The creek, said Possuelo, would grow wider as we followed it, leading us to the Jutaí—the river that would return us to civilization. It was a tantalizing prospect to consider, though one without much point. We were still weeks from nowhere, our contact with the rest of the world entirely severed. I struggled to stay focused on the here and now, putting one foot ahead of the other. That was the only way I'd ever make it home, to everyone I'd ever cared about and wanted to see again.

We stopped for lunch around noon, but there was no food. We sprawled in clusters of three and four on the damp forest floor. Most of the *riberinhos* kept their distance, smoking cigarettes, conversing among themselves. But the Indians revolved around Possuelo like planets around the sun, an audience that had grown to expect some kind of yarn or disquisition in moments such as this. He did not disappoint; it was time for a jaguar tale.

"I was out in the *selva*, hungry and alone," Possuelo began. "Finally, I'd shot a *mutum* with my long-bore .22. I tied it up in a tree and went down to the river to get some water." When he came back, the turkey was gone. "Strange, I thought, this looks like the right tree. Well, anyway, I figured a wild cat had taken it. Then about from here to there"—he gestured across a space of fifteen yards—"I see the back and shoulders of the 'cat' taking the bird away. I see it's a jaguar!"

By now Possuelo had everyone's attention. "I decide I'm going to make that animal pay for that bird, so I grab the rifle and head after it. I'm maybe ten meters behind when I lose sight of it. I look and look, but it's gone. Finally, I decide to return to the cabin. As I go to put the rifle away, I see the gun wasn't even loaded! Go figure what would have happened if I had caught up with that animal!" The Indians broke out in delighted cackles. It was a story they could appreciate; they'd all faced down jaguars. Jaguars were central to their lore and their myths, and jaguar attacks were often understood to be calculated attempts at assassination by shape-shifting enemy shamans.

Shortly after resuming the march, we came to a towering tree, its bark rippled with dozens of parallel grooves running vertically down its side. The mark of the jaguar. "See how she came here to clean her claws," Soldado said. Around the back side, most of the grooves were low to the ground, only a few gouges high up. "This is where the jaguar hung by her forepaws to clean her hind feet."

I conjured an image of the creature that had the size and power to pounce that high. I pictured the stepladder of Soldado's neighbor tossed aside, the bucket of rubber milk flying, and I imagined the horror of that moment when his life came to an abrupt end, ripped apart by the beast with those outsize claws. The grooves in the bark were fresh, still bleeding a reddish white sap, a graphic reminder that we'd entered not only the land of the Arrow People but the domain of the jaguar as well.

*　*　*

Midway through the afternoon, the sun broke through the clouds. Golden rays streamed through the foliage in a dazzling kaleidoscope of greens and yellows dancing on the forest floor. Soldado led the way through a tangle of head-grabbing vines, slashing away at the thicket. We emerged into a clearing commanded by a huge envira tree. Long strips of its shaggy bark had been peeled away from the trunk. A hole had been scooped in the ground at the base of the tree. *"Índios bravos,"* Soldado pronounced gravely, his sunken eyes studying the forest beyond. "They've been here."

We tromped through what appeared to be an abandoned banana grove, the low trees set in a patch of wild elephant grass slouched under the weight of their large, drooping leaves. Several had been slashed repeatedly at the base with what must have been a very dull ax. *"Capoera,"* said Soldado, looking around. A fallow garden. Ivan Arapá picked his way ahead of us beyond the clearing, suddenly crying out in a loud whisper: *"Pegada!"* A footprint was pressed into the mud. It was so well formed that you could distinguish individual toes. Still, it was old enough—from the day before yesterday, Ivan calculated—to presume a minimum margin of safety between us and whoever had left it. The men now fanned out in all directions, like a search party scouring the woods for a lost child, scuffing up leaves, looking for clues.

For nearly three weeks, we'd been bushwhacking through primeval forest to reach one of the most remote places on Earth, which made Soldado's next find all the more astonishing: a well-worn footpath snaking its way back through the forest. Unlike the nearly invisible path Possuelo had pointed out days before, this was as plain as day, like the Appalachian Trail.

We burst through dense thicket into a sunlit clearing to behold a dozen low-lying palm-roofed huts. It looked like a temporary hunting camp, probably from the previous year. "Indigenous groups don't always travel in large groups," Possuelo said. "Sometimes just a family comes out—a man, a woman, three kids, a brother-in-law—maybe six or seven people. They might stay here a week or so, then move on." I knelt down on hands and knees for a look inside one of the shelters. They were low to the ground, like pup tents, more suited for Hobbits than for full-grown human beings. At the edge of the clearing, a pair of V-shaped jawbones sat in a cleft of a low tree. The bones were covered in a fine green moss, but the molars sat intact in their sockets, white as ivory. The front teeth were set at a sharp protruding angle from the bone, like those in a donkey's snout. *"Anta,"* said Ivan Arapá. Tapir. He moved in for a closer inspection. Why the tapir jaws had been left this way, nestled in the crotch of a tree, was anyone's guess. Maybe some kind of totem, Possuelo surmised.

On the other side of the huts, Tepi and Binã Matis discovered a large ceramic pot buried in a mound of dried leaves. They hoisted it up for all to see. It was perfectly round, blackened with soot, large enough to hold a half gallon. Its walls were expertly shaped, uniformly thin; no casually thrown piece of clay. "This is the first time I see one of their *panelas,"* said Possuelo. He took it in both his hands. "Heavy," he said. "Difficult to carry." It raised new questions about the Arrow People, attesting perhaps to a more sedentary existence than we'd imagined. Were the *flecheiros* the simple hunter-gatherers, unchanged since Vespucci, that Possuelo had earlier suggested? Or had they rather descended from a more striated agrarian society—shattered and uprooted like the Marubo who had fled into the far corners of the rainforest? Thus hidden away in this jungle citadel, had they since reclaimed a measure of stability, marking a return to a more settled existence, the fruit perhaps of Possuelo's own work to protect them?

And another promising sign: the apparent absence of booby traps. Isolated tribes under pressure from intruders often littered jungle trails with spiked pitfalls, concealed beneath thin layers of leaves and branches. To guard against nasty foot injuries, FUNAI personnel working in places like Rondônia, where scattered indigenous groups were under constant harassment, lined their boots with PVC inserts. Here, the only punji-like sticks we'd encountered were those left by our own trailblazers as they swiped at saplings to clear our way forward.

We picked up the trail again where it led away through a pair of high trees. Not far beyond them, we came upon a chunk of masticated sugarcane lying on the ground. Nearby lay several clumps of white fiber—possibly cotton, possibly the lining from the pod of a kapok tree.

"Zarabatana! Zarabatana!" the Matis blurted excitedly. A blowgun.

The tufts served as wadding to pack a dart in a blowgun's chamber, Tepi explained. This was how we came to discover that the *flecheiros* in fact had other weapons—not only arrows—in their arsenal.

"Where are the others?" demanded Possuelo in a shouted whisper.

"Farther back," the Matis said in unison, pointing over their shoulders.

"They need to catch up," Possuelo groused. "Everyone has to stick together now."

A short way farther on, a piece of coiled vine lay at the foot of a tree. It was a simple contrivance, used by forest people to bind their ankles together to shimmy into the treetops. The tree bore shallow indentations, where the strap had pressed into its soft bark. Just a few steps ahead, we found fresh footprints in the mud. "This is from *agora*," Soldado said. "From right now!"

Possuelo read the skid marks and said: "He climbed the tree, saw us, came down, and took off running." We moved forward in silence. Possuelo turned back and whispered: "Maintain visual contact with the man ahead of you at all times. Pass the word back!" Just in front of Possuelo, Soldado signaled with his machete ahead and to the right, toward a gap in high elephant grass that opened toward the river. "I saw something, over there!" he murmured. "Like a shadow moving!" We stopped, cocked our ears. Possuelo took a tentative step forward, cupped his hands to his mouth, and called out: *"Whoooa! Whoooa!"* Only the forlorn cry of the screaming piha replied.

We followed the path another twenty strides—then Possuelo hissed: "Turn off here!" He instructed Txema to leave a "Turn Right" signal for the others to follow—a bunch of snapped-off saplings that would make clear which direction we'd taken. Within five minutes we arrived at the banks of an *igarapé* some fifty feet across. A tree spanned the channel, most of its trunk submerged just inches beneath the surface. Using a succession of long poles passed back and forth for balance, we crossed along the log, the swift current rushing over the tops of our boots, pulling on our ankles.

We plopped down on matted brush atop the bank, basking in the late-afternoon sun. A dazzling blizzard of butterflies—yellow, brown, and orange—danced all around us. It seemed as if we'd entered a land of magic. But Possuelo's face had gone dark. "They know we're here now," he said. "No question about it." For the first time since the expedition began, he strapped on his revolver.

CHAPTER 16

Ours Guns, Our Germs, and Our Steel

THE MATIS LED THE WAY forward. Suddenly they pulled up in their tracks and pointed ahead, toward a cluster of trees beyond the sawgrass. Possuelo raised his hand for silence. From off in the distance came a muffled, excited babble, unintelligible but unmistakably human. With hushed commands, Possuelo called for the Kanamari to come to the front of the column. Word was relayed back into the thicket, and soon Márcio and Remi appeared.

"Call to them in Kanamari," Possuelo instructed. "Tell them we're friends, and we mean no harm." The Indians cupped their hands and shouted toward the tree line. We strained our ears to listen. The distant murmuring ceased. Possuelo signaled the Matis to follow suit. They called out, but there was no response. Finally the Marubo took a turn. Again, nothing but the cry of the screaming piha.

Suddenly, without command and without explanation, our ranks broke. Everyone lurched forward, trouncing through the high grass in hot pursuit. In the excitement to catch a glimpse of the wild Indians, all discipline and sense of reason fell away. The sunlight danced like liquid gold on the river as we ran and ricocheted sideways in blinding flashes through the silhouettes of trunks and branches. Soldado and Paulo Welker cut left and made straight for the river, some two hundred yards away. Possuelo held straight to the parallel course. I was torn: Whom to follow? In a split second, I decided to follow Possuelo. Bad choice. Within moments, we heard shouts behind us, coming from the direction of the water. It was Paulo Welker. *"Over here!"* he yelled. *"Over here, they're crossing the river!"*

Soldado and Paulo Welker were heaving deeply, hands on their knees, by the time we reached the bluff above the river. Behind them rose the upended roots of an enormous tree that had fallen into the water. Another tree of similar dimensions had fallen from the opposite bank, some thirty yards distant, and the two trunks met halfway across the river to form a single span, in the shape of a shallow V, like a bridge that had taken a direct hit in the midsection and had collapsed into the water. Vines had been strung between the barren branches that protruded vertically from the prostrate logs to form a handrail. Clearly, this was a regular transit point for the *flecheiros*.

"I saw one!" Welker gasped, still struggling to recover his breath. "He was naked, with long hair. Broad shoulders. Strong. He ran across the bridge. Disappeared into the woods." He pointed across to the far side of the river.

"There were two of them," corrected Soldado. "They were naked—but for a string tied around their waists." As he had done before, Possuelo commanded the Indians to call out toward the high trees across the river. He cupped his hands and hooted, the Indians pleaded, but there was no response.

"Who's carrying those small pots we brought along for gifts?" Possuelo called out. José, Soldado's son-in-law, stepped forward. "Take three of those pots and shine them up nice," Possuelo said. "String them here at the bridgehead. It will be our way of saying thank-you." Soldado yanked a creeper from a nearby tree, then strung it through the handles of the cooking pots. He and José pulled the cord taut and tied off both ends to low-hanging branches. The pots dangled invitingly, about waist-high off the ground.

When it came to the business of giving gifts to "untamed" Indians, the presentation could be just as important as the presents themselves. Positioning them up off the ground made it clear that they were actual gifts, offerings of peace to their intended recipients, not merely discarded objects. It was also a sign of respect, a symbolic way to *hand over* the presents without physically doing so. For Possuelo, every gift he'd ever left at an attraction altar or on a remote jungle path was situated in a historical context that dated back to Portuguese navigator Pedro Cabral's first encounter with native Brazilians in 1500.

"The act of giving gifts . . . is perhaps the most ancient means of demonstrating peaceful intentions, especially when peoples of different languages come face to face," Possuelo wrote in his memo to FUNAI colleagues on the fundamentals of a successful attraction campaign. *"Since that first contact in the Age of Discovery to this day, all that we've done has been a repetition, with variations imposed by time and circumstance, of Cabral's initial gesture."*

The shiny aluminum pots left at the bridgehead offered a novel twist. The objective was simply to avoid attack, not to make contact—to show friendship, not to seduce the Indians into giving up their way of life. "Will it work?" I asked. "Hard to say," Possuelo replied. "Many times they destroy the presents to demonstrate their rage at the white man."

The anger would hint at some previous atrocity perpetrated on the Indians, for which the FUNAI team bore no blame, other than the fact of being emissaries from the same outside world. Wooing natives from the bush took finesse, requiring *sertanistas* to decipher the varied responses to their overtures—and to adjust methods accordingly. Indians might take knives and machetes, for example, but refuse a sack of sugar, hinting at the possibility that ill-intentioned whites may have poisoned them with arsenic-laced sweets in the past. They might leave crude relics of axes or scissors carved in wood, to signal their desire for more of these commodities. The Parintintin routinely accompanied their taking of gifts with harrowing war cries and showers of arrows, suggesting to Nimuendajú their need to impart an air of pillage to the process, to see the objects they were taking not as handouts, but as trophies of war. Besides smashing gifts, Indians might show resolute repudiation by leaving behind a dead animal at the offering hut, perhaps even a monkey for its obvious resemblance to the human form, heart impaled with an arrow like a voodoo doll.

Once the pots were in place, Possuelo rose to his feet. He wanted to put distance between us and the Indians, as quickly as possible. *"Embora!"* he barked. "Let's get moving!"

We followed the river, cutting in and out of the woods between patches of shadow and dazzling sunlight. We trudged across the sandy bed of an incoming creek through a swirling cloud of orange and yellow butterflies. We dashed up the banks and stumbled back into the forest twilight. We'd been on a fast march for a half hour when Possuelo ordered the column to halt at a bend in the river that looked down on a long white beach.

"The Arrow People have three *malocas* up ahead—there, there, and there," he said, pointing across the river at scattered intervals to the north and northeast. "We could keep walking for hours and not get any farther away from them. We'd better just camp here." He was certain the two Indians who'd crossed the bridge were shadowing us from the far side of the river, following our every move. They would soon head for their village, he was sure, to report every detail of what they'd seen. "Listen up!" he shouted for all to hear. "Everyone down to the beach, on the double! And bring your rifles!"

On the reconnaissance flight over the area prior to the expedition, Possuelo had made note of the locations of every clearing he'd observed and how many huts were in each. Extrapolating from the number of huts and their relative sizes, he figured each village to hold no more than fifty or sixty people. That made for seven or eight able-bodied men in any one settlement—probably too small a number for them to risk a strike. Of much greater concern was the chance that the Arrow People could mass forces from several outlying *malocas* for a more concerted and deadly assault. That would take more time, but the clock was already ticking. "There is nothing to keep them from setting up an ambush for us farther downriver," he said. He hoped to preempt such notions right now, by showing the Indians what we had—in terms of men and weapons.

Gaunt as scarecrows in our tattered fatigues, we stumbled out of the woods, the expeditionaries lugging their rifles. "Spread out down

the beach," commanded Possuelo. "Let them see that we are many."
We staggered along the shoreline, feet slipping in the loose sand. We
turned to face the towering wall of trees on the opposite bank, no
more than a hundred feet away. "Stand up straight, look strong! Hold
your guns up high!" Possuelo ordered. "Let them see how well armed
we are." Rifles came up off hips and shoulders, tilting toward the ma-
nila tufts of evening clouds that drifted overhead. Of course, Possuelo
had no intention to turn our rifles on them. He'd sooner have died
than fire upon the Arrow People. But he needed them to think that
we might. It was an odd combination: gifts on the one hand, guns on
the other. The carrot and the stick. We stared across the river into the
trees beyond the far bank. We saw nothing but the high wall of jungle,
though we could feel their eyes upon us. All we could hear was the incessant flow of the water and the rush of blood pounding in our ears.

*   *   *

We pitched camp on the bluff above the water. Possuelo issued a general ban on the discharge of weapons. "No hunting," he announced.
He dispatched the Indians—the Kanamari going upstream, the Matis
and Marubo going down—to fish for our dinner. "Stay along the riverbanks!" he yelled after them. "Take your rifles and ammunition!" In
case of trouble, he instructed, they should fire warning shots to summon help. He then ordered Tepi and Remi—one a Panoan-speaking
Matis, the other a Katukinan-speaking Kanamari—to keep lookout on
the beach, in case the Indians appeared on the far bank. "If they come,
do not invite them across to visit," he said. "Don't tell them we have
machetes and gifts for them. Tell them: 'We're just passing through.
We're leaving, don't worry.'"

Both fishing parties returned in less than an hour, laden with
dozens of orange-bellied piranhas. Besides the fish slung on their
shoulders with strips of vine, Wilson and Alfredo were carrying their
overturned camouflage jungle hats in both hands, leathery *tracajá* eggs
overflowing the brims. Possuelo was livid. "I didn't tell you to gather
turtle eggs!" he scolded. "The Kanamari don't like it when whites

come to your villages and steal eggs from your beaches. It's the same here. We're in the house of the Arrow People. We have to respect what is theirs." They slunk off into the woods at the far end of the encampment, where they'd thrown up their hammocks, still clutching the hats filled with the pilfered eggs.

We dined on the piranhas' flaky white meat—tasty enough, but laced with bones. In our famished state, the threat of choking on a piranha bone was the most dangerous thing about them. It was safe to bathe in the swift-flowing rivers, even with piranhas all around. They would attack only if they smelled the blood of an open wound, or if they'd been stranded in a still-water lagoon after floodwaters receded and they'd run out of food. Our own hunger was so intense, it required steely discipline not to inhale the spiny bones along with the meat.

"All right, everyone, listen up!" Paulo Welker stood before us as we slurped up the last drops of broth. Sentries would be posted throughout the night in rotating shifts, he said. He looked exhausted. His cheeks were hollow, his skin a pasty white. His blond hair, limp and greasy, hung to his shoulders. He held up the same whistle Possuelo had shown us the other day. "If there's an attack, the sentries will blow this." He pounded a nail into the tree behind him and hung the whistle on it. "If you hear that whistle, drop to the ground immediately. Grab your backpack, use it as a shield." Next he showed us a red flare gun. "I also have this *sinhalizador*." In the event of an attack, he said, he'd fire it to scare off the Indians. But with heavy jungle pressing down from above, it was hard to see how the gun would do anything other than ignite a wildfire in our midst.

From his clipboard, Welker read off the teams and their assigned hours: *Odair/Amarildo: nine to ten; Remi/Márcio: ten to eleven; Damã/Tepi: eleven to twelve;* and so on. Matis were paired with Matis, Kanamari with Kanamari, whites with other whites. When he finished, Paulo Welker said: "Now, take a look around. Check the path back to your hammock, see if there are roots or anything you could stumble on in the dark. Make note of where they are. Remember, no flashlights. That will make you a target. For those doing guard duty, check the list now to see who comes immediately after you. Know where they're sleeping, so you know where to find them."

As the last light faded from the sky, Welker made the rounds along the encampment's perimeter, conferring with the men in low murmurs. He eventually stopped at my hammock. "If they attack, they'll probably come from either this side," he told me, pointing out into the gathering shadows on my right, "or from over there." He swept his finger in the opposite direction, like a knife slicing the darkness. That was bad news for me; I'd occupied the most exposed position of the entire bivouac. But with night already drawing its stranglehold over the jungle, it was too late to uproot and move elsewhere. From the direction of the river came the spooky, reverberating chorus of *cururu* frogs: a wavering hoot that faded in and out and went on and on, somewhere between the creepy sci-fi theme from *The Outer Limits* and the long, lonely whistle of a distant train passing in the night. "Be alert!" Paulo Welker said, then vanished into the shadows.

I lay in my hammock, replaying what Possuelo had said about the three *malocas* across the river. Had their runners spread the news to all of them, and perhaps beyond to more distant settlements? Were the Arrow People now gathered in the flickering glow of their own campfires, locked in fierce debate over how to respond to this unprecedented intrusion? I pictured fiery young braves strutting in the dim light, warning with wild gesticulations of the imminent danger, urging a preemptive strike, while older and wiser tribesmen and women pleaded for a cautious wait-and-see approach in soft, measured tones.

We spent the night in fitful sleep, straining our ears to catch the snap of a twig or the rustle of leaves, anything that might signal the approach of the Arrow People. Sometime in the predawn, I awoke from a troubled doze to a peculiar song lilting through the jungle. It sounded like someone blowing across the reeds of a panpipe, playing a scale up and down, sometimes so faintly it was drowned out by the spontaneous sigh of the forest. Just when I thought it had died out, it would start up again. I wondered if it might be their way to signal one another, portending a possible strike. Apprenticing themselves to the birds and animals they hunted, tribesmen could mimic with startling precision the cries, mating calls, or songs of just about every creature in the forest and use them to attract prey, coordinate movements, strike fear in the hearts of their enemies, even cover the screams of their victims. But sentries were posted, I tried to assure myself. Unless they'd already been silently picked off, or had themselves fallen asleep. I eventually pushed aside these paranoid thoughts and tumbled back into an uneasy slumber.

Movement in camp began well before the first gray light seeped down through the foliage. I could hear the hushed voices of Mauro and Paulo Souza, sticks breaking, and the now-familiar *whoosh, whoosh, whoosh* as they fanned the fire with the lid of a cooking pot. Everyone was up early. We slurped unsweetened black coffee and nibbled on our ration of two soda crackers. Powdered milk had long since vanished. So too had the sugar. Mauro's corn bread was a distant memory. We were constantly famished. Many had acute dysentery. Some, like Soldado and Raimundo, were racked with malarial chills. Their faces had acquired a green patina, as if infested by a thin layer of jungle moss. But hunger was the greatest affliction. I'd done some rough math and figured that we'd been burning around 6,000 calories a day. Our scant rations must have averaged no more than 800. There was a notable exception: Orlando. He remained every bit as robust as the first day I'd met him. His broad chest and muscled biceps seemed to suggest he was eating well, and rumors had begun to spread about access he had to a private stash of evaporated milk, with his father's connivance. "Haven't you noticed?" Soldado whispered. "He's the only one who hasn't lost any weight. He's actually *fatter* than before."

As the campfire lapsed into smoky embers, Possuelo called everyone together. There was probably no one who didn't figure he was going to discuss the grave danger we faced and announce corresponding countermeasures. But he had something more personal to say.

"Orlando turns eighteen today," he began. "It's a matter of great satisfaction to me . . ." His voice cracked. His eyes were wet like the morning dew that dripped from the leaves. There was a long pause.

Orlando looked across from the far side of the clearing, where he sat on a rotting log. Possuelo composed himself, then continued. "Orlando is here. He's eighteen. That's great." He opened his mouth again. Nothing came out. Orlando, tears streaming down his cheeks, strode across the clearing and flung his arms around his father. We sang "Happy Birthday" to Orlando, a zombie chorus in shredded camouflage, several of the men parroting the motions, clapping their hands rhythmically to our tuneless song. Possuelo presented Orlando with his birthday gift, a single piece of candy, wrapped in a green leaf. "Forgive the weakness," he said to us as he dabbed his tears with the sleeve of his fatigue shirt. Warmth and mirth were not in great supply among the assembled guests; derisive sidelong glances were. I was nonetheless touched by the moment: father sharing a very special birthday with son. They'd remember it forever, provided they survived. Whether Orlando was actually tapping some secret source of sustenance, I didn't know. There was no proof, other than his well-chiseled physique. I wasn't sure I'd even hold it against Possuelo if he were slipping Orlando extra provisions on the sly. With my own birthday two days away, I couldn't help but think of my own boys, and what I'd be willing to do for them in similar circumstances.

The men packed up, waiting for the signal from Possuelo to move out. I looked around at the campsite as it emptied out: the desperate loneliness of the naked tent frames, stripped of their tarps, the barren benches circled around the fire that would soon be extinguished. We were leaving nothing behind we hadn't found here, or at least hadn't carved out of the forest. Still, there was plenty for the Arrow People to ponder: the tent frames, the benches, the stairway with its railing leading down to the river, the rickety platform of inch-thick sapling trunks built out over the water where we washed and bathed.

"Do you think the Arrow People will have a look around here after we leave?" I asked Possuelo.

"They'll be in here within ten minutes."

"Will they be nosing around, looking for clues about us, like we do at their camps?"

"Com certeza," he replied. "Most assuredly. You can bet on it."

"What do you suppose they're thinking?"

Possuelo fixed me with a look of dark foreboding, then said: "I imagine they're thinking that their enemies have arrived."

There was really only one reason our camp—or what we left behind of it—looked different from any of theirs: steel. Our freshly honed axes and machetes enabled us in minutes to transform the wilderness, as if by magic, into a small village, with lean-to, stairways, and furniture. Steel was precious. Without it, the same job would have taken days, weeks even. Which was why Possuelo turned next to Paulo Welker and directed him to leave a brand-new machete and a hunting knife as gifts for the Arrow People.

"It's not much," Possuelo said with a shrug. "One knife and one machete for eight or nine men. But they'll serve the purpose." I watched Paulo pull the sheathed blades from his knapsack and prop them on a log near the dying embers of the fire.

"If you just want to leave them alone," I asked, "why are you giving them this stuff? Aren't you just contaminating their society?" I was baiting Possuelo, but it was a legitimate question.

"The point is not to change the way they live," he said. "It's to demonstrate our peaceful intentions. A knife and a machete are not going to change their ecology."

An interesting choice of words: *change their ecology.* It was a novel idea, for me at least, the notion that people could *have* an ecology, in the same way they could have a way of life or a daily routine. It suggested that human beings were *a part* of the complex system of interactions among living organisms that made up an ecosystem, rather than *apart* from it or opposed to it, that people actually had a role in equilibrating that system, rather than destroying it. In fact, it was possible that significant stretches of the forest we'd been trekking through were "anthropogenic"—previously managed or altered in some way by humans.

But there was something more significant about Possuelo's approach: it broke with a five-hundred-year history of wooing, cajoling,

assuaging, subduing, or otherwise manipulating the aboriginal populations not only of the Amazon, but of the entire length and breadth
of the Americas. Conquistadors sought plunder; missionaries, the conversion of souls. Settlers wanted at their land, prospectors their gold.
Anthropologists sought to unravel their cosmologies and genealogies
and peer into what they imagined to be the distant origins of human
society. When not using force to bludgeon the natives, all used gifts
of seemingly magical provenance—metal, mirrors, clothing, beads—
to seduce them. Possuelo sought nothing, and in turn he gave little.
He was just passing through. He didn't want the locals to fret, didn't
want to uncover their secrets, didn't want to know much of anything
about them, except to know they were doing fine. And if they were
not, then he'd see what he could do about it. What he offered was
at once nothing and everything, something so huge and intangible
they'd never know he'd even given it to them—the chance to endure,
to survive another day, to replicate their way of life, a way of life that
had all but vanished from the rest of the planet.

He didn't know the ethnicity of the Arrow People, what language
they spoke, or what gods they worshipped. He didn't want to know.
That was the stuff of anthropology, and it could be gleaned only by
making contact, which was why he was so often at odds with its practitioners. "Once you make contact," he'd told me, "you begin the process of destroying their universe."

Only the year before, I'd visited isolated Yanomami villages in Venezuela's Upper Orinoco to gauge the lasting impact among the natives
of one anthropologist in particular. Michigan native Napoleon Chagnon claimed to have made several "first contacts" among Yanomami
villages, or *shabanos,* set deep in the Siapa highlands along the border
with Brazil, dating back to the 1960s. Chagnon became a rock-star
anthropologist with the 1968 publication of his groundbreaking ethnographic study, *Yanomamö: The Fierce People,* which became standard
reading on college syllabi. Chagnon had lived among the Yanomami
for months at a time, bedecking himself in war paint and feathers, taking hallucinogenic snuff with their shamans, insinuating himself into

their social fiber. He plied reluctant tribal informants with axes and machetes in exchange for the names of the *kamakari*—their deceased relatives—in order to construct the genealogies he needed for his research. It was taboo to utter the names of the dead, but Chagnon told the tribesmen: *"I will pay you for your sadness."*

The genealogies formed the basis for Chagnon's most controversial, neo-Darwinian assertion: that the most violent men tended to have the most offspring with the greatest number of women, thereby propagating their genes most successfully. Inhabiting a dog-eat-dog, Hobbesian world of black magic and perpetual internecine warfare, the Yanomami came to represent for Chagnon a virtually intact primitive society—"our contemporary ancestors," as he put it—that seemed to offer a glimpse into our deepest past, with dark implications for modern-day debates on the nature of humankind.

Those who took issue with Chagnon's pugilistic views of the Yanomami seemed to find a perfect post-Vietnam rejoinder in news that emerged from the Philippines in the early 1970s. A team of anthropologists and journalists reported the sensational "discovery" of a primitive tribe called the Tasaday, who were purported to inhabit a network of caves in the secluded forests of Mindanao. So docile were the Tasaday, the visitors gushed, that the tribesmen had no word for war, no concept of an enemy, nor any notion that their stone tools could be used as weapons. The world was desperate for such news. Soviet tanks had crushed the Prague Spring. American B-52s were carpet-bombing Indochina. The Tasaday seemed to offer reassurance, a story of human origins that painted us in essence as decent, benevolent creatures. The gentle Tasaday. Noble Savages. The peacenik's cavemen.

Chagnon's critics charged that his very presence among the Yanomami fomented the strife he claimed to observe—an anthropological variation on the Heisenberg uncertainty principle. Young Yanomami men willing to spill tribal secrets to Chagnon in exchange for machetes and other trade goods could accumulate unprecedented wealth and move directly into positions of power, upending a social contract that had bound their society together for thousands of years. By the time

I visited the Yanomami three decades later, they were zooming up and down the Orinoco and its tributaries in outboard-powered skiffs. Shotguns were rapidly replacing the bow and arrow as the weapon of choice among tribal hunters. Entire villages were relocating from the highlands to riparian mission posts in order to gain access to trade goods and remedies for deadly malaria outbreaks their own *shaporis* could not cure.

The younger men knew some Spanish, and they'd acquired a taste for Nike shoes, Ray-Ban sunglasses, and the red-and-black caps of the Chicago Bulls. So fevered was their quest for the White Man's stuff—and so widespread the conviction they'd been cynically exploited for years for the private gain of others—that Chagnon's old informant, now an aging headman, demanded nothing less than a brand-new outboard motor, preferably a Yamaha-40, as payment for an interview. Talk about changing their ecology!

The same story has played out with depressing familiarity every place on Earth where Western culture advances into the domain of age-old indigenous societies—in the Americas, Africa, the Arctic, Australia. The specifics may vary, but the central theme does not. In northeastern Australia, the introduction of steel axes by missionaries among Yir-Yoront aborigines led to the complete collapse of their ancient culture within a generation. Trade relations disrupted, taboos violated, myths shattered, age and gender roles overturned—such is the transformative power of our technology.

Our guns, our germs, and our steel. It was enough to make you think twice about leaving a single machete for the Arrow People.

CHAPTER 17

The Day of the *Maloca*

W E MOVED OUT INTO a gloomy morning, with glimpses of a milky white sky leaking through the canopy. Possuelo had instructed Paulo Welker to leave the gifts but seemed otherwise oblivious to the delicate situation in which we found ourselves. The only business taken up at the fireside convocation was Orlando's birthday. There had been no special instructions for the day, no reminders of how to respond to a possible ambush. Perhaps the old man was jaded. He'd been here before, on the knife edge of contact, and maybe he just took it for granted that everyone else had been, too. Now, ten minutes out of camp, my daily incantation behind me, I thought of saying something to him, specifically about Wilson and Alfredo: *Shouldn't we have made sure they were at the head of the column today?* They'd continued to lag behind on a daily basis, despite Possuelo's admonitions. Paulo Welker, it seemed, had also chosen to ignore orders to bring up the rear, which, in turn, rendered meaningless Possuelo's other command, for everyone to maintain visual contact along the entire length of the column.

It seemed to me that all those orders bore repeating. But who was I to say? I held my tongue, deferring to Possuelo's experience, figuring him to be a far better judge of what needed to be said or done, or what didn't. We traipsed across the level ground of the Jutaí's floodplain with Soldado and Txema leading the way, flailing into the underbrush. While the river twisted and turned in its convoluted course toward the main trunk of the Amazon, we pursued a straighter course dictated by

Possuelo's compass. The waterway receded from view as it meandered away from us, only to reappear twenty minutes later, as a bend brought it back toward us, a broad silvery sluice streaming light through the trees.

We emerged from the thicket onto a well-trodden footpath. Possuelo paused to check his compass. "Hmmm," he said. "It's going the same way we are. Let's follow it for a while." We'd spent weeks bushwhacking through near-impenetrable jungle, but this trail was remarkably straight and clear, like a superhighway by comparison. As we clipped along at double time, it was impossible to escape the sense that invisible eyes were upon us. Birds cried back and forth from the depths of the jungle. Soldado paused. "That's not a bird," he said ominously. "They're signaling to each other. They're watching us."

Within minutes, we came upon fresh footprints. The tracks were pressed deep into the soft red earth. They led away in the same direction we were going, roughly north by northeast, and disappeared around a distant bend. The steep walls of the impressions in the mud, and the long spaces between them, suggested the full stride of a runner bearing urgent news.

We continued, haunted by the uneasy feeling of unseen eyes upon us. Possuelo froze in his tracks. A freshly broken sapling dangled across the path before us, hanging by a shred of bark about four feet off the ground. It appeared as though someone had wrestled the young tree barehanded, finally managing to crack it before doubling it over the path. In itself, the makeshift gate could not halt a toddler, much less our column of three dozen well-armed men. Still, it bore a message—and a warning—that Possuelo instantly recognized.

"This is universal language in the jungle," he whispered. "It means 'Stay out. Go no farther.' We must be getting close to their village." He wheeled around and with a silent, dramatic wave, directed the column to veer off the path at a right angle into the dense undergrowth on our flanks. "This is as far as we'll go on their road," he said. "Soldado, mark our trail for the rest to follow."

We trudged on through boot-sucking mud, dodging branches that swarmed with fire ants, tunneling through the thicket. We reached the steep banks of a narrow black-water creek, where Possuelo called a halt to give stragglers time to catch up. Several of us hopped the creek and scampered partway up the far bank before dropping to the ground, facing the others across the ravine as they staggered in, two and three at a time, and collapsed under their loads. The creek was like hundreds of others we'd splashed through over the past three weeks. It was about eight feet across, shallow along its amber edges, where you could make out the sandy bottom, which was rippled like a washboard by the gentle current and eventually vanished in the depths of a swirling pool formed by a fallen log. One by one, we slid down the loose, dark earth, dipped our cups into the honey-colored water, and drank.

Possuelo took a seat on the forest floor straight across from me. A thin stream of blood trickled from a small gash below his knee. He'd been wearing the same pair of khaki shorts since the start of the trek, exposing his bare legs to all the scratches, insect bites, and lacerations the rainforest had to offer. Orlando brought him a cup of water.

"What did you make of the broken sapling?" Orlando asked, his weird German hat screwed backward atop his head. "Looked like whoever did it had nothing to cut it with."

"It was their way of communicating with us," said Possuelo, slapping a mosquito on his arm. "They don't want us anywhere near there. They must be very frightened. And we want to do exactly as they say." After all, frightened people can be the most dangerous: cornered, pressed to lash out.

As the minutes ticked by and Possuelo took a head count, it became clear something was amiss. We were short two men: Wilson and Alfredo. At first, we chalked it up to the usual foot-dragging; they'd show up soon enough.

But a full hour passed. Bawdy jokes and idle banter gave way to a tense silence, as Possuelo stole glances at his wristwatch with a deepening scowl that seemed to rival the gloom of the forest.

"Damn it!" he snarled. "These guys are holding us up! A total lack of discipline!" He turned to Welker and said: "Paulo, take Chico and

José and the other Kanamari and go find them." Nicolas left with
them, and I scrambled to catch up. But they'd gotten too much of a
head start. In a minute, I found myself alone, jungle pressing in on all
sides. I called out once. A second time. Nothing. The underbrush was
so thick I couldn't see my own feet when I looked down. I acquired
an instant appreciation for the Arrow People's practice of snapping
off *quebradas* to mark their trail. Another minute may have given me
the chance to overtake the rescue team, or, far more likely, to get completely lost. Still with some sense of where I'd come from, I chose to
turn back. I heaved a sigh of relief as Orlando and the other men came
into view along the embankment.

Another twenty minutes passed. Though it was approaching noon,
and we were only a few degrees off the equator, I'd begun to shiver in
my sweat-drenched fatigues. Where had the search party gone? Why
hadn't *they* come back? Had they met the same fate as Alfredo and
Wilson? Half the men on one side of the creek, half on the other, we
offered a shocking mirror image to each other from opposite sides of
the ravine: pale and haggard men, faces drawn in hunger, weary eyes
just now starting to register an incipient fear stirring within each of us.

"Tepi, Txema," said Possuelo at length. "Take five Matis and go see
what's going on." The Indians grabbed rifles and ammunition pouches
and vanished through a blur of foliage.

"If they actually see the—," I began to say, but Orlando cut me off.

"They won't see them," he said. "Even if they go all the way to the
maloca, they'll find it empty. Everyone will have fled into the forest."

"It's their system of security," Possuelo agreed. "They scatter into
the forest. There's no one in that *maloca* right now. We pose too great
a danger for them. They've been watching us. They've been just ahead
of us, watching everything."

It seemed Orlando had absorbed many lessons from his father,
both on this trip and on other forays. Possuelo scratched his beard
and stared blindly out into the forest at our flanks. "Think about it,"
Possuelo said. "Why do these Indians run from us? Why do they not
welcome us with open arms and kindness, as they did when the first

Europeans arrived? It's because contact with the white man has invariably meant ruin."

It was a point Possuelo had been hammering for a good twenty years. *"Today, isolated though they be, these people know the consequences of our advance,"* he wrote in the 1981 memo. *"Actions which may seem to us to be most benign and civilized are experienced by them as acts of aggression. Their hostility thus aroused, they become evermore resistant to contact."*

When Francisco Pizarro and the Spaniards first rode their horses into the Andes five hundred years ago, the bewildered Inca took them to be *viracochas*—immortal, godlike beings from another world. As recently as the 1930s, tribal highlanders in New Guinea thought the white Australians who came looking for gold in their streams were their own dead ancestors. The handful of Mashcos who survived the Fitzcarrald massacres and their descendants who remain in hiding to this day would appear to have no such illusions. As if the fear were embedded in their tribal DNA, their successors continued to shun contact with outsiders more than a century later. The same could be said for other isolated tribes as well, as though they'd developed a heightened suspicion of contact—refusing all gifts, spurning all overtures, fleeing deeper and deeper into the jungle. What would they do when they'd gone as far as they could go, when they felt they'd run out of room and could go no farther? Perhaps the Arrow People had just reached that point. True, the jungle around us was vast, but maybe we'd inadvertently pushed them into a corner. And now, with our force fragmented into four separate groups, the numeric superiority meant to dissuade them from launching an assault had evaporated.

There was rustling in the brush. Chico emerged, out of breath. He and the others had gone back to the point where we'd earlier veered off the Arrow People's path. It was there that they picked up the trail of Wilson and Alfredo. "It was easy to see their footprints," Chico panted. "They're wearing the Kachutes." He meant the tennis shoes that had been issued at the start of the expedition. Their tracks, he said, went straight past the makeshift barricade and kept right on going.

Either the two porters had missed the conspicuous blazes left by

Soldado to mark where we'd steered off the path, or they'd simply chosen to ignore them. Their footprints continued on, winding through
a huge *roça*—a jungle garden—sown with cane, cotton, manioc, and
plantains. "It was amazing," Chico said. "It was as big a *roça* as I've ever
seen." The tracks went onward, into the very center of a village—more
than a dozen thatched-roof houses set in a large clearing. The Kachute
imprints went straight through the village and out the far side, where
they disappeared into the woods. As Orlando had predicted, none of
the Arrow People remained in the village; they'd apparently all fled.
Possuelo had been listening quietly to Chico's account. Now he boiled
over. "What kind of shit is this?" he raged. "I can't fucking believe it!
I'll never work with any Kanamari—ever again!" With that, he grabbed
Soldado and said: "We're going to find out what's going on. Everyone
else stays here."

Perhaps it was the definitive manner in which Possuelo addressed
us, or maybe it was the fear of walking out into a shower of poison-
tipped arrows. But for whatever reason, I stayed right where I was
rather than follow them. I was cold, wet, and shivering in the forest
twilight, sharing an impending sense of doom with the others who
remained.

"Paulo Welker is anxious to make contact," Orlando sniped after
Soldado and his father had gone. "It will be great for his career, a
feather in his cap." No one said a word. "They could have gotten to
the *maloca,* found no one, and decided, *Let's just go a bit farther, see what
we find.*" His voice dripped with sarcasm. "But who knows how far you
can go before the arrows start flying?" Indeed, for all we knew, that
moment had already arrived.

We sat in apprehensive silence, damp and chilled, for what seemed
like another hour, though it was probably no more than twenty minutes. Time, beginning to play its tricks.

José now appeared through a tangle of lianas, brandishing a number of artifacts purloined from the village. Among them was a broken
arrow, its razor-sharp point fashioned from fire-hardened bamboo.
"We found these in their *maloca,*" he said. He also held up a filter,

made from interwoven fibers set in a wood frame about the size of a tambourine, used to make *caisuma* brew. Lastly, José showed us a two-foot-long section of a shattered blowgun, together with a blowgun dart, confirming Tepi's hunch that the Arrow People also possessed the *zarabatana*. *The more to kill us with,* I thought. "It's dangerous now," José concluded. "The Kanamaris' footprints just disappear on the far side of the *maloca*. And we've taken things that belong to them. We've invaded their homes. They have arrows, they have poison. They feel violated." And for all we knew, they had Wilson and Alfredo.

* * *

By the time Possuelo got to the Arrow People's *maloca*, his worst fears were confirmed. Not only were Wilson and Alfredo missing, but half the expedition was parading through the houses, picking things up to examine like they were curios in an exotic boutique. The huts were significantly larger than the Hobbit-size dwellings at the abandoned hunting camp. The peaks of their thatched roofs were ten feet high, and they sloped all the way down to the ground. Each could comfortably accommodate a family of five or six. Several campfires still smoldered near the center of the clearing, obviously abandoned in haste. The Arrow People must have bolted only minutes before our men first arrived. They'd left behind heaps of smoked meat—tapir, capybara, crocodile, peccary, sloth, and several different kinds of monkey. There were palm fruits, turtle eggs, and roasted caterpillars. Nine body-length ceremonial masks, made from long strips of envira bark, had been draped across the top of a thick log with the same care one might reserve for laying out a bridal dress. The heads of several wild boar were positioned atop a large stump, buzzing with flies. Clumps of recently trimmed, jet-black hair were scattered beneath another stump, along with splashes of *urucum*—annatto dye—the scarlet paint Amazonian tribes smear on faces and bodies for special occasions, like feasts and war. Inside several houses, blackened monkey heads were nestled in the rafters.

"Take nothing from this village!" Possuelo shouted. They were trespassing here, he knew, just as though they'd barged into a stranger's house. "Look here, Sydney!" Paulo Welker shouted from the entrance to one of the huts. He wanted him to see what José had mentioned to us: a large clay vat, brimming with curare, the sticky black poison that, when painted on the point of an arrow or dart, asphyxiates its victim within minutes by inducing paralysis. It had been concealed beneath a pile of leaves, evidently too cumbersome a burden to be carried on the fly. And something else—a pair of heavy, hand-carved wooden staffs. Each was nearly four feet long and tapered toward the bottom. Possuelo recognized immediately what they were: ax handles. The precious ax heads were gone, but they'd left the handles. Those could easily be replaced; the steel axes could not. How and where they'd acquired the axes was a mystery, but it became suddenly evident how the Indians had managed to clear such a wide breach in the forest cover. Scores of tree stumps littered the clearing. Most were no more than a foot or so in diameter, but there were a few kingpins—four feet thick—whose toppling made the whole settlement possible. Their weapons were gone, too. No bows, no quivers, only the fractured arrow and damaged blowpipe. And their hammocks—not a single one left in any of the houses. It looked like they were prepared to keep their distance, to sleep out in the forest if necessary, even abandon the village altogether if they had to. It most likely wouldn't have been the first time they'd had to run for their lives. It pained Possuelo to think of the families cowering in the nearby woods—the angst of men with families to protect, the desperation of women trying to hush children and babies. From where he stood in the center of the small village, he could smell them. It was the smell of wood smoke on human skin. And the smell of fear. The fear of being backed into a corner. That's when he understood it could come at any moment: a barrage of deadly arrows. The hair on the back of his neck stood on end. Indeed, the fear was mutual.

The fate of the entire expedition and especially that of Wilson and Alfredo—if they were still alive—hinged on calming things down. The Marubo and Matis called out into the forest: *Please don't kill our friends with your arrows!* Possuelo was going to have to get everyone out of the village. But first, he looked around for signs of struggle, any clue that might reveal the whereabouts of the wayward Kanamari. Strange, he thought, that neither of them had fired his rifle to call for help. Ivan Arapá led Possuelo down the path on the far side of the *maloca*, pointing to the spot where the Kachute footprints vanished. It was uncanny. The footprints were there, and then they were gone. No skid marks, no indication of dragging feet. It was as though they'd been yanked straight off the trail and bundled into the woods. He thought of their families back in Massapê, and the promise he'd made to their mothers to bring them home safely. How was he going to explain himself to them? What was more, his entire mission hung in the balance. All it would take was an incident like this for enemies everywhere to seize the initiative: *What is it with these naked savages and their bows and arrows, anyway? Time to civilize them, put clothes on them, get them out of the way. Make their lands produce.*

"Go back to where the others are," Possuelo told Paulo Welker. "It looks like the Kanamari have been killed. Maybe they've been captured. Go back and warn the others. Tell them to prepare for an attack. Who knows what could happen at this point. I'll be right behind you."

* * *

Paulo Welker now approached through the foliage, looking gaunt and ghostly, his fatigues hanging like oversize sacks off his frame. He brought fresh orders from Possuelo: Everyone move to the far side of the creek, clear the brush, form a defensive perimeter. A defensive perimeter? With visibility reduced to near zero by the monochrome of greens and browns surrounding us, the notion of a defensive position was absurd, even laughable. Except no one was laughing. I pictured the *flecheiros* advancing tree by tree, their barefoot steps drowned out by the pounding of my heart, pulling within striking distance before we could even know what hit us.

"Anyone who thinks this is a joke, take a look at these things we brought from the village," Paulo Welker said. He took the broken arrow from José and held it up for all to see. "And they have lots and lots of curare." This time, I took more notice of the arrow's flat, barbed point. It was indeed stained black with the poison. Whether they would actually have used it on us would have been a matter of some debate, had there been time for such trifles. Applied to the tip of a dart or arrow, the potent asphyxiant makes even a superficial graze fatal, sufficient to send a monkey tumbling from the treetops, or to drop a peccary dashing in full flight through the woods. When it enters the bloodstream, the poison's active chemical, d-tubocurarine, blocks the transmission of nerve impulses to the muscle, precipitating paralysis and halting the victim's ability to draw breath. Survival would have depended on an emergency tracheotomy followed by as much as three hours of artificial respiration until the poison's effect subsided. Under current conditions, in the middle of the jungle, I'd sooner have died from the curare itself. But beyond the fearsome and perhaps fanciful tales propagated by early Amazonian explorers about the so-called "flying death," there is little in the historical record to document the use of curare in warfare. That did not mean it hadn't been put to such use. Nor did it mean that the Arrow People wouldn't resort to it now if they felt they had to; they may have left that vat behind in the village, but the arrows they took with them into the forest could well have been treated with it already.

Members of the other search teams trickled back through the gap in the underbrush, everyone commenting on the fate of the missing Kanamari and what they'd seen in the village: the smoking fires, the mind-boggling assortment of meats, the masks draped on the log, the traces of red *urucum* paint. All agreed the Arrow People must have been preparing a feast of some kind. "Maybe a war party," Paulo Welker quipped darkly, "for us."

"This is serious," said Soldado, just now returning with Possuelo. *Coisa seria* was how he put it. A serious matter. It was especially unnerving to hear the unflappable Soldado make such pronouncements. His exhausted eyes had lost all their sparkle. They may as well have been peering out from the sockets of a bare skull, so spent was his flesh. Most disturbing, he said, was the way the tracks of Alfredo and Wilson had just vanished. One step they were there, the next they were gone.

Ivan Arapá stepped forward to demonstrate, covering his mouth with one hand and drawing an imaginary vine around his neck with the other, how the *flecheiros* could have grabbed them from behind, gagged them, and yanked them straight off their feet into the undergrowth. He didn't speak a word, but he didn't need to; the pantomime said it all.

"Either they've killed our men or they've taken them prisoner," Possuelo said, nodding. He was clearly shaken. He surveyed the closed jungle around us and saw a death trap. If the Arrow People had killed the two Kanamari, they could already be moving to encircle us for an all-out attack, before we could avenge their deaths. Revenge would have been the last thing on our minds, but they would have had every reason to expect it.

"We have to get out of here," Possuelo said. "Maybe the Indians will let them go. But we can't wait here for them. We'll move to more advantageous terrain and wait. We'll pitch camp near the river, see if they appear. Anyone have a better idea?" It was the first time in five weeks that I'd heard Possuelo solicit advice from anyone. No one had any. He laid a hand on Márcio Kanamari's shoulder. Tears welled in his eyes. "We had six Kanamari, and now we have four," Possuelo said. "And I am very, very sad." Márcio hung his head, saying nothing. Then suddenly snapping to, as if from a trance, Possuelo barked: "Let's get out of here—now!"

We rose to our feet, hoisted our loads, and ran. The jungle jerked past in a blur, sunlight fading in and out as we raced across the forest floor. Not a word was spoken. Our exotic fact-finding mission suddenly had become a run for our lives, the hunters now the hunted. We stumbled over roots, ripped through overhanging branches, anything to dodge the potential line of sight of an Indian taking aim with an arrow—poison-tipped or otherwise.

No one knows for sure if the bow and arrow migrated out of Africa with the first Homo sapiens, making it a weapon universal to our species, or if so-called "projectile-point technology" later developed on separate continents, as human beings fanned out across the globe. Scholars have long theorized that it may have developed first on the steppes of Central Asia and spread east and west from there. The archaeological record is unclear, with arrowheads appearing deep in the striated layers of excavation sites around the world, then disappearing, only to reappear in subsequent epochs. Few cultures seem to have developed without it. But if the use of bow and arrow was not entirely universal to the human condition, it was uniquely human. The use of pointed projectiles gave our forebears the upper hand to push aside other hominids, like the Neanderthal, and it greatly expanded the number of animals they could kill. It allowed our ancestors to enter new and unfamiliar habitats—deserts, tundras, mountains, and plains—and to emerge as the "apex predator" on top of the food chain. The bow-launched arrow was, in short, a game-changer with huge consequences for our species.

Projectile-point technology was particularly well suited for human survival in the tightly closed forests of the Amazon, even more so in consort with the various admixtures tribal herbalists had discovered for paralyzing prey or bleeding them to death: blowguns for taking vertical aim at canopy birds and monkeys, arrows for shooting sideways through the trees at ambulatory, four-legged targets. And two-legged ones as well. Arrows may have been no match for the repeating rifles in the village clearings and along the beaches where the rubber bosses' armies struck. But gunmen who pursued fleeing Indians into the forest soon found themselves enveloped in a terrifying world of moving shadows where they did not belong, picked off silently, one at a time, by an enemy they could not see and could not hear. Small wonder it's been the impulse of whites on every frontier to level the forest.

Chests heaving, hearts thumping, we plunged through maddening tangles of thicket. We crossed a succession of streams, some tight and shallow, others wide and deep, requiring bridges to ford. At one creek, a slippery log angled up from water level to the top of the far bank, about twelve feet high. Orlando lost his footing as he started across. He let out a grunt and fell into waist-deep water. Still on his feet, he staggered backward past me and slammed full force into the bank, unleashing an avalanche of loose dirt that poured onto his head and shoulders and down the open neck of his shirt. He fixed me with a stunned, wide-eyed stare, and I looked down, half expecting to find an arrow drilled into his gut. He collected himself without saying a word and waded through the water to the other side.

We shuffled through a carpet of brown, desiccated leaves, kicking up a rhythmic *shuh-shuh, shuh-shuh* as we went. And then, Nicolas let out a gasp and tumbled to the ground in front of me. *"Merde!"* He'd stepped in a well-concealed rodent's burrow. Clutching his knee, he limped on, but a short while later, we had to stop. He was trembling. I laid him down on his back, gave him some water to drink. As we waited, sprawled in the leaves, word spread through the ranks that telltale Kachute footprints had been sighted along the river. Possuelo dispatched a search party of Matis to look around, but they soon returned empty-handed. The tracks doubled back on top of each other, and there seemed to be some question as to whether they'd been left by our own group, by Wilson and Alfredo, or by someone else entirely. Whoever was making those tracks, they were making them fast.

"Soldado," called Possuelo. "Go after them. If you can't catch up, fire your rifle to signal them." The gunfire could have further incited the Arrow People, but under the circumstances, it was a risk Possuelo was willing to take. He clapped his hands together and pointed his face up into the light now streaming down through the canopy, as if beseeching God.

"The *flecheiros* could have stripped their clothing after killing Wilson and Alfredo," Chico smirked darkly. "They could have taken off their stuff and put the shoes on. It would be something new for them, something to try out." The suggestion was plausible enough to go unchallenged; no one said a thing. From the distance came the muffled blast of a shotgun. Then another. Soldado signaling to our lost comrades. "If ever there was a time I felt like caning someone, it would be right now," Possuelo said. "Rondon used to do that, flog men when they disobeyed. It was later banned."

Nicolas had stopped shaking. He was feeling well enough to resume the march, which we did. On a bluff overlooking the river, Possuelo shouted: "We'll stop here for the night!" Then word filtered in that Soldado had indeed found Alfredo and Wilson, but uncertainty lingered. Where were they? Why was it taking them so long? Most of the encampment's infrastructure was already installed before Soldado appeared through the trees, followed by an apologetic-looking Alfredo, head bowed. Wilson brought up the rear, his loping step and cheery smile betraying no trace of contrition or remorse. Possuelo glowered, hands on hips, but otherwise said nothing. He was clearly far more relieved than angry. But what I noticed right away, and Nicolas must have, too, was that they were carrying only their rifles. Their backpacks—*our* backpacks—were missing. It seemed impolitic to ask, but Alfredo was carrying all my field notes in that bag. And the two hundred rolls of film Nicolas had shot so far on the journey were in the knapsack in Wilson's care.

Standing with eyes downcast before Possuelo, like schoolboys called to a reckoning with the principal, they gave a very sketchy account in barely audible half-sentences. Apparently they'd come to wonder if the Arrow People weren't some long-lost relatives, separated from the Kanamari in the upheaval of distant times. Bringing up the tail end of the column, they decided to breach the *flecheiro* roadblock and head for the village. The first inkling of trouble came in the *roça*. They beheld its size, the sheer diversity of crops. It wasn't like the gardens their people tended. When they reached the village, they heard the Arrow People shouting from the forest. They panicked. It suddenly dawned on them that scores of arrows could be pointed straight at their chests. Spooked and lost, they lurched down the trail and flung themselves headfirst into the brush to throw off any would-be pursuers. The maneuver certainly fooled our trackers. Once off the path, they ditched the backpacks and took off running.

"They thought they were being chased by the *flecheiros*," Soldado laughed. "When I shot in the air, they finally realized who it was."

"What about our bags?" Nicolas finally brought himself to ask. "I've got very important stuff in there. All my film. If it's lost, we'll be in real trouble."

"Big trouble," I seconded.

"We hid them," Alfredo said. "We covered them with leaves. We get tomorrow."

"We'll pick up the bags tomorrow," Possuelo agreed. It may have seemed coldhearted to be asking about our stuff only moments after Wilson and Alfredo had returned from the dead, and in a way, it was. But if all our film and notes from the previous five weeks were missing, we didn't have a story. The entire ordeal would have been for naught. Still weeks from nowhere, we'd be condemned to finish out the trip with no prospect of getting published upon our return. The thought of our things sitting unattended overnight in the jungle, not far from the Arrow People's *maloca*, was almost too much to bear. I had visions of the Indians rifling through our packs, stripping film from their canisters, trying to decipher the scribblings in my notebooks. But there was nothing to be done about it for now. At least we were all still alive. And I had everything I needed for the night: hammock, a change of clothes, my flashlight.

The call went out a short while later for everyone to assemble at the main campfire, and we made our way down. Smoke wafted up through the trees. Fish sizzled on skewers. Water had begun to boil in the cauldrons suspended over the blaze. Possuelo stood, back to the fire, in khaki shirt and shorts. I couldn't help but notice how much thinner he'd become since the start of the journey. Still, compared with many of the slouching skeletons gathered around him, he retained a solid build and astonishing vitality.

"I'd say to our Kanamari friends that you were born again today," he began. "The Arrow People could have killed you. They could have run you through with their arrows." He fixed his stare on Alfredo and Wilson. "We'll never know exactly how close you were to dying today, but I can assure you it was close."

A log snapped in the fire, raising a spray of sparks. Possuelo looked around at the circle of faces. "We're not here to see them or to get to know them, or to call to them," he said of the Arrow People. He was speaking in that slow, clear diction he used in moments like this. "We're here to see if they use this land. We're here to make sure loggers, fishermen, and hunters don't come in here. I'm here to register their location and to take that information back to Brasília. So that no one will ever enter here again—ever!"

Silence fell over the gathering, punctuated by the crackling fire and the pulsing song of insects. Possuelo launched into a recounting of the day's extraordinary events. The foray had amounted to a flagrant violation of his orders. So too had the removal of certain artifacts from the *maloca*, even the broken ones. He didn't mention Paulo Welker by name; he didn't need to. It was tantamount to looting, Possuelo said, and the Arrow People would have felt doubly violated because of it—first by our invasion of their village, and then by the theft of their belongings.

Possuelo had to know that his career could have come to an abrupt and ignominious end today; a violent incident in the village could have erased a lifetime of toil, and even beyond that, left his legacy in tatters. Perhaps that was why he was so clearly elated as he stood there before us at the edge of the campfire, a man in the autumn of his life with what amounted to a new lease on it. Besides, the near-disaster had generated a wealth of information, all of it positive, that would otherwise have remained unknown.

"Here the Arrow People are living well," he said. "You could see it in the village. They hunt, they fish, they grow food. They must be healthy. Their babies are probably fat; their mothers must have lots of milk. They have feasts. They are happy. They don't ask anything from the white man. They don't need us!"

Some of the things the men had observed raised more questions than they answered. How had the Arrow People come to cultivate sugarcane and bananas—two crops that originated in South Asia and had been brought to the New World by Europeans? Early explorers had made similar discoveries, astonished to find nonnative species thriving in the gardens of isolated Indians. The plants had been traded from tribe to tribe, it turned out, adopted as staples in remote areas never seen by outsiders. The Arrow People likewise could have acquired them from other groups, perhaps generations ago. Or they could have raided the gardens of settlers in more recent times. Either way, for Possuelo, the crops signaled the depth of their resourcefulness.

The equating of primitive culture with backwardness has been so ingrained in the popular mind that even so-called "civilized" Indians on the lowest, most marginal rungs of society invariably believe themselves to be superior to their isolated brethren who remain in the bush. But Possuelo was calling that whole construct into question. The Arrow People were in no way inferior to any tribe. On the contrary! Their near-complete independence from the white man's world was to be admired, even emulated.

"You saw for yourselves, the Indian doesn't need the white man to live," he went on. "He knows how to make arrows, blowguns, ceramics, curare. He has everything he needs to live well. Once the white man enters, Indians forget how to do things their way, the old way."

The day's events had proven to be a vindication of Possuelo's policy, highlighting the inextricable link in his view between pristine habitat and uncontacted tribes. They went together, hand in hand. What enabled tribes to prosper in isolation from the global economy was a healthy and intact environment from which they derived their livelihood. In protecting the isolated tribes, as Possuelo had said, he was protecting enormous stretches of primeval forest.

It took me a few moments to process the significance of what had happened.

I couldn't shake a vague sense of disappointment that there hadn't been more, that we hadn't seen the Arrow People, that we hadn't— dare I say it?—made contact. But Possuelo's sense of elation was as contagious as the diseases we could have passed on to the tribe. For that very reason, contact would have amounted to a colossal failure, ushering in the demise of the people we were there to save. We had remained true to the mission. Flirting with disaster, we had triumphed.

Behind Possuelo, the last traces of daylight had drained from the sky. Luminescent moths zipped through the trees, like miniature space vehicles navigating the shadowy spires of a futuristic Ridley Scott dystopia. The frogs began their spooky evening chorus.

"Our work here is beautiful, because they don't even know we're here to help them," Possuelo said. "The best thing we can do is to stay out of their lives." He stared into the fire. We all stared into the fire. "Now we're going to continue our work and continue our journey. We're all going to get out of here alive."

Above: Sydney Possuelo

Right: Kanamari child, Itaquaí River

Below: Expedition boats moving up the Itaquaí River

Above: After the big boats turn back, the expedition continues in shallow-draft skiffs

Below: Members of the Alípio Bandeira Expedition *(author bottom row, far left)*

Above: Caiman awaits butchering in Kanamari village

Right: Kanamari returning from the hunt *(Márcio center, Wilson at right)*

Below: FUNAI riverboat pilot Adelson Pereira Brás

Matis scout Ivan Arapá

Left: Matis scout Kwini Marubo

Below: Marubo scouts Adelino *(left)* and Alcino *(right)*

Above: Soldado

Right: Matis scout Txema

Matis scout Kwini
Montac

Above left: Alfredo Kanamari
with piranhas

Above right: Wilson Kanamari
with a red-tail catfish

Right: Cooks Mauro Gomes
(left) and Paulo Souza *(right)*

Possuelo and Orlando
plotting coordinates
for the expedition

Tepi and Soldado, with tumpline head strap, prepare to move out

Left: Hobbit's table: mushrooms filled to the brim like champagne flutes

Below: Matis scout Ivan Waça before crossing a stream on a chopped-down tree

Raimundo *(left)* and Soldado *(right)* with monkeys for dinner

Right: Typical jungle bivouac

Below: The author fording a stream in the Javari Valley Indigenous Reserve

Left: Ivan Arapá discovers a tapir jaw left in a tree cleft by the Arrow People

Below: Binã *(left)* and Tepi Matis *(right)* with a ceramic pot left by the Arrow People

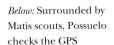

Below: Surrounded by Matis scouts, Possuelo checks the GPS

Above: A primitive canoe belonging to the Arrow People

Left: The main camp

Left: The author's Brazilian jungle boots

Opposite: Tepi at work on the Matis canoe

Kwini Marubo
fans fire
beneath the
canoe

Prying open
the hull while
wood is hot

Men haul the
canoe from
"shipyard" to
river

Right:
Canoes
newly
launched
on the
Jutaí River

Left: Matis
canoe with
thatched canopy

Above: Possuelo
aboard the Matis
canoe

Left: Canoes
move downriver
in early-morning
light

Left: Kwini Marubo with a boar's head

Below: Soldado *(left)* and Raimundo *(right)* with pirarucu

Below: Photographer Nicolas Reynard on the bow of the Matis canoe

Right: Tsohom Djapá tribesman recently contacted by Kanamari Indians

Below: The gold dredge *Gabriel,* seized by the expedition on the Jutaí River

Below: Kanamari village on the Jutaí River

Amazon sunset

Wallace interviews Sydney Possuelo

PART III

The Imperative to Survive

CHAPTER 18

Reprovisioned

T HE NEAR-ENCOUNTER in the village had convinced Possuelo of the need to put as much distance as possible between us and the Arrow People, as quickly as possible. He wanted them to understand that we were just passing through, with no intention of sticking around. A three-day forced march ensued. On the first day, Alfredo and Wilson led us straight to the backpacks. Luckily, they were still there, though so ill-concealed—with a single palm frond draped over each—it was a wonder they were. On the afternoon of the next day, we came across unsettling evidence that the Arrow People were not only following us, but perhaps had even leapfrogged ahead of us. Looking down through low-hanging branches, we sighted a primitive canoe moored along the riverbank. The *coshu* was fashioned from three hollow *paxiuba* trunks lashed together at bow and stern with sturdy vine. The multiple trunks seemed to provide balance, as well as room for a decent-size contingent. It was similar to a craft Korubo warriors had reportedly used recently to cross a river to attack a rival tribe.

I went down to the water's edge for a closer look. The palm trunks were about eight feet long and crudely split open along the top to create the multiple hulls. The vertical poles that pinned the craft to the bank, Possuelo said, were also the means to propel it. The canoe's pilot would stand, using the long shaft to push off the river bottom. Why the Arrow People would have no paddles was a mystery. They seemed to have the steel to carve them. Perhaps it was a question of know-how;

if they'd never seen one, the idea of making a paddle might not have occurred to them. From the looks of it, the canoe had been moored very recently, earlier in the day, maybe the day before. There could be little doubt about it: they had to know we'd be coming this way, too.

Of greater concern, Possuelo said, was the location of three more *malocas* along a creek that joined the Jutaí farther downriver, on the opposite bank. We'd eventually have to pass through a tight constriction there, within easy range of the Arrow People's projectiles. In fact, we wouldn't really be clear of their territory—and a potential ambush—until we'd made it through that last passage in our own canoes, a still-distant prospect.

The *flecheiros* were hardly our only worry. The vegetation was as dense as any we'd seen. The men were sick, dispirited. Soldado continued at the front of the column but barely had the strength to slash forward into the thicket. At one moment, he suddenly jumped back. *"Cobra!"* he cried out. We pressed in for a look. A thick bushmaster, one of the Amazon's deadliest snakes, was coiled beneath a branch only a few feet in front of us. "Orlando, shoot it!" Possuelo shouted. Orlando shouldered his .22 and took aim. The occasion really called for a shotgun, but Possuelo seemed intent on giving Orlando the honors. "Make sure you hit its head!" father instructed son. *KUH!* Orlando's rifle cracked. He missed. Now the snake's tail was shaking furiously, like a black angry flame. The bushmaster had no rattle, but its sibilance could be heard just the same, its tail vibrating against the brush. Orlando took a second shot. Missed again. Wide-eyed, Possuelo looked about, seized a dead branch, and brought it down on the viper. On the upswing, the stick got caught in the overhanging branches. Possuelo ripped it free and flailed with wild abandon. At last, he subdued the snake with a bone-crunching coup de grâce, driving the blunt end of the pole into its triangular head.

That final day of the march had a last test in store for us—a slippery log bridge stretching across a major *igarapé* feeding the Jutaí. We were nearly at the creek's mouth, making it all the wider—nearly fifty feet across to the far side. As had become standard operating procedure,

Soldado and Txema went across first to clear the way. They spread
three long balancing poles out at equidistant intervals along the span.
A separate tree grew out from the near bank at a twisted angle and
nestled low alongside our bridge. It looked like it might provide some
extra balance on the initial stretch, until you could find your footing
and move across. Possuelo, just ahead of Nicolas and me, bent down to
lay his hand on that support and yanked it back immediately. *"Porra!"*
he cursed. It was covered with vicious red ants.

"You thought you were just having to cross a bridge," Nicolas said,
turning to me with a slightly manic laugh. He seemed to have fully
recovered from the tumble he'd taken a few days back. "But no, it's
also covered with ants! After this, you'll make a great contestant for—
what's the name of the show—*Survivor?*" By the time I'd reached the
other side, I was a trembling mess. There had been nearly two dozen
equally harrowing bridge crossings in the past three weeks. But it was
the last we'd have to endure. An hour later, as we crouched in heavy
foliage overlooking the river, Possuelo called out: "Clear the brush!
We're making camp here!"

As Possuelo had envisioned from the beginning, the time had come
to build the canoes that would take us from the wilderness. We would
do it here, in the place we came to call the "main camp," a pivotal location that marked the beginning of the expedition's next phase. The
trek was over. And none too soon. The men had grown increasingly
restive. Raimundo and the other *riberinhos* had retreated into a small,
sullen clique. Any sparkle had long since drained from his smoldering
eyes. If he or any of the others had possessed the energy or the daring,
or if they'd been unified enough to pull it off, conditions would have
been ripe for rebellion. Perhaps if the eye-rolling Francisco had still
been with us. Good thing he wasn't.

The axes and machetes rang out; the underbrush was cleared away
and hauled down the embankment. Huge trees fell. The men attacked
the forest with newly found vigor. Soon a long swath along the river
was swept clear of brush. Then the men cleared the banks, hacking
apart the fallen trees. They followed the huge branches out into the

river. Submerged to their armpits and even up to their necks, the men pushed the foliage out from shore. Entire trees were cast adrift. Huge clumps of leafy vegetation floated out into midstream. Like toy boats launched on the current, they were swept downriver and around a bend, inexorably pulled toward the mighty Amazon, the same course we were to follow in the days ahead.

As trees fell along the bank, powerful rays of afternoon sunlight flooded in, bathing us in a splendor and warmth we hadn't experienced in weeks. Billowing clouds caught the pink light as the sun began to fade. I stood atop the bank marveling at the otherworldly hue of the twilight. I fought back the urge to cry. It was overwhelming. After all the hardships we'd endured and the dangers we'd faced, we'd made it through! Everyone was alive, no serious injuries, all members of the expedition accounted for. It was truly extraordinary.

The euphoria did not last long. Between Possuelo's foul moods and the ongoing perils we faced, morale rapidly evaporated amid a complete sense of isolation. Perhaps, too, it was the release from the intense pressures of the march. As awful as the conditions on the trek had been, the daily demands had kept everyone focused. Besides, the column's single-file configuration had been ideal for keeping a distance from whomever anyone wished to avoid. For most, that was Possuelo. Now, there was no escape.

*   *   *

"Base, base, base. Expedicão, cambio!" Paulo Welker was trying to reach the base in Tabatinga on the two-way radio. "Expedition to base, expedition to base, over!" All around him, men were continuing to make improvements to the campsite. This would be different from the other bivouacs, more permanent, since it was anticipated we'd be here up to two weeks. The ground throughout the entire camp was swept clear. All but the largest trees were uprooted or chopped down. The remaining trunks shot upward like giant uprights supporting an enormous ceiling high overhead.

The encampment stretched the length of a football field along the Jutaí's right bank, extending a hundred feet back into the forest. Our hammocks occupied a semicircular formation along that far perimeter. With forked stakes pounded in the ground and a square frame of saplings, Chico and Amarildo erected a small table for me beneath the shelter of my tarp. Now that we'd reached the end of the trek, Alfredo had made himself scarce, the Kanamari taking up a spot on the very opposite end of the campsite. I decided I wouldn't ask him to do anything unless I absolutely needed it. For the first time in three weeks, I spread out the contents of my bags—cameras, notebooks, film, first-aid kit, clothing.

The entire site was bustling. Log benches were installed around the main campfire, enough to accommodate the entire expedition. A rounded, palm-thatched shelter that resembled a huge turkey tail went up over the fire pit. The men constructed a command post—a thatch-roofed lean-to with a solid, rough-hewn table and benches set within it—that overlooked the river. Paulo Welker was seated there now, barking into the radio mike, trying to raise the base across nearly two hundred miles of unbroken jungle: "Expedition to base, expedition to base, over!" The radio's wire antenna had been strung to the top of a thirty-foot pole. The device had been virtually useless for the past three weeks. Now, with the wide break in the forest cover afforded by the Jutaí, it was hoped we could establish a tenuous connection to the control post and the FUNAI base in Tabatinga.

Possuelo hovered nearby, barking orders. He cut a laughable figure, stripped to his tight-fitting Speedo, wild tufts of hair sprouting from his temples. But no one was laughing. It should have been a joyous occasion, the weight of the trek lifted from our shoulders. But Possuelo was in a foul mood, and everyone skulked about on tenterhooks. Even those who had nothing to do tried to look busy, lest their apparent lassitude provoke Possuelo's ire.

"Everyone, listen up!" Possuelo shouted. "We've got an important announcement!" My ears pricked up. *Ah,* I thought, *here's where we get the inspirational speech, reflecting on where we've been and what still lies ahead. Now's when he lays out the plan for the next phase of the journey.* We gathered around.

"We have two latrine areas," he began. He pointed into the woods at either end of the clearing. "We can't have people taking a piss all over the place. It will draw all kinds of vermin." Before, when we were on the move each morning, it hadn't really mattered. But Possuelo wasn't content just to leave it there. "If I catch anyone taking a piss anywhere near the camp, I will personally and publicly humiliate him! Is that clear?" It felt like we were in a kindergarten with an abusive teacher trolling the aisle looking for knuckles to rap. We'd have laughed in his face had there been a means of escape, some boat or plane to hop: *Oh yeah? Well, fuck you! I'm outta here!* But there was no way out.

Nor was it possible to escape the impression that we'd awoken from one bad dream only to find ourselves in another even worse, imprisoned in a penal colony of Franz Kafka's making. That we were in the midst of constructing semipermanent installations backed up against the high jungle wall lent credence to the idea. Amid the thatched structures stood a jagged stump where a large tree had been taken down. It did not take an excessively fertile imagination to picture it as a whipping post where Possuelo intended to dispense justice.

Given our location, only three days' hike from the Arrow People's *maloca,* I had also expected Possuelo to say something about our security. After all, the *flecheiros* could still be massing forces for an attack. It was likely they had either followed us along on this side of the river or had shadowed us from the far side. Alcino Marubo even reported finding fresh footprints on a beach near the camp. More likely than not, they were watching our every move.

We needed to get out of there as quickly as possible. But we were too exhausted to continue marching and too far upriver for a boat of any size to extricate us. The summer dry season—or *verão*—was well into its second month. The Jutaí's waters were dropping by a few inches a day. There was a chance we could be stranded by the diminishing waters. Even if we weren't, the longer it took to build the canoes, the farther downstream we'd have to paddle before even a shallow-draft boat could reach us.

Possuelo put out a call for ax heads. Though a few axes had been used on a daily basis through the trek, most had been carried without handles in the bottom of backpacks. Six of them found their way to a tarp spread out before Possuelo, together with an equal number of adzes. Chico and José set to work, carving long handles for the tools.

Such a sizable inventory of the magical tools could yet prove to be an irresistible lure for the Arrow People. "They get their hands on our steel," Possuelo said, "and they'd be happy for the rest of their lives." And we could have gotten stuck there for the rest of ours. To see that that didn't happen, a rack was constructed for the equipment near the main campfire. "All the axes and adzes will be returned to the rack at the end of the day!" barked Possuelo. "No exceptions."

Back at the command post, Possuelo and Welker did some quick arithmetic and sketched some diagrams. To transport thirty-four men and all our gear, Possuelo figured, we would require two canoes, each between fifty and sixty feet long. "We'll divide the men in two teams," Possuelo said. "All the Matis and the Marubo on one team, the Kanamari and *riberinhos* on the other." The first would be commanded by Txema, the other by Soldado. "Let's have a race to see which side builds the best canoe the fastest. Where's Soldado?" His eyes searched the clearing. "Soldado! Txema! Come here!"

Each team would scout the forest for a suitable tree, then report back. "Nothing too valuable," Possuelo warned. "Something decent, but not precious. And make sure your trees aren't too far from the water. We don't want to have to build a five-mile highway to get the canoe to the river. Now, grab some men and get going!"

Possuelo turned to Paulo Welker and said: "Let's find out what we have left for provisions." There was a cold edge to his voice. Nicolas pulled me aside. "He's pissed off at Paulo for taking the things from the village," he whispered. "You know—the arrow tip and blowgun. Sydney didn't want anyone taking anything from the houses." To try to smooth things over with the Arrow People, Nicolas said, Possuelo had left another batch of aluminum pots behind, perched on the same log where the bark masks had been draped.

Paulo Welker spread out on a single tarp all that remained of our dried foodstuffs. It made for a pitiful sight: six leaking bags of coffee, eight kilos of manioc flour, twelve packs of spaghetti, their brittle cellophane bags cracked open. It was time to order an airdrop.

When Paulo Welker finally got through to base on the radio, he relayed the list of provisions we would need: sugar, salt, margarine, tobacco, beans, rice, farinha, powdered milk. *Yes!* I thought. Black coffee had gotten almost too monotonous to drink. So had the tepid river water. "Sydney," I asked, "would it be possible to include a bunch of powdered Kool-Aid packets? I'd be happy to pay for it."

Possuelo snatched the mike away from Welker and relayed our coordinates. The drop was arranged for the following afternoon. Kool-Aid would be included. Having been reduced to spectral waifs, we should have found the prospect of an imminent airdrop nothing short of miraculous. And in a way, we did. But we were soon to find out that this evident salvation was also a curse; once we were flush with victuals and supplies, any sense of urgency Possuelo might have had to get us home would evaporate.

"Positivo, positivo!" he bellowed into the mike. "That's correct, enough of everything to last us six weeks." Six weeks? It was now just the end of July. That meant we couldn't hope to reach Tabatinga before mid-September! Summer was already going to be completely shot, that I knew. But now, it seemed, the boys would start the new school year without me. And I wouldn't be present for any of the important choices Sarah was going to have to make about where she was going to work and live, about what would happen with us. I didn't even know if there would be an *us*. The days and weeks seemed to stretch out into an indefinite future, like a mirage constantly fleeing toward an unattainable horizon.

Having settled along the bank of a major river in lowland jungle, we were once again beset by a catalog of insects: ants, fleas, flies, mosquitoes, wasps, the insatiable *piums*. My hammock was the only sanctuary from the onslaught. Yet its impregnability was increasingly in doubt. Our gear had been pushed beyond the limits of its intended use. Everything was falling apart. I'd been lucky the jungle boots had made it through the trek, just barely. The soles were separating from the tops; my orthotics had fallen to pieces. My backpack was in tatters, and my camera bag was reduced to shredded canvas. Most distressing, the hammock was showing signs of serious fatigue, with a long tear spreading along the bottom, just parallel to the Velcro trapdoor. I'd taken to covering the rip with a poncho to keep the insects at bay. It was only a matter of time before the hammock gave out altogether.

The rainy season was long behind us, but cloudbursts still descended daily, often with little warning. Thunder grumbled, and suddenly the sky would go black as pitch with lightning flashing all around. Wind ripped through camp. Palm shards hurdled through the air. "Scotch, watch out for falling trees!" yelled Mauro as the forest churned, trees swaying wildly. I frantically hoisted my hammock up and ducked my head beneath the tarp. Lightning cracked over the river with a pulsing, ghostly flash, like a high-tension line gone haywire. The rain beat down with a deafening roar, the leaves of the forest suddenly joining in an enormous percussion ensemble, a million drumheads rumbling in counterpoint to crashing cymbals of lightning. Through the downpour, I could barely make out Mauro scarcely fifteen feet away, clutching his shelter as the wind whipped his shirt, like a sailor in a gale clinging for dear life to the mast of his ship. The thunder eventually drew off, leaving us to slacken our hold and stare dumbly at the dripping mess the deluge had left in its wake.

* * *

Soldado's team located a towering *samaúma*, a cousin of the kapok, ten minutes away, back through the jungle behind the campsite. "Let's go have a look," Possuelo said. Despite its majestic stature as a crown tree of the canopy, the *samaúma* was not regarded as a valuable hardwood.

It was susceptible to infestation and eventual rot. Nonetheless, it had been heavily logged throughout the Amazon in recent years, as lumberjacks depleted more precious timber and turned to less desirable species that could be milled into cheap plank wood or pulp. It was also highly buoyant, which made it ideal for our purposes. Nicolas and I followed Possuelo into the forest.

Above its sprawling buttress roots, the tree was four feet thick and soared high into the canopy. To reach the main trunk above the roots, the men had already erected ten-foot-high jungle scaffolding—poles lashed together with vines—around the entire base of the tree. Possuelo signaled his approval, and Wilson and José clambered to the top of the wobbly platform and took up positions on opposite sides of the trunk. The strokes began haltingly as the pair, barefoot and barechested, found their balance on the makeshift scaffold. Soon enough, they found their groove, laying into the colossus one swing after another, huge wood chips flying in every direction. Backs glistening with sweat, the two reached a hypnotic rhythm: *ka-chunk, ka-chunk.*

Two hours later, as José and Wilson whittled the trunk precariously close to its tipping point, Soldado turned to me and said: "With a chain saw, we could have brought it down in half an hour." The hand-swung axes might have represented a throwback to a bygone era, before the internal combustion engine vastly amplified our ability to build—and destroy. But they were still light-years beyond the rudimentary technology available to most isolated tribes. The tree would not have yielded, ever, to anything less than a steel ax. No wonder steel had shown itself to be such a seductive temptation; no wonder tribes had invested it with supernatural properties.

The tree let out a slow, terrible moan as it wobbled on its stump. José and Wilson leapt from the scaffolding as everyone dashed for cover. The tree came down in an earthshaking crash. It hauled several neighboring trees with it and unleashed clouds of fungal dust and swarms of bees, their wings glinting in the sunlight that suddenly poured into the clearing, as though the roof of a dark movie theater had collapsed during an afternoon matinee. It was moments before anyone dared break the terrible silence that ensued. And then, machetes and hatchets in hand, the men climbed atop the toppled giant, clearing away its limbs like a horde of Lilliputians subduing their vanquished prey.

* * *

The airdrop came the following day, bringing work on Soldado's canoe to a temporary halt. The open field nearby, dotted with palms and young saplings, was to serve as the drop zone, and the whites and Kanamari were summoned to prepare signal fires to guide the airplane to its mark. Two fires were burning at either end of the field by the time I got there. Chico and José were tending the fire on the far side of the clearing. At the near end, Amarildo and Alfredo were stoking the pyre with green branches. Thick clouds of smoke drifted up through the trees. Raimundo lay sprawled on the ground nearby, naked except for shorts and boots, oblivious to the ants crawling along his chest. It took effort to recall the robust, gung-ho adventurer I'd first seen six weeks ago on the Itaquaí. His muscles were now slack, his lifeless eyes drawn back into his skull. Paulo Welker slumped against a tree.

"Look at me, Paulo, I'm wasting away," Raimundo said. "If I had known it would be like this, I never would have come. This is like slavery. He does whatever he wants with us. I've never been so humiliated in my life as I have by this guy." Raimundo didn't seem to care who was listening. Paulo Welker nodded.

"Hey, Amarildo!" he called out. "More green branches. More smoke!"

Raimundo flicked an ant off his shoulder. "God knows what other shit he has in store for us," he went on. "I wish that plane would have a net hanging down I could grab on to. I'd leave here right now." That Raimundo could openly voice such insubordinate thoughts was a measure of how badly things had deteriorated. At least fresh provisions were on the way.

From the distance came the faint drone of the approaching aircraft, growing steadily louder. "More smoke, more smoke!" Paulo Welker shouted across the clearing. Amarildo and Alfredo heaped green branches on the bonfire and fanned frantically with long palm fronds. They let up in time to release clouds of dense smoke that wafted through the trees just as the plane came over. *Vroooooom!* The foliage blocked my view, but from the racket I could tell it was just off the treetops. "Fire off the flares!" yelled Paulo Welker. Amarildo ran to the center of the clearing and let loose a round. It lurched from the barrel and burst red above the trees. "Fan the fires! More leaves, more smoke!" Welker screamed. We could hear the plane banking, heading back. The wind shifted, carrying the smoke sideways through the trees. It was hard to picture how the plane was going to find its target. "Watch out! Take cover!" Even Raimundo pulled himself off the ground and dove behind a tree. "These airdrops can be dangerous," Paulo Welker said as we peered out on the clearing. He'd known a FUNAI scout who was killed during an airdrop. "The package landed right on his head."

There was a loud crack as the first package slammed into the branches. It was followed by a distant thud, a second bundle landing at the far side of the clearing. "Right on target!" Amarildo called out. We were draped around a massive tree trunk, peeping out like shy kids in the folds of their mother's skirt. The airplane looped back again. It was like we were being strafed with dummy rounds. This time I saw the bundle tumble end over end like a bomb just before it smacked into a tree, exploding on impact, unleashing a shower of plastic tubs the size of bricks. "Looks like margarine," said Amarildo. "That's correct," Welker said. "It was on the list we radioed to Tabatinga."

I caught a glimpse of the plane on its next run: a blue single-engine Cessna, swooping in just above the treetops. I even saw the pilot silhouetted in the glass bubble of the cockpit, or thought I did. In my semi-delirious state of deprivation and isolation, I pictured myself piloting that magic carpet, liberated from this suffocating jungle, winging my way back to Tabatinga, no more than an hour away. I glanced over at Raimundo, hugging a nearby tree. His eyes scouted the gaps in the canopy, hungry for another peek at the aircraft. I recognized the longing in the way he looked at the plane, perceiving it, as I did, as a kind of emissary from a distant world that seemed to have all but forgotten us.

With each low pass, the plane dumped two or three more bundles, some landing intact in the clearing, others crashing into branches to earsplitting effect. What were the Arrow People making of all this: the signal fires, the high-pitched whine of the winged craft as it swooped in low, its multiple excretions? Certainly it hadn't gone unnoticed. The plane swooped down and dumped two more packages on its way north. The roar of the engine receded to a distant drone. This time it wasn't coming back. Its faint thrum finally faded out altogether, drowned in the rhythmic refrain of the insects, leaving us to retrieve the cargo and our yearnings.

* * *

Back at camp, Mauro was crouched on the dock, disemboweling monkeys for dinner. He hacked off their limbs and pitched them into the current with the banal airiness of a gardener tossing aside clumps of sod. A dozen vultures had taken up residence at the bend in the river a few hundred yards below the camp, slouched in the foliage like a hideous set of matching tree ornaments. They were soon joined by a snow-white buzzard that I took at first to be albino. *"O urubú rei,"* said Mauro. The king vulture. Not that it was actually the king; it was the name of the species, all white with some black trimming on the ends of its feathers. Like its all-black comrades, it sported a can-opener beak perfectly suited to tearing tough hide to get at the soft tissue of a carcass. But here, Mauro had already spared them the work.

Atop the bank, Paulo Souza was placing the last of the stores from the airdrop on pantry shelves that had been built for the purpose. He was performing his duties with meticulous precision, using the burlap wrapping from the bundles to line the rough wooden surfaces that would receive the stores—everything from cans of candied guava to bags of rice.

"Scotch, look!" he said, holding open a sack for my inspection. "Kool-Aid!" I peered inside. It was an incredible sight. There must have been close to a hundred envelopes in a rainbow assortment of flavors—grape, orange, lemonade—all with the trademark smiling pitcher on the side. "I'll mix some up tonight with dinner!" He lowered his voice to a conspiratorial hush. "And, Scotch," he said. "Check this out!" A yellowish mass was oozing from a torn gunnysack that lay on the ground behind him, margarine packed in plastic tubs that had shattered on impact. Shards of white plastic protruded from the goop like broken teeth. He was under orders to salvage the margarine, repacking it in ziplock bags. He stole a furtive glance, stuck his finger in the margarine, and gobbled it up. "Go ahead!" he implored. "Try it!" I buried the entire length of my grimy finger in the soft, golden essence and crammed it in my mouth. I'd never tasted anything so good.

That was the thing about the airdrop. It brought us rice and beans, coffee and milk, tobacco and even Kool-Aid. It provided a fleeting sense of connection to the world beyond. But it opened a passageway to whole new depths of subterranean intrigue, of which I'd only just taken the first taste. And it could not alter the fundamental equation, that we were stranded in the far wilderness, cut off from the outside world, beholden to the erratic temperament of a brooding tyrant. In a way, it left us feeling even more despondent, as if, in the fading of the airplane's motor, we sensed a more definitive abandonment, like a lover's final, unspoken farewell.

the trunk in a tapering incision that would become the bow. He turned to Possuelo and said: "I chose this tree because it's tall and beautiful—good for canoe." Possuelo nodded his approval. *"É bom,"* he said. *"Agelim* resists water—and insects. This will be a very good canoe."

He took out a tape measure, hooked it on one end, and began stretching it along the trunk. It took four lengths of the measure to reach the far end, sixty feet in all, nearly as long as the Haida canoe at the American Museum of Natural History in New York.

Tepi walked along the top of the trunk with an old hand drill. He burrowed it into the hull and cranked until the bit reached a depth of three inches. He repeated this operation in three parallel rows at three-foot intervals along the entire length of the trunk. Once the log was flipped over and the team began hollowing it out, Possuelo explained, the holes would signal where the craftsmen should stop scooping. The perforations would both assure a uniform thickness to the hull and ensure that no one would gouge a hole straight through to the other side. Afterward, the holes would be plugged with pegs and pitch.

Nicolas decided he would take some aerial shots of the canoe-building process. He'd brought along—in the pack Wilson was hauling—a harness and ascenders to hoist himself into the treetops for just such an occasion. Maká Matis, binding his ankles with a lasso of creepers, quickly shimmied up a nearby tree, hauling on his shoulder a long coiled vine. In a matter of seconds, he was seventy feet off the ground, at the point where the main branches forked from the trunk. He let the line drop. Nicolas affixed his rope to it, and Maká hoisted vine and rope back up, slung it through the crotch in the tree, and quickly rappeled down.

Once Maká hit the ground, Nicolas stepped into the canvas sling and began his ascent. Soon he was snapping away from high off the ground. As the Matis labored to turn the trunk right side up, Nicolas's presence and his whirring motor drive seemed to have a galvanizing effect. It was as though they'd suddenly stepped onto a much larger stage than this secluded patch of forest, that they realized people

CHAPTER 19

Jungle Shipyards

THE MATIS IN THE MEANTIME had found a suitable tree some twenty minutes' walk downriver from the main camp. In no time, their comings and goings to the site had beaten a well-trodden, distinguishable path. It wound through high walls of bamboo that pressed in on all sides like a green tunnel, emerging at a bluff overlooking the river. The trail then plunged back into the woods, crossing a narrow stream and weaving beneath a stand of soaring, moss-covered kapoks and cedars. A few days' rest from the trek had left my legs wobbly and sluggish as I followed Possuelo on our first visit to the Matis canoe.

We could make out the hollow *clunk, clunk* of axes at work as we came out into a clearing where an enormous *agelim* tree of marbled red and white wood lay on its side, stripped of its bark like a naked carcass. At one end of the clearing, the tree's stump rose to a height of twelve feet, still enclosed in jungle scaffolding like an imprisoned sentinel keeping watch over its own truncated body. At the other end, the tree's canopy crown lay in a jumbled mess of branches and smaller trees hauled down with the fall of the majestic *agelim*.

"Scotchie!" exclaimed Ivan Arapá, ax in hand, as he saw us entering the clearing. He regarded me with his trademark smirk and handed me the ax. "Scotchie coming to work?" I laughed. "I'd be completely worthless," I said. "Worse than worthless." It was true; there was no point in even offering to help. All I could have done was either botch the canoe or hurt myself, maybe even both. Ivan was cutting away at whom they'd never know would see what they were doing, that it had greater meaning than they'd ever before assigned it, or at least had a *different kind* of meaning, not wholly intrinsic to the process itself. *"Quan!"* yelled Txema. *"Quan!"* shouted Ivan. "Now!" Amid loud grunts, the men heaved in unison. With each small increment, they shoved wedges beneath the log to secure it. Finally, they managed to turn it all the way over. Nicolas lowered himself out of the tree. "Wow, great pictures!" he said.

A half hour's walk away, work was in full swing at Soldado's canoe. The bittersweet scent of sap and freshly cut wood mingled with the odor of dampness and rot as we approached. The toppled *samaúma* was nestled in growing mounds of ocher-colored wood chips and sawdust that ran along its entire length. Alfredo, Odair, and Soldado were spread out along the top of the leviathan at ten-foot intervals, hollowing out the interior with axes and adzes. Muscles rippled, axes rose and fell. So sure were the men of their aim, they didn't bother wearing boots, even as their sharpened blades struck into wood only inches from their feet. Those not atop the log stood knee-deep in wood chips on its flanks—scooping, gouging, sculpting. Slowly, the canoe's form was taking shape in this jungle shipyard. It was a sight to behold, frontiersmen and Indians together, engaged in an ancient art that had all but vanished from the face of the Earth. I couldn't help but think of my boys. They would have been amazed. It was a thought that occurred to me with increasing frequency on my travels, the feeling of regret dampening the sense of wonder that otherwise attended my forays into parts unknown.

* * *

I awoke from a dream in the middle of the night. I'd been desperately trying to call Sarah from a pay phone. The phone was jammed. I slammed down the receiver and ran into the street, accosting strangers, giving them her phone number, pleading with them to call her. That's when I woke up, sweating. *Jesus.* I tore open the Velcro trapdoor and went out to take a leak. The silver light of a full moon poured through the trees, casting long shadows through the campsite. I made my way toward the corner of the encampment, where the trail led off to the latrine. I rounded the thick tree that marked the corner and started down the path into deep forest shadows. Just then, I pulled up short, straining my ears. I heard something, coming from across the river. A distinct, deliberate knocking, as though someone was rapping a tree with a club. It stopped, then started again. What was it? Didn't anyone else hear it? It seemed so real. Was I hallucinating?

I passed Soldado's hammock. No movement there. Sound asleep, I supposed. Halfway down the trail, I decided I'd gone far enough. The forest snapped and popped, as though everything were growing so fast you could hear the bark stretching. A twig cracked. Leaves shuffled. I made my way back in pallid moonlight, passing Soldado's hammock once again. I rounded the bend at the edge of the campsite, wrapping my hand and forearm around the thick trunk as though I were swinging around a pole. Yuck! Something wet and mushy. I flicked on my headlamp. The tree was crawling with thousands of termites. Several dozen were crushed into my shirtsleeve, their wriggling body parts enmeshed in the cloth.

I made straight for the river. I squatted on the shaky platform built out over the water and dipped in my sleeve. In an instant, fish roiled the water, gobbling up the squashed insects. Such was the terrifying competition for life here in the Amazon.

I rose and looked out across the Jutaí. In the dim light, the scene had a soothing effect, the very tableau of serenity: the chirring insects, the silver moon suspended above the trees, its mirror image shimmering in the current, the gentle and incessant lapping of the water. It begged for contemplation and quiet conversation, and I allowed myself to picture the nighttime dock at Lake George this time of year, dragging out a pair of Adirondack chairs, a few tumblers, a round or two of whiskey. It was a pleasant illusion. The same moon would be hanging in the sky, that same mysterious light dancing on the water. In my mind, the dark outline of the high jungle wall on the opposite shore morphed into the mountain ridge rising above the far side of the bay. August on the lake; there was nothing like it. Why, I wondered, hadn't I come down here before at this silent hour?

Then, from somewhere behind me came a faint rustling, a quiet splash. My hair stood on end. One thought came to me: *anaconda!* Sharing a smoke with Soldado at his hammock earlier, he'd warned me to be on the lookout: "Watch where you're walking at night. After it rains, the *sucuri* comes out." *"Sucuri?"* I'd asked. "Anaconda," Soldado had said, giving me a knowing, ominous look. By now, I'd heard many tales from my companions, how the anaconda trolled the riverbanks looking for prey, especially solitary ones caught unawares at the water's edge. Like the Korubo girl, snatched in broad daylight opposite the FUNAI base from the beach where Sobral had been murdered. Adults were by no means exempt from the anaconda's list of targets, Soldado had said. The serpents grew thirty feet or more in length. They struck like lightning, seizing their victims, hauling them out into deep water to drown them and crush them in their powerful coils. Then they'd unhinge their jaws and slowly, obscenely, swallow their prey. Heart thumping, I bolted up the riverbank, vowing to never again be caught out alone in the dead of night.

That was easier said than done. Dysentery had struck, and you never knew when you might have to make a run for it. In any other circumstances, particularly in the sophomoric witlessness that so often attends all-male gatherings, the greasy farts and mad dashes to the latrine would have been occasions for hilarity. Now, they heralded a plague that threatened to reduce us to ghoulish skeletons. My water-purification tablets were long gone. Soldado was shitting streams of blood. A half dozen others were fending off debilitating fevers. Nearly everyone had the runs. The airdrop had delivered much-needed supplies, but they weren't finding their way into our meals. Dozens of family-size cans of Nestlé powdered milk had been among the provisions. But when we lined up the next day in the dawn chill for Mauro to ladle our coffee, it was black.

On those first nights after the airdrop, the prospect of Kool-Aid with dinner sent a surge of excitement through the encampment. But the purple-tinged concoction that was supposed to be grape-flavored was so weak it didn't even begin to mask the dreary taste of silt and rotting foliage. "That's the way Sydney told me to do it, Senhor Scotch," Mauro said later. "Two envelopes per pot." One-eighth the normal strength. Maybe Possuelo was just trying to make it last. But within a few nights, the Kool-Aid disappeared altogether without explanation. We were back to plain, unadulterated river water.

In the midst of the trek, it had seemed like it would never end: the scramble to get up in the predawn chill, hastily pack up, head out into an uncertain day. The only sure things were sweat and peril, filth and fatigue. We all figured *anything* would be an improvement. But with the imperative of the march now behind us, we were beset not only by swarms of insects and physical decrepitude, but also by relentless boredom and scheming.

The camp was rife with rumors of theft and hoarding. Stores disappeared from the pantry shelves. The Kanamari believed the whites had unfairly monopolized the supply of the vile Fumo Coringa tobacco that had come in the airdrop. The milk vanished. Orlando was said to have pilfered several cans. Paulo Welker seemed to be the source of much of the gossip, particularly when it was aimed at Possuelo or Orlando. Possuelo in turn put out the word that Paulo Welker was on the take. He leveled no direct accusations, but he let things slip out, mostly through Nicolas. "Don't say anything to anyone, but Paulo Welker is stealing milk," Nicolas told me one morning, as though he were letting me in on a big secret. He must have noticed the look of surprise on my face, for he added: "That's what Sydney says." It was interesting to pick up these juicy tidbits of intrigue from Nicolas. He opened a window into Sydney's thoughts that would otherwise have remained closed. My relationship with Possuelo wasn't nearly as cozy, and I didn't want it to be. I tried to steer a middle course among the factions. If I could have avoided him altogether, I probably would have by this point. But I still needed his cooperation—not only for my own survival, but for the story I was there to write. Like the topographic maps of the land we were traversing, there were still large uncharted spaces in my knowledge of Possuelo. I needed to get more on his thoughts, on his personal history, on the reasons for the choices he'd made and those he was making even now. It became a source of constant anxiety. But when I tried to pin him down, he was often coy and elusive.

Most rumors and backbiting seemed to pivot around the question of provisions—who was getting how much of what. But there were other unknowns: how long the expedition would last, what undisclosed missions might still await us downriver, and when we could expect to reach Tabatinga. Possuelo refused to divulge more than vague prognostications, fueling speculation that he had plans for further privations that could even have the potential to spark revolt were they to be made known among the rank and file. "I prefer not to make predictions or live by a set calendar," he'd say. "There is no set date for anything."

"Think about it for a second," Paulo Welker said to me one afternoon, pulling me back into the bush where we could not be seen. "We've found all the vestiges to prove where the Indians are. He's got all the information he needs to take to Brasília to make his point. So why not head straight for Tabatinga?"

We were beset by an epidemic of angst-filled dreams. The pitter-patter of raindrops one night provided the rhythm for a nightmare from which Nicolas awoke, believing it was raining *tracuá*, the nasty ants pouring down everywhere. Vengeful, knife-wielding monkeys returned to torment Mauro's sleep. And Possuelo dreamed of suffocating in the river at the hands of a faceless stranger. "I never have nightmares. The last one I had was when I was a teenager," he complained in the morning with an air of bewilderment. He conceded that he was on edge. "I've been lying in my hammock thinking about lots of things. We're in a risky area. This is a risky place." His candor was surprising. So too was the revelation. I'd thought the danger had passed. But the Arrow People were still around, he said, "watching everything we do." Did I have something in my medical kit that might help him get to sleep more easily?

My own dreams were so tormented, I couldn't tell which was

worse—sleeping or waking. I showed up at my old house on Christmas Day, and no one, not even my kids, would acknowledge my presence. In another dream, a former boss ridiculed my decision to set off on a long trip. "You'll never make it in this business," she said. Two nights later, I pressed the Playback button on a friend's answering machine and found a message from Sarah I wasn't supposed to hear. She'd acquiesced to her mother's plans for her to marry some guy in Ohio. I was frantically searching the Yellow Pages for the Columbus area code when I awoke. Most unnerving of all was a dream that, for its sheer content, should have been a comfort: Sarah standing in a doorway wearing a black kimono I'd given her on her birthday. Her hair was blond and gleaming, her smile lovely and radiant, and she looked out from that doorway with angelic serenity. Others might have taken solace from such an image. But in the circumstances, it produced the contrary emotion, so closely did it resemble one of those paranormal experiences people are always claiming to have of loved ones appearing in dreams to bid farewell at the very moment they're dying somewhere far away, as if to say, "Don't worry about me. See? I've never felt better. I'll see you later, when you get to the other side." Was it an affirmation of her love, or a premonition that something awful had befallen her? I shook it off and brought my focus back to the penal colony, fenced in as we were behind high walls of jungle, the one that towered directly behind us and the other that rose above the far side of the river like an enormous green tidal wave about to break over us.

We continued to work and take meals together as a single unit. But blood ties exerted a greater hold on camp life as time went on. The Matis were the most cohesive and unflappable of all the factions. Nothing seemed to bother them. They'd built their shelters in a row alongside one another. They hunted together and shared their cheerful, high-pitched banter, which remained unintelligible to the rest of us. Now they were even building their own canoe together. The two Marubo Indians, Adelino and Alcino, were first cousins as well as brothers-in-law. They were thoroughly inseparable. The Kanamari likewise stuck together in their own fellowship. The whites were the most fractious. You had the Amazonian frontiersmen, like Soldado, Raimundo, Amarildo, and the rest of the *riberinhos*. Paulo Welker increasingly attached himself to this group, having lost Possuelo's confidence. And then there was the tight-knit triumvirate: Possuelo, Orlando, and Nicolas. I drifted among the various factions, cracking jokes, picking up gossip. But essentially, I was alone. Profoundly, unalterably alone.

The men would return in the late afternoon from the construction sites, deposit axes and adzes at the rack, and line up for dinner. Afterward, we'd file down to the river to rinse off plates and spoons. The "dock," made of two-inch-diameter sticks, lying side by side and supported by poles pounded into the river bottom, could hold only two or three men at a time. A greasy sheen would form on the surface, where the water boiled with fish attacking the morsels of rice that floated into the current.

When night enveloped the jungle and the frogs began their otherworldly chorus, Possuelo would hold forth by the campfire, offering his disquisitions on the state of the universe to whoever would listen. Usually it was only the Matis and the Marubo who remained after dinner, the whites and Kanamari having already trundled off to their hammocks to smoke, scheme, or wax nostalgic about home in the company of their respective clansmen. I would hang for a while, not anxious to retire too early.

"You can see today how beautiful things are here," Possuelo started in one night. "There are lots of fish. There are many animals. Everything is beautiful. Do you remember what it was like before— when the whites came here and took everything? When no one stopped them from doing whatever they wanted?" The Indians nodded, their faces aglow in the orange light of the fire. Their ragtag camouflage, together with their clamshell earrings and bamboo-shoot whiskers and the deep wilderness that pressed in around us, seemed to lend an air of timelessness to the moment, as though this scene could have unfolded sometime in the distant past, two or three hundred years ago, here or somewhere else, far to the north perhaps, on the upper Connecticut or the Missouri, or south toward the Argentine. Possuelo rose, stirred the ashes, and fed another log to the flames. The fire popped. Sparks drifted up into the overhanging branches, seeming to mingle with the stars that winked through the gaps in the tree cover. He turned back to where the Matis were sitting, but he remained on his feet.

"You must say NO to the white man!" Possuelo implored, his tone suddenly acquiring an edge of desperation. His bulging eyes flashed in the firelight. "Tell him: *We don't want loggers, we don't want fishermen, we don't want hunters here! The fish are for us to eat! The meat is for us to eat! The turtle eggs are for us to eat! For us—the Matis, the Marubo, the Kanamari, the Korubo, and yes, the Arrow People, too! The monkeys are for us! The boar, the tapir, the turkeys—they are for us!'* Tell the white man to stay out! Tell him: *'We don't want you here anymore!'*"

It was curious that Possuelo should feel the need to do this kind of politicking. After all, the Javari Valley Indigenous Land was a done deal. It wasn't like other places in the Amazon, where industrial fleets from Manaus and Belém were laying dragnets across the entire widths of rivers, sucking up every last fish. It wasn't as though whole communities were on the run here from the whine of chain saws, as was the case in places like Rondônia and Maranhão. Moreover, there was an effective grassroots indigenous movement within the Javari. The reserve, in fact, had been decreed partly in response to agitation from the Indians themselves.

Still, the same indigenous leaders who had demanded the expulsion of whites ten or twenty years ago weren't so young anymore. Many were already gone. The allure of the bright lights downriver—the boom boxes, the Nikes, the laughter lilting from street-side barbecue joints—exerted a pull on the younger generation as inexorable as the current that swept past their backwater hamlets. Some might even be tempted to conspire with whites to traffic in the Javari's riches.

And yet, Possuelo had another, even greater concern: that one day the protections that he and other like-minded activists had fought so hard to put in place—not only in the Javari, but in the lands of the Yanomami and Kayapó, the Cinta Larga and Zo'é—could be overturned by a change of government in Brasília, opening the floodgates to the pent-up fury of jobless laborers and profiteering bosses. He sought to instill the will to resist among the Indians, the readiness to fight for what was theirs, were that day ever to come.

I went down to the river to brush my teeth before turning in, secure in the knowledge that my companions were awake and close by. I could see the fire's glow lighting up the trees atop the bank, and I could hear the soft murmur of their voices. I crouched on the platform and just as I was dipping my cup into the river, something hit the water—*ker-plunk!*—with the same sound and splash a golf ball would make. Ripples radiated out along the surface. At first I figured it was some kind of fruit dropping from an overhanging tree. Then came another, even closer. *Ker-plunk!* And another, and again one more. Too many, too close, too fast. They couldn't have been random nuts or palm fruits dropping in the river. It was as though someone were teeing up 9-iron shots from the other side of the river, and dropping them closer to the pin with each stroke. *Plunk.*

Was it the Arrow People? A solitary Indian, or were there several? Were they trying to frighten me? Or were they playing? Maybe both. One thing seemed clear: If they'd wanted to kill me, they could have done so. Whoever was lobbing those stones or palm fruits or whatever they were had certainly pulled close enough to nail me in the chest with an arrow. The river was only a hundred feet wide; I was well within range from the far side. What were they trying to say in this unspoken language? If they'd wanted to frighten me, they could have taken more drastic measures. Perhaps it was a kind of mischievous knock on the door: *We've got our eyes on you!* Whatever they were trying to communicate, I didn't think it prudent to linger any longer.

Rejoining the fold around the fire, I decided to keep what had happened to myself, at least for the moment. I wasn't entirely sure I'd actually seen and heard those splashes. It was like so many reports of sightings of wild Indians that seemed to abound in the Javari, glimpses of painted bodies and moving shadows on the edge of the forest, gone in an instant, leaving witnesses to wonder what they'd seen, or if they'd

seen anything at all. Yet the more I thought about it, the more convinced I became that I had, in fact, experienced an odd sort of contact
with the People of the Arrow.

"I've seen that kind of thing before," said Possuelo in the morning when I decided to mention the strange events of the night before.
"Only those weren't stones they were throwing. They're a kind of little
coconut. It could be they're trying to frighten us without actually injur-
ing us. It could be their way of saying: 'Okay, you've been here long
enough. Get moving, time you got out of here.'"

He'd experienced the same thing while bivouacked on the Arara
Contact Front in the early 1980s. The natives would wait until dusk,
then launch barrages of *babassu* nuts at Possuelo's team as they huddled by the campfire. "The nut's very hard and heavy," he said. "One
of those hits you, you don't forget it. The intent was to hurt us, to
make us go away. Of course, we didn't." They didn't, because the objective was to make contact, whether the Indians wanted it or not. "Or,"
Possuelo said, pausing while he thought, "they could be trying to draw
our attention."

This last possibility was especially intriguing, and it raised a whole
new host of questions. It was clear from the instances when they'd fled
from us—across the bridge, from the village—that we'd aroused the
Arrow People's deepest fears. But now that we'd crossed their land
without torching their hooches or firing upon them with our thun-
dersticks, had trepidation given way to curiosity? What if they actually
wanted release from their isolation? Maybe the Arrow People weren't as
joyous, vibrant, and free as Possuelo liked to imagine. What if paradise
was not in the here and now for Indians still fortunate enough to be living in isolation, as Possuelo believed? What if, as some critics alleged,
they were actually steeped in a nasty and brutish twilight, enduring
an excruciating isolation from which they sought escape? Didn't Possuelo's project—imposing this kind of reverse-apartheid to partition
off the outside world—amount to a holier-than-thou approach similar
to that of the missionaries whose zealous proselytizing he so despised?

Didn't he presume to know, with the same cultural arrogance as the catechists, what was best for his native charges?

That might be true, Possuelo conceded, but he wasn't taking any choice away from the Indians. If they wanted contact with the outside world, they had a strange way of showing it. Everything they did suggested a deliberate decision, an act of self-determination, to shut themselves off from the rest of us. The point was to let them decide if they wanted contact, on their own terms, in their own time, not to force it down their throats. Even so, it wasn't a choice he would be inclined to encourage. Contact was a Pandora's box, filled with calamities that few of the Indians could even begin to imagine. Then again, maybe they could. Maybe that was why the last tribes were so adamant in refusing contact. The Arara or the Parintintin who made off with knives, machetes, and axes from the *tapiri de brindis* had no idea what taking that bait would ultimately lead to. Epidemics were just the beginning. Once they were crippled by demographic shock, their lands were easily overrun. They often lacked the will or the strength even to feed themselves, let alone to resist. The survivors were soon corralled on marginal parcels, bereft of the traditions and know-how that had sustained them for thousands of years, despised by the society that had hoodwinked them with a boundless flow of gifts and promises of a better life. In the wake of contact, the Parakanã endured eleven relocations at the hands of the SPI and later FUNAI, as their land was carved up by the invaders and their numbers dwindled to a third of precontact levels.

For a number of *sertanistas,* contact became not a triumph but a tragedy. Wellington Figueiredo notched eight "first contacts" of his own and had taken charge of the Department of Isolated Indians during Possuelo's two-year reign as FUNAI president. Toward the end of his career, he'd come to be "terrified" by the prospect of first contact. On one expedition, a colleague suggested they should hide the Indians rather than contact them. He agreed. If only they could have. Contact left *sertanistas* as troubled and traumatized as combat veterans, having to contend not only with the spectacle of mass death, but also in some cases with the near-certain knowledge that they had been the bearers of the deadly illness. Indeed, the disasters occasioned by contact could overwhelm even the most seasoned, well-prepared field agents.

"So what do you do when you know in advance they're going to get sick?" Possuelo said. "If you know they're going to end up with pneumonia, eye infections, diarrhea, you get prepared to assist them. You think you'll be able to take care of them." Possuelo had made such preparations for the Arara—doctors at the ready, nurses, medicines, even a helicopter to evacuate the most infirm. There was one thing he hadn't thought of. "I didn't have the cooperation of the Indians," he said, fixing his gaze on the trees beyond the river. The Indians fell ill predictably enough, but they didn't come to Possuelo for help. Instead, they fled into the forest, further spreading the diseases. "It's not always enough to have everything at your disposal if you don't have the cooperation of the Indians. Because without it, you don't know if you can help them. Preparation doesn't mean success." Though it could mean the difference between outright extinction and mere decimation.

It was not only the mass die-offs that burdened the conscience of FUNAI agents. There were also countless cases of their own inadvertent bungling and insensitivity, moments they wished they could take back and do over again, things for which apologies were wholly inadequate. Like the time Figueiredo made a Guajá boy extinguish his tribe's firebrand—the torch they used to light their fires. Figueiredo's team was racing against the clock, trying to get the small band of Guajá they'd just contacted to a FUNAI post for medical treatment. But the boy was slowing their progress, falling behind to tend to the precious embers—blowing gently on the coals, shielding them from the wind. With night fast approaching, Figueiredo grew exasperated. "Tell him to put it out," he told his Guajá interpreter. He turned to the boy. "Here," he said. "Look." He pulled a Zippo from his pocket and flicked it open. A flame jumped out. The Indians drew back in fright. Translation was unnecessary: *If you can carry fire in your pocket and summon it magically at the snap of a finger, why bother with a clumsy torch?*

Without a word, the boy snuffed out his smoldering stick, and the march resumed at a faster clip. But with each step, the boy seemed to withdraw deeper into himself. By the time they reached the post, the spirit had gone out of him. It wasn't until later that Figueiredo realized the enormity of what he'd done. That flame had been handed down from generation to generation, a sacred trust that bound the tribe to their past, to their ancestors, and to the future, when the boy would have passed the torch on to his own child. In an instant, Figueiredo had snuffed all that out. His intentions were pure, at least he thought so; he wanted to get the Indians to medical care quickly. But the more he thought about it, the more he sensed an underlying, unconscious arrogance in his own gesture: *See? Our way is so much better than yours.* He'd unwittingly begun the same assault on the Guajá's values and identity that plagued every tribe following contact. Such incidents ended up haunting many *sertanistas* to their dying days, Possuelo said; trying to save the Indians, they'd succeeded in hastening their demise. Figueiredo himself came to believe that *sertanistas* were not so much agents of contact as "agents of tragedy." When Possuelo proposed to gather all *sertanistas* in Brasília back in 1987 to chart a new course for the profession—and a new policy toward the uncontacted tribes— Figueiredo was among his most ardent supporters.

* * *

"Let's go check on the Matis," Possuelo suggested, tiring of the conversation. It still felt strange to be walking upright through the woods with no loads on our backs, no creepers tugging at our ankles, along a footpath now worn by repeated trampling. There was no way to get lost. The trail through the woods was plain as day, reminiscent of the pathways laced with gnarled roots and carpeted in pine needles the color of copper that followed the Lake George shoreline.

Nicolas suddenly appeared through a screen of lianas, coming toward us from the other direction. It almost seemed as though we were casual weekend hikers, bumping into one another on a trail, except that in one hand, Nicolas brandished a hatchet. "The Matis gave it to me," he said, taking a practice swipe in the air. "They said there's a jaguar around looking for food." He grinned sheepishly. "I'm not sure it will do me much good, but I wanted to get going, and nobody would lend me a gun."

When Possuelo and I reached the clearing, five or six Matis were standing inside the canoe, ripping and clawing at the wood with axes and adzes. "Four more days, finished," Ivan Arapá promised. He invited me to take a seat inside the hollowed-out log. My eyes could barely peer out over the gunwales. The hull was narrow. Even at its midsection, I could barely extend my elbows. It made no sense. How were so many people supposed to fit in this torpedo-shaped craft? Guessing my thoughts, Ivan said: "Later we will open with fire. Make the canoe wide." I didn't understand what he meant. I would soon enough.

CHAPTER 20

The Tipping Point

THE DAYS BLURRED ONE INTO ANOTHER. I'd awake
to the predawn shivers and the murmurings of Paulo Souza
and Mauro as they prepared breakfast. The air would be cold
and damp, mist swirling on the river, when they'd bang on an empty
pot and shout out: *"A comer! A comer!"*

Like inmates in a chow line, we'd cue up grimly to await our rations. A pair of macaws might wing past, momentarily breaking the
silence with their shrieks. An earful of the raucous avian life of the
jungle—the yelping toucans and chattering parakeets—strongly suggested a direct link with the dinosaurs. In fact, everything about the
forest—from the squawking birds and ravenous fish to the Spanish
moss that dripped from the trees like ancient beards—seemed to
underscore our circumstances as puny beings in a primeval world of
colossal dimensions that would finally, at the time of its choosing, swallow us whole. Possuelo's latest eulogy to Percy Fawcett from just a few
nights before would still be fresh in my mind: *Wouldn't it be better just
to disappear.* . . . It was hard to say if Possuelo was trying to spook us or
if he genuinely believed that vanishing in the jungle would help secure his place in the exalted temple of Brazil's great explorers. If these
nightly disquisitions suggested anything, perhaps it was the creeping
mania of an aging man obsessed with his legacy. If he was just trying
to buck us up with a bit of humor, the sidelong glances that flashed
around the fire made it clear that the jokes were falling flat every time.

Nicolas and I attempted to send messages to the outside world via the radio, just to let our families know we were alive. Each of us wrote simple messages in Portuguese and handed them over to Paulo Welker. He, in turn, read them over the tenuous airwaves to Tabatinga. Then, we hoped, someone would know how to make a collect international call, and relay the message. After listening to the excruciating interchange between Welker and Siqueira or whoever was on the other end, I came to regret the effort, wondering what might come out if the message ever reached the States, like that campfire game called "telephone," in which a sentence is whispered from one person to the next, only to end up back at the beginning in comically mutilated form. Except in this instance, the results might not prove to be so humorous. I pictured my grief-stricken parents, installed in their wing-back chairs in the living room, trying to arrange for consular staff to retrieve my remains.

On the fifth day of construction, Soldado supervised the delicate process of rolling over his team's canoe. Amid a chorus of groans, the men nudged the beast, inch by inch, into its own knee-deep bed of wood chips and sawdust. Once it came to rest facedown, Soldado's crew swarmed atop its shaggy gray back and began stripping away its bark in a flurry of flying axes. The canoe was nearly fifty feet long, ten feet shorter than the Matis craft. But the rest of the trunk was not going to waste. On the margins of the clearing, Raimundo and José were at work with their machetes, sculpting four-foot lengths of the blond wood into sleek paddles with round, foot-wide blades that tapered at the bottom to a sharp point. Amarildo and Chico were like-wise fashioning wide, smoothly finished boards that would eventually become the seats to be fitted inside the canoe.

At lunchtime three days later, Soldado announced they would set fire beneath their canoe that afternoon, a procedure that would soften the wood and enable the men to pry open the hull, key to creating a buoyant and balanced vessel. It was an event I didn't want to miss. But I'd already promised the Matis I'd check on their progress. So I figured I'd dash there first, then accompany them to Soldado's canoe. Surely they'd be going there to help. I quickly scarfed a hunk of smoked boar and a slug of river water, then raced to my hammock to get my boots.

I was still lacing them when I saw Tepi and Ivan Arapá grab the last of
the axes and vanish into the forest. "Hey, guys, wait up!" I yelled across
the campsite.

Clipping at a near-run down the trail, I thought I would quickly
overtake the Matis. "Tepi! Ivan!" I yelled. There was no response. I
kept at it, plowing through the green tunnel that marked the halfway point to the Matis canoe. I cupped my hands, shouted again. No
answer. I plunged onward. I felt relieved as I reached the slope that
led up into the clearing. *Strange,* I thought. There were no voices. No
thunk of axes on wood. Nothing.

The canoe lay unattended in the middle of the clearing, its hull
long and sleek, like a wooden submarine in a Groton shipyard. Shit! I'd
misunderstood. The Matis must have gone directly from lunch to help
Soldado! I'd have to retrace my steps all the way back. Until word had
spread of the jaguar's presence, I hadn't thought twice about strolling
the path to the Matis canoe. With nil chance of getting lost on
the well-worn trail, I'd been lulled into a sense of safety that was not
altogether appropriate for the circumstances. Sure, a submerged fear
was operative at all times, a fear that something horrifying could be
lurking, waiting to pounce. But the fear remained largely tucked away,
especially with so many well-armed companions around. Not anymore.

Alone and unarmed, I started back. I looked about for some rocks
to perhaps hurl in self-defense, then realized I would find none in
these woods. I recalled running into Nicolas on the same path a few
days before, and how he clutched that hatchet in the vain hope of
fending off jaguars. "They're intelligent animals," Possuelo had said
after we took leave of Nicolas. "They know we're around, going back
and forth." Returning along the same trail only heightened the danger. A predator, having seen me on the way out, might now be biding
its time, preparing an ambush for my return.

The wind rustled the treetops—perfect cover for an animal's advance through crackling leaves on the forest floor. I picked up the
pace, taking advantage of the momentary racket to conceal my own
steps. I peered out into the dense wood and its dizzying verticals of

trunks, saplings, creepers dangling everywhere like a hall of mirrors. It occurred to me that I'd gone slack with the Jungle Prayer in recent days. Perhaps I'd forfeited a crucial edge of protection. I looked about for some kind of weapon, finally locating a stick with some heft and a razor-sharp point that had been left at the side of the trail by the swipe of a Matis machete. More likely than not, it would have been completely useless in my hands. Still, it was something. The wind gusted again and shook the high treetops. My step quickened. Back home, we had an educational board game I'd play with the boys, called Predator and Prey. But this was an education of an entirely different order. *Christ,* I thought, *what a way to spend a Sunday afternoon.*

By the time I reached Soldado's canoe, a dozen men were spread out along either side. Everyone was present—Matis and Marubo, Kanamari and whites. They laughed when I told them what happened. "Scotchie walking alone in the forest?" Ivan shook his head in mock disapproval. "No good. Scotchie stay here with us." I'd never been happier to see them.

Quads flexing and biceps bulging, the men slid the hulk inches at a time through the woods toward the river. A twelve-foot-wide road had been cleared all the way to the main camp and on to the river—in all a distance of five hundred yards. The towering, moss-flecked trees that pressed in on both sides and the freshly hacked stumps littering the way called to mind an ancient Roman road in the far reaches of the empire, maybe the hinterlands of northern Gaul. Blur the vision, take away the tropical heat, and this could have been Europe two thousand years ago.

"We'll make the fire here!" Soldado yelled. Clearing the path had produced mounds of firewood the men had piled along the route. By the armload, they dumped the wood beneath the canoe's overturned hull. Soldado made his way along the length, setting the wood ablaze. Soon, the entire vessel was shrouded in thick gray smoke. Bright orange flames licked at the edges of the gunwales. "We need wind!" shouted Soldado. Amarildo and José vanished into the trees and reappeared moments later dragging ten-foot-long palm fronds.

Silhouetted against clouds of billowing smoke, three or four men spread out along both sides of the vessel, beating the air with the huge palm-leaf fans. Giant flames shot up as the men jumped back. Heat scorched the air like a blast furnace. It seemed as though the entire canoe would incinerate. But the blaze diminished, giving way to an acrid smoke like burnt toast. Working in unison, leveraging the tree with stout poles on either side, the men brought the canoe upright. Its interior was thoroughly charred. Heat roiled up in shimmering waves. Dressed only in bathing trunks and boots, Soldado grabbed an adze and began raking the smoldering embers out onto the ground. I now understood why they'd moved the canoe before setting it afire. The piles of wood chips and sawdust back at the construction site could have burned for days, perhaps even igniting a fury that could have blazed out of control.

The moment of truth had arrived. With the wood rendered pliable by the searing heat, the men now began to stretch the hull, using two bifurcated branches—like huge, upside-down tuning forks—to grip the facing gunwales. Grabbing hold of thick vines lashed to the butt end of each fork, four or five men pulled in opposite directions with all their might. Little by little, the hull creaked open. As they moved down its length, other men followed, jamming saplings cut to length on the spot to prop open the stretched-out hull. "Easy, easy!" Possuelo urged. A bit of overzealous tugging could split the canoe apart, a demoralizing outcome that would have profoundly negative implications for the expedition and for our own security.

Gradually, reluctantly, the wood gave way. Cracks opened lengthwise with excruciating groans, but none was deep enough to damage the integrity of the hull. Ropes slackened, muscles relaxed. Before us stretched an enormous dugout canoe—rough-hewn and soot-blackened, but otherwise intact. The hull's width had doubled. The midsection was even wider, with enough room to accommodate three men abreast. Age-old know-how combined with collective muscle had produced the craft that would carry us back to our loves, our lives, and the comforts of civilization. Or so we hoped. Compared with the quaint *coshu* the Arrow People had parked on the shore upriver, this was almost a battle cruiser.

A similar scene unfolded the next day at the other canoe, with a slight variation. First the Matis turned the hull on its side, and then they set a series of fires within. Amid the roar of fire and incomprehensible shouting back and forth across the hull, the Matis tipped the hulk on to its belly. Tepi jumped atop the hull, his silhouette nearly vanishing in thick curtains of smoke. It drifted into the canopy and splintered the sunlight into a dazzling design of radiating shafts. The men turned their gaze skyward and gawked.

With our departure imminent, we began preparations for a new phase of the journey. Hunting parties were dispatched. The Kanamari shot a tapir so enormous they had to hack it into eighths before lugging it back to camp. Its tasty meat sizzled on skewers, free for the taking. Alfredo returned with two dozen large piranhas, strung together through the mouth and gills. New fires sprang to life, more firewood was chopped, smoking racks were erected to cure fish and meat. The air was abuzz with anticipation. We couldn't wait to get out of there.

Work continued on both vessels. More paddles had to be carved, benches installed. Soldado's canoe was ready to launch. A final three hundred yards separated the vessel from the river. To the ring of axes and cautionary shouts, trees cracked and fell. Trunks were stripped of branches and laid crosswise in the road as rollers to ease the behemoth's passage. Lining both sides of the canoe like bare-chested pallbearers, the men dragged it down the tree-shrouded boulevard, slipping between sunlight and shadow as they came. *"Embora!"* Soldado shouted. The men strained in unison. The canoe lurched forward, rolling atop the logs, barging its way into the main camp like some huge, ungainly beast. On it came, past the tool rack, past the command post, to the bank, where it pushed its nose out over the top, until fifteen feet of its length hung way out over the embankment. Suddenly reaching its tipping point, the nose dipped, and the entire canoe followed, rifling down the bank and hitting the river with a tremendous explosion. It knifed its way under and filled with water. The men dove in, grabbed the gunwales, and rocked the craft back and forth. Curtains of water sloshed out, rinsing away the soot that had blackened the interior. The water finally drained from its hold, the canoe achieved full buoyancy, floating magnificently on the sparking, sunlit river. All fourteen men clambered aboard, paddles in hand. To a chorus of cheers and hollers, Soldado's canoe took its maiden voyage halfway to the bend upriver and back, the men stroking with unbridled zest. After ten long days, we suddenly had a fifty-foot canoe beached on the shore beneath the camp. It would hardly have seemed more unlikely to find a Mercedes-Benz parked there.

Next morning, the Matis were ready to launch their enormous vessel. Nicolas and I reached the clearing in midmorning, just as Ivan Arapá shouted: "*Quán!*" Most of the expedition was here, including all the Matis, the whites, and the Kanamari. Eight men on a side, they nudged the craft through a narrow passageway littered with stumps. It ground to a halt against a large palm. Maká staggered down the hill, an eighty-pound log on his shoulder, and wedged it beneath the bow. The men rejoined the effort. The canoe suddenly popped free and came barreling down the hill, scattering us in all directions. There would have been no surviving a run-in with such a giant; it must have weighed as much as a small tractor-trailer. It came to rest against a cluster of trees fifty feet above the river. Kwini, dapper as ever with his jaguar whiskers and brilliant white earrings, grabbed an ax and laid into the offending trees. A third of the canoe was hanging precariously over the river. With the trees finally out of the way, the Matis pivoted the hull sideways, providing a diagonal trajectory down the bank to the water. It was a delicate operation; unlike the buoyant *samaúma* of Soldado's canoe, the *agelim* was so dense it would not float when submerged. If the canoe hit the water at too steep an angle, it would sink straight to the bottom, lost forever.

"*Quán! Quán!*" The men freed the vessel. It rocketed down the bank at heart-stopping speed. It hit the river with tremendous force, a minor tsunami breaking over the bow. The water rushed into its hold, smacked against the stern, and ricocheted back toward the front. But it soon settled, reflecting a sliver of the dreary whiteness of the sky over-head. By the time it came to equilibrium, the hull was a third of the way filled with water, but the craft had held its own. Ivan Waça jumped aboard with a newly carved paddle, wide as a spade, and began slosh-ing the water out in sheets. Within ten minutes, the craft was emptied. All the Matis hopped in and took seats. "Scotchie, come on!" shouted Ivan Arapá, seeing me hesitate at the shore. "Get in!" He slid over to make room. The last of the tools were loaded on, paddles were handed out, and all laid into the water with gusto. As I looked up into the trees, I realized that this was to be my final exit from the construction site of the Matis canoe. I would never again return to camp along the well-trammeled footpath I'd come to know so well: the bluff overlooking the river, the tunnel of high bamboo, the dense thicket that could so easily have provided concealment for a *flecheiro* ambush or a jaguar attack.

The water rushed beneath the hull as we paddled upstream. A sense of expectancy built as we rounded the final bend and the camp-site came into view. I pictured a triumphant arrival with elated cries rising from the shore. There was nothing. Possuelo barely looked up from his perch at the command post. Only Orlando showed interest, running down to the river, camera in hand, to pop off a few snaps.

I climbed up the bank to find Possuelo in his Speedo, slumped over the radio. He was in a foul mood. Soldado lay in a hammock behind him. His malaria chills had intensified, and he'd been turned inside out with dysentery. His ability to travel was questionable. Pos-suelo had spent the past two hours, he said, trying to reach the base in Tabatinga. Apparently Siqueira had taken an extended lunch break. *"Filho da puta,"* Possuelo muttered. "No one takes his job seriously. Son of a bitch!" Before the radio got packed up, he needed to confirm our eventual rendezvous with the *Kukahá*—one of the four riverboats that had brought us up the Itaquaí. This time, Possuelo said, we'd all have to squeeze aboard a single boat.

He spread his map out across the table while the men gathered around. If all went according to plan, the boat would retrieve us more than two hundred miles downriver, where a tributary called the Curuena joined the Jutaí. His finger traced a convoluted line of twists and turns. The planned date of rescue: August 18th. It was now the first day of August.

We'd depart the next morning. "We'll go back to the same routine we followed before. Around two or three in the afternoon, we'll make camp along the river. We'll hunt, eat, make *farofa* to take with us the next day." There were three places of special interest downriver that he planned to check out. First stop: the border of the Javari reserve, where we would clear brush along both sides of the river, to create the illusion of vigilance, at least for a few months, until the banks were reclaimed by the jungle. The idea was to encourage would-be intruders to halt at the boundary. Something of a vain hope, Possuelo acknowledged, until a permanent outpost could be erected on the Jutaí. The second stop: Kanamari settlements from which rumors were emanating of villagers making contact with, and possibly enslaving, members of the isolated Tsohom Djapá tribe. Possuelo needed to investigate and discourage further efforts by the Kanamari to "tame" isolated groups that might be in their vicinity. Last, once we met the *Kukahá,* Possuelo planned a side trip up the Curuena, which doubled back inside the Javari Valley Indigenous Land, to expel an old man and his family who had refused to leave when the reserve had been decreed. He needed to see if they were still there, and if they were, to evict them. "But before any of that," Possuelo said, "a large *igarapé* will join the main trunk of the river about an hour below here. That creek leads to three *malocas* of the Arrow People. We need to be vigilant when we pass. If the Indians have anything planned for us, that would be the place where they'd try to do it."

For now, it all retained an air of unreality. I fixed my gaze downstream, beyond the roosting vultures, to where the river cut left and disappeared beyond a high wall of jungle. It was now only hours before we'd be on the move once again, following the inexorable flow of the current. Anxious as we were to get out of there, it did mean giving up the many comforts of routine. Who knew what awaited us around the bend and the hundreds of other bends we'd journey through in the days and weeks ahead? What fresh hardships, what improbable encounters? Yet, we'd made it. We'd endured the worst of the isolation. We now had our transport, our means of escape from the jungle. From here on, we'd be moving forward, heading home. As the sun sank beyond the trees, throwing the river into shadow, I anxiously returned to my hammock to pack.

CHAPTER 21

East with the River

A GRAY MIST DRIFTED ACROSS THE WATER. Down below, the vessels were loaded and ready to go. The Matis canoe measured sixty feet, thirteen feet longer than Soldado's craft, which meant it would carry more men and a greater load. The Matis had added a palm-thatch awning amidships to protect gear and provisions, effectively cutting the canoe into separate sections fore and aft—each with four or five rows of paddlers.

We loitered by the command post, paddles on shoulders, awaiting Possuelo's orders. Behind us, the campsite stood naked and empty. "See how sad it feels when people leave a place," said Possuelo, taking in the scene for the last time. "It's interesting, the human presence, what it does." You'd have thought we'd spent the time of our lives here. Still, Possuelo's words rang true. We hadn't even departed, and it already looked like the loneliest, most godforsaken outpost on Earth, like a colony on a lost planet, abandoned to a climate too hostile to endure.

"What about the Arrow People?" I wondered. Wouldn't they be in here checking the place out soon enough? "Just as soon as we leave," said Possuelo. I pictured the Indians swarming the campsite, studying the structures with intense curiosity, running their fingertips over the cleft ends of saplings and boards where factory-fresh blades of steel had left their mark. They'd walk out onto the small dock, rock back and forth on it. They'd check out the lean-to with its split-log table and walls. They'd sprawl on the long benches that flanked the fire pit.

Maybe they'd smash it all to pieces. Maybe they'd decide to move their *maloca* here.

I took a seat near the stern of the Matis canoe, on the bench that abutted the rear of the thatched awning. It required me to face backward, my back to the awning, without a paddle, looking straight into the faces of the seven Matis spread out on the canoe's final four rows. Soldado lay under the awning behind me, groaning. He was feeling too frail to travel aboard the vessel he'd built. Here, he could at least stretch out in the shade of the canopy and drift in and out of fevered sleep.

We shoved off and eased out into midriver. The current caught the bow and brought it about. Dozens of yellow butterflies danced along the bank. The men dipped their paddles and soon fell into syncopated rhythm. I took a last look back at the encampment—the empty tool rack, the command post perched atop the bank, the high, thatched turkey tail where smoke from a dying fire wafted through the trees. To the rhythmic stroke of the paddles, we rounded the bend, and the main camp vanished from our sight forever.

We glided past the high white beach, where some footprints, presumed to be those of the Arrow People, had been sighted by the Marubo on our first day at the main camp. We passed the bluff opposite, where Possuelo and I had idled away an hour one afternoon, tossing sticks to a school of playful needle-snouted fish. We passed the gash in the forest through which this same canoe had barreled down to its launch only yesterday. It was as though we were watching our own recent history slide by in a moving diorama. And then, we slipped into unknown territory. Macaws screeched from the treetops. A kingfisher crossed the open water, wings pumping. We came to rest on a sandbar farther downriver, the canoe scraping bottom as we pulled ashore. The Marubo scouts hopped out and dashed up the dune, returning moments later with their floppy hats brimming with leathery *tracajá* eggs while gulls stared with disheartened eyes into the pillaged nests.

Our way was soon blocked by an enormous tree that had tumbled off the left bank at a 45-degree angle. Despite the odd angle, it still stretched across the entire width of the river. The trunk yielded in due course to Wilson's barrage of rapid-fire ax strokes, administered from the bow of Soldado's canoe. He needed to chisel only halfway through the log to create a channel deep enough for the canoes to slide through.

By nine o'clock, the sun was out in full force—raw, blinding, scorching. We sought the lip of the river, where overhanging boughs offered a cool sanctuary. A black bird cackled from the treetops. A pair of shrieking brown jacamars—black, with white chests, and long black beaks—zipped low across the water. Branches of submerged trees reached up from the water like gnarled, arthritic fingers, while heavy beards of Spanish moss hung low over the river. Huge spider-webs glinted in the sun. A jet-black toucan with a bright orange bill took flight downriver and came to rest in the crown of a distant tree.

We paddled by the mouth of a large stream that entered the river from the northwest. From upstream came the familiar catcall of a screaming piha, the first we'd heard since leaving the headwaters weeks ago. Its off-key song called out from the depths of the woodland each time we passed the confluence of an *igarapé*, as though the creeks opened a fleeting channel into a now-distant memory, a place we'd come to know intimately in another life, but which had since withdrawn behind the imposing palisades that lined the river, refusing to disclose any further secrets. We navigated the choke point without incident—no *flecheiros* on the bluff waving good-bye, or waiting in the underbrush with bows drawn. Just the jungle and its utter indifference to our presence. It was as unceremonious a departure as our arrival had been weeks earlier, when we came upon the first clues to their existence. To the despondent cry of the screaming piha, we took leave of the land of the Arrow People, once and for all.

Clouds gathered in fantastical shapes over the river and brought relief from the searing sunlight. After weeks of forest gloom, my skin had been drained of all pigmentation. In the jungle, I buttoned sleeves and neck to protect myself from insects; now I did so to shield my pasty skin from blistering burns. In anticipation of this eventuality, I'd packed a single bottle of sunblock, which I now applied to exposed outcroppings—nose, ears, backs of the hands—with miserly judiciousness. Ivan Arapá watched intently as I did. He nodded at the bottle. I couldn't refuse. Soon it was making its way around the back of the canoe, each of the Matis smearing a dab on his face and neck before passing it on. By the time the bottle got back to me, it was practically empty.

Off to port, an old weather-beaten frame structure sagged in the midday sun. "Kanamari," Ivan Arapá stated. "For drying *peixe*—fish." The shack was made from machined planks, clearly not of the Arrow People's making. The Kanamari had long ago established a series of footpaths that led from their villages on the Itaquaí through here and on to their former settlements on the Juruá. Indians could still use the paths legally to enter and exit the reserve. But the thoroughfares also offered ready-made routes of trespass for white poachers—loggers, fishermen, jaguar-skin hunters—outlaws by definition, whose disposition to open fire on unwanted "savages" or launch punitive raids on their *malocas* could never be underestimated. That was one of Possuelo's chief concerns, though everything we'd seen so far pointed toward stability and security for the Javari and its indigenous inhabitants.

Ivan Waça squeezed past me and ducked under the thatched canopy. Soldado groaned and rolled over. Ivan emerged seconds later with a soot-blackened banana leaf, neatly folded like a tamale wrapper. He opened it to reveal a brownish-white gelatinous goo. *"Dendo,"* he said in Matis. *"Peixe elétrico."* Electric fish. Eel. I took a taste. It had the liquid consistency of caviar and a smoky fish taste, like lox. It was delicious. Eels were fairly common in the Amazon, though it wasn't all that easy to spot them. We did see a few in the final days of the trek, as they floated near the surface in a shady glen on the edge of the Jutaí. "Look!" Possuelo had pointed down to the water. "Electric fish!" I crouched, my face just feet from the surface, but saw nothing. "Are you blind? Right there!" Finally I'd caught sight of a flicking tail. There were two of them, perfectly camouflaged in the flotsam adrift in the shallow eddy: dark brown, square-jawed, three feet long, thick as sticks, which was exactly what they looked like. "Very dangerous," Possuelo said. "One of those wraps itself around your leg, its shock can kill you." All 600 volts of it. But dead and broiled, the fish was an absolute delicacy. I scooped a handful with my unwashed fingers and greedily sucked it into my mouth. I wasn't sure how I might have rated its worthiness under more civilized conditions, on a restaurant table cloaked in white linen, say, but under the circumstances, the Amazon eel was delectable, a radical departure from our usual fare.

We pulled off the river in the late afternoon. I staggered from the canoe and immediately took a tumble on the wet, slick sand. The Matis howled. I picked myself off the ground, trudged up the bank. It took a moment for the eyes to adjust to the darkness of the forest, like going straight from a high-altitude glacier into an unlit, windowless shack. Campsite construction was in full swing. Machetes beat back the thicket. Trees fell. After a two-week lull, we were back to the routine of putting up overnight bivouacs. At least now we could do it without all the filth and exhaustion. There were no clothes to wash, no boots to scrub, then dry over the fire, less angst to darken our thoughts.

The feeling was much like that of hostages recently freed from long captivity. Turtle eggs were handed out—four each. I gained a fifth when Paulo Welker played "guess which hand?" and I won. I placed my share in a pot to boil together with a dozen others. Pork livers dripped succulently on spits over the fire. Skewers of fish roasted over red coals. Paulo Souza stirred the cauldron. It was full of boiling pork. Back in the shadows between the trees, the Indians lit ancillary fires to smoke fish, meat, and eel.

"Did Scotchie see the *jacaré*?" asked Ivan Arapá after dinner. "The caiman—it's down by the water, waiting for Scotchie." It was well past dark, and I was just about to turn in. Instead, I slid into my flip-flops and followed Ivan down the bank. My flashlight batteries were weak, the beam barely carrying fifty feet. "There!" Ivan shouted. I jumped. At the outer limits of the flashlight's capacity, a mere stone's throw away, lay the croc, its eyes glowering red, its mouth curled in a malicious smile.

Lightning was flashing intermittently through the trees as I made my way back to my hammock, the thunder's roll nearly constant. I'd just climbed into bed for the night when a chorus of shouts erupted from the direction of the Matis shelters. I stumbled out into the darkness once again, catching a glimpse of the path in the next stab of lightning. As I approached, the shouts turned to hoots of laughter. The scene was astonishing. Kwini stood at the base of a tree, barefoot and nearly naked, brandishing a smoldering stick. Ten feet above him, a shaggy animal with stout limbs, about the size of a large monkey, was making its way slowly up the tree. Its glacial pace seemed to suggest a halfhearted attempt to elude Kwini's reach. The other Matis, reclining in their hammocks, poked their heads out from the roofs of their low-lying shelters, their faces aglow in the light of the fire, taunting their friend.

"Pusen," Ivan Arapá said in Matis in response to my quizzical look. Then he added: *"Preguiça em branco."* Literally, he'd said "In white, sloth." In other words, in Portuguese. It was how the Matis and many tribes in Brazil referred to Portuguese—"the white man's language."

Sure enough, with the next jolt of lightning, I could make out her splayed, three-toed feet. She had somehow become separated from her infant, which could be heard bleating plaintively out in the darkness, desperate and heart-wrenching. The mother was trying to descend the tree to reach her infant, but Kwini wanted none of it. He was curing a rack of boar meat, and he didn't want anyone—or anything—to get near it.

Fundamental decency would have seemed to dictate yielding a path for the mother to reach her baby. Not so with Kwini. The sloth began to descend once again, this time headfirst, craning her neck to look around with sad, intelligent eyes. She'd nearly reached the base of the tree, and I thought she was finally going to make it, but Kwini grabbed a burning stick and chased her back up the tree, sparks flying as he whacked the trunk.

"Stop!" I cried out. Too late. She was already in full retreat—as full a retreat as any sloth is capable of—plodding back up the trunk in slow motion. The first drops of rain began to pelt down through the canopy. I hoped the sloth would give it one last try. This time, I would physically interpose myself to clear the way for her safe passage. But now the sky broke open in full downpour. I could still make out the baby's whimpers as I reached my hammock, but soon they were drowned out in the thunderous deluge. I prayed the baby could hold out through the drenching night and outlast the importunity of our intrusion. Maybe after we finally left, mother and child would be reunited. I lay in my hammock as the rain beat down, recalling the gruesome scene weeks earlier, when Orlando shot the mother monkey and left her infant son alone to fend for himself. Mercy, it seemed, was very much in short supply in the Amazon.

We awoke to a gray and chilly morning. There was no sign of mother or baby sloth. I hoped they'd managed to find each other in the middle of the night. Mist hung over the river as we boarded the canoes and shoved off. I resumed my position in the rear of the Matis canoe, still feeling revulsion over the previous night's ordeal. At least they hadn't killed the sloth. I wondered why not. "Matis no eat *pusen?*"

"*Sim, come,*" Damã replied. Ivan Arapá nodded. They liked sloth meat.

"Then why didn't you guys kill the sloth last night?"

They shrugged. That was all I could get out of them. It turned out that Possuelo had issued an order weeks ago to kill no sloth. They were a threatened species, he'd told them, and a virtually helpless one at that. The only time they should ever hunt *preguiça* was to save themselves from starvation.

The sun elbowed its way through the clouds and chased the fog from the river. I traded places with Ivan Arapá and took his paddle. It was exhilarating to glide downriver in a vessel of such scale: ten oarsmen on either side, all pulling to a single, mesmerizing rhythm. The paddle blades dipped and rose, dipped and rose, flashing in the sunlight, trailing droplets that pattered in ringlets on the water and dissolved. We hit a straightaway and lapsed into contemplation of the sky, blue and enormous, doubled in size by its identical twin reflected on the river's surface.

As if from nowhere, the rival canoe came abreast, and the race was joined. The cry went up: *"Quán! Quán! Quán!"* Snapped from our stupor, we dug into the current in a flurry of paddles. Soon both canoes fell into the same beat, and we continued side by side, exulting in the certain knowledge that we were on our way out of the jungle. It would take time to get there, but every stroke took us farther downriver, ever closer to our rendezvous with the *Kukahá* and on to the mouth of the Jutaí, where it joined the mighty Solimões—the Amazon River itself. There we'd turn upstream on the home stretch, bound for Tabatinga and journey's end. But there were still hundreds of miles of river before us.

The rear of the Matis canoe was a gallery unto itself, cut off from the forward half by fifteen feet of low, thatched canopy. Reaching the front—shared by the rest of the Matis with Possuelo and Nicolas—was a formidable task that required climbing through the dark enclosure on all fours, over mounds of tarpaulin-covered gear, with multiple opportunities to stub a toe or even break one, bang a shin, or cut open the palm of a hand. It was an excursion to be avoided if possible, which only heightened the sense of isolation between fore and aft. Seven of the Matis were in the back section, along with myself, Chico, and Soldado—who continued to waste away in the canopy's fetid enclosure.

Pressed against the thatched awning and facing four rows of Matis faces for hours at a time, I came to observe their features in the minute detail afforded by what was, in essence, an ongoing staring contest. I couldn't help but notice—in their high cheekbones, their sparse and wispy beards, and the epicanthic folds of their almond-shaped eyes—the unmistakable traces of a lineage that stretched back to the Mongolian steppe. In their tattered jungle hats and camouflage fatigues, they had the look of a derelict band of Hmong guerrillas on the upper Mekong, circa 1965.

I came to bear the brunt of an incessant stream of fatuous jokes that pinged around the back of the canoe. Seven sets of eyes were on me at all times, studying my every move, smirks already curling the corners of their mouths in anticipation of the next jibe. When I took off my shirt to get five minutes of sun, Ivan Arapá was ready with a comment. *"Scotchie pusen shitaro,"* he said, pointing at the hair on my chest. "Scotchie has chest like sloth."

We slid ashore at another beach; the Indians were anxious to hunt *tracajá* eggs. They combed the beach in pairs, each starting from opposite ends of the *praia,* walking toward one another gently, heel first. Where the sand ceded slightly beneath their heels, they would stop to dig. Ivan Arapá and Tepi, along with Alcino Marubo, had strikes. They returned to the boats with broad smiles and hats brimming with eggs.

As we made ready to leave, Possuelo called out: "Scott, come sit with me for a while." He patted the bench beside him. He was in good spirits. He brought out a cutting board and a hunk of smoked pig. He carved off a piece and handed me the knife. Even cold, the meat was lean and moist, like southern barbecue.

"August is the best time of year for travel here," Possuelo said, studying the jungle as it drifted past. "It's the month of transition to summer. The rains have stopped, the water is still high enough for canoe travel. The living is easy." So it seemed, compared with what we'd been through. High above the river to the east, clouds gathered in rich white tufts.

We came to a bend in the river. Possuelo pointed to the left at a long white dune that ran along the shore. "Notice how there's almost always a beach on the inside of the turn, and a high bank on the outside." Suddenly it made sense, how floodwaters would hurtle downstream in the rainy season, channeled through the bends by the steep embankments, sometimes more than thirty feet high. Once the bank could resist the onslaught no longer, it would give way, sending two-hundred-foot giants tumbling into the current. Some might block the channel where they fell. Others would be swept farther downriver, coming to rest miles downstream in a haphazard jumble that bedeviled all forms of navigation.

Once free of the precipitous inclines in their places of birth, the rivers of the western Amazon meander across vast expanses of virtually level ground. The Amazon River itself drops a mere 279 vertical feet along its last 2,500 miles from Tabatinga to the Atlantic. Every tributary offers such a serpentine infinity of twists and turns that it takes nearly three miles of actual travel for every one represented on a map. "But you'll see as we go farther downriver," Possuelo said, "as more water flows in and the volume of water increases, the gentler the bends will get, and the longer the *estirãos*—the straightaways."

In this part of the world, he said, *riberinhos* and Indians alike measure distance not by kilometers or miles but by bends in the river, or the number of beaches. "So you ask someone, 'How many beaches away from here do you live?' It's the same as asking how many bends in the river. You ask how many miles or kilometers, and they'll tell you they don't know."

Our descent of the Jutaí presented a kind of mirror image of the earlier journey up the Itaquaí. I saw what Possuelo meant about the increasing volume of water. With each passing stream or *igarapé* that joined the river, the wider it became, and the deeper. On the Itaquaí, the reverse process had unfolded: the farther upriver we went, the narrower the channel became, the more entombing the jungle canopy. The Kanamari settlements thinned out, then gave out altogether. Now, each bend in the Jutaí and each straightaway led us farther away from the secluded domain of the Arrow People, through a similar sort of no-man's-land, toward the edge of the civilized world and its dreary frontier settlements. Like the Itaquaí, those squalid outposts abutting the Jutaí wilderness were also settled by Kanamari.

"We've left the Arrow People behind," said Possuelo. "But they still venture down this far, in their little *coshus*. Here's where you begin to run into Kanamari. It's transitional territory here, belonging neither to one nor to the other." He'd no sooner spoken those words than we rounded a bend, and there in front of us, no more than two hundred yards away, was a small canoe, bobbing in the current. Paddle flashing in the sunlight, the little craft took off, trying to outdistance us.

It was a futile undertaking. The Matis struck out double time, pulling oars with reenergized vigor. We rapidly gained on the smaller craft. "You can see the first reaction out here is to flee," said Possuelo, shielding his eyes against the glare. We could make out a lone adult in the front of the canoe. Three children sat behind him, rigid and motionless, as if resigned to an unkind fate. "You can feel their fear from here."

We pulled abreast. *"Boa tarde!"* Possuelo stood, hands on hips. The father looked up from his small canoe, a hesitant smile on his gaunt, wrinkled face. There was no question that he was Kanamari. He wore no shirt, just a pair of faded cutoffs several sizes too big, bound at the waist with a piece of rope. The kids were scruffy, likewise dressed in tattered shorts. I guessed their ages to be about six, nine, twelve—roughly the same ages as my boys. They gaped at us with undisguised amazement.

"W-we're just out looking for *tracajá* eggs," the man stammered, struggling to regain his composure. He nodded upstream. "There are the wild Indians up there. The headwaters belong to them. *Não quer mansar*—they don't want to be tamed." It seemed a bit odd for an Indian to speak about other Indians this way, a tacit acknowledgment that his own people had already been "tamed." He exhaled a silent, tearless sob. "We thought maybe you were . . ." His voice faltered, and then he finished his thought: "the Arrow People."

We laughed. Small talk ensued. They were camped a short way downriver. I looked inside their tiny canoe. There wasn't much: a few turtle eggs on a palm leaf, an old ax, a five-foot-long harpoon topped with a barbed steel point.

"Do you know who I am?" Possuelo asked at length.

"Sim," he replied. *"Você é Sydney."*

Other than the fleeting glimpse of the *flecheiros* on the bridge, they were the first people we'd seen besides ourselves since leaving Pedras six weeks ago. We were in the middle of nowhere, still a half day's journey beyond the most isolated outpost on the Jutaí, and one of the most isolated anywhere on Earth. Yet even out here, the Kanamari knew Sydney Possuelo.

The man's name was Renato. He and his boys were camping with their mother and some relatives a few beaches downriver, and he offered to take us there. He paddled alongside us, piloting his tiny craft from the bow, its gunwales barely clearing the water. The blade of his paddle was wide as a snow shovel, and with it, Renato maintained a surprisingly good clip.

"This is a grand transmission of knowledge," said Possuelo, nodding toward the father and his sons. "They go out together, learn how to fish, learn how to hunt. Their stories are passed down orally." Possuelo was certain our appearance would enter that body of lore from this day forward. "This is a fantastic experience in their lives—thirty-some-odd people all the sudden coming around the bend in two enormous canoes. They'll never forget it."

Back in June on the Itaquaí, it was clear enough: we were coming upriver from the civilized world, envoys from the metropole, welcomed as heroes. But to materialize from the far side of the frontier had an altogether different effect, so bewildering that we might as well have been returning from the far side of the grave. Our provenance from upriver, the sheer size of our vessels, the number of hands on board with their odd mix of jungle camouflage and native adornments— all combined to stir a reaction perhaps not unlike that produced by the appearance of the Long Ships off the Frankish coast a thousand years ago.

Cries of hysteria rang out from the riverbank as we rounded the next bend. With flailing arms, two women herded a clutch of naked toddlers off the beach, stealing panic-stricken glances back over their shoulders. Smoke drifted lazily from a palm-thatched shelter on the top of the bluff, providing a snapshot of the domestic tranquillity we'd just shattered. Renato swung his tiny canoe out into view of the shore, cupped his hands, and called out in Kanamari. The high grass rustled. Heads poked out here and there to look around. Finally reassured that we meant them no harm, the women and children stepped out from the thicket as we disembarked in waves of shimmering heat and buzzing flies. The skins of a dozen giant pirarucu fish lay stretched out all around us on the beach, pale and ghostly in the blinding light. One of the world's largest freshwater fish and one of the most endangered in the entire Amazon, the pirarucu is an ancient creature, with a narrow snout leading to a long, streamlined body that ends in a round, simple tail. Mature adults reach up to ten feet in length and can yield as much as 150 pounds of succulent meat. The ones that lay at our feet—gutted and opened like butterflies to cure—were seven to eight feet long.

The sand was loose underfoot as we scaled the dunes to the simple hut where Renato's people were encamped. Hammocks hung languidly from the beams. Large chunks of fish were roasting on three separate fires. Horseflies the size of hummingbirds buzzed about. One by one, the Indians drifted back: half-naked women with red *urucum* dye smeared on their faces, skinny men in threadbare shorts, barefoot kids with sun-bleached hair and distended bellies.

"I thought you were *índios bravos*," Renato laughed. "We were thinking we were all going to die." Heads nodded in agreement amid nervous giggles. They were amazed to find Kanamari among us. Wilson, Alfredo, and the others drifted off beyond the hut to exchange confidences with their fellow tribesmen. They were equally astonished by the presence of an American. They refused to believe I was from the United States, even after I indulged their repeated requests to speak in my native tongue. At length, they convinced themselves that I was speaking *inglés,* or at least something that wasn't the "white man's language"—Portuguese.

"That's a lot of pirarucu just for yourselves," Possuelo said, nodding toward the fish curing on the beach. His tone was mildly disapproving, like a schoolmaster gently scolding an errant student. "Pirarucu for the community, fine. Selling pirarucu, no good."

The Indians were free to hunt and fish within the bounds of the Terra Indigena all they wanted, for their own consumption. But amassing a surplus to sell in commercial centers beyond the reserve was illegal.

"It's just for the community," Renato stammered. "I swear, Senhor Sydney."

Pirarucu had already vanished from broad stretches of the Amazon, victim of the soaring demand for its exquisite, flaky meat. It's an air-breathing fish that must surface every fifteen minutes or so, making it easy prey for harpoon-wielding fishermen. Besides the delicious meat, the fish are highly prized for their bony tongues and scales, which make excellent rasping boards and nail files. It had been listed in 1975 under the Convention on International Trade in Endangered Species of Wild Fauna and Flora (CITES) as an endangered species, but Brazil had only recently gotten around to protecting it. Pirarucu fishing had been banned in nearly all parts of the Amazon, and undercover agents were busting eateries in Manaus and Belém, where the fish turned up as daily specials. Like most other resources in the Amazon—from timber and minerals to exotic animals—the largest remaining repositories of the fish were found on Indian lands. The temptation was almost irresistible for cash-strapped natives to dry it, salt it, and smuggle it to buyers outside the reserve.

"They're lying," Possuelo whispered as we made our way back down the hill and boarded the canoes. "Of course they're going to sell it. I don't approve, but I understand. They've been completely abandoned by FUNAI. They have no other means to earn the money they need to buy a knife or a machete." A number of Kanamari trailed us in their small canoes, like minnows streaming in their mother's wake. "They want to be a part of the event," Possuelo said. "Maybe get a handout." Except we had almost nothing to hand out. Unlike our journey up the Itaquaí, when we were flush with supplies, we were now virtually bereft of wares to ease our passage through the communities downriver.

Storm clouds were gathering beyond the treetops to the south, their underbellies black and swollen. Lightning flashed. Thunder boomed. The Kanamari bid farewell and turned back, leaving us alone to face the coming squall. The wind came up, and the rain began. We could hear it first, pounding down on the forest across the river, then advancing in a white line, straight as a ruler, coming at us across the water. We were lashed by icy torrents, as though a hidden hand somewhere overhead were upending endless crates of cold, liquid marbles, whipping the surface of the river into a frenzied, pearly froth. We came to a large tributary entering the Jutaí from the left, and we turned up it.

We paddled into a gray and godforsaken land, devoid of color, past sandy shores guarded by the wreckage of fallen trees. Scraggly branches protruded from the water in solemn, twisted shards, like tank traps set on a beachhead awaiting an invasion. I'd never thought the Amazon could look like this.

Possuelo sat soaked and shirtless, water pouring from the visor of his jungle hat. "Look over there!" He pointed into the treetops off to the left. A band of a dozen monkeys—silhouetted black against the ashen sky—was swinging through the treetops. This sideways angle afforded a very different perspective on the monkeys than peering up at them from below. They flung themselves fearlessly into the air at dizzying heights with the exuberance of seasoned trapeze artists. The leaves shook like maracas as they sprang from perch to perch and tree to tree, advancing together through the canopy, on their way, so it seemed, to nowhere in particular.

The Matis studied the troop with keen interest. I expected them to pull the canoe over any second and disembark, rifles in hand. But the paddling continued, each collective stroke taking us beyond the range of the carefree primates, much to my relief. When we pulled off to camp for the night twenty minutes later, it was on the opposite bank. Too much trouble for a hunting party to cross the water and double back. The monkeys had been spared. The rain scarcely relented, and we were forced to pitch camp in the midst of the downpour, shivering and miserable.

We had turned up the Igarapé Daví—a black-water creek that stretched back into territory that had been hotly disputed between whites and isolated Indians of unidentified ethnicity until the reserve was decreed. It was only at dinner, as we huddled with chattering teeth beneath crude thatching thrown up over the campfire, that Possuelo revealed why we'd come here: to find out if the native population— Arrow People or whoever they were—had repopulated the Daví's headwaters.

The next day, Paulo Welker would depart with ten men in the Matis canoe to explore the Daví for signs of isolated Indians, looking for snapped-branch *quebradas,* footprints, lean-tos, the usual stuff. It was to be a quick hit and run, nothing exhaustive. "You should be back here in four days," Possuelo told Paulo Welker. The rest of us would wait.

Meanwhile, some kind of infestation of bugs was eating away at Soldado's canoe. Possuelo ordered the Kanamari to take it across the creek and submerge it, hoping prolonged immersion would eliminate the pests.

* * *

Paulo Welker's party returned unexpectedly on the afternoon of the third day just as the sun was beginning to set. Toucans were yelping from the treetops. A flock of blue macaws was flying past in wing-to-wing formation. And the canoe bearing Welker and his party appeared from around the bend upstream. They looked surprisingly well rested. "We found some old *capoeiras*—abandoned gardens," Paulo Welker said, climbing the bank to report to Possuelo. "That's all. Nothing recent." He made no attempt to explain how they'd managed to cover so much ground in so little time.

Possuelo didn't even look up from the campfire. "Huh," he said icily. "I thought the Indians would be using the area again." He had no further questions. He seemed not the least bit curious. The truth emerged later that night, leaked to Possuelo from the Indians who went on the mission. They'd gone just a few hours up the Daví in the canoe, set up camp on a choice spot, and spent two days gorging on supplies pilfered from the airdrop. Together with the bogus journal entries he filed to cover his tracks, it was an offense that would end up costing Paulo Welker his job. Why Possuelo didn't send him—or someone else—back to do a proper survey wasn't clear. Most likely because of our desperate condition and the need to keep moving. Anyway, there was no guarantee he'd get any better results without going himself, which apparently he didn't want to do.

We departed the next morning at first light. It was a relief to get on the move again. Every rhythmic stroke meant another ten yards down the river, closer to home. The two days of underwater submersion appeared to have driven the pestilence from Soldado's canoe. Soldado himself seemed to be enjoying at least partial recovery, though he remained aboard the Matis canoe with us, alternating between naps and short spurts of paddling.

Three days had passed since we'd seen Renato and his family, five since we'd left the main camp behind. It was getting on noon of a picture-perfect day. Clusters of rich, milky clouds scattered the sunlight through a cobalt blue sky. Stiff from hours slumped on the hard bench of the canoe, I stood up to stretch. I looked around: the high forest walls, the honey brown river disappearing around a sweeping bend up ahead, another just like it now behind us. And then, over the heads of the rear oarsmen and above the treetops, I caught sight of a small white scratch on the deep blue sky. It soon resolved into a jetliner, etching a pair of perfectly parallel contrails. As the jet came in our direction, the curvature of the Earth afforded the illusion that it was climbing vertically up through the firmament.

"Mira!" I shouted. The jetliner was now cutting its way straight across the top of the sky. The Matis shielded their eyes to look. The aircraft itself seemed little more than a tiny gray speck, propelled as if by magic across the heavens. Were it not for the lines of vapor it trailed in its wake, the plane would surely have passed unnoticed. It vanished into a bank of brilliant white clouds and reappeared on the other side.

"It's very big, isn't it, Scott?" said Soldado. I was surprised by the question. It only now occurred to me that Soldado had never seen a jetliner up close.

"About two hundred people can fit inside," I said with a nod. The serendipitous appearance of the aircraft—and the fantasies that attended it—offered a fleeting respite from this rough-and-tumble world where for weeks I'd been the bumbling novice to these jungle-hardened men. It was like an emissary sent from *my* world, something I actually knew a little bit about. "It's traveling at about a thousand kilometers an hour," I said. "From where we are here, up to there, it's about ten thousand meters—ten kilometers." Everyone stared in amazement.

"You'll be on one of the planes soon, won't you?" Soldado said.

You know it, man. One of those big beautiful starships is gonna be taking me home. I allowed myself that momentary, impulsive thought. But I heard the wistfulness in Soldado's voice and saw the sorrow in his soft brown eyes. For the first time I realized that this seemingly interminable trip would indeed have an ending. And that it was likely, however intimately I'd come to know some of these men, however unforgettable the experiences we'd shared together, that I would never see any of them again. "Yes," I said. "One just like that."

Soldado looked back up at the plane. *"Debe ser bonito,"* he said. "Must be nice, to be on one of those." He looked at me searchingly, like he was just awakening to an avenue of thought he'd never allowed himself to venture down, that he had never really known to exist—the idea that he could escape this life, maybe start a new one somewhere else. Not that he actually would. This was his land. His people lived here. He'd have been just as lost amid the honking horns and whoosh of traffic on Broadway as I'd have been here without him and the rest of this crew.

"So how do you get to your home from here?" he wanted to know. "Where does the airplane go?"

First I'd fly from Tabatinga to Manaus, I explained. Two hours. Then a plane from Manaus to Caracas, four hours. I'd change planes in Caracas, get on a different one bound for New York, eight hours. All told, about fourteen hours on three different planes. The Matis had ceased paddling, leaning in to listen with intent ears.

It sounded ridiculous, defying all sense of proportionality. Sitting in this ancient mode of transport—nothing to move us forward but paddles, muscle, and the current—we could hope, in the next fourteen hours, to navigate twenty bends in the river and advance maybe ten miles along the face of the map. New York, on the other hand, was five thousand miles away.

The plane vanished far beyond the treetops, bound for who knew where, its vapor trail dispersing in the wind. "So how much does it cost?" Soldado asked. "How much from here to New York?" I knew before I answered that this would be where the magic ended.

"Round trip is 3,000 *reais*," I said. About $1,500.

"That's more than we earn in a year," he said, spitting in the river. "You can't buy anything with our wages. *É uma miséria.* A pittance."

The plane might as well have just fallen from the sky. To preempt thoughts that I might be some obscenely rich dilettante who flitted around the globe to his heart's content, I hastened to add: "But I don't pay for it. The company pays."

It seemed to get me off the hook. The men went back to paddling, and I joined in. It was the only way to get from here to there. In my case, to get from here on the river to up there in the sky, aboard the big bird that would carry me home.

"Scott's going to forget all about us," Soldado sighed. He stopped rowing to light a cigarette. He must have thought I led a wildly glamorous life. Compared with his, I suppose I did. But I couldn't help but feel that his was the nobler. His feet were firmly planted here in these forests. I was just passing through, a day-tripper of sorts. He'd had to stand and fight for everything he had; I could always get on a plane.

"No," I said. "I will never forget."

The words came out frail and feeble, like I didn't really believe them myself. I wished I could have come up with a less restrained response, more suited to the occasion: *Are you fucking kidding me, Soldado? You think I'm ever going to be able to forget this?* But the moment passed, and I let it go.

CHAPTER 22

Borderlands

W E MADE GOOD TIME, if such can be said of paddling canoes on a flat, meandering river. On the map, we were advancing about fifteen miles a day; in reality, it was more than thirty miles of convoluted twists and turns. We soon came to the first permanent Kanamari settlement on the very edge of the Jutaí frontier—a half dozen thatched huts set atop the left bank. Word of our impending arrival had evidently preceded us, for the residents betrayed no fear, streaming to the beach to greet us.

Many had painted their faces red with *urucum,* flourishes of black polka dots, and swirling curlicues. From above us came the familiar wail of the women's welcoming song: a bucket of frothy *caisuma* was on the way. The Indians lined up to take their fill. I ducked out, having endured too many days and nights of dysentery already, with no medicine left to quell renewed digestive turmoil.

We plodded up the bank to the community, called Yarinal, home to about ten families. Its shabby palm-roofed huts stood atop pylons spread out on a sandy plain covered with chigger-infested scrub. A short man, face painted a brilliant scarlet, watched us in silence from the notched log that served as a stairway to one of the shacks. He was attired in a flimsy nylon bathing suit, and he sported a short-sleeved khaki shirt, emblazoned with a crimson patch over the breast pocket. Boy Scouts of America, it read in English. "Boy Scouts?" I asked him. "Do you know where that shirt is from?" He smiled at me with a blank stare. He spoke no Portuguese. A gaunt man approached from across the clearing, the visor of a ball cap casting his leathery face in deep shadow. His polyester slacks had been cut off at the knees and crudely mended with a hodgepodge assortment of colored thread and patching. "I am Geraldo," he said, "one of the village elders." He told Possuelo the community had been "completely abandoned" by FUNAI. "They've done nothing for us here." The public health agency was even worse. "They're thieves. They pocket the money and live the high life down in the city. They never come here."

We stood in the clearing under the blinding light, swatting flies, listening. There was no invitation to sit somewhere, or to get out of the sun. Geraldo reeled off a list of items the community needed desperately: shotgun shells, medicine, diesel, machetes, cooking pots, fishhooks, salt.

"I saw lots of salt up there," said Possuelo with a doubtful tone, nodding upriver in the direction of the fishing camp where Renato and his relatives had been curing pirarucu.

"We've been leaving salt upriver for the *índios bravos*. Fishhooks, too," said Geraldo. "They take the salt but leave the fishhooks." So it was true; these Kanamari *were* making contact with the isolated tribes. As Geraldo spoke, a third man approached, bearing a clutch of bamboo arrows and a long wooden bow. He cut a spectral figure, his emaciated frame swimming in a white shirt five sizes too big. His thick black mane fell to his shoulders, bangs cut straight across his forehead. A thin wisp of a mustache covered his lip and an equally scant tuft of long whiskers clung to his chin. I guessed he was in his early forties. He walked with a bowlegged gait, and the toes of his muddy feet were splayed in the manner of a forest dweller who had never worn a pair of shoes in his life.

"This is one of them," Geraldo announced, like a zookeeper showing off a rare species. "One of the wild Indians. He's *manso* now—tame. We tamed him." The Indian nodded with a faint smile, understanding nothing. Possuelo was incredulous.

"A few years ago, when I was here, they told me: 'Senhor Sydney, there's a group of *índios bravos* upriver, all naked,'" Possuelo said.

"They asked if I wanted to see them, and I said, 'No!' Now look what's happened." He smacked himself on the side of the head, as if to say: *How could I have been so stupid?*

The man's name was Aruá, and he was here with his wife and two children. There were others here as well, including the man in the Boy Scout shirt I'd initially taken for Kanamari. I could have spent hours—days even—imagining the various scenarios by which an Indian who'd just emerged from the bush on the very edge of the civilized world could have come into possession of a shirt from a scout troop somewhere back in the States.

The Boy Scout had drifted off, but Aruá remained, his dark eyes wearing a look of dazed incomprehension. The one thing he seemed to understand was that Geraldo was talking about him. "It was I who led the taming effort," Geraldo said with unabashed pride. "We lured them from the forest." With a series of gestures and unintelligible utterances, Geraldo commanded Aruá to bring his family out for us to see. "They hunt and fish for us," Geraldo boasted. And they tended gardens for the community. Their language was similar enough to be understood by Geraldo's people.

They were indeed from the same Tsohom Djapá tribe we'd heard about way back on the Itaquaí. The Kanamari called them *tukanos*— the Toucan People—and it was clear they occupied a completely subservient position here. Most of the tribe—no one knew for sure how many—remained deep in the bush, probably in the Jandiatuba headwaters. In fact, there was no way of knowing if these Tsohom Djapá might also be members of that much-vaunted group we'd come to call the Arrow People. It was hard to say. No one yet knew the actual ethnicity of the *flecheiros*, leaving a lot of room for speculation. Orlando noted a striking similarity between the black-feather fletching on Aruá's arrows and the tail feathers we'd observed on the broken shaft taken from the Arrow People. "Exactly the same," he said.

Nicolas set about posing Aruá and his family in the doorway of Geraldo's shack. "I heard whites make lots of money taking photos of Indians and selling them on the outside," Geraldo said. The remark caught me off guard. It was becoming a common refrain among the more media-savvy tribes, who had started to demand payment from journalists before consenting to be filmed or photographed. In some Yanomami *shabanos,* you couldn't move without first presenting the headman with a Casio watch or a stack of broad tobacco leaves. The Kayapó and Panará had begun to charge stiff fees, hundreds of dollars, for access to their communities. But I was surprised to hear it out here, where *jornalistas* were a scarcer commodity than the goods Geraldo was seeking from Possuelo. Nicolas ignored him and kept snapping away. After he finished, I motioned for Aruá to sit back down in the doorway. I wanted my own photograph to enshrine the occasion.

If the presence of the Tsohom Djapá in the village was not Possuelo's worst nightmare, it was close to it. A cursory glance around revealed a precarious health situation: children with the sniffles, adults with hacking coughs, complaints of fevers, stagnant pools of water ideal for the propagation of malaria-bearing mosquitoes. Renato had told us that illness was rampant in the Kanamari villages; five Indians had died on the upper Jutaí in the past few weeks alone. Aruá and his relatives stood a fifty-fifty chance of sharing the same fate in the months ahead, vulnerable as they were to the same contagions that had wiped out dozens of tribes before them. "I'll make a deal with you," Possuelo told Geraldo. "I'll send a boat up here with knives, fish-hooks, and gasoline for you. I'll send cartridges, medicines, cooking pots, hammocks, mosquito nets. I'm your friend; my word is good." He laid a hand on Geraldo's shoulder. "But in return you have to help me. Your people must stop trying to contact the *tukanos.* Leave them alone. Don't let anyone go up there. They're better off without us. They know the jungle, how to hunt. They don't need anything from FUNAI. If you let them come, soon they'll be asking for everything."

"That's what happened to us," said Geraldo with a nod of resignation.

"Leave them alone," Possuelo repeated. "When they're wild—*bravos*—everyone respects them. Once they've been tamed, no one does."

Possuelo's leverage was scant, and he knew it. He hoped the

message would have some effect. But he hadn't been here in years, and it was unlikely he'd be back anytime soon. He could send a boatload of stuff to the Kanamari, but it didn't guarantee anything. The distances were vast, resources in short supply. More to the point, the entire exchange between Geraldo and Possuelo seemed to highlight a central dilemma for tribes like the Kanamari, caught between the ancient ways they were quickly forgetting and a world of fast-moving boats, planes, and commerce that was passing them by. They no longer knew how to hunt with bow and arrow, much less how to make them. They'd been reduced to utter dependence on FUNAI's paternalism for manufactured necessities, such as shotguns and shells. And now, having run out of the latter, they'd recruited the Tsohom Djapá to do their hunting for them. Straddling the divide between civilization and the wild, the Kanamari belonged neither to one nor the other.

Before we took leave, Possuelo made one further demand of the assembled crowd: "If whites come here, do not trade with them. They will take all the fish from the rivers, all the animals from the forest. Soon you'll be left with nothing. If the white man comes, take everything from him, all his things, and tell him to get out."

The Kanamari roared with glee, as though sharing a delicious complicity with Senhor Sydney. After all, there was a time, before the legal impositions of the Terra Indígena, when the *kariwa* ran roughshod over the communities of the Jutaí, as Possuelo reminded them. The whites plundered at will; the Indians were powerless to stop them. But the joke turned out to be on Possuelo. Two days later, we would come to find out that even while Possuelo lectured the Kanamari on the incorrigible rapaciousness of *o homen branco,* they were harboring a river trader in their midst—"the Captain" was his moniker—come to buy their salted pirarucu and smuggle it out.

He passed along the shore below our encampment downriver the following night, his canoe laden with the dried fish, accompanied by a Kanamari woman we'd seen in the village. Paulo Welker spoke with them briefly. The Captain actually acknowledged he'd been hiding in the community during our visit. Possuelo shook his head in disgust when Welker told him about it the next morning. "I'll keep my part of the deal anyway," he said. It wasn't clear why Welker had done nothing to confiscate the fish or otherwise penalize the Captain. Perhaps Paulo had dispensed with any pretense of performing official duties, knowing as he must have that his days at FUNAI were numbered.

We drifted past a smattering of Kanamari settlements, stopping at some, passing others by. It was important for Possuelo to at least check in and say hello, since FUNAI so rarely showed its face here. Besides, Possuelo was anxious to trade an ax or a machete for a few sacks of *macaxeira*—manioc—or anything else that might qualify as food. We had enough meat to keep us going, but we'd run out of almost everything that had come in the airdrop. We came ashore at Nova Queimada, "New Burn," a village just taking shape in a clearing littered with freshly charred stumps and a jumble of fallen trees. The thatched huts were brand-new and still retained a golden hue the color of hay, not yet bleached to dreary silver by the merciless sun. Residents had recently abandoned Queimada, their old village, to escape the mysterious illness that was killing their people.

Children crowded around. In the short time we were there, they carved toy cameras from blocks of wood in imitation of ours and pretended to take our pictures. On the porch of one hut, a baby snowy owl blinked at us in the blinding light with forlorn eyes, tethered by his ankle to a perch. A woman emerged from inside with an entire bunch of ripe bananas, maybe three dozen in all, and offered them to us. I inhaled mine in two bites, the first taste of fruit I'd had in two months.

Like Sherman's troops marching to the sea, we'd taken on the ethos of a scavenging army in search of sustenance. Of course, to the limits of our abilities, we were still willing to pay, a circumstance that led Possuelo into a number of convoluted negotiations. He bartered an adze for manioc with one man who'd told us we could pick up the harvest at his garden three beaches downriver, only to find out once we got there that he'd meant three beaches *upriver*. Now six beaches away, we swallowed the loss and moved on.

The restrictions on commercial activity in the reserve did appear to be paying off for the wildlife. Otters played hide-and-seek with us, popping their brown, knobby heads up from the water, vanishing as we approached, resurfacing at our stern. We were trailed by pink river dolphins with babies in tow. Shaggy capybaras, giant hamsterlike creatures with blunt muzzles and tiny ears, eyed us from the top of a bluff. An agouti, with the head of a squirrel and the powerful hind legs of a rabbit, scrambled up the bank at our approach. Herds of wild boar—*queixada*—foraged back in the forest, hidden from view. The Matis would be the first to detect them, sniffing the air, ears cocked, eyes peering into the jungle like searchlights. Rowing would cease. A prattling tremor would issue from the depths of the forest, like a distant stampede, punctuated by the clacking of the boars' fearsome jaws. Piglets could be heard squealing amid the snorting of grown-ups. Long after the Matis initially picked up the scent, I'd finally catch a whiff of the herd's musky odor wafting from the jungle.

Usually nothing more would come of such occasions. Possuelo would be loath to stop; it would be too early in the day to hunt, or we already had enough meat on board. We'd just keep moving, leaving the Indians squirming in their seats, like Marines on landing craft anchored offshore, itching for a fight. Then, late one morning when the pungent scent of peccary drifted our way, Possuelo gave the green light; we needed food. The canoes made hard for the left bank. The Matis scrambled for guns and ammo. "Scotchie, come with us?" said Ivan Waça, and motioned for me to lace up my boots. The Kanamari were already disembarking from the other canoe when our craft swept sideways into dense willows that hung out sideways over the water. We leapt straight from the gunwales onto their heavy overhanging boughs, which like catwalks conveyed us over the mudflats and onto solid ground at the top of the embankment.

I followed the Indians into the forest. The ground was covered with the imprints of peccary hooves, swirling patterns embedded in the soft earth. I couldn't tell in which direction the jumbled mess of hoof prints pointed, but the Indians showed no hesitation. The woods were heavy with their scent. We huddled in silence. Maká Matis and

Orlando would flank the herd from either side. Once in place, they would open fire and drive the animals toward us. Orlando said: "Scott, if the herd comes at you, climb a tree, remember how I said? Just high enough to get off the ground."

"*Queixada é muito perigrosa,*" said Ivan Waça. The boars are very dangerous. "When they're just walking around, no problem. But when they're angry, watch out! You've got to be careful." The hunters peeled away in groups of two and three. I stayed close on Ivan's heels as he high-stepped silently through the brush, back arched like a cat's, the very embodiment of the archaeological ideal of the "apex predator"— stealthy, smart, in possession of advanced projectile-point weaponry. We could hear the animals rooting about in the thicket, jaws clacking like a thousand castanets. It must have been a large herd.

From back in the forest came the muffled blasts of shotguns, followed by a growing drumbeat of stampeding hooves. The bristle-backed boars swept between the trees like a gray wave. "They're coming this way!" cried Ivan Waça. They were charging straight toward us, heads bobbing, tusks flashing. I'd picked out a tree and made ready to hoist myself out of the range of the marauding herd. Just before reaching us, the wave miraculously divided. One group swept to our right, the other to our left.

"This way, Scotchie!" Ivan shouted. We took off in full flight, bounding over roots, ducking branches. The animals were streaming past, left to right, no more than twenty-five feet away. Hundreds of them. Ivan leveled his rifle and fired into the flood of sprinting pigs. *POW!* Gunshots erupted all around us. It was pandemonium. Here and there, boars dropped in their tracks while the rest of the herd thundered on. We joined the chase. Ivan stopped, drew a bead, fired again. Another animal went down. More blasts rang out ahead of us, behind us. Finally, the last dozen or so peccaries charged past us through the gauntlet, grunting and squealing, their bounding rumps vanishing through a veil of dense underbrush.

It was over in less than two minutes. Ears still ringing with gunfire, heart pounding, I joined Ivan to retrieve the carcasses—eight in all. I was beginning to understand how Soldado could reckon from hearing gunshots a mile away what sort of prey was being hunted. A large sow lay at our feet, blood trickling from a hole in her flank. She was about four feet long and probably weighed about sixty pounds. Her coat was a crude weave of black and white bristles that combined to fool the eye from a distance into seeing a charcoal gray. Her brown, glassy eye stared blankly up at us. A yellow fang hung over her lower lip. Ivan stuck his forefinger into the wound and pulled it out, covered in blood like a dipstick. He buried his knife in her breast, sliced downward, then plunged in with both hands, pulling out coils of gray entrails.

The other hunters appeared through the trees, peccaries bound at the hooves with envira vine and slung on their shoulders, ready to return to the boats. We received a hero's welcome at the canoes when they saw us coming through the woods, bringing home the bacon. We'd been gone twenty minutes; we came back with enough food to feed everyone for the next three days.

*   *   *

When we'd gone a little ways downriver, Ivan Arapá cleared his throat to speak. "Scotchie, what's it like where you're from?" he said. "Tell us about it again, about the cars that go up and down." It was weeks ago when I first described New York's streets and skyscrapers one night around the campfire.

"The city is absolutely huge," I began, flinging my arms open to show just how big. "There are thousands of cars on the streets. Thousands. The houses are tall as the trees." Their eyes followed my finger as I pointed into the canopy. "They're so high, you have to ride on special cars that go straight up and down from the street to your house." Astonished whistles resounded through the back of the canoe. It did sound a bit like science fiction, kind of like *The Jetsons*, but I could think of no better way to describe it. The two worlds at times seemed so mutually exclusive that there was almost no jumping-off place, no reference point from which to begin a meaningful comparison. Each held a kind of fantastical, mythic quality in the eye of the other. I'd become a kind of unwitting time traveler, straddling separate realities, and I found myself growing susceptible to the same sense of awe my friends must have experienced when I described the far-off place where I was from. They had asked me to repeat the story many times ever since. Each time would produce the identical response. Smiles would tug at the corners of their mouths, and they'd sit with wide-eyed amazement; they never seemed to tire of it.

It occurred to me, belatedly, that I was treading perilously close to the kind of mystification of the white man's world that ultimately leads to the dissolution of indigenous societies and led, in the case of New York, from its initial theft from the Mannahatta for a handful of shiny tokens to the colossus I was attempting to describe. I wasn't saying anything that wasn't true, but then again, neither did Wellington Figueiredo when he waved his cigarette lighter before the eyes of the newly contacted Guajá. Had Possuelo been privy to the conversation, he certainly would have added a disclaimer, like: "Yeah, and the air is so filthy, you can hardly breathe. The water is poisoned. Every day, there are a dozen murders."

"Do you have rivers there, like this?" said Damã Matis. "And forests, with trees like this?" I hadn't been asked this before, and I had to think before answering. There is nothing more important to the Indians than the forest, and I didn't want to be glib. I looked around. There was the river, our highway through the jungle, the riotous vegetation with its mind-numbing monotony of greens and browns, the white sun pounding down from overhead.

"Yes, but the forest isn't green all year round." I told them about the changing seasons, that the trees are green only in the summertime. Then, I said, it begins to get cold, and the leaves turn all sorts of colors—yellow, red, and orange. Then they fall off, leaving all the branches bare. After that, I went on, it gets so cold that white stuff, called snow, starts falling—so much of it that it turns the land white.

I could see the men were trying to picture in their mind's eye what a white forest might look like. They laughed, shaking their heads. *"Não pode ser,"* said Ivan. "It can't be." Then it gets so cold, I said, that the rivers turn to ice, so solid you can walk on them. They exchanged glances in utter disbelief. It was so outrageous a contention, I couldn't possibly have made it up. "We have special shoes," I added, "with blades like machetes fastened to the soles. You can slide across the ice really fast." They laughed in delight. From then on, it was something they would want to hear about over and over, as if it might cease to be true if I failed to repeat it at least once a day.

* * *

The next morning, under a brilliant blue sky, we came to the confluence of the Jutaizinho, flowing in from the right. Its current was as turgid as the Mississippi's compared with the Jutaí's darker and clearer flow, and where the waters collided, they mixed in swirling galaxies of mocha brown and black. We had reached the boundary of the Terra Indigena Vale do Javari, as a battered plaque nailed to a tree atop the bank proclaimed.

FEDERAL GOVERNMENT
Ministry of Justice
National Indian Foundation
(FUNAI)
PROTECTED LAND
Indigenous Land Vale do Javari
Access Prohibited to Strange Persons
Art No. 231 of Fed Constitution
Art No. 18 Sec 1 of Law 6001/73
Art 161 of criminal code

I liked the part about *pessoas estranhas*—"strange persons." I pictured a boatload of poachers motoring their way upriver, stopping at the entrance to read the sign: *You strange? Didn't think so. Me neither. Let's head on in!* Of course, it basically meant No Trespassing, but by itself, a sign wasn't about to stop someone with criminal intent anyway. Nor would it stop the smugglers of contraband, like the Captain, who might simply avert their eyes and press on upriver, pretending they'd never seen it and pleading ignorance on the off chance that they got caught: *I didn't see the sign, Officer.* Or perhaps they were convinced of the rightness of their mission in the first place: *Hey, the Indians are begging for us up here. How else are they going to get what they need?* Some rust was eating at the edges, but otherwise the placard remained intact. Wonder it hadn't been shot full of holes. Ammunition was too precious, I supposed. But riotous undergrowth had laid siege to it, threatening its visibility and its value to potentially deter those with at least a passing respect for the law.

"Disembark here!" Possuelo shouted with cupped hands across to the other canoe. We steered over to the left bank and ran aground in the shallows. "We're going to do a bit of work. Grab your machetes!" The men attacked the foliage like an army of peons slashing through a high wall of sugarcane. Their bare backs glistened in the blazing sun while hornets circled angrily, looking for a chance to strike. This had been cleared only once before, Possuelo said, when the boundaries of the reserve were physically delimited a year ago. If he had the funding, he'd build a control post similar to the one at the Ituí-Itaquaí confluence right here. Until then, he hoped the sheer isolation would keep most intruders from venturing in this direction. That, and the willingness of the Indians to defend what was theirs. But that was more problematic.

"The Indians should be out here every few months, keeping this clean," said Possuelo as he watched the men advance through the brush, machetes flashing in the sunlight. "They need to get organized and understand the importance of protecting this." With a wave of the hand, he indicated he was talking about the entire Terra Indígena, in whose vast forests we'd been swallowed for the past two months. He pulled off his floppy camouflage hat, looked inside it as though he might find an answer there, then gently tugged it back on his balding pate. "The only problem is that by the time you get the Indian to understand that, he's stopped being Indian." *Ele deixa de ser índio.*

I thought back to the moment three weeks ago when we came

upon a sapling doubled over a footpath deep in the forest. Its message, in essence, was the same as this one: Access Prohibited to Strange Persons. It was a slapdash gesture, assembled in haste—no letters emblazoned on sheet metal, no allusions to statutes, constitutions, or criminal codes. But the crude roadblock was no less human an undertaking. It was a matter of scale—and perhaps a measure of how ungainly, complex, and abstract our own society had become by comparison. I thought I detected in Possuelo's words an acknowledgment of the central paradox of his work: He might wish the Indians to transcend their narrow tribal interests, to see themselves not just as Matis or Marubo, Kanamari or Tsohom Djapá, but first and foremost as *índios* in a common struggle. But as much as he wanted that, it was still *his* wish, not necessarily theirs, an abstraction that, no matter how salient and beneficial to their own interests, bore the indelible mark of a white man's mind. After all, it was the Kanamari who chose to ignore the Arrow People's sign. It was the Kanamari who were making contact with the Tsohom Djapá, though their methods were hardly different from those used by the *sertanistas*. Perhaps it would be the Kanamari who would one day make contact with the Arrow People. Maybe this very trip would serve to show them the way. What would keep the Kanamari, bored with village life and looking for adventure, from retracing our steps on their own at some future date? Possuelo could only hope they'd absorb the right lessons; he couldn't guarantee it. The world had grown complicated, and Possuelo was growing tired.

* * *

Before we shoved off, Possuelo ordered Paulo Welker to set up the radio and put up the antenna. He needed to speak to Siqueira and order the crew to ready the *Kukahá* for imminent departure. It would leave Tabatinga the next morning and head east down the Solimões to its confluence with the Jutaí some three hundred miles away. There it would turn south, up the Jutaí, and proceed toward our eventual rendezvous, still more than a week away. It was a good thing the boat was coming, and it was a good thing we were already on the river, moving downstream. The whites had reached their own borderline, the limits of their endurance, and hopping into the canoes every mist-shrouded morning at least rekindled their hopes of getting home. It provided a kind of safety valve, perhaps the only thing that kept the expedition from falling apart in the midst of isolation, monotony, and deprivation.

Even the hard-bitten frontiersman Soldado was near the breaking point. "We've still got cans of milk," Soldado whispered to me one day, repeating a rumor he'd picked up. "Can you imagine—forty cans? When was the last time we had milk?" He held me in the gaze of his dim eyes. "Sydney says I'm the best of the woodsman, that he couldn't do this without me," he continued. "But then when I'm weak and sick, he doesn't even ask me how I am." This was, in Soldado's estimation, the longest and most miserable journey he'd ever endured. "You know something else?" he said, lowering his voice. "The Indians might be having a bad time, too, but they don't speak up. They don't complain. That's why he likes them."

Word had it that Possuelo was holding back fifty kilos of sugar as well. Yet, every morning our coffee was black, unsweetened. The rationing seemed to defy logic, fueling gossip that Possuelo was planning other missions that he refused to disclose, that perhaps we wouldn't be heading home so quickly after all. In the absence of concrete information, speculation abounded, abetted by Possuelo's ongoing lapses into a dark netherworld whose unseen torments he seemed determined to inflict on the rest of us.

We paddled into the late afternoon as storm clouds gathered above the treetops. Thunder rumbled. We passed several locations that seemed ideal for a bivouac. From the middle of the river, the Matis could spot such sites, where the trees were free from *tracuá* infestation, the ground was firm, and the riverbank would support a stairway down to the water. *"Burrá,"* they'd say, and point into the forest. Good. But we kept going. Thunder crashed overhead with electrifying flashes. Wind tossed the treetops. Still, Possuelo signaled no intention to pull off.

Then the rain came, thumping down on the forest with a deafening roar. It swept upriver toward us, a white diagonal squall line. Gusts pushed the deluge in curtains back and forth across the river. The canoe was rapidly filling. Ivan Arapá handed me a rubber boot. "Bail, Scotchie," he said. When Possuelo finally ordered us off the river, I hopped the gunwales into oozing, knee-deep mud that sucked the flip-flops right off my feet. The campsite went up in the midst of the downpour.

Once I'd gotten myself situated, I sought shelter beneath the kitchen's large tarpaulin, where Paulo Souza was preparing the chow. He invited me to a piece of boiled *macaxeira.* I shrugged. It was steaming hot, but white and bland, not a particularly enticing treat. He cast about with a furtive eye and pulled back the lid on another pot, this time to reveal a big glob of margarine. "Scott, be quick!" he hissed. "Before anyone comes!" I stuck the hunk of yucca straight into the margarine and on into my mouth. I'd burned my tongue but wolfed it down anyway to hide the evidence. I was too famished to feel any sense of shame or remorse. I just didn't want to get caught. "Scott, I have to tell you something. Promise not to tell anyone?" He flashed me the look of the knowing insider, ever the tawdry riverboat gambler. "Paulo Welker stole twenty packets of the Kool-Aid for himself after the airdrop." That damned Kool-Aid had turned out to be a lot more trouble than it was ever worth. "And something else," Paulo Souza continued. "We still have lots of it, maybe fifty or sixty packets. Sydney told Mauro not to serve it anymore. Said it would spoil the men, make us weak." It seemed like the height of absurdity, a kind of gratuitous cruelty.

*   *   *

Midway through the next day, we pulled off the river at a clearing atop the right bank, where a solitary thatched house stood on stilts with a ladder that served as a stairway up to the main level. A woman was out in the yard draping laundry on a line. Wide-eyed kids huddled in the doorway. "Good morning, senhora!" Possuelo shouted from the canoe. "Is your man at home?" A sweaty, bare-chested man appeared from behind the house and introduced himself: "José Pereira. It's a pleasure to meet you." He invited us up the steps and into his house, a single room with a split-palm floor, about ten by ten. Pereira removed his ball cap, revealing a weather-beaten face lined with deep grooves and a furrowed brow. He slipped into what passed for a shirt, a gray flannel pajama top with red sleeves crudely stitched on to extend the length of the original short ones. Protection from the jungle's prodigious insect life.

The Pereiras were the first whites we'd seen since the journey began. The wife and husband lived here with four children. A three-year-old boy with startlingly beautiful luminescent green eyes sat beside me and put his hand in mine. Mucus flowed from both his nostrils. I fought the impulse to clean him up, not wanting to embarrass the parents.

"All the kids have colds." Pereira shrugged in apology. They ranged in age from one to seven, all skinny and grim-faced. None of them had ever seen a doctor. Neither had Pereira. In fact, in all his twenty-five or so years (he wasn't sure exactly how old he was), he'd never once made the trip downriver to the municipality of Jutaí, the only town on the entire river, located at the confluence with the Solimões. "It's too far," he said. Traveling straight through, day and night, in a motorized boat, he said, it would take at least seven days from here. His aging mother, who lived with them, went to see a doctor once in Eirunepé, on the Juruá. It took two weeks by foot and boat to get there, and two weeks to get back. That was fifteen years ago.

These encounters, first with the Kanamari and now with the *riberinho* family, had fostered the pleasing illusion that the comforts of civilization were at hand, that any day now we'd be kicking back, guzzling ice-cold Cokes around a table we could actually set our bottles on. But here with Pereira, reality reasserted itself with a stinging slap. Nearly three hundred snaking, scantly populated miles still separated us from the mouth of the Jutaí and the bright lights of the town bearing the same name, Jutaí, with its twenty-five thousand souls.

Possuelo had hoped to trade an ax for some course-grained manioc farinha, but Pereira had none to spare.

"Will you be coming back this way?" he asked.

"No, we're heading all the way down," Possuelo said. "Long way, right?"

"Longe mesmo," Pereira said, drawing out the words with a slow shake of his head, as though it were so unbelievably long that it strained the imagination. It was time to go.

CHAPTER 23

Rendezvous

EVERYWHERE THE RIVER was in the process of transitioning to the dry season. The level of the river continued to drop, leaving consecutive lines of dried and drying mud along the banks like rings on a bathtub. The trees had been dropping, too, from either side of the river, though by now the Jutaí was far too wide for a single tree to obstruct navigation. Some of the giants had fallen during the most recent floods, others years ago, their bark bleached to a dull silver, branches reaching up from the water like mangled appendages. Soldado pointed to a yellow marker perched on a pole high atop the bank. "That's used to mark the high-water line of the river," he said. It was nearly forty feet above our heads.

The air was thick with moisture, the light blinding white. A thatched hut, old and wilting, came into view on the top of the bank. Two giant pirarucus were drying on a wooden rack, their pallid meat curing in the blast-furnace heat of the sun. "Let's have a look!" barked Possuelo. We slid to the shore. Alcino Marubo, standing on the nose of the canoe like a harpooner, pitched a fifteen-foot pole into the sandy shallows. The craft thus anchored, it slowly swung about in the current, facing upstream as we jumped into the ankle-deep water.

An old man in a straw hat hobbled down from the shack with a hesitant gait. "Fear not," shouted Possuelo up the bank, seeing the man's reticence. "We come in peace." Unlike the Itaquaí, where FUNAI controlled the access and strangers were a rarity, it seemed that here the prevailing law was the law of the fist. The arrival of strangers often meant the arrival of problems. Government officials were greeted with equal reserve, either because they themselves were on the take, or because they might turn out to be incorruptible agents who would actually enforce the criminal code.

Did he have *macaxeira* he could sell us? Possuelo asked. "Nothing." The man shrugged. "Pack of boar came through, ate my entire patch." By now, he reached the shore and extended his hand to Possuelo. His name was José Santos, and he'd lived on this same bluff for forty years. "I've grown old here," Santos said with a wan smile, squinting into the bright sun, his dark eyes mere slits beneath white eyebrows so wildly overgrown they looked like paste-ons. Possuelo turned his gaze up the hill toward the house, where a pair of pirarucus were hanging like ghosts to cure from porch rafters and several kids stared apprehensively out through gaps between the shack's rough-hewn planks. He said: "How about salt—and maybe some of your fish? We've got some axes." Santos said he couldn't spare any, had mouths to feed. He did have ripe lemons if we wanted to send a crew back upriver to pick them. "Five beaches up," he said. Possuelo thought about it. Too far, he concluded.

Fish were getting scarce, Santos explained, ever since a fat cat called Carlão—"Big Carlos"—began coming up this way. "He brings lots of men in motorboats. They cover the entire river with their nets, from here clear across to the other side. They take everything." Big Carlos was also buying from the Kanamari, he said. Not just fish, but timber as well. "The Kanamari are cutting cedar for him," Santos said. "They go up the *igarapés* to cut the trees, then float them out at the time of high water." Carlos's team gathered the trunks on the banks, then sawed them into fifteen-foot-long sections, called *toras,* and corralled them into huge rafts to float downriver to the sawmills of Jutaí.

"When we came up here to shut down the Javari and get the whites out," Possuelo said, "we found three hundred *toras* in a single creek, waiting to be taken out. That was just one creek!"

Santos nodded. "That's how it was." Santos said Carlão was buying pirarucu from the Kanamari for a mere 20 *reais,* roughly $7 each for an entire fish. It didn't seem possible. One of the Amazon's most ancient and magnificent creatures was being decimated for a pittance. Its hardwoods were being looted for pennies on the dollar. Delimiting the Terra Indigena had gone a long way to stanch the hemorrhage up this way, but the pressure was constant, always nibbling at the edges. Enforcement alone could never work; the distances were too vast, personnel and resources too scarce. There had to be another way, some kind of alternative that would give the cash-starved peoples of the Amazon—Indian and non-Indian alike—a stake in its preservation.

"How far to the Curuena?" Possuelo asked. The name had acquired the ring of mythical resonance for us, like the Promised Land, where we were scheduled to meet our salvation—the *Kukahá*. Santos took a long look at our canoes, the ragged oarsmen, our blistered hands. He knit his brow. "Rowing from early morning till night, I'd say three days."

"You know the old man, named Heleno?"

"Yeah," Santos said, nodding. "Don't really know. Know of him."

"Is he still living up there on the Curuena?"

"As far as I know," replied Santos.

"Well, we're going to pay him a visit. He's squatting on Indian land, and I'm going to get him out of there."

Santos pulled on the brim of his hat. *"Boa sorte,"* he said. "Good luck."

* * *

The days seemed interminable, rowing for hours on end along the high jungle walls, blistering sun beating down. The canoe had taken on a nauseating odor. We were beset by clouds of insects, so thick I went back to wearing long pants, long sleeves, and boots at all times. Nights were equally trying. We camped at a site overrun with *tracuá*, after Possuelo skipped over several ideal locations. He didn't even bother to come to the campfire that night, leaving the rest of us to dance around to keep the ants off while we tried to eat.

"He did that last night *por gusto*—for pure pleasure," Soldado whispered to me the next morning. "You see how many good places we went by that he ignored?" That Possuelo might be inflicting misery on us by design was a disquieting thought, but there seemed to be no other explanation.

We finally reached the Curuena, as Santos had predicted, three days after we'd pushed off from his shores. Thunder was barreling in a darkening sky in the late afternoon, and it looked like we were in for a drenching. Then we caught sight of a long sandbar jutting out from the low, jungle-strangled bank to our left that marked the mouth of the incoming tributary. It entered the Jutaí at an oblique seven-o'clock angle, its current so powerful that it pushed our canoes sideways as we crossed in front of it. The Jutaí's right bank loomed high above us—a forty-foot vertical cliff topped with towering trees that ran unbroken down a long straightaway that seemed to go on forever.

There was no sign of the *Kukahá*. We paddled along the high wall, Possuelo standing atop his bench, hands on hips, as he studied the cliffs like an ancient mariner looking for a place to put in on a foreign shore. The paddles dipped in unison and we followed downstream to their rhythmic pulse and the low rumble of thunder. One by one, Possuelo rejected potential landing sites. "Ground's too low" or "Too many trees blocking the shore." Where a huge kapok had fallen diagonally down the bank and into the river, Tepi and Kwini hopped off and scampered up the enormous trunk and then through a jumble of brush to the top of the bank. *"Burrá kimo!"* they shouted moments later. "Perfect!"

We clawed our way up the embankment, heaved our bags over the top, and stood on the edge of dense forest. The rain had held off, and now in the magical hour just before day's end, the clouds cracked apart, giving way to a syrupy golden light that streamed in through the trees. Eleven days after departing the main camp, we'd reached the rendezvous point. The canoes had served their purpose.

At least we were on dry, level ground, with no *tracuá*, and plenty of firm trees for hanging our hammocks. Our individual *barracas* were spread out in clusters beneath the towering kapoks. My site occupied a niche in a buttress-rooted tree at the end of a cul-de-sac, just beyond those of Possuelo, Nicolas, and Orlando, about a hundred feet from the main campfire. By sunset, the way down to the river was complete, an engineering feat that included three zigzagging flights of stairs, each with a banister, and a total of forty-three steps etched into the cliff. A long catwalk over the mudflats led from the stairs to a sturdy washing platform built out over the water.

From the top of the bank you could see for at least two miles straight down the river and nearly the same distance back up the other way. It was hard to believe we were looking out on the same waterway that we'd first stumbled upon as a narrow *igarapé* twisting through dense jungle so many weeks before, that we'd crossed heel to toe upon a slippery log one morning, and that we had later stared across with pounding hearts, certain in our knowledge that invisible eyes were returning our gaze from the forest on the other side. That same river was now spread out before us, a vast silver sheet nearly three hundred yards wide, running straight as a desert highway into the distance.

The unobstructed line of sight across the river and over the treetops on the opposite shore allowed for clear radio reception from the north and northwest, meaning with both the Tabatinga base and the Ituí-Itaquaí outpost. A thatched kiosk was hastily constructed at the top of the bank, the two-way radio was positioned on a high table inside, and its antenna was strung up into the trees. Here Possuelo installed himself, one foot resting on a tree stump, his elbow leaning on the table, as he barked commands into the handheld mike.

The *Kukahá* had started up the Jutaí only that morning, from what Possuelo could make out. He suspected the boat pilots—Pedro Lima and the old Tikuna Adelson—had done more in Jutaí City than simply refuel, as per his instructions. Otherwise, they'd have departed the night before. "Cretins," he groused. "Never do as they're told." But he was in good humor all the same, in the mood to entertain. Watching him work the radio was like having a front-row seat at the Improv. He'd commandeered the Afrika Korps hat from Orlando, and it sat cocked sideways atop his head, the brim comically askew. He rolled his eyes in mock exasperation when speaking to Danilo aboard the *Kukahá* and cracked brutal off-mike jokes at the expense of Siqueira, on the line in Tabatinga, who had just repeated something perfectly obvious for the third time. He cursed Francisco, manning the outpost at the confluence, for rambling on about some irrelevancy or otherwise missing the point. This was the other side of Possuelo—funny, charming, engaging, even compassionate.

A pair of long benches had been installed alongside the command post, looking downriver. When they weren't off hunting or chopping wood, the men would hang out there, enthralled with Possuelo's antics. But I'd lost all interest in hanging out, retreating into morose introspection. Never had I experienced time moving at such an agonizingly glacial pace. I had the sense that my life was falling to pieces, and that I couldn't even start picking them up or see how they'd fit back together until I got home. Home? I didn't even know where that was. I didn't know where Sarah was, if she'd decided to take a job elsewhere, whether I'd be moving there to be near her. I thought of the boys constantly. I didn't know how I was going to manage to stay in their lives, and I didn't even know how I was going to earn a living when I got back. It all sounded so absurdly complicated that I couldn't even begin to explain it to anyone. So I kept it to myself.

The anguish was no doubt exacerbated by a gnawing hunger that never seemed to dissipate, no matter how much greasy wild boar or bony smoked piranha I'd try to stuff in my mouth. The menu had grown so monotonous I could barely stomach any of it anyway. Even tightening my belt all the way, it was difficult to keep my pants cinched to my waist.

Midway through the following day, we were draped languidly over the benches at the top of the bank, the men engaged in fatuous banter, when a shout went up: *"Kukahá!"* All fell silent. We strained our ears. From downriver came the faint thrum of a sputtering engine. We rose to our feet, staring down the long straightaway, the water smooth as glass reflecting the deep blue sky and high white clouds. The boat appeared far downriver, a tiny speck bobbing in the midst of that vast convergence of sky and water. It had the outline of a classic Amazon riverboat, and it sliced the water like a knife at its pointed bow, trailing a perfect V-shaped wake that stretched across the entire width of the river. It was a sight to behold.

We could scarcely contain our excitement, but as the boat drew near, it resolved into a small, single-deck vessel, much like the low-lying *Sobral*. An official-looking emblem adorned the side of its cabin, but not that of FUNAI. It was rather that of FUNASA, the much-maligned public health agency. Three bewhiskered men stood in the boat's open doorway on the port side, arms folded, staring out on the river. They passed without saying a word, their eyes barely seeming to register our existence. Not even a hand was raised in greeting.

"Brutes," spat Possuelo. "You'd think they'd stop to see if anyone here was sick—or dead." Dead would have seemed more likely, given our hollow-eyed, spectral appearance. Which was probably why the boat continued on its way, churning upriver, indifferent to our fate, its wake spanning the breadth of the river's glassy surface. It might have helped had we offered even the simplest welcoming gesture to the FUNASA men, a smile or a wave of our own, rather than returning their gaze with stone-cold stares of contempt.

It would be two more days before the *Kukahá* made its appearance. Two more nights around the campfire with Sydney Possuelo. To be fair, had it not been for his oratorical acumen, our nights would have devolved into mindless chitchat, punctuated by long silences. Instead, we got Possuelo. His anti-Western, antiwhite diatribes were standard fare at his nighttime disquisitions: the litany of European-perpetrated atrocities, the white man's sordid quest for wealth and status, the glaring inequalities and injustices, our cavalier disregard for the planet, our gross overconsumption of its resources.

The whites drifted away after dinner, no doubt feeling inadequate to the task of conversing in such abstractions. Perhaps, too, they suspected Possuelo was implicitly lashing out at them, that these evening rants were a camouflaged extension of the more overt brow-beating they endured in the daytime hours.

Yet for all his discursive heavy-handedness, Possuelo was not an ideologue, at least not in the common sense of the word. His social critiques were sui generis, of his own hand; he was too much the icono-clast to adhere to anyone's party line. Nor was I ever singled out for vilification because of my nationality. Brazilian, North American, Por-tuguese, Spaniard, or Englishman—it made no difference; we were all part of a single sickly scourge afflicting the planet. Among shades of white, Possuelo did not discriminate. He judged you on the strength of your merits and your weaknesses; for the most part, you were in for a protracted exercise in ego deflation.

He did have a powerful point: the original Americans were un-doubtedly better off before our European forebears arrived at their shores. And if there were still some final holdouts, like the Arrow Peo-ple, who refused to join the rest of the world, didn't they have the right to be left alone, to live the way they and their ancestors always had? Of course, there were plenty of people who didn't think so: officials who believed Possuelo was denying the natives the "right" to assimila-tion; gold prospectors who claimed to be bringing the "benefits of civilization" to the forests they plundered; evangelizers who lamented the departure of Indian souls for a "Christless eternity" even while introducing, inadvertently or not, the deadly epidemics that hastened their departure from this Earth. Together, they amounted to an impla-cable foe that stirred the depths of Possuelo's rage.

"If Indians were to declare war on the whites tomorrow," Possuelo told me that night after everyone else had turned in, "I'd take the In-dians' side. That's what's in my heart." I got the feeling that he actually would have welcomed the prospect, were it not so obvious how disas-trous the outcome would be.

When the *Kukahá* did arrive two days later, it was without ceremony. We watched in silence from the top of the embankment as Pedro Lima nosed the boat to the shore alongside the platform. Danilo and Adel-son dropped the gangplank and made their way up the long stairway.

"*Com licença*—with your permission," Danilo said with mock formality upon reaching the top. "You may enter," Paulo Welker said. He was the same old Danilo—rotund and jovial. But as he looked around at the sullen faces and sunken chests, he hardly seemed to recognize us. It was as though he were beholding an entirely different group of men from the one he'd taken leave of two months earlier on the Itaquaí River. The smile faded from his lips.

"How many outboard boats did you bring?" asked Possuelo, peering down at the *Kukahá* and the launches it trailed in the stern.

"Two."

"I ordered you to bring three."

"We could only come up with two that had functioning motors."

"Amazing," Possuelo sneered. "No one ever does what I ask." A more blasé reception for a rescue team could scarcely have been imagined.

Adelson appeared at the top of the steps. He looked around as if searching for a familiar face in a crowd of strangers. When our eyes met, he did a double take.

"My God!" he cried. "Look at Scott! He's so skinny!" He looked me up and down. *"N-nossa!"* he stammered. "My God! Looks like you've had a hard time!" We embraced. It was good to see Adelson. I'd enjoyed our long talks up in the wheelhouse of the *Waiká* as we inched our way up the Itaquaí. I looked forward to renewing our friendship on the way down the Jutaí. He looked none the worse for wear, dressed in his ragged denim cutoffs and signature bush hat, still sporting the sparse tuft of long whiskers on his chin.

We bounded down the stairs and boarded the boat. The galley counter was stacked with eggs in industrial-size cardboard trays, four dozen to a carton. A pot of carrots was on the stove, a sack of onions in the corner. The first vegetables we'd laid eyes on in more than two months. Possuelo was upstairs in the master cabin, where frigid air blasted from the AC unit. He was trying to engage his Globalstar phone, but the signal was weak and kept failing. As I passed back through the galley, Paulo Welker grabbed me by the arm and spun me around. Without a word, he shoved a heaving spoonful of Hershey's chocolate powder into my mouth. How could I refuse? The sensation was intense, as though taste buds long dormant had suddenly been revived. Welker put his finger to his lips to indicate silence; this was to be a shared little secret. I'd seen that gesture before. Ah, then I remembered: back in the jungle on the trail of the Arrow People, when he signaled me to hush. How far we'd traveled since then. How far he'd fallen from grace.

All around, the place jumped with activity. Men rowed the canoes to the far side of the river, where they were upended, submerged, and scrubbed. Possuelo planned to take them back to the Ituí-Itaquaí post; in the meantime, he ordered their insides scoured, dried, and coated with burnt motor oil to ward off infestation. The *peci-peci* outboards on the small boats roared to life, with Amarildo and Pedro ferrying men back and forth to the canoes, where Soldado was supervising the restoration effort. In a matter of minutes, a sleepy patch of wilderness had been transformed into a bustling hub.

Despite the arrival of the *Kukahá* and its galley cabinets bursting with provisions, the evening's menu remained unchanged: smoked pork and *macaxeira*. But it didn't seem to matter. The mood had lightened, the air charged with anticipation. Hearty laughs punctuated the mealtime banter. As the men wolfed down the last morsels of dinner, Possuelo pounded on his tin bowl with a spoon. "I know everyone is wondering what's going to happen next," he said. "Here's what we're going to do. There's an old man named Heleno who lives with his family up the Curuena. Some of you heard me asking about him on our way downriver." The men pressed in close to listen. "He's still living inside the Terra Indígena. I'm going to take a small detachment with me tomorrow. We're going to go up there and see what we can do about getting him out."

The Curuena River snaked back into the depths of the Javari reserve, and its headwaters harbored several isolated indigenous groups, including at least one *maloca* of Arrow People. Heleno Texeira and his wife had been squatting on public land there for fifty years, Possuelo said, and his family now included children, grandchildren, and great-grandchildren. He'd acquired a reputation as a maverick frontiers-man, manning a lone outpost in a jungle rife with untamed Indians. Heleno and his kin were the only whites who'd managed to avoid ex-pulsion when the Javari reserve was decreed. Apparently they'd yet to receive due compensation for their house and crops, and they weren't leaving until they did.

"They are not bad people," Possuelo said, taking care to make eye contact with the Indians. "But they are living in indigenous territory. It belongs to you, the Indians. As long as they stay there, other whites will think it's all right for them to go, too. They'll say: 'Heleno's there with his family. Why not us?'"

The Texeira homestead could become a flash point for violence, Possuelo continued, the target of an Indian attack that could invite reprisals. "As long as they remain there, contact could happen at any moment. Whether the contact is violent or peaceful, it will be the same for the Indians—ruinous!" It was time to round up the old man's ex-pansive family and get them out.

CHAPTER 24

The Old Man and the River

W E LOADED THE LAUNCHES from the back of the *Kukahá* in the early-morning fog. These were not the same long, thin boats that had taken us to the far reaches of the Itaquaí. They had the same *peci-peci* outboards to navigate shallow waters, but these boats were shorter and stouter, with squared-off sterns like normal punts. With only two boats rather than the three Possuelo had requested, he'd selected a scaled-down detachment—ten men in all—for the Curuena mission. The roster included Soldado; the skinny and cheerful Amarildo; the two Marubo; Márcio and Remi Kanamari; the riverboat-gambler cook Paulo Souza; and boat pilot Pedro Lima. Nicolas and I rounded out the roster. I had packed the bare necessities: a change of clothes, my hammock, and my tarp. I left the rest of my stuff suspended in bags from the crossbeam of my shelter. We'd be back in four or five days, Possuelo figured.

In the meantime, Possuelo wanted the Matis and Kanamari staying behind to continue their intertribal fraternizing, the better to build the pan-Indian consciousness he sought to instill. "You should go fishing together, hunting together, keep learning words in one another's language," he told the Indians, who had gathered to see us off. "This is important. United—Matis, Kanamari, Marubo—you are strong. You can keep the white man out so you have plenty to eat and can live happily. Have fun together, become good friends. Do you understand?" The Indians nodded. "And another thing . . ."

I didn't wait around to hear what the other thing was. I dashed up the ladder to the master cabin on the upper deck, where Possuelo's Globalstar was charging in its cradle on the desk. I dialed Lake George. The boys would have made it there by now, and my parents would be there, too. Voice mail picked up; too early for anyone to be awake. I left a message, saying I was all right. I made one more call, to Sarah. My heart pounded as I heard the phone ringing on the other end. And then, an automated voice answered. The line had been disconnected. She'd left New York.

"Where's Scott?" boomed Possuelo from down below. No time for another call; it would have to wait. I scrambled down the steps to find everyone waiting for me, the skiffs all loaded and ready to go: backpacks, foodstuffs, weapons, fuel. We even had the old chain saw. I tumbled into a seat in the bow alongside Adelino Marubo. Nicolas and Paulo Souza were right behind us, followed by Márcio and Remi. All the way in the back, Pedro Lima manned the outboard. The other skiff was piloted by Amarildo, with Possuelo and Alcino Marubo on the middle bench, and Soldado at the bow.

We turned up the Curuena, water smooth as glass. The mood was cheerful and relaxed, especially since Possuelo was in the other boat. We filled our cups with steaming coffee from a thermos. The can of chocolate powder made its way around the boat, everyone taking a turn to shove a spoonful in his mouth, ducking to stay out of both the wind and Possuelo's line of sight. "Make sure Sydney doesn't see!" said Nicolas. He peeled a carrot and handed half to me. I chomped with gusto.

The sun broke through the clouds. Shrieking blue macaws flew wing to wing across the water, their yellow breasts aglow with light bouncing off the water. We fell in behind the other skiff and slid into its wake. The river's glassy surface offered up a spectacular mirror image of the towering walls of jungle and a cloud-mottled sky that seemed to go on forever. After days of laborious paddling at a snail's pace, it was an undeniable thrill to be gliding without the slightest effort through this vast waterworld, feeling the wind on our faces, experiencing the forest zipping past on our flanks, and watching the ever-shifting reflections of sky and jungle receding on the water before us.

We pulled even with a brilliant white beach and the first suggestions of human presence: footprints that led from one pillaged turtle nest to another.

"*Nawa*—white man," Adelino said.

"How do you know?" I asked.

"I don't," he replied with a vague smile. But he was probably right. This far downriver, it was unlikely to be anyone else. Adelino had pocked cheeks flanking a broad, bulbous nose, and his jet-black hair stood in artlessly groomed clumps, as though it had been clipped by a hedge trimmer. Unlike many of the Indians with us, he knew his age—thirty. He could even read and write a little, thanks to the New Tribes missionaries in Rio Novo, for whom literacy was part and parcel of coming to know the Word of God.

I hadn't spoken much with the Marubo in the past two months. For the most part, they were quiet and taciturn and kept mainly to themselves. But sitting with Adelino in the front of the skiff afforded a chance to get better acquainted. Like just about everyone else, he was looking forward to getting home. "There will be very big party," he said. "Everyone gets dressed up with macaw feathers, armbands, necklaces. The *caisuma* is very sweet. Everyone dances."

It turned out that Adelino's real name, the one he used among his people, was Washakama. It was not uncommon for Indians to have both tribal names and "white" ones, which they used in their dealings with the outside world. It was their way to keep their distance, perhaps even to protect their spirits, from corrupting influences. The Matis employed few such aliases, but among the Marubo and the Kanamari it was common practice. Possuelo never used their indigenous names, always their white ones. I understood this as a show of respect for their boundaries. Following the example of the Villas Boas brothers, Possuelo was emphatic in his refusal to "go native" in any way. He maintained a distance. He never participated in their sacred ceremonies or attempted to uncover tribal secrets. When it came to native names, I followed his example. I came to know our companions' indigenous names, but I did not use them.

Adelino was already thinking about collecting his wages and the shopping spree that would ensue in Tabatinga and Leticia. Along with ammunition for his shotgun, Adelino planned to buy household goods—pots, plates, spoons, soap, fishhooks—and presents for his wife and two children. The shotgun shells were essential to his ability to provide for the family. Only the Marubo elders still knew how to make the stiff but supple long bow and the fletched cane arrows tribesmen had hunted with for aeons.

Adelino said he liked Possuelo, especially because he had thrown the whites out of the Terra Indigena. "Before, there were lots of *brancos*—loggers, fishermen, hunters. They took everything—the animals, the wood, the fish. They cut down the kapoks and the cedar. Now there are lots of animals—boar, *tracajá*, monkey. Now the river has many fish." Clearly where Adelino was concerned, Possuelo's teachings had not been for naught. Without intact forest, the Indians had nothing. Environmental protection was central to their survival.

* * *

Early in the afternoon, a large frame house came into view off to the left, set back against the woods atop a gently sloping bank. We cut our engines and drifted toward the shore, our arrival greeted by a pack of snarling mongrels. "These dogs bite?" Possuelo shouted up the bank. "Yes, they do," came a voice from somewhere up the hill. A wiry man in cutoffs and a loose-fitting shirt came out from behind a line draped with laundry. He loped toward us with a lazy shuffle like he had all the time in the world. The dogs yelped and bared their teeth. Possuelo went for his holster. "We might be obliged to put a bullet in one of these animals," he said, "if you don't get down here and control them."

"The name's Marinaldo," the man said, reaching the shore and calling off the dogs. They turned tail and scampered off. Marinaldo was built solidly. His open shirt revealed rippling six-pack abs. Bulging arteries laced his forearms. Possuelo stood in the boat, pumping him for information: Were there hunters upriver? Loggers? Were they floating logs downriver? "Not many," Marinaldo said, shrugging. "Everything's calm." There were three more houses farther upriver, he reported. The very last one belonged to Heleno.

"The cripple?" said he. "Missing part of his leg?"

"That's the one," Possuelo confirmed with a nod.

Marinaldo looked at our boats. "You won't make it there today," he said. "Maybe not even tomorrow."

We barreled on at full throttle, cutting in and out of a labyrinth of submerged trees, zipping past a succession of high shimmering beaches. We passed one house painted white, set idyllically against the forest. As the sun began to drop low in the sky, we passed the second house. Only Heleno's remained. We kept on, racing to get as far upriver as possible before nightfall.

We camped that evening in an enchanted glade, with soft, sandy soil and strange, low-lying trees with sideways-growing trunks from which we suspended our hammocks. Fireflies winked, and luminescent moths cruised through the gathering dusk. From deep in the forest came the bleating of nighthawks, shrill and monosyllabic, like baby cats. Suddenly a man in a brilliant white shirt appeared in the twilight, coming toward us like a ghostly apparition. *"Boa noite!"* He called out. The man's name was José. His handshake was firm. He was one of Heleno Texeira's sons, he said, on his way back to the family home. He'd heard we were heading in the same direction. The conversation was polite. "No one has ever come to measure the size of the house, or to inspect the crops to determine our compensation," he said. Possuelo invited him to stay the night, but he refused. "Need to keep moving," he said. "But I'll see you up there soon." He went on his way, standing in a tiny dugout canoe, poling it upriver end over end, vanishing into the night.

After a simple dinner of pork and *macaxeira*, I went back to the river's edge to wash up. I squatted there, water lapping at my feet, oblivious to any lurking danger. I heard a voice behind me: "Watch out for the caiman." It was Possuelo. He flicked on his flashlight. Jesus! A pair of red eyes glowered straight at me, no more than fifty feet away. It was a monster, judging from the wide gap between its eyes. "Watch out, Scott," Possuelo said. "He could have eaten you for his dinner."

We were out on the river at dawn. Within an hour, we came upon a canopied canoe drifting downstream. Two young men stood in the vessel, fore and aft, poling it through the shallows. A motor, wrapped in plastic, was cocked at the stern. "No gasoline," explained the guy in the back. Possuelo grilled them: What were they doing? Where were they going? Any hunters upriver? What about the guy who lives at the fork in the river—is he up there?

"The cripple?" said the guy in the back. "Yeah, he's there."

The Cripple. He was beginning to acquire legendary status in my imagination: Heleno Texeira, the grotesquely maimed villain, conducting his quest for global domination from a forbidden hideout deep in the jungle.

The channel continued to narrow, the way forward clogged with downed trees at every turn, their barren limbs twisted in strange contortions. At the confluence of a black-water creek that entered from the right, we passed a plaque marking the boundary of Terra Indigena and took a right where the river forked. We were back in Indian Country. We slowed to a crawl to get past enormous branches that hung low out over the water, everyone sprawling facedown as the brittle limbs snapped and raked across our backs. We skidded across trunks submerged just beneath the surface, Pedro deftly yanking the prop again and again just in time to spare the propeller.

We'd already ventured ninety miles up the Curuena, according to the map, double that in actual distance, and still no Heleno. "You can see how hard it is to keep an eye on things up here," said Possuelo when we stopped on a beach to stretch. "The area is larger than many countries in Europe." Why anyone would choose to live so far from the comforts of civilization in such radical isolation from the rest of the world was beyond me, especially with nothing standing between him and the unvanquished tribes upriver.

Which was exactly why Possuelo wanted them out. There was a good chance the Texeiras were logging upriver from their house, Possuelo thought, bringing them ever closer to a violent clash with the Arrow People or some other group—the uncontacted Tsohom Djapá, perhaps. "To get the valuable timber, you have to go deeper and deeper in, farther and farther upriver. The farther you go, the greater the chance of a *choque* with the Indians."

Perhaps even more troubling was the chance that Heleno's family could suddenly find themselves playing reluctant hosts to organized crime—heavily armed drug traffickers or timber mafias commandeering their home as a springboard for deeper penetration into the jungle.

* * *

The Texeira compound turned out to be both far more modest and far more spectacular that I had envisioned. Early on the morning of our third day, we came to a fork in the river, and took the south branch. Just ahead, what appeared to be the main house rose on the left bank, a steeply crested thatched structure set in the shade of a luxuriant mango tree. The house stood atop stout ten-foot pylons, and behind it rose a cluster of majestic *acaí* palms. Six canoes were moored to uprights on the shore out front, like cars in a driveway. One was completely filled with peeled *macaxeira*—sweet manioc—soaking in water, the prelude to grinding it for farinha. The home was flanked by a large banana grove on one side and neat rows of manioc, their leafy, knee-high tops stretching back to the edge of the forest. Chickens squawked. Kids ran barefoot through the yard amid squeals of laughter. José stood out front, wearing the same brilliant white shirt we'd seen two days before. "Welcome to Igarapé Lobo!" he called. "That's what we call it here. Come on in!" The lair of Dr. Evil this was not.

"Pedro, take the Marubo and Kanamari for a look around upriver," Possuelo said in a low hush. "See if there's anything unusual. Be back here in an hour or so."

A notched log served as the stairway up to the front door. I followed Possuelo up the steps. A diminutive man with unkempt gray hair sat crumpled in the middle of the split-palm floor, a single leg folded beneath him. A four-day stubble covered his gaunt face. Twisted horn-rimmed glasses dangled at an odd angle from his nose, thick lenses magnifying a pair of sad brown eyes. A tattered purple T-shirt that read FREE LOOK in English in big block letters hung from his sagging shoulders. I guessed he was about seventy years old.

"You're just in time for *café da manhã*—breakfast," said Heleno Texeira. We approached to receive his handshake, taking pains to step atop the crossbeams so we wouldn't fall through the thin flooring. A stiff deerskin and an old guitar hung from the rafters above his head. Shirts, shoes, and an old Singer sewing machine were tucked into crevices against a waist-high partition that walled off the sleeping quarters behind him.

"So you've come to kick us out?" said a handsome, rail-thin woman in a faded gingham dress, raising her voice from the kitchen alcove off to the left where she hovered over a steaming pot. "The government exists for one purpose—to take everything away from you." Her name was Amazoninha—"Little Amazon"—and she was Heleno's wife of fifty years. She handed each of us a plate of steaming pancakes smothered in wild honey, along with a cup brimming with *café com leite*. It was like magic; we'd traveled to the ends of the Earth for a stack of piping hot pancakes! As I ate, a mangy bird with long legs and neck—a gray-winged trumpeter—pressed its head against the back of my hand with endearing insistence. If I stopped stroking it for even a second, it would nudge me with its downy crest. I hadn't experienced such tenderness in a very long time.

"Officials will come here, and they will pay you," Possuelo said at length. "They will measure your house. They will measure the size of your *cultivos*. You will be compensated accordingly: a square meter of planted *macaxeira* is worth so much. But you will have to leave. You won't be compensated for the land, because that's property of the *união*—the union." As in the States, the "union" meant the federal government. "All you have to do is move down below the plaque, outside the Terra Indigena, live there for five years, and the land will be yours." That was one interpretation of the law, which was nebulous enough on the issue of squatters' rights to be a source of ongoing feuds and land wars across the Amazon.

"We've been here for forty-eight years," Amazoninha said. She didn't need to say the rest: *A lot of good that's done us.* They had forty thousand *macaxeira* plants ready to harvest and another three thousand they'd recently planted. In another time and place, the Texeiras would have been hailed as model citizens, environmental stewards, exactly the kind of decent, hardworking settlers an Ohio-born nun named Dorothy Stang was organizing farther east in the state of Pará to resist powerful ranchers who were razing the forest to plant pastureland for their cattle, a crusade for which she would eventually pay with her life. Unfortunately for the Texeiras, they had no way of knowing when they settled here that this small patch of forest in which they would invest a lifetime of toil would one day be declared off-limits, whatever claim they might have had to it null and void.

Behind Amazoninha, the kitchen ceiling was caked with the soot of countless cooking fires. Rows of old powdered-milk cans, dozens of them, were wedged against the blackened roof. Spoons and toothbrushes were stuck in the thatching. Frying pans, cooking pots, and big metal washbasins hung by their handles from the rafters above a table spread with a red-and-white-checked oilcloth. The yellowed pages of newspapers and old drugstore calendars papered the kitchen walls. It looked like a tropical version of a Walker Evans still life.

Heleno had arrived here from the Juruá as a young homesteader, he said, invited to tap rubber for a man named Mario Ferreira, who claimed to own everything along the entire length of the Jutaí back in the day. Heleno brought along Amazoninha and their firstborn son, then only months old. "All the rest were born here," he said, still sitting in a heap in the middle of the floor. When the boys were old enough to work, they joined Heleno on his daily rounds to milk the rubber trees. He hired local Indians to beef up the workforce. More than once, they clashed with untamed tribesmen upriver. "The last time was more than ten years ago," said Heleno. "More like twenty," interjected José, who had been sitting quietly in the corner. "Four were killed on each side—four of them, four of us." It was a startling admission, followed by a long silence.

If Possuelo required any further reason to get the Texeiras out, he'd just heard it. He didn't care how long ago it had happened. Without definitive expulsion of all the whites, violence would erupt again; it was just a matter of time. History had demonstrated graphically enough, on the Upper Amazon and elsewhere throughout the Americas, that a single well-organized reprisal raid could obliterate a whole village, wipe out the last remnants of an entire tribe, and no one on the outside would even be the wiser. All screams were smothered, all evidence was snuffed out, in the vast depths of the jungle. Not that the Texeiras would do it. But they could find themselves unwitting accomplices. The white presence, ipso facto, was a threat.

Did the Indians still come around? Possuelo wanted to know. Heleno shook his head. "You know, Indians don't attack whites just because they like to or because it's their nature," Possuelo said, imparting a quick civics lesson. "They do it because, in the past, whites burned their villages and razed their crops. They'd kill the Indians that didn't get away." He spoke strictly in generalities, not wanting the Texeiras to think he was imputing guilt.

It was clear in any case that Heleno's fighting days were long behind him. It had been seven years since his foot had been shattered when a grandson accidentally discharged a shotgun he was cleaning. It took ten days and nights full-out in a motorboat to reach the hospital in Jutaí. By the time Heleno got there, the gangrene had spread most of the way up his leg. There was no choice but to amputate.

The grandkids and great-grandkids were growing antsy, jumping around in the grown-ups' laps, fixing us with bright, cheery smiles. They were way too young to comprehend the ill tidings we bore for their family and their future.

All told, I asked, how many people lived here? "Hmmm. Let's see," said José. He pulled a calculator from his pocket. He seemed to be racking his brain as he entered computations on the keypad, mumbling all the while. At last he looked up and said: "Seventeen."

Maybe it would work out for the best, Heleno said with a sigh. They'd move to the city; the young ones could go to school. "We knew it would come to this one day," he said with abject resignation. "We'd have to leave." But the idea seemed to fill him with dread. "The city is for people who have a job. No one's going to hire me. The forest is where someone like me belongs." He offered me a cigarette. I took one, then fished around for a light. Before I could stop him, he hopped up on his one leg and came across the floor to me, lighter in his outstretched hand. There seemed to be no end to the man's graciousness. "It's been good here," he said. *"Boa de mais."* Better than anything he'd ever known or would ever know again. As he looked out the open doorway, past the mango tree and out beyond the yard to the river, I could see it all reflected in his big Coke-bottle glasses. His small piece of paradise. Still, his voice betrayed not a trace of bitterness.

"Hey, Sydney!" Pedro called from the shore. He'd just returned with the others.

Possuelo rose to his feet. "The people will come soon," Possuelo said. "Be ready to leave." He started across to the doorway, then turned back. "Do you need fuel? I'll trade you forty liters for two sacks of your farinha and a basket of *macaxeira*." Heleno nodded. They had a deal.

I bent down to say good-bye to Heleno. He would not be coming down to see us off. "Farewell, *meu querido*," he said, wrapping my hand warmly inside both of his. "All the happiness in the world for you." *My dear one*—did I hear him right? It was one of those encounters: an hour spent with a complete stranger you will never see again who touches your life in a way you will never forget.

At the bottom of the notched log, Amazoninha laid a bony hand on my forearm. *"Felicidade para você,"* she said, echoing her husband's sentiments. I couldn't help but wonder where all this goodwill sprang from. They wanted nothing but the best for us. They should have wanted us dead.

We climbed into the boats and backed out into the current. Pedro gunned the throttle. Amarildo's skiff followed in our wake. Heleno's wife, his children, his grandchildren, and their children spilled out of the doorway, down the ladder, and onto the beach, waving as we disappeared around the bend. We regrouped a short way downstream, on the sandy shore of Igarapé Lobo. "As soon as I get back to Brasília, I'm going to get the paperwork moving to get them out of here," Possuelo said.

We resumed the journey, dodging through the submerged trunks, half-sunken branches, and floating logs. Once the Texeiras left Wolf Creek, and no one was around to remove the fallen trees, the channel would soon fill in, making navigation all but impossible. Access to the world beyond would shut down, and the Indians would once again reign supreme over the forest.

CHAPTER 25

The Gold Dredge

SHORTLY AFTER LEAVING Indian land behind, we roared past a canopied boat where two men reclined in hammocks, sleeping or pretending to sleep. We didn't give them a second thought, until a few hours later, when we came upon an enormous creature—long and twisted, yellow and green—bobbing on the surface. It was floating belly-up, knotted upon itself like a thick firehose, nearly thirty feet long. Its flanks were adorned with large yellow spots outlined in black, and it was bloated through its midsection like it had been pumped with air.

"It's an anaconda!" shouted Nicolas. Soldado vaulted into waist-deep water to untangle the dead serpent, grappling its slimy girth as he flipped it upright. Its head sprang free to reveal a large bullet hole. A nauseating stench enveloped us like a noxious cloud.

"It was those two idiots upriver," Possuelo said.

"A *sucuri*," said Soldado, wrestling with the ungainly monster, oblivious of the reek that had the rest of us gagging. "This kind of anaconda will flip a canoe right over, then squeeze you to death. I've seen it." Not that this one would have. Its belly was full; most likely, it had been lolling on the bank, digesting a pretty decent meal, when it was shot.

"What's the point in killing a magnificent creature like this?" said Possuelo, incredulous. "It posed no threat to them." Now he wished he'd stopped to find out what those guys had been up to, and why they were hanging out so close to the border of Indian land. He didn't like it. Acts of such gratuitous violence seemed to reveal a deeper, underlying contempt for life, as far as he was concerned, especially troubling when its perpetrators were loitering at the very doorstep of the protected area.

"Let's get out of here," Possuelo said.

When we got back to the Jutaí encampment, Orlando and Paulo Welker were huddled around the campfire, discussing a news clip they'd seen on the television aboard the *Kukahá*. CNN had obtained video purporting to show Osama bin Laden at a terrorist camp of undisclosed location, conducting ghoulish experiments on dogs to demonstrate the deadliness of some nerve agent he had come to possess. There was the evil bin Laden, a sadistic smile creeping across his face, like the Penguin or the Joker from some comic-book farce, threatening to poison Gotham's water supply. Behind him, dogs twitched and fell motionless.

Over the years and decades, Possuelo had found it best to shut himself off from the outside world while on expedition. He never took a shortwave radio with him, never bothered trying to keep up with world events. "What for?" he said. "What good would it do to know that India and Pakistan are threatening each other with nuclear weapons?" This first bit of news certainly bolstered his argument; it would have been hard to imagine a more depressing initial welcome back to the larger world. Could it really be possible that we were all connected, everyone on the planet, by six degrees of separation? It all seemed so far away from here, too huge a leap to contemplate. But oddly, my "connection" to bin Laden was clearly traceable: a close friend had interviewed him in an Afghan cave in 1996. We were thus separated by a mere two degrees. What about the Arrow People? Where was the trail of six knots that could possibly have bound me to them? We'd followed a path that led right into their village, but they'd fled just in time to preserve the fluid and invisible frontier that kept us apart. It was the same line that ran through the shadows and across the creek beds and maybe right up to the front door of Heleno's lonely outpost upriver. We'd been mere paces from the *flecheiros*, probably more than once; we'd likely even hovered in the sights of their drawn arrows. Yet in a very real sense, the Arrow People remained more removed than the bearded men holed up in the caves of the Hindu Kush. Maybe there was a connection through Wura, the Kanamari back on the Itaquaí, who claimed to have once visited a clan he called the "Capybara" so long ago. Perhaps through Aruá of the Tsohom Djapá, or his friend in the Boy Scouts shirt whose name I did not know. But then again, maybe not. Maybe six degrees couldn't get us to the Arrow People; maybe not even thirty. Maybe it would take going back two thousand generations, to the time when our common ancestors left Africa, to find the link. Perhaps that is the essence of what it means to remain uncontacted: to be that uncoupled from the global village. Too many degrees of separation to count. You couldn't get there from here.

* * *

A loud commotion carried up to the top of the bank from the water's edge. Soldado and Raimundo had just come ashore in a canoe, with an enormous pirarucu. They'd strung it up by the mouth to a pole, and they hoisted it over their heads like stretcher bearers to keep its tail from dragging on the ground. Soldado had shot it with his rifle upriver, when it came to the surface to breathe. But they had only just suspended the fish from a pair of forked poles when the command went up: We were leaving. The fish would have to be loaded aboard and cut up later. By the fire, Paulo Souza was breaking down cardboard boxes, dumping them in a heap on the smoldering coals. He seemed oblivious to the danger of spreading fire to the thatched canopy that had sheltered the hearth these past several days.

As the engines roared and the *Kukahá* pulled back from the shore, Paulo Souza's mound of garbage atop the bank caught fire with a spectacular whoosh that jumped into the thatching overhead in a roiling orange fireball, which quickly subsided. For days now, a dozen vultures had been keeping a grim vigil in the nearby trees. The ruffling of their wings had provided an unsettling backdrop to the trilling of insects at dusk and in the predawn hours. Their moment now arrived. They swooped down on the riverbank with brazen effrontery and, as if to make a mockery of our vain pursuits, seized control of the abandoned dock without even waiting for us to retreat from view.

I went to the upper deck to stretch out on the hard floor. It was the first time I'd been able to set my back down on a level surface in more than two months. I made my way fore to the wheelhouse, where a few plastic lawn chairs were scattered about. Sitting there looking down on the water as the jungle slipped past, I felt as though I were on a magic carpet ride.

Down below, the Kanamari had fallen asleep on the floor in a single heap, heedless of the throbbing engine that convulsed the floor with an unrelenting reverberation. Out on the bow, Orlando and Pedro were playing poker on Possuelo's laptop. Paulo Welker sat alone on the poop, headphones from a Walkman clamped on his ears, sucking a gourd of yerba maté through a metal straw. The two canoes and the aluminum skiffs were tethered to the stern, and the Matis had retreated to the shady sanctum beneath the canopy of their canoe. It was as though they'd become so attached to the vessel they'd built and conducted downriver that they couldn't bear to be without it.

* * *

Late in the afternoon, we passed a thatched shack off on the left bank. Soldado, Pedro, and José hopped into a skiff and peeled away from the *Kukahá* for a look, hoping to buy or trade for some tobacco. The men returned empty-handed. "They took off," said Soldado. "Ran into the woods." Their panic was measured in what they'd left behind on the dining table: Six plates with their place settings had been laid out, along with platters piled with meat, fish, and turtle eggs. "They probably thought we were IBAMA," said Soldado. He was referring to the Brazilian Institute of Environment and Renewable Natural Resources, Brazil's environmental protection agency. "They think it's better to have their stuff get confiscated than to get arrested." Everything on that dinner table was *prohibido,* in Soldado's words, from giant slabs of pirarucu to piles of *tracajá* eggs.

"It's amazing." Possuelo shook his head. "Everyone hides from everyone else out here. The Indian hides from the white man. The white man hides from other whites. No one can trust anyone. It's a devil's confusion." No sooner had he spoken these words than we drifted by another solitary hut presenting the same aspect of quick abandonment, not a single face peering from a window nor a silhouette darkening an open doorway.

We traveled into the night, Soldado and I hanging with Adelson at the wheelhouse on the upper deck. Lightning flashed beyond the horizon. Two scrawny men stood barefoot in the thicket off to starboard, opposite a high white beach. Their small canoe, tied to the bank, bobbed in our wake. "They're guarding the beach," Soldado said. "*Tracajá* will lay eggs tonight." I wasn't sure how he knew that, or how the men on shore knew it. But Soldado was absolutely certain of the words he spoke.

That may have explained why so many caimans were patrolling the shallows as well. Their glowering eyes burned red like coals in the darkness, four or five pairs at every bend, caught in the beam of Adelson's spotlight. "*Muito jacaré,*" Adelson said, his beak of a nose and long whiskers highlighted in the backwash of the light. "They look hungry." A nighttime tumble overboard was to be avoided at all costs; you'd have stood little chance of making it to shore alive. And it could have happened so easily; the railings around the upper deck barely reached knee height.

Riverboats provide the backbone of the Amazon's public transport system, and it's a wonder there aren't more stories about such mishaps in the papers. They probably happen on a daily basis, too common to merit the ink, except when an obscenely overloaded vessel tips over and hundreds go missing. I'd once met a nurse from the public health service in the Kayapó village of Gorotire whose three-year-old son had gone overboard on the Xingu River on their way to her posting. She had been preparing dinner on the deck, as everyone does on the public boats, when the boy ran off. "Ciao, Mama," he'd told her. She thought he was just playing a game, but when she turned to look for him a second later, he was gone. She searched the entire boat in mounting panic, calling, shouting his name. The captain refused to turn the boat around, saying there was no point. She got off at the next stop and doubled back, but she never found him, not even the body. She continued on to the Gorotire; she'd signed a contract. Besides, she told me: "I had nowhere else to go."

* * *

In the galley, Mauro and Paulo Souza were getting dinner ready. A jet of steam whistled from the pressure cooker, blending with the roar of the *Kukahá's* 125 horses. We were clipping along at nearly twelve knots. Laughs and elbow jabs rippled through the chow line that snaked around the main deck. Everyone had a freshly scrubbed look, the result of a bucket bath with real soap and shampoo, followed by a change of clothes. Alfredo, sporting clean fatigues and a recent buzz cut, could have been an army recruit heading home on leave. Amid snickers and guffaws, we waited for our dinner of steamed rice and succulent pirarucu.

Later on, I missed out on a place to hang my hammock, ending up on the floor, vibrating all night long to the throbbing engine. I got up in the middle of the night to find Mauro still at work in the galley, just pulling trays of fresh biscuits from the oven. "Here, Mr. Scotch," he said with a wink, handing me a piping-hot roll. "Be quick, b-b-before anyone sees." There seemed to be no end to the conspiracy and intrigue.

The trip downriver proceeded monotonously, the jungle sliding past, the river growing wider. There were still hazards to navigation— strong crosscurrents, hidden sandbars, and huge logs that bobbed just beneath the surface, like drifting contact mines. We hit one so hard that the vessel lurched and began to list, forcing us to pull off on a remote beach. The men dove beneath the boat and surfaced with its huge propeller. One of its blades was bent at a sickening angle. Danilo set up an impromptu foundry on the beach, pounding the blade back into place with a sledgehammer.

We pulled into an eddy flanked by high bulrushes at the mouth of the Rio Mutum—the Wild Turkey River—which entered the Jutaí at a sharp bend along the right bank. Possuelo peeled off in a skiff with Pedro Lima to visit a shack overlooking the confluence on a wind-tossed bluff. He returned twenty minutes later with reports that dozens of illegal gold dredges were operating far up the Mutum. They'd been up there for weeks, the locals reported, no sign of the law anywhere. It was just the kind of information that would tempt Possuelo to act. A seemingly pathological lust for gold had driven wave after wave of explorers and adventurers ever deeper into the Amazon over a five-hundred-year history, with incalculable environmental and social costs: innumerable tribes wiped out, enslaved, or set to fighting each other. Rivers poisoned, forests razed. Possuelo had seen the consequences with his own eyes among the Yanomami—the death and disease, the complete and utter bewilderment of a people overwhelmed by the stampede for gold. The *dragas* were merely the scourge's latest manifestation: floating rigs that laid waste to huge stretches of shoreline and spewed toxic effluents straight into the rivers. So destructive were the dredges that a permit was nearly impossible to obtain. But that didn't keep hundreds—if not thousands—of the machines from operating extralegally along the region's most remote and ungovernable waterways. Rarely did anyone try to stop them.

Technically, the rigs were operating beyond the bounds of Possuelo's jurisdiction, but that fact did little to deter him. "They may be out here today," he said, "but there's nothing to stop them from entering the Terra Indigena tomorrow." He went upstairs to get his Globalstar. All he needed was a go-ahead from the Federal Police. For Possuelo, it seemed too propitious an opportunity to let pass. He was close enough, relatively speaking, and he had nearly three dozen men—armed, in uniform, and effectively deputized—certainly enough muscle to tangle with the notoriously violent *garimpeiros*, or prospectors. We were hundreds of miles from nowhere; it could take years before a law-enforcement agency could muster such resources to challenge the outlaws on the Mutum again. But the *Kukahá* was crippled, the propeller barely functional. And when he failed to get through to the DPF on his satellite phone, Possuelo reluctantly decided to scrub the mission.

There was a consolation. His informants confirmed what Danilo had already told him: a dredge was operating a half day's journey downstream, along the right bank of the Jutaí. The *Kukahá* had passed it under cover of darkness on the way to meet us. Danilo was pretty sure no one on the rig had seen them. Also, contrary to Possuelo's earlier suspicions, the *Kukahá* had remained in Jutaí City only long enough to refuel. It had been nighttime, and few townsfolk would have noticed the vessel tied up at the waterfront, limiting the chance that word had spread of FUNAI's presence on the river. The stage was set for a surprise raid.

* * *

The window flaps on the *Kukahá* came up on a gray morning, mist drifting like smoke through the trees. The warning buzzer sounded and the engine sputtered to life. Hammocks were stashed as we started out into the sweeping current. We'd pulled off along the bank the previous evening to avoid any unseen and potentially crippling blow to propeller or rudder in the dark. Now, just past 5:30 a.m., the moon hung bright and low in the sky, pouring through the trees as though ensnared in the scraggly branches.

The dredge, it turned out, was no more than twenty minutes downriver. We rounded a bend, and suddenly it loomed before us through the fog: a weird contraption like something out of *Mad Max*—part West Virginia coal tipple, part Staten Island garbage truck—suspended over the water on a rusted hulk of a barge. Possuelo ordered Danilo to pull the *Kukahá* to shore, hoping we hadn't yet been seen. He strapped on his pistol. "Pedro, let's take the launch!" Pedro Lima dropped into the skiff, ripped the cord. The motor sputtered to life. "Give me two Matis—you, Tepi! Ivan! Let's go!" They climbed aboard. "Hey!" Possuelo shouted as the launch pulled away. "I want everyone in uniform! Kanamari, Matis, Marubo! All the *riberinhos*! Everyone! Look smart! Follow us in five minutes!"

No sign of life stirred on the dredge as Possuelo caught sight of its huge drill bit dangling from a high crane, vegetation caught in its teeth like rotting chunks of flesh. A battered, iron-hulled tugboat nestled in a slot to the barge's rear, a mangled relic of World War Two vintage that looked as though it had survived the attack on Pearl Harbor, barely. The monstrosity was topped by a gray, weather-beaten shack, the living quarters, whose upper story was peppered full of bullet holes and buckshot, eloquent reminder, as if Possuelo needed one, of the mayhem that invariably attended the business of alluvial gold prospecting in the Amazon.

"National Indian Foundation—FUNAI—Ministry of Justice!" he shouted. "We're coming aboard!" The main deck was empty. Possuelo bounded up the steel mesh stairway to the upper deck, where he found the crew, four men and a woman, reclining in their hammocks in a kind of open-air common room, yawning and rubbing their eyes as though awakening from deep slumber. But pings of hot metal from machinery just extinguished belied the charade.

They had no permits, no documentation of any kind for the dredge. "This is completely illegal," Possuelo told them. "Consider yourselves under arrest." The men were a disheveled lot: oil-stained clothes barely covered enormous guts, unwashed hair, bleary eyes. They followed Possuelo down the stairs, registering the presence of Indians in jungle camouflage with 20-gauge shotguns with the best poker faces they could manage. Still, they were unable to suppress the occasional smirk or sidelong glance that betrayed their true feelings toward these impudent intruders. By now, the barge was swarming with rifle-toting Indians in uniform, as Pedro and Danilo continued to ferry reinforcements from the *Kukahá* to the scene of the alleged crime.

The man in charge of operations called himself Antonio, and he was clearly the smartest of the lot. He was in his mid-thirties, with scraggly beard and an unruly mat of black hair barely contained by a faded ball cap. His weary brown eyes betrayed little of the malice his crewmates seemed to bear us. His torn khaki shirt was festooned with food and machine stains. His polyester slacks were maroon, the color of diseased liver, cinched at the waist with a big brass buckle. A lifetime of filth lodged beneath the nails on his calloused hands.

He seemed an eager host, as if to prove he had nothing to hide. The overseer of the dredge was a mysterious man who called himself "Paraíba," he said. "Comes and goes in a large boat, a couple of guards with machine guns. We don't know his real name."

"That's usually how it works." Possuelo nodded. "They cloak themselves in anonymity."

Every few weeks—never on the same day of the week, nor the same hour—Paraíba would appear with fresh supplies and take away the earnings. The latest haul, when he came the week before, was slightly more than twenty-eight ounces of gold. It seemed pretty clear that Antonio shared no great affection for the man he called Paraíba, nor for a line of work that demanded long stints deep in the bush, far from home. He and his crew had been digging into this same seam for two months now. He had a wife, two teenage kids, in Jutaí. "I was going to put in another month and get out—for good," he said with the dubious contrition of a man who can't believe his bad luck.

Antonio toured us around the dredge, which bore the name *Gabriel*. At the front of the barge, where the steel boom supporting the drill straddled a pair of rusty pontoons, a cesspool of fetid water, metal tailings, and upended trees lapped against a ravaged shore. The rig had chewed its way more than fifty feet into the embankment along a seam a hundred yards long. At Possuelo's request, Antonio climbed into the cockpit and fired up the machine. The entire barge shook. Diesel fumes tore at our nostrils. Antonio toggled the drill bit back and forth with the force of the rig's 315-horsepower torque, trying to free the chunks of thicket from its fangs. Effluent spewed out from an overhead pipe, cascaded into giant mesh screens, and gushed as sandy plumes into the river. "This is what happens to the forest when Indians sell off their resources to the white man!" he shouted, his voice barely audible in the deafening roar.

But of even greater concern was the separation process, in which mercury and cyanide were used to extract the gold from the ore. It would be dumped straight into rivers and streams, poisoning fish and drinking water. Where rivers ran past Indian settlements downstream from gold strikes, ulcers and suppurating sores were the order of the day. So were birth defects. The grieving nurse in Gorotire had delivered two stillborn babies in her first three months on the job. The fetuses' brains were growing outside their skulls. The Kayapó of Gorotire had made a deal with the devil; they got a cut of the action from the Maria Bonita gold mine upstream, but in return, their once-crystalline river was ruined forever.

The ringing in our ears went on well after Antonio silenced the machines. "I realize you guys are merely workers," said Possuelo at length. "But have you ever stopped to think about what you're actually doing—the destruction you cause, the pollution?" Antonio thought it best to remain quiet. Possuelo pointed a trembling finger at the drill bit as it dangled over a jumble of chewed-up trees and ravaged jungle. "Behold," he proclaimed, "the giant prick that rapes the Amazon."

"Possuelo!" Pedro shouted, holding up the Globalstar. "DPF on the line!" Possuelo took the phone from Pedro and disappeared around the corner, returning a few minutes later.

"My orders are to seize this *draga* and accompany it to Jutaí," he said, collapsing the phone's periscope antenna and shoving the device in his pocket. "I will turn you over to the Military Police in Jutaí. The Federal Police will come later to take custody." Possuelo cast a piercing look around at the crew. Only minutes before, they'd been gainfully employed, counting their 4 percent share as they drilled away at the riverbank and leached out the gold into dull yellow cakes the size of small muffins. That share came to about $650 a month, a small fortune for unskilled laborers in this part of the world. Now, they were effectively under arrest, their means of production impounded, tattoo-faced Indians loaded for bear prowling their decks.

"First time a dredge like this has ever been seized on the Jutaí!" Possuelo said with an air of triumph. Once the barge was turned over to the DPF, it could be tied up for years in litigation. A drop in the bucket, but a victory nonetheless, the result of catching the dredge red-handed. "I found them in the midst of an illegal act." Though technically, he hadn't. The engine had been pinging hot when he'd boarded the dredge, but Antonio had successfully shut it down. Still, it was rare to get even this close. Pirate operators nearly always managed to detect the arrival of authorities well in advance, working a network of informants on the radio, often counting on tipsters inside the police. Agents might show up at a bust, after days or even weeks of river travel, only to find the dredges innocently afloat in midstream, their crews lounging on deck as though they were on the vacation of a lifetime. Without hard evidence, there was little the cops could do.

This time was different. Kind of. There were certain details from his conversation with the Federal Police that Possuelo thought better of sharing with Antonio, like the fact that he'd stepped into a legal minefield. Without police forces present, Possuelo had overstepped his bounds; he had no real authority to make an arrest, or even a seizure. He'd gotten the go-ahead, but from a judicial standpoint, no action could be contemplated until the crew and the dredge were delivered into police custody. In the meantime, we'd be navigating in legal limbo all the way to the city of Jutaí.

The lone crew member who seemed not the least bit perturbed by the proceedings was Jessica Sampaio, the twenty-six-year-old cook. Attractive, with reddish brown hair cut in a bob and a trim figure, she remained casually aloof, sipping coffee and smoking cigarettes at the kitchen table upstairs. She drove a motorcycle taxi back in Jutaí, she said, and had been lured to the gig at the last minute with the promise of good money. It was a decision she came to regret early on: the solitude, the bugs, the crass, unwelcome advances from certain members of the crew. "I really didn't want to come out here," she said with a breezy laugh. "It will be nice to go home."

Not that she couldn't take roughing it, she gave me to understand. She'd grown up on the Javari River, gone logging with her stepfather deep in the bush, and even had a hair-raising run-in with "wild Indians" on the banks of the Ituí when she was still a girl. "They were all painted red," she said. "I remember they all had clubs in their hands." The loggers scrambled aboard their boat and made for midriver in the nick of time. The Indians followed along the bank, calling and waving, showing they wanted to trade one of their girls for Jessica. "It was scary," she said. "I'll never forget it."

The description of the episode left little doubt who the Indians must have been: the head-bashing Korubo of the Ituí River. She'd been lucky, and perhaps so too had the Korubo—both sides escaping the near encounter unscathed. As Sobral's own fatal meeting attested, it didn't always work out that way.

"Let's go, people!" Possuelo called. It was time for the dredge and the *Kukahá* to head downriver. "One thing," said Antonio, clearing his throat. "This machine is large and difficult to maneuver. My pilot doesn't know the channel. It's too dangerous to travel by night. We'll have to put in each day before dark."

Possuelo nodded. "We'll go at your pace," he said.

With the force of the Jutaí's current behind it, together with the full throttle of the derelict tug, the *Gabriel* glided downriver at remarkable speed. We slid in behind it. "Don't let the thing out of your sight!" Possuelo yelled up to Adelson in the wheelhouse.

The river broadened into a vast sheet of water with huge liquid vistas rolling on toward distant tree lines. The enormous surface offered up an unblemished mirror to a seemingly infinite sky, mesmerizing to behold. At times, the shore receded almost beyond our view, the trees along the shore reduced to a thin green line dividing water from sky. Flying fish skidded over the water in desperate flashes of silver, pursued by pink dolphins.

Clouds turned from gray to purple to electric pink as a spectacular sunset unfolded. Lightning flashed on the horizon like distant artillery. In the flat light of dusk, the dredge angled off toward the right shore, putting in for the night. We drifted farther off and pulled off five hundred yards downriver.

We awoke to the blare of the alarm that preceded the rumble of the *Kukahá's* engine. *"A draga vai embora!"* came shouts from up top. "The dredge is leaving! *Vamos, vamos!"* The window flaps came up as the *Gabriel,* crane and pulleys ablaze with signal lights, bore down on us from upstream as if driven not by human hand but of its own accord, harboring intentions to overrun us or, given a second choice, outrun us. Now we fell in beyond the barge in the half-light of dawn, hitting a straightaway that seemed to go on forever, a silvery moon still hanging over the indistinct shapes of the trees.

* * *

Everyone was thinking of home. The Indians spoke of the grand fiestas that awaited their return, the *riberinhos* of planting their crops and renewing the Sunday soccer rivalry between their tiny hamlets of São Rafael and São Gabriel. They were going to kick each other's asses, they vowed with slaps on the back. But wary eyes and furrowed brows seemed to belie the whites' jocular veneer. A sense of foreboding and quiet dread lingered just below the surface. After all, they'd gone off to work for one of the most despised agencies in the entire Amazon, second only to IBAMA, the environmental protection service. They faced resentment, perhaps even reprisals, when they got back home. As Possuelo had said, all of them could find themselves *homens marcados* upon their return.

The usually ebullient Amarildo was especially morose and withdrawn. It turned out that he had been among the victims of the harrowing assault in the channel outside Tabatinga—the same incident Francisco had told us about on that first morning back in June as we raced upriver to catch up with the expedition. He'd been with a brother, a cousin, an uncle, and an aunt, returning home from a fifteen-day fishing trip. In a rush to get home, they took a shortcut through the secluded channel, where three men in a speedboat cut them off.

"They took us back deep into the *furo.* Then they took all our stuff— the fish, our shotguns, the motors," Amarildo said. "They pointed their guns at us, and told us to keep our heads down." The bandits intended to execute them, but they pleaded for mercy. "We said we were poor people with children to raise." The gunmen let them go.

As soon as they got back to Tabatinga, Amarildo and his uncle went to the police. But the cops shrugged, said they had "no conditions" to pursue the case. So they hired two civil policemen, offering them $150 each to "break" the bandits and get their stuff back. There was something odd about the way he lowered his voice and looked askance when he said it.

"What do you mean—break them?" I asked.

"Kill them," he said.

"*Kill* them?"

"Yeah, because if you don't, they'll get out and come after you."

The rent-a-cops did arrest the culprits two days later as they attempted to sell the outboard motors in the waterside market. But with bystanders milling about, they were not able to "break" the suspects. Exactly as Francisco had described, the assailants had spoken Spanish while staging the holdup, Amarildo said. But they turned out to be Brazilian, from a gang called Metralha—"Machine Gun"—that operated with impunity in the triboundary region. "The police are afraid of them." As if to prove Amarildo's point about the criminals coming after them, the accused told his uncle at the police station that they would find him and kill him the day they were released, which probably wasn't far off. That's when Amarildo joined the expedition and got out of Dodge. He had no idea what fate had befallen his uncle in the meantime. "I'm afraid to go back," he said. "It's dangerous for me in Tabatinga. I'm well known there." *Poor Amarildo,* I thought. *So young to have grown so old so quickly.*

* * *

Upstairs in the air-conditioned cabin, Possuelo was sprawled on the cot, weighing his options. It had been four days since we'd seized the *Gabriel.* We would be arriving in Jutaí the next morning. By now, he reasoned, word had gotten out downriver. The Federal Police would have notified the local deputy of the PM, the Military Police, which functioned as a regional agency, akin to our state police. The news would have leaked out into the broader community. Probably the owner—whoever it was—had already found out. In fact, it was likely the deputy had been the one to tell him. "These guys cozy up to the police. At the end of the year, he'll slip the deputy 300 *reais* with a wink and say, 'Here, get something nice for your woman.' That's how these guys work. That's how they obtain privileged information."

What concerned Possuelo was what the owner might do with that information. It wasn't that big a stretch to picture the guy conscripting an ad-hoc force to wrest control of the dredge in the middle of the night, before we could turn it over to the police. "Or maybe they just come up in a speedboat, try to start up the engines of the *draga*, and take off with it." He stroked his beard, thinking.

"He may know that you don't have police authority up here," said Orlando, who was stretched out on the other bed, arms folded across his chest.

"Yeah, but I do have the manpower and the guns," Possuelo said. "He might not know that. It would be better if he did." Better, for the deterrent value, though it could also simply serve to incite him to up the ante. "In any case, if he comes up here, either he'll need to bring ten men armed to the teeth with Uzis, Kalashnikovs, or he'll have to bring a force double the size of ours."

He got up, went to the door, and bellowed out into the darkness: "Paulo Welker! Come up here!" He ordered Welker to post sentries in pairs in hour shifts throughout the night, exactly as we'd done in the heartland of the Arrow People weeks ago. No small irony, considering this was the eve of our return to "civilization." It was as though we were entering enemy territory.

*   *   *

"So," I asked after Welker withdrew, "is gold mining really the most destructive activity in the Amazon?" It was one of those leading, insipid questions journalists resort to on occasion, with no purpose other than to elicit a juicy quote that might enliven their otherwise dull reportage, or to cloak their own assertion in someone else's words.

"I don't like that way of thinking," Possuelo said, his eyes narrowing. "That's like asking: Which smells more—one piece of shit or two? Take deforestation. You cut down the forests, and you destroy the flora, the fauna, the rivers. Gold extraction is concentrated along the rivers. It pollutes the water, kills off the fish. It's all the same shit. It all stinks equally."

Tomorrow on our way downriver, Possuelo said, we would pull alongside the dredge and lash the *Kukahá* directly to it, in case of a possible showdown. "We'll be tied to them, but we'll all stay aboard our boat. If the owner shows up, then I'll send the men to take it over *tudinha*—entirely." He clapped his hands loudly, to show just how decisively the operation would be executed. It had been a few years since the attempted assault on the control post, but it was still fresh in Possuelo's mind. Three hundred men had turned out to torch the base. No one knew how it might have ended that day had the police not been there to drive off the rabble with their helicopter. None of that anger had subsided in the borderland communities. If anything, it had continued to mount, like steam in a pressure cooker, awaiting release.

As first light filtered through the fog, the dredge's engine could be heard upriver, coughing, then sputtering to life with a muffled roar. "Adelson, start the engine! *Embora!*" shouted Possuelo from the rooftop, where he'd been supervising repairs to the boat's antenna. The ungainly beast came toward us through the mist. Adelson laid on the throttle, and we joined the chase. Possuelo summoned Paulo Welker. "Take the skiff, go over there, and dismantle those boats." He pointed to a pair of outboard-powered launches that trailed behind the dredge. "Pull them out of the water. Take their motors off, and flip them over. I wouldn't want them to think they might be able to take off on us."

We'd never know if Antonio and his crew might have bolted if given the chance. They never got it. Possuelo ordered his plan into effect. We pulled alongside the dredge and tied up. By midmorning, we were approaching the city of Jutaí, *Kukahá* and dredge bound together side by side. Excitement reigned on deck, tempered with apprehension. How would the city receive us, the captors of their fellow citizens? Most likely, we figured, with less than open arms.

Possuelo came down from his cabin, where he'd been drawing up paperwork for the police. "Let's take the fast boat and go ahead," he told Nicolas and me. He wanted to get the judicial process started, and he wanted to find someone to fix the propeller. We boarded the skiff, and Danilo opened the throttle. Before long, the first hints of human habitation appeared in the distance: green meadows, scattered ranchos, and finally the zinc rooftops of warehouses glinting in the midday sun.

CHAPTER 26

Civilization and Our Discontents

L OGS BOBBED IN THE SHALLOWS, forcing Danilo into a wide sweep to approach the docks, which were made of large floating rafts connected by gangways to the shore. Sawmills and warehouses clung to the high embankment. As we plodded up the plank stairway that led to town, machines screeched from an open-air lumber mill, a frontal assault on ears and nerves. At the top of the steps, a wooden gate opened to the back room of an empty restaurant with ceiling fans and cheap plastic furniture. We walked through the restaurant and out onto the street. It seemed a strange way to make our entrance to civilization, through a back door.

We walked in silence, along a row of kiosks, grocery stores, a freshly varnished assembly hall of Jehovah's Witnesses. A pickup truck sailed past. My legs were weak and wobbly. It had been days since we'd last set foot on solid ground. We passed tin-roofed clapboard homes, doors wide open, townsfolk swinging in hammocks on their porches. We must have made a pitiful sight—our faces gaunt, boots in tatters, clothes stained and shredded.

I felt a muted exhilaration. Here it was: the Outside World! Jutaí was a tiny rat's nest of a place, but a few months in the wilderness has a way of altering standards. If civilization meant automobiles, telephones, stores crammed with consumer goods—we had arrived. It was August 28, the seventy-sixth day since Nicolas and I had departed Tabatinga. I half expected a brass band and confetti. I wanted to scream out: *Hey, everybody, look! We're here! We made it!*

The door to the police delegate's office was locked. "He already knows we're coming," Possuelo said. "He's probably down at the waterfront." We started back. But as we sauntered past the patio of a luncheonette, the aroma of beefsteak and fries wafting in the air, Danilo spoke up: "Sydney, let's stop and get a drink, at least. You guys haven't seen any of this stuff for months." We pulled up chairs. The time had come to quench my obsession. When the waitress came to take our order, I ordered an ice-cold Coke.

Guzzling it down in no time flat, I was left with a vague sense of dissatisfaction; it hadn't quite measured up to expectations. I ordered another. Same thing. My companions—Nicolas, Possuelo, and Danilo—were gabbing away about something or other. The jaunty beat of Brazilian *brega* blared from the sound system. For all the illusions of freedom our society promotes, rarely do we have the chance to step outside it long enough to gain some distance. Beyond the fatuous talk about liberty and the price our founders paid for it, I wondered: How free were we if we'd become so dependent on the comforts produced by industry that we couldn't do without them? How free was I, that the first thing I wanted and had been craving for weeks was a sweet and fizzy caramel-colored beverage that came in a bottle with a scarlet label and passed itself off as the Real Thing?

May the Arrow People never come to know it. As long as they had streams unsullied by mercury and sprawling woodlands rich with animals, they could remain beyond our reach, beyond the swirling vortex of consumer society and the machinery that manufactures our wants, creates our needs, serves us our ice-cold beer. May they never come to know the squalor of their brethren, not only in Brazil but all across the Americas, who have been sucked in, then spat out and left to wander dusty frontier streets or the hopeless, crack-infested subdivisions on the rez, filthy and destitute, the objects of scorn and derision. What they had could not be measured in dollars or Brazilian *reais*. They could never be adequately compensated if they were ever to lose their freedom. I could think of no better reason to applaud Brazil's efforts—however flawed, enfeebled, or underfunded—to protect them. As the

Possuelo-led *sertanistas* pointed out in their 1987 petition to spare the last isolated Indians from gratuitous contact with civilization, the tribes were the patrimony not only of the nation, but of all humanity.

*   *   *

A half hour in the embrace of civilization and I could feel the old anxiety gnawing in my chest. The music thumped nonstop. I wanted to get out of there. We paid the bill and strolled down the block to the crest of the bank. Straight across the Jutaí, unbroken jungle rolled away into the distance. Bright, rippling clouds hung suspended, as if by some supernatural sleight of hand, over the infinite green flatlands. Closer at hand, just beyond the tin rooftops that lined the shore, the Jutaí's darker waters opened out to a vast channel of rich brown, bounded by a thin, far-off line of trees. The Solimões. At long last, the Amazon!

We found both the *Kukahá* and the *Gabriel* tied up at the floating dock alongside our outboard-powered launch. A slightly overweight man in his mid-thirties, with pomaded hair and aviator glasses, stalked about the deck of the dredge, glancing at his wristwatch with evident annoyance. He brightened at our approach, introducing himself with a faint smile and firm handshake: "Dr. Alysson Silva, police deputy, at your service." Possuelo steered him by the elbow toward the drill at the front of the barge. "You can really appreciate the impact of these things when you see them far upriver," said Possuelo. "The entire bank is scarred. There are sandbars and artificial channels, tons of earth displaced!" As if to impart a civics lesson to a dim-witted understudy, he added: "This would fall into the category of 'ecological crime'—*um crime ecológico.*"

The deputy asked to see Possuelo's documents—a warrant from the DPF perhaps, or an order from a federal judge. "We're coming straight from the jungle, man." He was struggling to keep his cool. "This dredge was apprehended in flagrante delicto. We had no prior order for its seizure. It's my understanding we didn't need one."

Silva scratched his well-oiled head, as though the ordeal were beyond his pay grade. The dredge was rumored to be owned by a wheeler-dealer out of Manaus, one Moysés Israel. He rarely came this way, Silva said, though he claimed to own "the entire Jutaí." That was quite a claim, considering the size of the municipality—twenty-seven thousand square miles, bigger than the state of West Virginia, extending all the way back to the boundaries of the Terra Indigena. Silva's force consisted of a mere five agents, and a lone pickup truck. Without a single boat to patrol the district's myriad waterways, his agents effectively went nowhere; the municipality's entire network of roads petered out in rutted dirt tracks just beyond town.

Relatively new in town, Silva often found himself seeking advice from Mayor Asclepíades de Souza, a crafty politician who'd earned a local following for his frank, shoot-from-the-hip style. De Souza laid out the situation for me in his cavernous office at City Hall.

"Moysés Israel has his fingers in everything," said de Souza. "He controls the entire trade in illegal timber on the river. Anyone who cuts down a tree must sell it to him." The mayor was affable and articulate, a trim man in his mid-forties with kinky brown hair, a hawkish nose, and heavy eyebrows. True to his reputation, de Souza didn't seem the slightest bit cowed by the region's big power brokers. Perhaps he wielded so little power himself that he posed no real threat to their operations. The municipality had never been able to collect a dime in taxes from Israel, he said. One of his companies claimed ownership of tens of thousands of acres of woodlands that had been confiscated and incorporated into the Terra Indigena Vale do Javari, and he was seeking restitution.

From the standpoint of governance, de Souza painted a grim picture of his domain: gold dredges that slipped upriver under cover of darkness to ply their illicit trade, fish-packing plants that befouled the waters with heads and entrails, Peruvian drug traffickers with wads of cash pulling into port to fuel their fast boats. The outlaws, he said, were as elusive as guerrillas. "If you go out to find them, you're just wasting time and gasoline. They have radios, Globalstar. They know more than we do." The creation of Terra Indigena complicated everything, said de Souza. On the one hand, it deprived the criminals of access to untold reserves of timber and gold. On the other, it was strangling the local economy, pushing residents toward joining the criminal syndicates. "It's a trafficker's paradise here," he lamented, walking me to the door.

I found most of the crew gathered at tables on the same patio where we'd downed our drinks earlier. Amarildo, Soldado, and Adelson were there. Both Ivans—Waçá and Arapá, Tepi, Txema, Nicolas, Paulo Souza, the riverboat gambler, and Mauro with his bushy mustache and ruddy cheeks. Remi and Márcio Kanamari had pulled up chairs. Bystanders stared wide-eyed. It wasn't every day they saw such a spectacle: the Indians with their cat whiskers and earrings, dressed in camouflage uniforms, sipping Cokes in the company of white men. Far less benevolent were the icy glares and menacing taunts that came from the open-air bar next door. A raucous, beer-swilling group had assembled there. In their midst sat the disheveled crew from the gold dredge.

"What do you suppose they want me to do now," shouted one of the suspects, his voice dripping with sarcasm, "steal to make a living?" His huge gut protruded from an unbuttoned shirt and pressed obscenely into the side of his table. His eyes were green as emeralds, and they bore straight into me with an alcohol-fueled glint. The guy hadn't spoken a word the morning we boarded the dredge. The beers, it seemed, had loosened his tongue.

"We're honest, legitimate people," he said, never taking his eyes off me. "But we can't make a living. I'm going to have to start sticking people up to feed my family."

A motorcycle taxi pulled up to discharge the passenger on the back—police deputy Alysson Silva. Then, as if lifted from the script of a bad sitcom, the driver dismounted and removed her helmet, and shook loose her reddish brown hair. It was Jessica Sampaio, the cook from the *Gabriel*. She remained alongside her bike, joining neither our group nor the increasingly boisterous gold dredge crew.

"Bad news," Silva said, taking a seat. He'd been scouring the town for a recruit to guard the *draga* until the DPF showed up to take charge.

He'd spoken to five different men—all decent, law-abiding citizens, out of work, in need of money. But despite the good wages Silva tendered, every one declined. "Fear," Silva said. "Everyone's afraid."

Tracy Chapman was playing on the juke: *Baby, can I told you tonight? Maybe if I told you the right words. . . .* I was flooded with emotion—so happy to have reached the shores of civilization. But what kind of civilization was this that we'd returned to? And my friends, these people gathered around the table, I'd come to know so well, to whom I had entrusted my life, who had shielded me from mortal dangers, what would become of them? What were the chances I'd ever see any of them again? Crowded House came on: *There is freedom within, there is freedom without, try to catch the deluge in a paper cup.* The song had been on a compilation tape a Dutch friend had dubbed for me fifteen years earlier in Managua. Not long after that, he was shot dead while we huddled together during a firefight on a backstreet in El Salvador. *Hey now, hey now, don't dream it's over.* The music caught me off guard. Why was I still here and he was not? I'd lived, I'd lived to tell the tale. A tear had formed in the corner of my eye. I caught it before it got too far down my cheek, before anyone could notice. *Hey now.*

Word reached the table that the propeller had been fixed and Possuelo, down at the boat, wanted to get out of there. So did we all. The vibe had taken a decidedly toxic turn. A beer bottle shattered. Their families might have been at home starving, but the *garimpeiros* next door had no problem keeping their glasses full.

The proprietor was sorry to see us go. We'd been good business, for a day anyway. "When are you coming back?" she asked as I settled the bill. "Not sure," I said. "It might be a while."

*   *   *

We turned west and entered the mighty Amazon, motor straining against the current. Out on deck, Possuelo and I watched the lights of Jutaí recede in the distance. He'd left the dredge in Silva's hands, hopeful the deputy would show some resolve. "I like the fact that he's new in town," Possuelo said. "He hasn't had time to be compromised by local interests." If he could just hold out long enough, the Federal Police would get there and take charge. Still, the pressure to release the dredge was sure to be intense. The owner himself was rumored to be arriving in his private aircraft in the morning.

Adelson was up in the wheelhouse, directing the *Kukahá* west toward Tabatinga, still five days away. The propeller had been fixed, but the rudder had also taken heavy damage. The boat was in a delicate state. Another grounding might leave us stranded on mudflats far from help. "It's always interesting"—Adelson smiled mischievously— "traveling on the Solimões. You never know what to expect." The same could be said for anywhere in the entire Amazon Basin, I thought.

Behind us, the lights of the city faded to a pale glow beyond the horizon, as though the moon were about to rise there. The river was broad and sprawling, nothing like the snaking Itaquaí or Jutaí. Wide as it was, Adelson hugged the shore to the north side where the channel was deepest. He turned the watchtower spotlight on the riverbank and probed the darkness with its circular beacon.

The river narrowed to a mere hundred yards. "A channel between the islands," said Adelson calmly. I stood alongside him in silence, content to watch the silhouetted cattails slip past along the bank and to feel the motion of the boat beneath my feet as it battled the current. An enormous sky opened before us, uncrowded by forest sentinels. We churned upriver at seven kilometers an hour. On the Jutaí, we'd been gliding downriver three times as fast. Adelson had pulled the night shift and planned to be up all night. "Go get some rest, Scott," he said. "I'll be fine."

Down below on the main deck, hammocks were wedged into every square inch, bodies suspended one over the other, crisscross fashion. I slid sideways into my hammock, careful not to nudge anyone awake, and I nodded off to the white noise of the engine's din.

We were awakened in the middle of the night by shrieks coming from the galley: *"Noooooooooo! Aooooaaaaah!"* The screams were truly bloodcurdling, as though we'd awakened to an actual murder in progress. It was Mauro, who'd slung his hammock in the kitchen, just steps away. The men made light of it: just the monkeys, slicing his dick off yet again.

"He's dying!" came one voice from the darkness.

"He's already dead," said another.

"It's the *macacos*," a third said. The monkeys.

"No, not monkeys," said a fourth. I recognized the voice: Ivan Arapá. "It's the *flecheiros*!"

Everyone laughed. I did as well. Soon the others drifted back to sleep, lulled by the incessant throb of the engine. I lay in the dark, heart still thumping. Mauro had been one of the very best mates on the entire journey—always of good cheer, always showing genuine concern for others. He had been sure to save my portions at countless meals when I was running late and others had already lined up for seconds. "Here, Senhor Scotch," he'd say with a wink as he ladled out my share. His hair was always a tousled mess, his mustache droopy, his eyes sleep-deprived. It was impossible not to feel a special fondness for him and his endearing stammer, to appreciate his basic goodness. He hadn't dismembered a monkey in weeks. But in his dreams, the animals lived on, turning the tables on their butcher in a bloody coup d'état, reenacted nightly. Mauro's peace of mind, it seemed, figured among a growing list of casualties from our journey to the far side.

* * *

I was up early, bringing a cup of coffee to the wheelhouse for Adelson. A pink sunrise was on the river, none of the gray mist that cloaked the smaller rivers in early morning. Adelson looked like he was ready for a break, his eyes bloodshot. Even his bush hat was wilted. We were back in the main channel, by all appearances, for it must have been three or four miles across to the northern shore from our position hard on the bulrushes to our port side. A flock of yellow parakeets streamed out across the water and melted back into the thicket amid riotous chirping.

Soon the sunlight turned white and blinding, its brightness doubled by its enormous reflection on the water. Adelson leaned into the wheel and angled the *Kukahá* sharply to the right. The force of the current pushed the boat sideways, downriver. "Dangerous shoals," he said with a sly smile. He flexed his fingers as a cat would its paws. "You have to be able to feel the river."

The Amazon River—or Solimões, as Brazilians call the stretch from Manaus to the Peruvian border—is in a constant state of transformation, continuously rearranging the landscape on its flanks. Islands appear in midstream where last year there were none. The seasonal floods carve brand-new channels in the riverbed and close off others. Entire villages vanish where long stretches of riverbank suddenly collapse. Navigating the Amazon is more art than science, the ability to read the currents of far greater use than familiarity with nautical charts. Following a hunch, Adelson crossed the river, perpendicular to the flow, and sought the way upstream through a fresh maze of islands.

Compared with the unbroken line of towering giants that had shaded our travels through the upper tributaries, the trees here were stunted dwarfs, none higher than fifty or sixty feet. The best had been logged out aeons ago. I wondered what it must have been like when the first Europeans laid eyes on it. If even a page of their chronicles is to be believed, it must have been a sight to behold: spectacular flora and fauna, native communities of staggering size and density. Friar Gaspar de Carvajal, chronicling the descent of renegade conquistador Francisco de Orellana and his band of Spaniards in 1542, described village after village crowding the banks, the sedentary population so dense that "not but a crossbow shot" separated one settlement from another. A far cry from today's interspersed huddles of weather-beaten shacks, punctuated by long, lonely stretches of tangled jungle and thicket. Recent years have seen archaeologists and anthropologists recalibrate their estimates of the Amazon's precontact population to many millions of native inhabitants before disease and conquest emptied rivers and forests.

Two or three days' travel downstream from here, Orellana's troop squared off against a legion of archers of mythic ferocity—women all, according to Carvajal, himself wounded in the shower of arrows.

Only the tremendous roar of European firearms and the devastating accuracy of their crossbows managed to drive off the attackers. Farther downriver, one of Orellana's men was felled by a curare-tipped arrow. The shocking sight of their comrade gasping for air sowed panic among the survivors and marked the first such incident ever recorded—a white man succumbing to the dreaded "flying death." Ferocious feminine warriors, poisoned arrows, monstrous beasts that devoured men whole: it all seemed larger than life itself. Henceforth, the massive waterway came to be known to the rest of the world as the "River of the Amazons."

We passed the day in a semiconscious, trancelike delirium, minds numbed by the vaporous heat and the incessant throb of the engine. We drifted into that strange holding period toward the end of a long journey, when the mind has already departed but the body hasn't yet been able to follow. I wandered the decks, squeezed past my expedition mates with an apologetic smile, letting slip a sophomoric obscenity for lack of meaningful conversation. For all intents and purposes, we'd already said our good-byes. Only the engine's roar filled the embarrassed silence of having nothing left to say.

We plowed up the broad Solimões into the setting sun. Off to the north, storm clouds were rising over the jungle. The river stretched out before us, here and there hemmed in by narrow peninsulas coming in from the left or right. Several hamlets slid past: single rows of huts wedged between forest and shore. At the center of each stood a whitewashed clapboard church with a modest steeple topped by a plain wooden cross. One village had the good fortune to be crowned with a high *açacu* tree whose branches burst over the embankment like an enormous umbrella. A crowd gathered beneath its lovely orange blossoms to watch the curious spectacle of the *Kukahá* and her ghostly crew limping by on the way upriver.

A spectacular sunset ensued. Thin ribbons of clouds glowed neon orange against the deepening blue sky. This had always been my favorite part of the day, especially in the Amazon. The searing heat was gone, and a cool breeze swept the deck. The electric lights hadn't yet come on that would obliterate the twilight and draw us into our smaller world. The sun, on its way to somewhere else, would issue an invitation to gaze off toward the far horizon and ponder the mysteries that lay beyond. "It's like a dream, isn't it?" said Possuelo, who had joined me at the bow of the upper deck. "In fact, this whole thing will soon feel like a dream. I find that the intense experiences of these expeditions have a dreamlike quality to them. You're left thinking afterward: Did that really happen? Did I really live that?" We hadn't reached the end yet, but I understood what he was talking about. So divorced are such experiences from our everyday lives, it strains the mind to believe they ever happened. Already the journey was acquiring a sense of the unreal. How time had dragged in the depths of the jungle. I knew the day would come when it would seem like all of it had happened—*snap, like that*—in a split second.

*   *   *

On the main deck, Kwini lay bundled in a hammock, pale and listless, running a high fever. Possuelo had seen too many Indians needlessly succumb to treatable illnesses over the years; he was not about to leave Kwini's fate to chance. We pulled in at San Antonio Içá, at the mouth of the Içá River, just past nightfall. We escorted Kwini from the harbor along a garbage-strewn street that led diagonally up the embankment, past music shops blaring *forró* and *brega,* past appliance stores with front windows jammed with glowing television screens, all tuned to the same channel. We entered a street clogged with motor scooters and honking cars, finally reaching the hospital on the far side of the main square.

A doctor appeared thirty minutes later. He was a squat man with wiry hair, dressed in a soiled white smock that came to his ankles. He was chomping on an apple. Possuelo had a sense of déjà vu, the frustration of sitting in hospital waiting rooms with Indians he'd brought in from the bush, encountering the blatant racism that so often attended such experiences—the refusal to treat, the willful neglect. He'd once pulled his gun on hospital security guards when they tried to eject a gravely ill Guajá woman from an emergency room. Another time, he put a choke hold on an orderly who failed to tend to a tribesman. "I think I can be a dangerous man sometimes," said Possuelo, a touch of surprise in his voice, as though the thought had never occurred to him before.

Mercifully, this visit proceeded without altercation. After checking Kwini over, the doctor ordered intravenous antibiotics. "Intestinal infection," he said.

"That would be the diagnosis for all of us," said Possuelo, not even half joking. He was undoubtedly right. Passing by an old scale with sliding weights in the hallway, I climbed on: 76 kilos, 167 pounds. I'd lost 33 pounds since the trip began.

We left San Antonio Içá in gray weather the next morning. In the wheelhouse, Soldado was sharing a cup of coffee and a smoke with Adelson. There was nothing to eat for breakfast but crackers; Mauro and Paulo Souza were sleeping off a night on the town that had ended in indescribably ugly drunkenness. Only after we'd rejoined the main trunk of the Amazon did I remember something that had been on my mind: Soldado's mother. We'd come within a few hours, no more, of the Santa Crucian village where she lived. Why hadn't Soldado gotten off and gone to see her? "Too complicated," he said, training his sad eyes on the jungle. He took a deep drag and blew the smoke into the wind. "Besides, I have no money. I'll only get paid when we get to Tabatinga. I'll go another time." It had already been thirteen years. I couldn't imagine when "another time" might roll around. Father abducted at the age of nine, never to see his birth family again; himself, uprooted by his own parents at age eleven to join the crusade of a charismatic zealot; years later, forced by FUNAI to abandon the home he'd spent years trying to rebuild. Soldado's life made mine seem like the epitome of stability.

Things were reaching the boiling point on the main deck downstairs. First Paulo Welker ordered the men to turn over their expedition gear: rifles and ammo, backpacks, machetes. "Put them in piles! Knapsacks here, tarps over there, camouflage over there in the corner!" There was grumbling; the men had expected to keep some things, like tarps and uniforms. But far worse, Welker then announced a search of personal belongings. Some things had gone missing, he said, and they had to be accounted for. The whites were incensed. The expedition was on the verge of complete meltdown. Had we not been in the final countdown, reprisals of some sort would almost certainly have followed.

It turned out to be Paulo Welker's last official act as head of the Javari Valley Ethno-Environmental Protection Front. After the inspection, he was summoned upstairs to Possuelo's cabin. He returned minutes later. "As soon as I arrive in Tabatinga, it's all over," he said and sighed. "The *filho da puta* fired me." I felt bad for him. He was a decent guy. A bit weak-willed perhaps, probably not well suited for the job. As a liaison between Possuelo and the rest of the expedition, particularly the other whites, he'd been put in an extremely tough position. But he meant well. He'd even been quietly planning a party for our last night to celebrate Possuelo's long and illustrious career. Mauro and Paulo Souza were going to prepare a special dinner, bake a big cake. We would all sign a T-shirt for Possuelo to commemorate the Alípio Bandeira Expedition, one of the most ambitious in FUNAI history. It would bring closure to the grueling months together and provide a final affirmation of our fellowship. "By the way," Paulo Welker said, "the party's off."

It had been Possuelo who'd ordered the inspection. The Matis had complained that someone was stealing their personal effects. If anything had indeed been stolen, the culprit concealed it well, for the inspection produced nothing but another dose of ill will.

Possuelo himself remained out of sight in his cabin, a reclusive Captain Queeg. That evening he sent word down with Orlando, inviting Nicolas and me to dine with them on the upstairs deck. He'd laid out a table with chairs behind the wheelhouse and served a dish he'd prepared himself, using the dried pirarucu Soldado and Raimundo had caught back at the Curuena. The meat was tender and delicious; the conversation, less so. "I can't stand the sight of them," said Possuelo of the white *riberinhos*. "I never want to lay eyes on them again in my life." He reserved especially harsh words for Paulo Souza, whom he'd caught stealing an egg from the galley. Souza had denied it, saying it was a turtle egg he'd gotten from the Indians. "I felt the yolk on the spoon," Possuelo hissed, "and I knew it was a chicken egg. The fucking liar, I can't look at him anymore. I won't even let him serve me."

The vitriol was shocking. All bearings had been lost; all sense of proportion gone. Just two days separated us from Tabatinga, and crates of eggs still crowded the galley counter. They'd soon go bad if *someone* didn't eat them. It was a far cry from the morning of July 15, Orlando's eighteenth birthday, when Possuelo allowed himself to break down in front of the men. I couldn't begin to imagine that kind of sentimentality now.

The weather mirrored the mood aboard ship. Ashen clouds hung low above the river as we pressed on the next morning into a strong headwind. Up ahead, the carcass of a seven-foot-long caiman bobbed upside down in midstream. A vulture pranced obscenely on its swollen yellow belly, taking flight at the last instant as we bore down.

Adelson called me to the helm midway through the day. "Scott, I want you to see something," he said, pointing to a row of huts at the mouth of a wide creek to the right. "Over there is Vendaval. Remember the story I told you about Quintino Mafra? The boss who'd ruled over the Tikuna like a feudal lord? His house was there." Adelson nodded toward a bluff where a schoolhouse and a water tower stood.

"Where's the house?" I asked.

"It's gone now," Adelson said.

After decades of despotic rule, soldiers and FUNAI agents raided the compound in the early 1980s. Adelson's own father had played a key role, going to Manaus to denounce the abuses. The house was incinerated during the outpouring of pent-up rage that followed Mafra's arrest. Now, dozens of tin-roofed shacks crowded the edge of a wide lagoon, fringed by banana trees, papaya groves, and tall, swaying palms. A family crossed the water in a small canoe, father upright at the helm, poling end over end. It was the very tableau of serenity. Clearly, some things had changed for the better.

*   *   *

Three flags snapped in the breeze upon a bright yellow floating dock off to starboard: the green and gold of Brazil, the tricolor of Amazonas State, and the black and gold of the Federal Police. A cement-block fortress, also painted gaudy yellow, squatted atop the forty-foot embankment. We'd reached Anzol, the DPF checkpoint for all boat traffic traveling to and from the border with Colombia and Peru, just a day's journey upriver.

A crisp-looking Sergeant Fradique Queirós was on duty. He was in his mid-thirties, with pressed black fatigues, close-cropped beard, and green eyes. A tiny woven-palm cage sat on the counter next to him. Two green parrots squatted inside, cocking their heads and eyeing us with innocent curiosity. His agents had just seized the birds from a pair of down-and-out men in a motorized canoe. Would we be willing to deliver the parrots to IBAMA in Tabatinga? he wanted to know. Their wings had been clipped; they could not be returned to the wild.

It would have been too much trouble to detain the men, said Queirós. They were small-time poachers, not even worth the time to write up the paperwork. The police had merely impounded the birds. Far more sinister syndicates were plying the waterways of the Upper Amazon, trafficking in everything from cocaine and exotic wildlife to precious hardwoods. Checkpoints such as Anzol were critical to efforts to stanch the flow of illicit cargo. But Queirós had at his command just a handful of agents to inspect the dozens of boats that pulled into his docks every day. It sounded depressingly familiar. "We can only conduct a search if we have grounds for suspicion," he said. With the temptation for payoffs high, the DPF had taken to rotating agents in from distant posts on thirty-day shifts. Queirós himself was from the state of Maranhão, 1,800 miles away.

Of course, the cops were hoping to catch—or at least deter—the major crime lords and the big shipments of drugs, timber, or animals. But, as the case of the baby parrots attested, poverty and desperation are fueling much of the environmental crime in Amazon. Twelve million wild birds and animals are poached in Brazil every year, according to IBAMA. Well-positioned dealers—like Moysés Israel, "Big Carlos," and "the Captain"—may have grown fat on the trade. But the desperadoes raiding the nests and felling the timber, like the Kanamari of Queimada or the two-bit poachers nabbed by Queirós, are driven by more basic imperatives, like the need to put food on the table.

We took the parrots with us. But once we got outside, Possuelo said: "I'm not turning them over to IBAMA. They'll just sell them." He'd take them to the Javari control post, where the birds were sure to make lively mascots.

The day passed quietly. The men were subdued, speaking in whispers. Everyone was ready to move on, as if we'd overstayed our welcome by years. Our last dinner was delicious—a beef stew Mauro whipped up, served with rice and beans and farinha. It was dished out unceremoniously, without the slightest whiff of nostalgia. This was to be the night of Possuelo's party. He didn't even come downstairs to eat. Out on the bow, the *riberinhos* took their dinner in silence.

The weather finally cleared as darkness fell, and we moved through an ethereal landscape of trees, water, and wide-open sky. I kept my eyes to the fore, seeking the faint glow on the horizon that would signal our approach to Tabatinga. The heavens overhead burned with pulsing stars in unfamiliar constellations. Only one did I recognize: the trusty Southern Cross, hanging low off the port bow.

* * *

I was jostled awake in the predawn hours: men brushing past my hammock, long strides across the deck, whispered shouts. The engine was silent. I looked at my watch: September 3, 3:20 a.m. A faint light came from the galley. Most of the hammocks were nowhere to be seen. Only the Kanamari were still asleep. I found the Matis at the bow, staring

beyond silhouetted trees and sheds toward the glow of the city lights.
In the shadows, I recognized our location: the FUNAI boathouse we'd
departed from so many weeks ago.

On my way back to pack up, I ran into Soldado. Nicolas had already bolted for a hotel in town, he said. "The Hotel Anaconda, in Leticia." That figured. I'd catch up with him later. Most of the whites had
packed up and gone. There would be no good-byes. Besides Soldado
and Danilo, the only one left was Paulo Souza, just then shouldering
his belongings. *"Vou embora!"* he said. We shook hands, and he was
gone. I went back in and hastily threw my stuff together. I climbed the
ladder up to Possuelo's cabin, where I'd left my money and cameras.
I thought he might be asleep, so I tapped lightly on the door before I
opened it. "Come in." I heard Possuelo's weary voice in the darkness. I
fumbled for the bag beneath his cot and grabbed my stuff. "See you,"
I told him, knowing we'd meet later in town.

I joined Soldado and Danilo on the bow. Nicolas had somehow
managed to get a lift, but Danilo said it was too early to find a cab into
town; I'd have to wait for daylight. "Where'd everyone go?" I asked.
"They got their salaries and left," Soldado said. "Bad news," I said.
"Muito ruim," Soldado agreed. A disaster. The worst he'd ever seen.

The Indians were all still here, many still asleep. They'd have to wait
for another day or two for the *Kukahá* to take them home. That would
give them time to shop in town. Alfredo was at the stern, hanging out
with Wilson and Márcio. *"Bak!"* they intoned cheerily. Good! I took
Alfredo aside and counted his salary into his hand. The same amount
Possuelo paid everyone else: 640 *reais,* about $320. "Don't spend it all
in one place," I admonished. He nodded and slipped the money into
his pocket. It occurred to me that he might need some guidance when
he went into town to shop. But I didn't want to seem patronizing. We
remained, even at this late stage, straitjacketed in our roles.

Out on the river, families paddled past in the darkness in their
small canoes. A tugboat version of the *Kukahá,* with the same lines and
railings, pushed a barge upstream, engines bucking against the invisible but inexorable current. Boats pulled away from floating docks to

join the growing flow of traffic on the Amazon. Parakeets streaked across an overcast sky, celebrating the dawn of a new day with their riotous shrieks. I finished my coffee, smoked one last cigarette with Soldado, and got ready to go.

We stood at the top of the gangplank. I looked one more time into those sad, noble brown eyes. Had it not been for Soldado, I might well have perished out there in the jungle. Certainly the journey would have been much more difficult to endure.

"I'll see you again," I said as we embraced.

"Promise?" he said.

"Promise."

*   *   *

After showering and devouring a proper breakfast at the Anaconda, I delivered two bags of laundry to the front desk. "Have them boil these clothes for an hour," I told the receptionist. "You have no idea where they've been." The phone rang just as I returned to my room. It was Possuelo down in the lobby with Orlando. They'd come to find me and Nicolas. "Scott," said Possuelo. "Let's go out for a look around, have lunch." I couldn't think of three people I less wanted to be with at that moment. "Okay, I'll be right down," I said, not sure why I agreed. We wandered the streets to the blare of car horns and drifting fumes of black exhaust. Pedestrians pushed and shoved on the crowded sidewalks. We bought the morning paper and stopped at a bustling coffee bar. The big news: FARC guerrillas had attacked a Tikuna settlement called Puerto Nariño a half hour upriver, killing two and wounding two others. Colombia's three-way war, pitting leftist rebels against the government army and right-wing paramilitaries, had devolved into a nightmarish campaign of brutality. As the war spread into the remotest valleys in the Colombian Amazon, the remnants of the country's last isolated tribes were being flushed from the bush, dazed and starving.

We ducked into a sandwich shop for lunch. The conversation was lame, stilted. After weeks on end together, there was nothing to say. I just wanted to bolt. We got sundaes at an ice-cream parlor. As I went to pay, I realized in a heart-stopping flash that my notebook was missing. It must have been a measure of my unease, for I misplace things of import—like the cell phone back in New York—only when feeling inordinately stressed. But in more than twenty years of reporting, at times under extreme duress, I'd never lost or misplaced a single notebook. Field notes are a reporter's currency, more valuable than a wallet or even a passport. Those can be more or less easily replaced; notes cannot.

What was worse, I didn't remember when I'd last had it with me, whether I'd been in Tabatinga or here in Leticia. I peeled away from the others to retrace my steps. I stopped at the coffee shop, the newsstand, the sandwich place. Nothing. I heard a shout from over my shoulder: *"Bak!"* I looked back. Márcio Kanamari smiled from across the street. He sported brand-new clothes and a bright white bandanna wrapped around his head. Even from the distance, I could see he was beaming. I would have liked to stop and hear about his adventures in the big city. But I had to find that notebook. I waved and turned the corner. It was the last I ever saw of him.

The receptionist at the hotel was sympathetic. "Why don't you go to the radio station, señor?" he said. "You can put a bulletin on the air. If you offer a reward, maybe someone will come forward."

The station was just down the street. At the front desk, I filled out a classified form with all the details: "Scott Wallace (which they would pronounce *Escote Guálas*), a writer for *National Geographic,* has lost valuable field notes from his journeys in the jungle. Please bring the notebook to Hotel Anaconda to claim a $50 reward." But Radio Caracol only broadcasted to the Spanish-speaking audience in Leticia. How was I to reach the Portuguese speakers in Tabatinga? I asked one of the cabdrivers outside, thinking he might have an answer. "I know a guy over there who has a truck with loudspeakers," he said. "Makes his living advertising. You know, political campaigns and product propaganda. You could pay him to go through the marketplace in Tabatinga reading your announcement."

We pulled up outside a modest home on an unpaved backstreet. A Toyota pickup was parked in front with two large megaphones mounted on the roof of the cab. I handed the guy the message to read, paid him, and sent him on his way out into Tabatinga's streets.

When I got back to the Anaconda, a middle-aged woman with a kindly, wizened face was waiting for me in the lobby. Her name was Blanca, and she sold lottery tickets on the street downtown. She'd found the notebook on the windowsill at the coffee shop. "It looked like something important," she said, "but I didn't know exactly what it was." Then she heard the announcement on the radio. *"Gracias, mi amor,"* she said, tucking the cash under her apron.

* * *

I was more than ready to head for home. But Possuelo wanted to visit the Korubo he'd contacted six years before. They now occupied a *maloca* near the FUNAI control post at the gateway to the Javari. We crossed back to Tabatinga the next morning in a depressing drizzle. The stairway down the embankment was slick. We bounded across the same plank to the FUNAI boathouse that had marked the beginning of our journey nearly twelve weeks before. Wilson and Alfredo were inside, sitting on the floor. Alongside them, a Sony sound system the size of a large suitcase pulsed with green and red lights to the pounding beat of *brega*. It represented the entirety of Alfredo's earnings, blown in an instant.

I pictured the scene at the appliance store the day before while we were so pointlessly wandering the streets of Leticia. Alfredo had been left to fend for himself in an alien world. He must have been bedazzled by the thump of the boom box's speakers, its flashing lights, and the promise it seemed to offer for good times to be had back home. *Bak!* he must have thought, digging into his pocket. *And look, I have just enough to pay for it!*

"Burrá?" Ivan Arapá said, nodding with disgust at the stereo. "What's his woman going to say? No presents for her. Nothing for the kids." It must have dawned on Alfredo that he'd made a huge mistake,

for he was staring through the boathouse door out into empty space, as if in a catatonic stupor. "Alfredo," I called. He didn't look up.

"Someone should have offered some orientation," Danilo said in my ear. No kidding. I cursed myself for getting caught up with Possuelo and Nicolas. Surely this sort of thing must have happened at the conclusion of other expeditions. Why hadn't Possuelo issued some guidelines? Or why hadn't he organized a collective shopping trip or something? Maybe it had to do with the weird time of night we'd arrived in Tabatinga, the fact that some had already bolted, while others stuck around. Maybe he was just too burned out, like everyone else. Thoroughly burned out.

To make matters worse, Alfredo's sound system ran on current, not even on batteries. It would be virtually worthless in Massapê, where they had no electricity. "Alfredo, listen to me," I implored, laying a hand on his shoulder. "You've got to take this back to the store. See if you can get your money back." That seemed like a long shot. "At least ask if they'd exchange it for one that runs on batteries." He nodded. I looked around. "Someone should go with him," I said, raising my voice.

But I couldn't. Possuelo, Orlando, and Nicolas had already taken their seats in the speedboat. Danilo started the engine. "Alfredo, take this." I pressed my Swiss Army knife into his hand. *"Muito obrigado.* Thanks for your hard work. Good luck." It wasn't much, but it seemed to take the sting away, at least for a moment. I climbed into the boat, and Danilo threw it in reverse. Alfredo slowly hoisted his hand in a kind of wave. He managed a faint smile. And then, we were gone.

CHAPTER 27

Meet the Head-Bashers

THE CLOUDS DISPERSED as we cruised upriver through splotches of sunlight. The channels beyond Tabatinga were virtually unrecognizable, so low had the water dropped in the past few months. The *furos* where Amarildo and his family had been assaulted were no longer passable. We had to take the long way around. The baby parrots rode in the back, alongside the Yamaha-85, terrified of the engine's blare, poking their heads in desperation through the spaces in the wicker cage, looking for a way out.

It was midafternoon when we reached the base. Antonio Carlos greeted us with a big smile at the top of the stairway. He pointed to pole beans and fat watermelons growing below the catwalk. "I told you we'd have beans and melons here," he said.

Now that the floodwaters had receded, it was much easier to fully appreciate the base's strategic position at the confluence of the two rivers and the long stretch of beach across the way, where Sobral had perished five years before.

Thunder was grumbling in the distance. Dark clouds threatened rain. But Possuelo wanted to get moving. He cupped his hands to his mouth and called: *"Embora, pessoal!* Let's go visit the Korubo!" We shuffled down the steps and climbed back into the boat. With us were Antonio Carlos and a FUNAI medic named Oliveira. Two Matis working at the base, Chapu and Tumin Tucum, shoved the boat off and hopped in. Both carried shotguns. "They have a family relationship with the Korubo," Possuelo said. "That's why they're coming with us."

Both the Matis and the Korubo are Panoan-speaking tribes, and Matis
scouts were instrumental in helping Possuelo make peaceful contact
with the Korubo in 1996. There had also been the mixing of blood,
owing to an incident from the period before contact, when the Matis
kidnapped two Korubo girls. They'd been raised in the tribe and had
eventually given birth to children of their own. The Matis always served
as interpreters and intermediaries between the Korubo and FUNAI,
helping to maintain an atmosphere of trust.

It was a short jaunt up the Ituí. Within fifteen minutes, we pulled in
where an Indian boy stood completely naked in a dugout canoe leaning on a pole. "That's Te-oh," said Oliveira, who'd been making daily
excursions to treat the Korubo for a variety of ailments.

We sprang from the boat into soft mud and started down a path
flanked by soaring kapok trunks of enormous circumference. Once
again, we were in the domain of primeval forest. Te-oh led the way,
followed close behind by the Matis with their rifles. Since the death
of Sobral, no one was permitted to visit the Korubo without an armed
escort. Oliveira, just ahead of me, lugged a large plastic tackle box that
served as his medical kit. "Hey-hey, ho-ho," we sang loudly as we moved
along the path in the shade of soaring monoliths. An answer came
from up the path: "Hey-hey, ho-ho."

Thunder growled. Dogs barked. We entered a broad clearing dom-
inated by a huge hut with palm thatching that ran from its twenty-foot-
high peak all the way to the ground, giving the shelter the appearance
of an enormous bale of hay. We ducked through a low, narrow entrance—a safeguard against surprise attack—and emerged in the deep
gloom of the *maloca*. The air was thick with the smell of wood smoke.
As my eyes adjusted to the dark, I made out a woman swinging in a
hammock near the entrance. Something nudged my calf: a baby peccary. Two small monkeys loped along a neatly swept earthen floor.
The woman in the hammock had thick black hair, cropped in a bowl
cut, with bangs hanging at midforehead. She was completely, unself-
consciously naked. Red *urucum* paint streaked the upper half of her
round, matronly face, around her eyes, and across her nose. An infant

suckled at her bare breast. She was robust, built like a linebacker, and I guessed she was in her early forties. "Sydney!" she beamed. "I adore you!" Tumin stood to the side, gun in hand, translating to Portuguese. This was Maya, and she was, in essence, the chief of the clan.

"Everyone listens to Maya," Possuelo said. He made sure Tumin translated everything he said back to Korubo, so the Indians would know we harbored no secrets. Possuelo knelt alongside her, and she grabbed his beard playfully, stroking it with affection. He seized her arm and made like he was going to chomp it. Howls of laughter came from the shadows. I could see now that several others were gathered around, adults and children. Some swung in hammocks strung between the uprights that held up the roof. Others squatted on the floor. One man held a toddler in his lap. A woman by his side held a younger baby in her arms.

"Washmä," she said, pointing to herself. She was Maya's oldest daughter and the mother of the child killed by the anaconda on the beach opposite the base. It appeared as though she'd been successful in reconstituting her family in the ensuing years. The infants quietly poked at each other. A monkey crawled up and down their arms, across their heads, down their shoulders. As my eyes adjusted further to the darkness, I could appreciate the truly cavernous dimensions of the hut, with its towering peak and single chamber that extended nearly fifty feet to the far end, where light seeped through a low opening like the one we had entered.

Possuelo spoke of our expedition, and of the *índios bravos* whose village we'd entered. He described the large gardens, the houses, all the different kinds of meat the Indians had prepared, as though they were getting ready for a big party. He hadn't wanted to enter the village, he told Maya, but he'd had no choice; two of our men—also Indians—had gone missing, and we'd needed to find them.

"Did they have clubs?" Maya asked.

"No," Possuelo replied. "Just arrows and *zarabatana*—blowguns."

She seemed disappointed. I understood why. Maya had led her band away from the main body of Korubo several years earlier, following a violent spat that saw her first husband killed. Some warriors objected to her subsequent marriage to Shi-shu—a slight man who was now sitting off to the side—and they were forced to strike out on their own. But the clan was small, only twenty-three members, not enough to ensure the longevity and viability of the group. Despite any lingering animosities, Maya's group would probably seek to rejoin the larger tribe at some point in the future. The older children were reaching puberty and would require mates beyond the confines of their single *maloca*. Having had no contact with them since the altercation years ago, Maya naturally was eager for news of the larger community. But the wild Indians we'd visited had no clubs; Korubo they were not.

"Let's go outside," Maya said with a sigh, rising from her hammock. We ducked through the low portal and out into blinding daylight. We sat on a pair of thick tree trunks, toppled giants that lay in the shade of a shaggy banana grove. Maya asked my name again, and now she was repeating it over and over with a broad smile: *"Scotchie, Scotchie."* Now all the Head-Bashers started chanting my name in unison, falling over themselves with laughter like it was the funniest thing they'd ever heard. Where was I from? they asked. *"Estados Unidos,"* I said in Portuguese. The United States. *"Stassos Nidos,"* they repeated, roughly the equivalent of saying "Nited Stace."

Possuelo asked about the incident the Kanamari had reported during the journey, about the time when loggers killed Korubo on a beach somewhere and chased others into the woods. *"Nanutita,"* said Maya, counting on her fingers. "The white loggers killed three on the river," Tumin translated. The other adults spoke up, talking excitedly over one another. By now, our hosts included four women and an equal number of men, all nearly naked, all with bowl cuts like Maya's, bangs cut halfway down the forehead. Which incident was Sydney talking about? they asked. How long ago?

"When he was this high," said Possuelo, pointing first to Orlando, then to the toddler, to indicate when Orlando was the same height as the younger one, about fifteen years ago.

"Mepewe shawakayno," Maya said. She didn't remember.

"You would have been very young," said Possuelo, paying her a compliment. "Or it could have been the other group of Korubo."

"*Aí,*" she said. "We were already living separate from the others." Now she remembered: the incident on the Itaquaí, when the whites killed the Korubo. Like the rest of her people, she'd thought back then that the whites were but a handful, and she proposed wiping them out once and for all. She hadn't been present at the particular incident Possuelo mentioned, but she'd heard about it. It wasn't an isolated event; she and all the other grown-ups had survived gunshot wounds. They came forward, one by one, to show me their scars—on their backs, buttocks, and limbs. "This is where our doctors removed buckshot embedded in their hides," Possuelo said. "The loggers call the Indians to the shore. They say, 'Hey, we have food for you! Here, take some farinha!' The Indians come, and they shoot them." In at least one instance, the flour itself had been treated with poison.

"*Aí, aí,*" said Maya, nodding. That's right.

It would have been about fifteen years since Jessica Sampaio had fled from club-wielding Indians on an Ituí beach. It wasn't necessarily the same incident, but I wondered if she had chosen to omit certain details about her stepfather's logging operations on this river, just as Maya would have been inclined to skip over the particulars of her own people's less than tenderhearted conduct. Some twenty-six whites had perished at the hands of the Head-Bashers since the late 1960s along the Ituí and Itaquaí rivers. Three more had been kidnapped. Korubo losses had certainly been much higher, but then again, no one had been counting.

It was in this contentious atmosphere that Possuelo had moved to choke off access by outsiders into the Javari, then launched a succession of expeditions to contact with Maya's small band of Korubo. As with all attempts to contact isolated tribes, the effort was fraught with risk. Like the Arrow People, the Korubo had no way to distinguish "good whites" from those who meant them harm. Ever since the days of Rondon and Nimuendajú, helping Indians make this distinction has been a fundamental principle in the *sertanista*'s playbook.

Possuelo and his team doggedly pursued the Korubo, following their tracks deep into the forest. They found fallow gardens and abandoned *malocas,* and they came across camouflaged pitfalls the Indians had prepared for them.

"I spent a long time looking for you," Possuelo said to Maya with a playful wag of the finger, reminding her of those weeks and final days leading up to contact. "I left a pot and a machete out in the garden the first time, remember? You were inside the *maloca.* We were singing to you."

"We were listening," Maya said in her high-pitched voice, laughing. "I said to the others: 'They are calling to us.' Some were afraid. I wasn't. I said, 'They're singing to us. They must be friends.'"

"Es nano cho!" Washmä shouted, evidently repeating what she had said that day as they huddled in their hut, Possuelo's contact team just outside. Tumin translated: "I said: 'You come here!' I wanted you to come to us."

Possuelo began to sing a simple lullaby. From the radiant smile spreading across Washmä's face, I understood this was the song he'd sung the day they had met six years before. It was the song that had put the Indians at ease and disarmed them just enough for Possuelo to make his approach. And here they were now, reunited as old friends, reminiscing over that special moment when they'd first met. Except that, in this instance, the encounter had been of a different order of magnitude: that moment on the cutting edge of history when complete and utter strangers from separate universes stood face-to-face, looked each other in the eye, and recognized their common humanity. It had been first contact.

Possuelo was more animated than I'd seen him in weeks. He engaged the Indians with his bulging eyes and wild facial contortions, digging into his vast actor's repertoire of comic melodrama and vaudevillian slapstick, a born entertainer. He listened, in turn, to what they had to say, and they could tell he was listening. He had a knack for seeking out common points of reference and evoking shared memories. No matter if the Korubo inhabited an entirely different reality,

Possuelo possessed an uncanny ability to get inside their minds and their hearts. He made no mention of his old friend Sobral, nor did he ask after Sobral's killer, a warrior named Ta-van, who was noticeably absent from the meeting.

Oliveira broke open the tackle box. He dispensed cough syrup into disposable paper shot cups and made his way around the circle, personally ministering each dose. "They had 100 percent malaria here," Possuelo said. "There were twenty people in the *maloca* and twenty cases of malaria. Pneumonia, malaria, fever, cough, cold—they've had it all."

"When there's an outbreak like that, you have to come every day," said Oliveira. He had been coming here to see the Korubo on a daily basis for the past forty-five days. It was fortunate that the Korubo were close enough to treat them. Maya's group had planted gardens of corn and manioc in scattered clearings through the forest, and they migrated from one *maloca* to another as the crops came into season. They would soon be on the move again.

Maya grabbed a handful of red *urucum* berries from a clay vat at her feet, crushed them in her palms, and spat into them. She stood up and commenced smearing the scarlet paint on my forehead, my cheeks, all over my face. "That means she likes you," Possuelo laughed. Maya turned to Possuelo, gave him like treatment, then moved on to Nicolas.

"*Guantá,*" she said with a wave of her hand. "You go now." Her husband Shi-shu got up, their young daughter clinging to his back. They escorted us back down the path beneath the towering trees whose majesty and timelessness demanded respect. I felt a sense of awe wash over me, a feeling that defied articulation, that I was standing in a sacred presence.

At the top of the bank, we bid farewell.

"Ciao, Scotchie!" they said.

We returned downriver as the light faded from the sky. Storybook clouds glowed yellow in the far distance, their perfect reflections keeping pace with us as we glided along the smooth water of the Ituí.

And then in a blaze of orange and purple, the sun vanished behind a screen of silhouetted palms. It would be our last sunset over the jungle. By this time tomorrow, we'd be back in Leticia.

Back at the base, we stood on the deck looking out on the river in the gathering darkness. Cicadas started into their incessant, pulsating buzz.

"He was hit twice," Possuelo volunteered. The day's visit must have jarred something loose; he'd always been closemouthed on the subject of Sobral. "The first blow killed him. His head exploded. He died instantly." Possuelo hadn't been here at the time. Had he been, he was sure the incident would never have happened. The men had blithely ignored norms he'd established for conduct at the base: Carry rifles at all times in the presence of the Korubo and display them ostentatiously; never cross the river to visit the Indians in lesser numbers than theirs; and never allow yourselves to be surrounded, always deploying two or three men at a distance to keep watch.

In a sense, these same precautions had applied throughout the course of our intrusion in the land of the Arrow People. There was our strength in numbers, the conspicuousness of our rifles. Even our usual deployment in a single column would have prevented encirclement by the Indians.

When the Korubo had appeared that day on the far shore, singing and dancing arm in arm, Sobral and the others anxiously crossed over with gifts of bananas and farinha. They took their cameras to get some souvenir snapshots for their families back home. It seemed like one of those breakthrough moments, when recently contacted tribespeople demonstrate new heights of confidence and friendship. They didn't see the war clubs hidden in the grass at the Indians' feet. For Possuelo, the attack could be understood only in the context of a long history of persecution at the hands of whites in the region, dating back to at least 1928, when rubber tappers reportedly killed forty Korubo. They could be forgiven in Possuelo's mind, for they hadn't yet come to appreciate that all-important distinction between the FUNAI team and the other *brancos* they'd encountered in the past, the ones who made a sport of shooting them.

It was in that same place across the river, Possuelo said, that Wash-mä's five-year-old girl later perished—strangled and hauled away in an instant by a monstrous anaconda. The Korubo had come back, months after the Sobral incident, to receive treatment for malaria. They were camped on the high ground overlooking the beach. The girl waded into the water. It was midafternoon, broad daylight. "Everyone was watching," said Possuelo. "All the sudden, *whoosh!* Just like that, the anaconda grabbed her. Right in front of everyone. Took her and vanished beneath the water. They stayed over there for eight straight days, crying."

There was an odd symmetry to the two deaths, the fact that one was white and the other Indian; that one had died for reasons of history, the other taken by the hand of nature, though the Korubo likely saw supernatural powers at work in the anaconda's lightning strike. The tragedy of a young life cut short was amplified by the tribe's minuscule numbers—a people struggling to maintain viability and survive into the future. Yet, in a way, Sobral's death was no less tragic, for he, too, belonged to a vanishing breed—the backwoodsmen who stood between civilization's advance and its most defenseless victims. Both perished in a split second, when they least expected it. Surprise. It was what made life in the Amazon so intense, and at times, so terrifying. You never knew when death might reach out and strike. Just like that.

CHAPTER 28

The Overflight

THE WIND WHIPPED THROUGH the open doorway into the cabin as the Cessna bounced through a patch of gauzy clouds. The forest spread out below us, its broccoli-top canopy a greenish gray, laced with the brown waters of the Itaquaí twisting a thousand feet below. In the differentiated shades of brown, you could make out the shallows and the deeper channels in the river's sweeping S-turns, and the bright white margins that marked its beaches.

We'd left the Anaconda in Leticia an hour earlier, making our way out to the airfield for one last mission: a reconnaissance flight to retrace the expedition route. In a matter of minutes, we'd look down breezily from above on what had taken us months to grind out on the ground. The plane's rear door, on the right side of the fuselage, had been removed for the occasion, affording an unobstructed view for our cameras.

Belt cinched around his waist, Nicolas leaned halfway out the open door, wind ripping at his hair, wildly flapping his collar. Without the seat belt, he'd have gone straight out in the void. The morning was dazzling—bright sunlight, patchy clouds. We passed over lakes in the shapes of hearts, horseshoes, and squiggles that ran parallel to the river, old channels cut off by the receding floods. Within them swirled deep brown waters like heated chocolate in a vat.

Ducking in and out of clouds, we circled the base where the Ituí joined the Itaquaí. A riverboat was pulled fast to its floating dock—

the *Kukahá*! The Indians would soon be home. We followed the Ituí. A smaller skiff churned upriver, trailing a frothy wake on the brown water. "That must be our people!" Possuelo yelled over the roar of the wind and engine. "Look, there's the Korubo's *maloca*!"

We cut due south, resuming our route over the Itaquaí. Here and there, tiny hamlets of five and six huts hugged the shore. A large village appeared on the right bank with a log passageway leading from the river to several palm-thatched buildings. I recognized it instantly: Massapê. It was where we'd first met Alfredo and Wilson and where we'd recruited them to the expedition. What a difference, to be gliding over it from up here, knowing we'd be back in the city in an hour, not heading into the jungle for three months. It seemed both decadent and exhilarating to be winging our way above it all, unbound by the suffocating heat and the torpor that had attended so much of the terrestrial journey.

We turned west, away from the Itaquaí, jostled by the air currents. Down below, *igarapés* snaked back and forth, catching the sun's sparkle for an instant before they were once again snatched from view by the jungle. Faint ripples in the jungle canopy, all but invisible to the eye, marked the infinite hillsides and ridgelines that had so thoroughly punished us. I could tell where there were rivers before actually seeing them. I could make out where narrow *igarapés* twisted and turned without being able to see them at all. I'd never beheld the Amazon this way before. On scores of flights I'd taken over the rainforest—in jetliners, bush planes, even helicopters—I'd always looked down on a vast, largely undifferentiated mass of green, interlaced with winding rivers, going on and on to infinity. Now, I saw something akin to a living relief map, a unique synthesis of terrestrial and aerial perspectives. It was as though I were looking down on the rainforest with an entirely new set of eyes, my vision from up above informed by the footsteps I'd taken down below.

We hit a crosscurrent, and I caught an adrenaline rush as the plane suddenly dropped. We cut east now along the headwaters of the Jutaí.

"Look!" Possuelo cried. *"Índios bravos!"* He pointed down at what looked like a large brown scab spread out on the forest carpet. A cluster of several huts stood in the center of the clearing amid a crisscrossing of toppled trees, blackened earth, and what appeared to be banana groves. Smoke drifted from the thatched roofs in lazy swirls. And then suddenly, there they were: the People of the Arrow!

Dark figures scurried about like ants between the huts, no doubt spooked by the appearance of this droning monster overhead. I couldn't escape the sense of irony, even absurdity, of the moment. Three months in the wilderness, and I'd never laid an eye on the Arrow People. Forty minutes out of Tabatinga and here we were, looking down on them.

"Let's go lower!" Nicolas yelled from halfway out the door. We were circling clockwise over the village at two thousand feet, the plane banking hard, the better to get an unobstructed view. But we were too high to discern any detail in the outlines of the human forms below. "No lower than this!" barked Possuelo. "Any lower and you scare the shit out of them. I won't allow it."

The figures on the ground appeared to halt their frantic scrambling. They stood motionless now, as though staring up at us in a trance. How strange, to be looking down at them, and they in turn gazing up at us across this distance. It was almost as though we inhabited entirely separate universes. They knew virtually nothing about us, had no way of even knowing human beings were aboard this winged creature whose shadow had darkened their sky. About them, we did not know a good deal more. We'd come to know they were skillful hunters, masters of projectile-point technology, which had allowed them to reap the rich bounty of the forest. We knew they trekked seasonally through the jungle, following the rhythms of the rain and water. They cultivated manioc, banana, and sugarcane, and some kind of cotton as well. Somewhere along the way, they'd managed to obtain a steel ax or two, as their broad clearing so eloquently attested. Most important, as far as Possuelo was concerned, they appeared to be thriving in every way. Isolation, far from strangling them, had made them strong. For

Possuelo, this is what victory looked like: the Arrow People, holding forth in the Parallel Realm. Uncontacted. Untamed. Unconquered.

Still, I wondered if he found this arrangement entirely to his satisfaction. Didn't Possuelo want to know those people down there, and didn't he want them to know him, to stroke his beard, to laugh and call his name? Over the whistling wind and whining motor, I put the question to Possuelo: Don't you want to know them, meet them, shake their hands, and make friends?

"I prefer to keep things this way," he shouted back. "That they are there, and I am here, that we are separated by this distance and that we will never know each other." He looked down as the pilot leveled off the plane and the village vanished from view behind us. "I'm happy to know that they're taking care of themselves and that we, from a distance, are taking care of them."

We pressed on, now heading east, following the Jutaí. We passed straight over where the main camp must have been, but I didn't see the dock. Perhaps it had already begun to fall apart, or maybe the Arrow People had trashed it. Maybe I just missed it. I looked down on the treetops. Somewhere just below us was the trail we'd followed every day for nearly two weeks to visit the site where the Matis were building their canoe.

On the last afternoon before we started downriver in the dugouts, I'd followed Possuelo on the way back to the main camp along that well-worn thoroughfare. We'd made it to the place where thick bamboo formed a high wall that seemed poised to break like a wave over us. I stopped to ask him how long it would take for the path we were walking on to disappear, for things to return to their natural state. "In two years, this will be gone. You'll be able to detect some of these cuttings," he said as he grabbed a sapling sliced by a machete. Then he pointed out into the forest on our flanks. "But the trees will begin growing through here. It will all be grown over. The path will be gone. Five years from now, you'll never know we were here."

It was doubtful the Arrow People would forget us so easily. Perhaps for years to come they would recount to their children and to their children's children the story of the day their enemies arrived, just as they were preparing a big feast. They would tell of scattering in panic—warriors safeguarding women, children, babies—and how they watched as the odd-smelling strangers entered the village with their deadly weapons. Perhaps they would mention our offerings of friendship—the knives and machetes, the axes and cooking pots—and how those gifts gave strength to voices of caution and quieted those who called for strident defense of their jungle homeland. Or perhaps they would say it was the fear of devastating reprisal that stayed their hand. I hoped that we would never find out, that the answers to such questions would remain forever within the realm of our imaginings.

In any case, it was equally doubtful that we would ever erase from our own memories the wonders and the horrors we found in this forest we had slogged through, not to mention the invisible people it harbored. Nor would we forget the streams we forded, the hardships we endured, the friendships and the bitterness we shared in the course of exploring this bastion of untamed wilderness, one of the very last in the world. Yes, we could have just flown over it. But we would never have come to know it. We came, we saw, and we left it alone, the way it's been since time immemorial, and if Sydney Possuelo and those who follow in his footsteps have any say in the matter, the way it will remain for a long, long time to come.

Epilogue

DIPLOMACY WAS NEVER his strong suit. It was perhaps only a matter of time before Possuelo ran irredeemably afoul of higher authorities for acts of insubordination. That time arrived in January 2006, when he publicly lambasted Mércio Gomes, then in his third year as president of FUNAI.

Press reports had quoted Gomes as saying, in effect, that Brazil's Indians were demanding more land than they were reasonably entitled to. "It's too much land," Gomes said, according to a Reuters dispatch. He went on to suggest that the Brazilian Supreme Court set limits on Indian land claims.

A reporter managed to track down Possuelo to get his reaction. He was deep in the bush at the time, visiting the Zo'é tribe. He hadn't even seen the news dispatch himself; the journalist read it to him across the tenuous line of a two-way radio transmission. No matter. Possuelo held nothing back. "I've heard this discourse from ranchers, land sharks, prospectors, and loggers," he shouted back across the radio line to the reporter from *O Estado de São Paulo*. "But from the president of FUNAI, this is the first time. It's scary."

Possuelo said Gomes's stance was akin to that of an "environmental minister calling on people to cut down trees," and he called on Brazilian president Luiz Inácio Lula da Silva to clarify: was the head of FUNAI spouting personal views, or was this the official position of the federal government?

The answer came in little more than a week. Possuelo was sacked. But he refused to back down. "I have never been one of those nice workers who agree with everything that the government does," he said. Indeed, *nice* was generally not the first word that came to mind at the mention of Possuelo's name. But he could be very gracious. He made himself available to me every day for more than a week when I visited him in Brasília in December 2009. We spent long hours at his home and on the street. We discussed his career, his years in the bush, his thoughts on isolated Indians, and we spoke at length about our time together in the jungle.

In an effort to keep his hand in the game, Possuelo had formed his own NGO, the Instituto Indigenista Interamericano, dedicated to forging transboundary alliances among indigenous federations and Indian rights groups. He was routinely invited to speaking engagements abroad. But it was evident that he missed the old days and the central role he had played in shaping and carrying out Brazil's Indian policies. Far removed from the Amazon forests, the primordial cry of its parrots, and the Indians to whom he'd dedicated his life, Possuelo seemed like a caged animal amid Brasília's boxy glass buildings and manicured boulevards. He was doing his best to get on with his life, but he seemed to be chafing beneath the surface.

Possuelo could take consolation from the fact that others were carrying on the work he had begun. The entity he had been critical in shaping, the Department of Isolated Indians, remained in charge of protecting Brazil's last uncontacted peoples. Whatever its faults, and there were many, the system of identification, protection, and vigilance Possuelo had put in place was making a difference. The number of uncontacted tribes whose existence the department had confirmed had grown to twenty-six, and the department continued to uncover and compile evidence of previously unknown groups of wild Indians.

But disturbing trends hovered on the horizon. A killer drought in the western Amazon in 2005 had reduced river levels as much as forty feet, stranding hundreds of communities. Billions of trees had shriveled and died. Scientists called it a "1-in-100-year event," but an even more withering drought returned in 2010. Billions more trees perished, releasing their stored carbon. For the first time, the Amazon had become a net producer of greenhouse gases, rather than the world's most important carbon sink. Climatologists attributed the drying trend to warming sea surface temperatures in the North Atlantic and warned that we are "playing Russian roulette with the world's largest forest." The Amazon is in a danger of reaching a "tipping point," they said, beyond which its role as a critical buffer against global warming could begin to unravel.

The world's appetite for tropical timber posed a more immediate threat to the uncontacted tribes. Illegal logging in protected areas in Peru was pushing groups of Indians into Brazil, heightening strife among contacted and uncontacted communities at the headwaters of the Envira and Jordão rivers. Eager to generate employment and earn revenues on timber and hydrocarbon development, Peruvian president Alan García had thrown his country's Amazonian territories open to logging and oil and gas exploration. Citing a lack of hard evidence, he scoffed at the notion of uncontacted tribes. One official in the state oil company likened the tribes to the Loch Ness monster, a mere figment of the imagination concocted by environmentalists to sabotage Peru's economic growth.

The presence of isolated Indians, if confirmed in any given area, did pose a serious obstacle and potential liability to the profitable exploitation of resources, raising the specter of a political and public relations disaster. With billions of dollars of oil revenue hanging in the balance, speculation abounded that Peru might be turning a blind eye to illegal logging, allowing lumberjacks in effect to flush the jungles of *índios bravos*, to "take care of the Indian problem" once and for all.

Desperate to draw attention to the plight of the Indians, veteran *sertanista* José Carlos Meirelles took a photographer on an aerial survey of the border area in 2008. Possuelo had appointed Meirelles several years earlier to head the Envira Ethno-Environmental Protection Front, with jurisdiction over the westernmost corner of Brazil in the state of Acre. His bush plane swooped in over the *maloca* of an uncontacted tribe, prompting the Indians to launch arrows at the low-flying aircraft. The images of naked tribesmen brandishing bows and arrows electrified the world. Breathless headlines pronounced the discovery of a "lost tribe," but just as quickly denounced the whole thing as a "hoax" when Meirelles explained that he'd been monitoring the Indians for two decades. But there was no hoax. The Indians were very real. In effect, the media outlets had duped themselves; they didn't understand that a tribe could be observed from afar and remain uncontacted. Meirelles had never claimed the Indians to be "lost." He'd never used the word.

Two years later, Meirelles returned to the air over the forests of the upper Envira with a BBC film crew, hoping this time to lay to rest any doubt about the existence of uncontacted peoples in the border region. Loggers had invaded reserves set aside for isolated tribes in Peru, and efforts by Peruvian authorities to crack down appeared half-hearted at best. Perhaps only a media campaign that captured the attention of the world, Meirelles reasoned, could halt an impending disaster.

Outfitted with a stabilized zoom lens, the television crew was able to gather astonishing images of the same tribe that had been photographed in 2008, this time from high above the jungle. On the video, the Indians are seen looking out through the banana trees around their huts, curious but unfrightened, pointing at the distant airplane in wonder. "They are a reminder that it's possible to live another way," Meirelles told the BBC as he looked down on the Indians from the circling plane. "They are the last free people on this planet." When the video aired in early February 2011, it became an instant global sensation.

Comparisons to the box-office blockbuster *Avatar* were inevitable. Indeed, in the weeks and months following the film's 2009 release, indigenous rights groups hailed the resistance of the fictional Na'vi to corporate mining interests as an accurate representation of the struggles of indigenous people around the world. Director James Cameron traveled to Brazil in 2010 to lend support to Kayapó Indians fighting to stop a massive hydroelectric project planned for the Xingu River. But in the images of the uncontacted tribe, real life seemed to be imitating art. The BBC's high-definition camera imparted a dreamy, cinematic quality to the scene: the towering canopy trees, the smoke swirling above the *maloca*'s thatched-palm roof, the natives in brilliant crimson body paint stepping through the emerald forest. No grainy newsreel, this video had the look and feel of a movie, as if the Indians were peering out at the world from one of Cameron's own sets.

Peruvian authorities promised to clamp down on the illegal logging. For the first time ever, they committed to working closely with their Brazilian counterparts to protect the sensitive habitats of the isolated Indians. This welcome news notwithstanding, the Amazon's last uncontacted tribes are under mounting threat, the noose around them tightening. In the summer of 2011, heavily armed drug traffickers reportedly from Peru overran the FUNAI outpost in the Envira headwaters, forcing Meirelles and staff to flee for their lives. Returning with escorts from the Brazilian military, they captured one suspect, together with evidence that suggested the gang may have attacked the same isolated community so idyllically portrayed in the BBC's footage. A subsequent reconnaissance flight revealed that the *malocas* were intact, but their inhabitants were nowhere to be found.

On the eastern side of the Amazon, the forests harboring the last isolated community of Guajá Indians is under intense pressure from loggers, who in January 2012 stood accused of burning a girl alive to sow terror and drive off the natives. Meanwhile, the government of president Dilma Rousseff entered its second year committed to pushing forward with the controversial Belo Monte megadam on the Xingu, despite ongoing protests from environmentalists and Kayapó Indians. Not only will the $17 billion project inundate Kayapó land; it could also snuff out a recently sighted band of nomadic tribespeople, forcing them to flee into colonized lands where only hostility and violence await them.

FUNAI was in the midst of a major reorganization that had begun the previous year. With a dearth of fresh blood and many of the graybeards who'd come of age with Possuelo's retiring, the agency's long-term viability as an effective defender of Brazil's Indians was in doubt. At the end of 2010, Possuelo authored an open letter in defense of isolated indigenous peoples, calling on sympathizers around the world to raise their voices to protest the mounting assaults on the Amazon's beleaguered tribes and their lands. "The situation is critical," he wrote. "The isolated Indians must live. They are our purest essence, our most vital impulse."

There will be no pardon for us, said Possuelo, if we allow them to disappear.

Postscript

O N   N O V E M B E R   11, 2004, photographer Nicolas Reynard was killed when the plane he was shooting from crashed in the Rio Negro near Manaus. Prior to the accident, veteran pilot Paulo Miranda Corrêa had been repeatedly landing on and taking off from the river to allow Nicolas to take photographs out the open door on the side of the aircraft.

Among the things he was photographing that day was the private Embraer Sertanejo pontoon plane of Margi and Gérard Moss, a Rio de Janeiro couple who were at work on a project to gather water samples from lakes and rivers throughout Brazil. Pilot Corrêa and the Mosses were swapping places back and forth, one plane landing while the other circled overhead, the better for Nicolas to get dramatic shots of the Embraer. The Mosses grew worried when the plane carrying Nicolas failed to appear alongside them as they headed west over the forest from the Rio Negro. Doubling back, they spotted the wreckage on the river's surface and brought their own plane down for a closer look.

They quickly surmised that the other aircraft had hit the water at high speed. It had broken apart and was rapidly sinking. Gérard dove into the dark waters, desperately trying to free the crash victims. It was too late. The plane had already sunk too deep for him to reach the cockpit door. After repeated attempts, his lungs bursting, Moss was forced to give up.

And then, something both remarkable and horrifying happened. From the depths of the river, several 35 mm film canisters bobbed to the surface. Gérard gathered them up. When the Mosses later processed the film, they discovered beautiful images from that fateful morning, including a striking photograph looking down on their plane as it lifted off from the Rio Negro. The photo graces the cover of their book, *Brasil das Águas,* published in 2005. It was Nicolas Reynard's final shoot. He died, as he lived, doing what he loved most in the place where he had so boldly staked his claim—the Amazon.

Acknowledgments

Very special thanks to my editor at Crown, John
Glusman, for his keen editorial eye and his unflagging commitment to this project, not to mention his boundless patience and skillful editing, and to Domenica Alioto for her care and
dedication. I would also like to thank editor Charlie Conrad and Julie
Cepler and Ellen Folan for their tireless efforts to market and promote
this book. Thanks also to my agent, Deborah Grosvenor, who believed
in this book from the start.

I owe a debt of gratitude to Oliver Payne, editor extraordinaire
at *National Geographic*, and to Peter Miller, as well as to Chris Johns
and Bernard Ohanian. Huge thanks also to Stephen Byers and John
Rasmus at *National Geographic Adventure*. All of them, at one point or
another, have taken their chances with me and turned me loose in
the Amazon, trusting I'd make it home with an incredible story to tell.
I am grateful to Keith Bellows and Scott Stuckey at *National Geographic
Traveler* for their support, and to Mary Anne Potts of National Geographic Digital.

A great many people have offered generous assistance and their
insights about the Amazon and its indigenous peoples over the years.
In Brazil, I enjoyed the hospitality and friendship of Deocleciano Ben-
tes de Souza and his family. Paulo Adario; his wife, Amelia; and the
entire staff of Greenpeace in Manaus—including David Logie, Nilo
D'Avila, Marcelo Marquesini, and Coca Coehlo—opened their doors
to me, shared their lives and their knowledge of the rainforest and
its peoples, and offered inspiration by their example of cool, understated courage. Other Brazilians who imparted valuable lessons and offered a helping hand were Matthew Shirts of *National Geographic Brasil*,

José Leland, Mauro Sposito, Lilian Newlands, Paulo Barreto, Márcio Santilli, Moacir Melo, Enrico Bernard, Pingo Jerozolimski, Marco Lima, Haroldo Castro, Juliana Arini, Felício Pontes Jr., the Honorable Marina Silva, Father Ricardo Rezende, Bishop Erwin Kräutler, and the brave Sisters Jane Dwyer and Katya Webster, who carry on the work of Dorothy Stang, murdered for standing up to the men with the guns who pillage the rainforest.

Of course, this book would never have been made without the courage and the cooperation of Sydney Possuelo, who not only delivered me safely from the far side of the Amazon but welcomed me on multiple occasions into his home in Brasília and generously shared his ideas and friendship. We did not always see eye to eye, but I have known few people with greater intelligence, fearlessness, dedication, and integrity. For all that and more, Sydney, I am truly grateful. Thanks, too, to his wife, Soraya, and to Orlando Possuelo, a great companion who maintained good cheer even in the darkest hours of the trek. I also owe much of my understanding of the history of FUNAI and the mystique of its *sertanistas* to Wellington Figueiredo, the late Apoena Meirelles, Marcelo Santos, José Carlos Meirelles, Antenor Vaz, and Elias Biggio. Fabricio Amorim shared his enthusiasm, as well as his excellent research on the isolated tribes of the Javari Valley. I owe much to Leonêncio Nossa, a true companion and one of Brazil's finest journalists, and to Felipe Milanez, a great friend, investigative reporter, and seeker of justice for Brazil's beleaguered tribes. Inés Fraga provided generous assistance at the archives of the Museo do Índio in Rio de Janeiro.

Many extraordinary people have informed the pages of the book with their knowledge and wisdom, including Thomas Lovejoy, Adrian Cowell, Dan Nepstad, Adrian Forsyth, Vincent Carelli, Mari Corrêa, Fiona Watson, Pepe Álvarez, and Barbara Bramble. Many daring activists travel into the Amazon at considerable risk to themselves to document the destruction of the rainforest and its indigenous tribes. Among those who deserve special mention are David Hill, Chris Fagan, Gregor MacLennan, Andrew Miller, Scott Paul, Aaron Goldzimer, Trevor Stevenson, Andrea Johnson, Aliya Ryan, and journalist Willow Murton.

This journey really began with the publication of Patrick Tierney's *Darkness in El Dorado* and the eruption in the fall of 2000 of the so-called Chagnon Controversy. As a producer for CNN at the time, I led a television crew to northern Michigan to interview Napoleon Chagnon about his alleged misconduct among the Yanomami Indians, and I later traveled to Yanomami land in Venezuela on assignment for *National Geographic Adventure.* The cooperation of Chagnon and the Yanomami—not to mention that of anthropologists Terence Turner and Leslie Sponsel—was vital to the publication of my story on the controversy. As far back as 1992, I traveled into Kayapó territory with Terry Turner, a very able guide in my early efforts to grasp the complexities of Amazonia's indigenous cultures. Stephan Schwartzman has graciously provided a wealth of information and help over the years. He also took me into Terra Indigena to meet the Panará, once known as the fearsome Kreen-Akrore tribe, an experience I will not forget. Philippe Erikson, Silvio Cavuscens, Barbara Arisi, Luiz Antonio Costa, and Javier Ruedas have produced excellent anthropological and historical works on the tribes of the Javari, and their writings have informed this book. I owe much as well to Carlos Augusto da Roche Freire for his exhaustive study of twentieth-century *sertanista* history and to Beatriz Huertas Castillo for her work on Peru's isolated indigenous populations.

I am indebted to Blue Mountain Center in the Adirondacks and the Mesa Refuge in Point Reyes Station, California, for the precious gift of time and sanctuary to write amid lovely landscapes and wonderful company. Thanks to Peter Barnes, Patricia Duncan, Harriet Barlow, David Morris, Ben Strader, Chloe Brown, Alice Gordan, Sis Eldridge, and Diane McCane. I am grateful to the International Center for Journalists and Rob Taylor for supporting my work in Brazil with a Ford Environmental Reporting fellowship; to the Woodrow Wilson International Center for Scholars in Washington, D.C., for providing me with valuable assistance as a public policy scholar; to Paulo Sotero of the center's Brazil Institute; and to research assistants Kathleen Chalk, Laura Fassak, and Jasmine Heiss. I owe thanks also to Frank Ochberg,

Bruce Shapiro, Miles Moffet, Mike Walter, Deirdre Stoelzle, and the Dart Center for Journalism and Trauma.

Lectures at the Explorers Club in New York, Yale and Georgetown universities, Gettysburg College, and the CRITTER Salon in San Francisco helped me refocus my thoughts at critical junctures in the process.

Others have generously guided me as I grappled with the many issues raised in this work: anthropologist and ethnobotanist Wade Davis, anthropologist and geneticist Spencer Wells, and archaeologists John J. Shea, Rusty Greaves, and Michael Heckenberger. I also received valuable help from anthropologist Glenn Shepard, intellectual property rights expert Graham Dutfield, and naturalists Mark W. Moffet, Matt Finer, Ted R. Kahn, and Enrique Ortiz. Composer David Monacchi shared his brilliance and expertise in acoustic ecology and the sounds of the rainforest. I owe apologies to Carrie Regan for appropriating the title of her great novel, *Rumors of Savages,* for my opening chapter.

Brothers Jon Lee Anderson and Scott Anderson have been very generous with their advice, friendship, and moral support. I owe them both more than I could ever pay. Scott read part of the manuscript early on, and his comments helped me set the course for the rest of the work. For their camaraderie and support throughout this entire project and before, I have a number of other amazing friends and colleagues to thank, among them Bob Nickelsberg; Crary Pullen; Bobby Block and his late wife, Donna; Bill and Esther Gentile; Clifton Wiens; Carl Hoffman; Peter Bergen; Tresha Mabile; Margaret Bergen; Geoffrey O'Connor; Don Lange; Tim Loughran; Donovan Webster; Aaron Huey; Les Stone; Beth Wald; Ingrid Arnesen; Richard Chetwynd; Steve Nettleton; Rich Gorby; Stephen Cushman; John Fielding; Andrew and Leslie Cockburn; Victoria Churchville; Bill Evans; Billy Savett; Bucky Brown; Jake Cunningham; Drew Brown; and Frank Smyth. A topic as complicated as uncontacted indigenous cultures produces hundreds of hours of conversation, during which ideas were challenged, shaped, and transformed. Others who contributed to this process in one way or another include Meri Danquah, Kimball Stroud, Matthew Naythons,

John Silbersack, John Lantigua, Lou Adesso, Jonathan Halliwell, David Adams, Jim and Cece Doane, Sally and Ken Murray, Douglas and Betsy Cummins, Kevin Buckley, Phil Gunson, Christina Asquith, Fernando Batista, the legendary Paul Kantner, Paul Buckley, Jeremy Bigwood, John Bennett, Ioulia Siori, Carl Ginsburg, Helen Demeranville, Jerelle Kraus, Randy Credico, Jonathan Tasini, Tanya Dawkins, John Rebbeck, Ed Grefe, Susan Moon, Stan and Linda Cauldwell, Mark Dowie, Adriane Colburn, Chanan Tigay, Molly Antopol, Dara Grunwald, Joyce Weinstein, Dianna Cahn, Jean Rohe, Ravi Shankar, Kristin Jones, Immy Humes, Elizabeth Bailey, Emma Daly, Vera Witte, Suzie Humpstone, Santiago Lyon, Penny Owen, Bill and Debbie Liss, Richard Linnett, Pilar Larreamendy, Bill Clary, Steve Connors, Molly Bingham, Dan Meltzer, Maria Russo, Xavier Moscoco, Jonathan Badrian, Greg Honick, Mo Leypoldt, Madalyn Aslan, Mike Virtanen, Phil Brown, Ellen O'Grady, Kurt Hartwig, Q Gaynor, Jeff Sharlet, Nanette Burstein, Elizabeth Gettelman, Kate Levinson, Steve Costa, Kirsten Stolle, Charlie Castaldi, Gioconda Belli, John Carlin, Hans Ravesteijn, Matthew Campbell, Mike Reed, Lee Poston, Jag Bhalla, Terry Wingfield, Steve Warshaw, Bob Saunders, Joe Mezzanini, John Abounader, Ralph Martell, Alba Valle, and María de los Angeles.

Thanks are also due to Charlene Nemetz, David Heebner, Ellen Anderson, and the late Jim Barnett. Jesús Pérez Calderón first showed me the Amazon. George Schaller taught me to appreciate the sounds of silence. My late stepmother, Sherry Devers, greatly anticipated this book's publication. I am sorry I wasn't able to finish it in time for her to read. Bobby Coffey deserves special recognition for his daily encouragement when it seemed I would never find my way to the end of this story. The courage and wicked humor of the late Eithne McGuinness continued to resonate throughout the writing of this book. During my long absences and over many years, Hanka and Tomek Tomaszewicz have looked after my family with love and care.

Several other friends read the manuscript, in whole or in part, and deserve my heartfelt thanks for their efforts. They are Tamara Stonebarger, Amanda Carter, Andrew Cockburn, and Peter Bergen.

Clif Wiens and Arthur Allen gave especially careful reads to the manuscript, and they buoyed my spirits with their enthusiasm and suggestions. Jill Rothenberg and Mia Gallagher helped me organize my ideas very early in the process, and Margaret Knox and Meehan Crist furnished valuable editorial assistance. Jerome Cookson drew a great map.

I have been blessed with a number of truly remarkable mentors, without whom none of this would have been possible. Albert Bildner, a man of keen mind and big heart, first introduced me to the magic of Brazil and has watched my career unfold with unwavering support. Others of no less importance are John Peter Bermon, a solid rock in the foundation of my life, Nancy Clair, Enrique Sacerio-Garí, Bob Shacochis, Alice Elliot Dark, Susan Zirinsky, Bill Finnegan, Lawrence Van Gelder, the late Randall Gorby, and the late John Whale of the London *Sunday Times,* who counseled to write to the "sound of the inner ear." Peter Bloch, Kevin Buckley, the late Ben Sonnenberg, and the late Randal Ashley were believers and supporters of my work from early on.

One scholar of the Amazon stands out above all others—trailblazing historian John Hemming. His book *Die If You Must* proved to be a tremendous resource, and his comprehensive histories of the Amazon remain a guiding light and a benchmark to all of us who stumble after him in the dark.

A number of NGOs that dedicate themselves to the fight for indigenous rights have helped with important documents and information, including the Instituto Socioambiental (ISA), Amazon Watch, Cultural Survival, Save America's Forests, Conservation International, Environmental Defense Fund, World Wildlife Fund, and Survival International. Survival has taken the lead in waging a steadfast campaign for years on behalf of the world's uncontacted tribes. More information about Survival's campaign can be found on the Internet at www. uncontactedtribes.org.

I shall never forget my expedition companions—Matis, Marubo, Kanamari, and *riberinho*—who shared the joys and the misery of the long journey. Without them, I surely would have perished along the way. Soldado, Ivan Arapá, Alfredo Kanamari, and Tepi Matis deserve special mention. I hope that one day I shall see them again. I salute the indigenous peoples of the Amazon and along the planet's far-flung periphery, who are locked in a daily struggle for their lives and their lands. It is a struggle, in essence, for the preservation of the Earth and our own humanity.

Deep thanks go to my late parents, Robert and Flora Wallace, who first awakened my curiosity about the world and provided me the wherewithal to explore it. I only wish they were here to read this. Thanks, too, to my brothers, Christopher and Bruce, and their spouses, Martha and Paula, to their families, and to all my cousins and their children.

Thanks, affection, and love to my boys—Mackenzie, Aaron, and Ian—who have always been a source of delight and inspiration, a wellspring of tough questions and astute observation, and to their mother, Jennifer. Finally, my deepest thanks go to Margaret Walsh, my loyal friend and reader, ally and companion, who never wavered in the course of this entire process in her love and her belief in this book. Thank you.

Notes

PROLOGUE

Page

xiii The tribe had no immunity: Sydney Possuelo, interview. It was presumed, based on countless well-documented encounters with uncontacted tribes, that deadly epidemics would break out in the event of close contact with the tribe.

Note: I was with Possuelo every day, minute by minute and hour by hour, June 17 through September 7, 2002. Unless otherwise noted, all quotes or information attributed to Possuelo came from our daily discussions during this time.

1. A RUMOR OF SAVAGES

Page

3   Since then, my career as a journalist: I was a news correspondent based in El Salvador, Nicaragua, and Guatemala, 1983–90, reporting for CBS News Radio and a succession of print outlets, including Cox Newspapers, *Newsweek,* and the British dailies the *Independent* and the *Guardian.*

4   And then there was Sarah: Not her real name.

5   He'd just presided over a monumental and herculean task: William R. Long, "A New Call for Indian Activists," *Los Angeles Times,* February 9, 1993, http://articles.latimes.com/1993-02-09/news/wr-1380 1 latin-america/7.

6   After all, the germs we would carry: Ronald Wright, *Stolen Continents: The "New World" Through Indian Eyes* (Boston: Houghton Mifflin, 1992), 86, 123; David E. Stannard, *American Holocaust: The Conquest of the New World* (New York: Oxford University Press, 1992), 102, 129. Recent scholarship suggests that the earliest explorers of the interior of the New World, such as de Soto and Cartier in North America and Orellana in South America, unwittingly spread epidemic diseases as they traveled through the hinterlands. They are now believed to have left colossal losses in their wake without even realizing it, creating the impression in the next wave of explorers who followed decades or even centuries later that the continents' vast interiors were sparsely populated wildernesses ripe for colonization.

9   Scientists were just beginning to unlock: Bruce Gellerman, "REDD Path to a Green Planet," *Living on Earth,* September 11, 2009, http://www.loe.org/shows/segments.htm?programID=09-P13-00037&segmentID=6.

9   On satellite images never before available: "Satellites Show Amazon Parks, In-
    digenous Reserves Stop Forest Clearing," *Science Daily,* January 27, 2006, http://
    www.sciencedaily.com/releases/2006/01/060126200147.htm.

9   It was an area fast on the border of Peru: Vincent Brackelaire, "Situación de los
    últimos pueblos indígenas aislados en América Latina (Bolivia, Brasil, Colombia,
    Ecuador, Paraguay, Perú, Venezuela): Diagnóstico regional para facilitar estrate-
    gias de protección" (unpublished manuscript, January 2006), PDF file, http://
    www.ibcperu.org/doc/isis/687.pdf, 12. Unless otherwise noted, all translations
    of documents from Spanish and Portuguese are the author's.

10 Within one hundred years of the establishment: Kirkpatrick Sale, *The Conquest of
    Paradise: Christopher Columbus and the Columbian Legacy* (New York: Knopf, 1990),
    291.

10 Nearly a century had now passed: Nancy Rockafellar, "The Story of Ishi: A
    Chronology," University of California, San Francisco, last modified 2010, http://
    history.library.ucsf.edu/ishi.html.

2. SCRAMBLE TO THE AMAZON

Page

15 Sydney Possuelo was: Wellington Gomes Figueiredo (*sertanista* and former head
    of the Department of Isolated Indians, FUNAI), interview, Brasília, September
    19, 2002.

15 Since the late nineteenth century: John Hemming, *Die If You Must: Brazilian Indi-
    ans in the Twentieth Century* (London: Macmillan, 2003), 24.

15 The men (for they were almost always men): Figueiredo, interview.

15 In a very public resignation: Hemming, *Die If You Must,* 286.

16 Once an Indigenous Land: FUNAI Presidential Decree No. 1901/87, July 6, 1987.

    Note on *maloca:* The word refers specifically to a palm-thatched dwelling typical
    of indigenous communities in the Amazon. Since entire communities often live
    within a single communal dwelling, the word is often used interchangeably with
    aldea, or "village."

16 He'd gained renown: Carlos Augustino da Rocha Freire, "Sagas sertanistas: práti-
    cas e representações do campo indigenista no século xx" (Ph.D. diss., Univer-
    sidade Federal do Rio de Janeiro, 2005), 206, http://teses.ufrj.br/PPGAS_D/
    CarlosAugustoDaRochaFreire.pdf; Apoena Meirelles (retired *sertanista*), inter-
    view, Rio de Janeiro, September 21, 2002.

17 The Indians were said to inhabit: Fabricio Amorim, "Povos indígenas isolados da
    Terra Indígena Vale do Javari" (internal report, Brasília: FUNAI, Coordenação
    Geral de Índios Isolados, 2008), 9.

19 Though not explicitly articulated: Centro de Trabalho Indigenista (CTI), "Iso-
    lados," last modified 2004, http://www.trabalhoindigenista.org.br/programa_
    isolados.asp. The NGO CTI partners with, and channels foreign funding to, the
    Department of Isolated Indians to maintain the Ethno-Environmental Protection
    Project for Isolated Indigenous Peoples of the Brazilian Amazon.

20 " 'It's been eighteen years . . .' " Leonêncio Nossa, "Expedição amazônica busca
    tribos desconhecidas," *O Estado de São Paulo,* June 10, 2002.

24 Outlaws of all description: "Just Saying Yes," *Brazzil,* January 1997, http://www
    .brazzil.com/cvrjan97.htm; Erling Söderström, "The White Triangle: Anti-
    Cocaine Operations in the Javari Forest," Korubo, last updated 2001, accessed
    July 21, 2009, http://www.korubo.com/AMAZONDOC/coca.htm.

24 Between us, we had no more: Kátia Brasil, "Eleição colombiana motiva ação na
    fronteira, diz general brasileiro," *Folha.com,* May 22, 2002, http://www1.folha.
    uol.com.br/folha/mundo/ult94u41603.shtml. So concerned was the Brazilian
    military about Colombian guerrillas and narco-traffickers that the army launched
    a major operation along the triborder region in May of 2002.

26 The Andes rose up: Michael Goulding, Ronaldo Barthem, and Efrem Jorge
    Gondim Ferreira, *The Smithsonian Atlas of the Amazon* (Washington: Smithsonian
    Books, 2003), 15–19; "Andes Formation Was a 'Species Pump' for South
    America," *Science Daily,* January 11, 2009, http://www.sciencedaily.com/re-
    leases/2009/01/090109083451.htm.

26 With little stone: Eduardo Neves, "Amazônia—Ano 1000," *National Geographic
    Brasil,* May 2010, http://viajeaqui.abril.com.br/national-geographic/edicao-
    122/antigas-civilizacoes-amazonia-552374.shtml; John Hemming, *Amazon Fron-
    tier: The Defeat of the Brazilian Indians* (London: Macmillan, 1987), 11.

27 As it was: Hemming, *Die If You Must,* 544.

3. THROUGH THE CHOKEPOINT

Page
28 The Matis are one: Amorim, "Povos indígenas isolados," 9.

28 Like Lewis and Clark: Meriwether Lewis and William Clark, *The Journals of Lewis
    and Clark,* ed. Bernard DeVoto (Boston: Houghton Mifflin, 1953); Possuelo,
    interview.

29 On a FUNAI expedition: Barbara Maisonnave Arisi, "Matis e Korubo: Contato e
    índios isolados, relações entre povos no Vale do Javari, Amazônia" (master's the-
    sis, Universidade Federal de Santa Catarina, 2007), 41–42, http://tede.ufsc.br/
    teses/PASO0186.pdf.

29 The wooing of the Korubo: Possuelo, interview.

29 The entire Korubo tribe: Arisi, "Matis e Korubo," 17.

29 The Korubo group contacted: Possuelo, interview.

29 When discussing why: Possuelo, interview.

29 It would have been: Arisi, "Matis e Korubo," 39.

30 It was a crucial: Possuelo, interview.

32 At the dawn of the twentieth century: Hemming, *Die If You Must*, 1–13.

32 He had been the very first: Scott Wallace, "Into the Amazon," *National Geographic* 204, no. 2 (August 2003, 10).

33 Following in Rondon's footsteps: Memorandum, "Primer encontro de sertanistas, documento final," FUNAI archives, Brasília, June 27, 1987, 3–4.

33 Henceforth, the *sertanistas'* role: FUNAI Presidential Decree No. 1901/87, July 6, 1987.

33 More of the Amazon Basin: Scott Wallace, "Last of the Amazon," *National Geographic* 211, no. 1 (January 2007, 49).

33 There were reports: Eriverto da Silva Vargas (coordinator for CIVAJA, the Indigenous Council of the Javari Valley), interview, Atalaia do Norte, Brazil, September 9, 2002.

34 Beneath Rondon's photograph: Hemming, *Die If You Must*, 10.

34 Rondon himself: Ibid.

34 No fewer than 120 FUNAI: Paul Raffeale, "Out of Time," *Smithsonian*, April 2005, http://www.smithsonianmag.com/travel/Out_of_Time.html.

34 Among the most recent: Ibid.

34 The Korubo were exempt: Alcida Rita Ramos, *Indigenism: Ethnic Politics in Brazil* (Madison: University of Wisconsin Press, 1998), 19.

4. AT A BEND IN THE RIVER

Page

38 Literally meaning "canoe path": Charles W. Domville-Fife, *Among Wild Tribes of the Amazons* (Philadelphia: J. B. Lippincott, 1924), 169.

43 In an earlier epoch: Elsje Maria Lagrou, "Kaxinawá," *Povos indígenas no Brasil*, last updated November 2004, accessed November 19, 2010, http://pib.socioambiental.org/en/povo/kaxinawa/.

44 *TIME* hailed him: "The Amazon Ambassador," *TIME for Kids*, October 26, 1998, http://www.time.com/time/reports/environment/heroes/tfk/0,2967,tfk_possuelo,00.html.

44   Spain had recently awarded him: Ibid., 63.

44   A grant from the European Union: Possuelo, interview.

44   Journalists with limited: da Rocha Freire, "Sagas sertanistas," 144.

5. A TOPOGRAPHY OF STRIFE

Page

48   This was one of six: Brackelaire, "Situación de los últimos pueblos," 4.

49   It amounted to a clear expression: Glenn H. Shepard Jr. et al., "Trouble in Paradise: Indigenous Populations, Anthropological Policies, and Biodiversity Conservation in Manu National Park, Peru," *Journal of Sustainable Forestry* 29 (June 14, 2010): 253.

49   All told, the territories: Centro de Trabalho Indigenista (CTI), "Isolados."

49   In a heartbeat: da Rocha Freire, "Sagas sertanistas," 239.

49   It had been Possuelo's: Possuelo, interview; Figueiredo, interview.

49   Starting in the mid-1940s: Hemming, *Die If You Must,* 133–34.

50   Though the park was initially conceived: Ibid., 170–72.

50   Possuelo earned the brothers' definitive: Possuelo, interview; Moacir Melo (indigenist technician and former CBF agent), interview, Tabatinga, Brazil, September 4, 2002.

50   For their dogged efforts: Jan Rochas, "Orlando Villas Boas," obituary, *Guardian,* December 14, 2002, http://www.guardian.co.uk/news/2002/dec/14/guardiano bituaries.brazil.

50   The Xingu Indigenous Park: Wallace, "Last of the Amazon," 68.

51   But he would by the late 1980s break: da Rocha Freire, "Sagas sertanistas," 306.

51   For Rondon, it was: Ibid., 326.

51   For the Villas Boas brothers: Ibid., 299.

51   Not only had the Inca: Kim MacQuarrie, *The Last Days of the Incas* (New York: Simon & Schuster, 2007), 48.

51   Deadly pathogens undoubtedly accompanied: Stannard, *American Holocaust,* 47, 53.

55   In their totality: Hemming, *Die If You Must,* 638.

55   The Javari was the only: FUNAI, "Projecto Javari," Ministério da Justiça, last updated 2007, accessed July 7, 2009, http://www.mj.gov.br/data/Pages/MJDoE 56FE7ITEMIDF544570BEB0445988704857DFB7815A4PTBRIE.htm.

55   In other parts of the Amazon: Hemming, *Die If You Must,* 574, 640; da Rocha Freire, "Sagas sertanistas," 153.

55   In some instances, *sertanistas:* da Rocha Freire, "Sagas sertanistas," 227.

55   By comparison: Amorim, "Povos indígenas isolados," 9.

55   Regardless of where: Possuelo, interview.

56   Eighteen such sites: FUNAI, "Projecto índios isolados," Ministério da Justiça, last updated 2007, accessed July 7, 2009, http://www.mj.gov.br/data/Pages/MJ DoE56FE7ITEMIDE686F244540E4961BC3786AD6E76BE6FPTBRNN.htm; Amorim, "Povos indígenas isolados," 9.

56   So little was known: Fabrício Amorim, e-mail correspondence, May 27, 2010.

57   Brazil's constitution guarantees: Brazil Constitution, Article 231. Furthermore, the right to nonassimilation is enshrined in the United Nations Declaration on the Rights of Indigenous Peoples, adopted by the General Assembly, 2007, with 143 votes in favor (including Brazil), 11 abstentions, and 4 against: the United States, Canada, New Zealand, and Australia. Article 8:1 of the declaration reads: "Indigenous peoples and individuals have the right not to be subjected to forced assimilation or destruction of their culture."

57   But landgrabs: Monte Reel, *The Last of the Tribe: The Epic Quest to Save a Lone Man in the Amazon* (New York: Scribner, 2010), 37.

59   A series of technological advances: Adam Hochschild, *King Leopold's Ghost: A Story of Greed, Terror, and Heroism in Colonial Africa* (Boston: Houghton Mifflin, 1998), 158–59.

59   Exploration of the Amazon . . . had been largely confined: F. Bruce Lamb and Manuel Córdova-Rios, *Kidnapped in the Amazon Jungle* (Berkeley: North Atlantic Books, 1994), vii–viii.

59   With labor in short supply: Michael Edward Stanfield, *Red Rubber, Bleeding Trees: Violence, Slavery, and Empire in Northwest Amazonia, 1850–1933* (Albuquerque: University of New Mexico Press, 1998), 40.

59   The plantation lords became a law unto themselves: "Bolivian Natives Tortured," *New York Times,* July 13, 1912, http://query.nytimes.com/mem/archive-free/pdf ?res=9C00E1DF1630E233A25750C1A9619C946396D6CF.

59   Patrons struck deals: Beatriz Huertas Castillo, *Indigenous Peoples in Isolation in the Peruvian Amazon* (Copenhagen: IWGIA, 2004), 145.

59   Slaving expeditions trolled: Lamb and Córdova-Rios, *Kidnapped in the Amazon Jungle,* 104, 123.

59   Entire villages were kidnapped: Stanfield, *Red Rubber, Bleeding Trees,* 56–57.

60   Exports of Amazonian rubber quadrupled: Ibid., 21.

60   The decade from 1897: Ibid., 97.

60   Rubber exports from estates controlled: Ibid., 105.

60   Witnesses at Arana outposts told: "Saw Wholesale Murder in the Amazon Rubber Fields," *New York Times*, August 4, 1912.

60   The Indian population under Arana's charge: Jordan Goodman, *The Devil and Mr. Casement: One Man's Battle for Human Rights in South America's Heart of Darkness* (New York: Farrar, Straus & Giroux, 2010), 186.

60   Deliberately stoking internecine conflict: Michael F. Brown and Eduardo Fernandez, "Tribe and State in a Frontier Mosaic: The Asháninka of Eastern Peru," in *War in the Tribal Zone: Expanding States and Indigenous Warfare*, eds. R. Brian Ferguson and Neil L. Whitehead (Santa Fe: School of American Research Press, 1992), 184–85.

60   With the express purpose: Fritz W. Up de Graff, *Head Hunters of the Amazon: Seven Years of Exploration and Adventure* (New York: Duffield & Co., 1923), 57.

61   Finding himself at a loss: Goodman, *The Devil and Mr. Casement,* 258–59.

61   Some Indians never: Huertas Castillo, *Indigenous Peoples in Isolation in the Peruvian Amazon,* 21; Wallace, "Into the Amazon," 10.

61   On one of his early expeditions: Possuelo, interview.

62   Some of the isolated groups: Brackelaire, "Situación de los últimos pueblos indígenas," 15–17.

62   Tribes that had been: Figueiredo, interview. Figueiredo described an indigenous group of fifteen to twenty Indians in a "situation of constant flight" that he and another *sertanista* had been trying to contact before they were wiped out by loggers: "We found abandoned *malocas,* along with bows and arrows, pots, baskets, hammocks. Very characteristic of a group on the run." He explained the dynamic that leads an uprooted tribe to extinction: "The women stop having children. Under these conditions, why have children? The older men lose their ability to run, climb mountains, cross rivers. The younger ones are strongest, but they're in a state of total demoralization. It's contradictory. On the one hand they don't want to live; on the other, they don't want to surrender."

62   Others had sufficient numbers: Spencer Wells (geneticist and anthropologist), interview, March 15, 2010. A human population requires a minimum of fifty to a hundred people to maintain genetic diversity and future viability, according to Wells, who heads the Genographic Project at the National Geographic Society.

62 For the most obscure groups: Brackelaire, "Situación de los últimos pueblos indígenas," 15–17; Amorim, "Povos indígenas isolados," 36.

62 The Arrow People were also known: Fabrício Amorim (Department of Isolated Indians, FUNAI), interview, Brasília, December 9, 2009; Amorim, "Povos indígenas isolados," 19, 24.

62 Lévi-Strauss famously joined: Claude Lévi-Strauss, *Tristes Tropique: An Anthropological Study of Primitive Societies in Brazil*, trans. John Russell (New York: Atheneum, 1972).

62 Napoleon Chagnon set out: Scott Wallace, "Napoleon in Exile," *National Geographic Adventure* 4, no. 3 (April 2002): 52–61, 98–100.

62 But the hostility of the tribes: Silvio Cavuscens, *Pela sobrevivência dos povos indígenas do Vale do Javari* (Manaus, Brazil: CEDI, 1986), 9.

63 In the years leading: Ibid., 57; Amorim, "Povos indígenas isolados," 19.

64 The Indians clubbed one: Valdeci "Soldado" Rios (backwoodsman), discussion with author, aboard the *Waiká*, Itaquaí River, Brazil, June 19, 2002.

64 Indians willing to resort: Wallace, "Into the Amazon," 11.

64 Their traditional way: Hemming, *Die If You Must*, 638.

6. WHITE RIVER, BLACK NIGHT

Page

68 There would have been: I witnessed the DPF's demolition squad planting charges and blowing up a clandestine airstrip, Fazenda Limão, state of Pará, Brazil, February 8–9, 2006.

68 But the narcos: Mauro Sposito (coordinator of special operations, Brazilian Federal Police) and Antonio Ricardo Villaça (special agent, Federal Police Demolition Squad), in discussions with author, Fazenda Limão, Pará, Brazil, February 9, 2006.

69 In the fight: Villaça, interview.

69 But the Federal Police: Possuelo, interview.

69 Detractors within the agency: Apoena Meirelles, interview. This was not the personal opinion of Apoena Meirelles; he was reporting what others inside FUNAI were saying about the Department of Isolated Indians under Possuelo's command.

Apoena was the son of renowned SPI *sertanista* Francisco Meirelles and one of FUNAI's most accomplished modern-day *sertanistas,* credited with several "first contacts." He was killed in an armed robbery at an ATM in Pôrto Velho, Brazil, in

2004 while in Rondônia to mediate a dispute between Cinta Larga Indians and miners who were prospecting diamonds on their land. In light of the sensitive nature of the assignment and the high stakes, friends suspected the killing may have been politically motivated, cloaked in the appearance of a common crime. He was not related to *sertanista* José Carlos Meirelles.

70 Then there were people: Sposito, interview.

71 Fawcett was a hard-bitten explorer: David Grann, *The Lost City of Z: A Tale of Deadly Obsession in the Amazon* (New York: Doubleday, 2009), 130.

71 Could the natives have suffered: Ibid., 153–55.

72 In 1951, Orlando Villas Boas announced: Hemming, *Die If You Must*, 83.

74 Recent reports warned: Stan Anonby and David J. Holbrook, *A Survey of the Languages of the Javari River Valley* (Dallas: SIL International, 2010), http://www.sil.org/silesr/abstract.asp?ref=2010-003.

74 Loggers had conducted: Arisi, "Matis e Korubo," 81.

74 Head-Bashers . . . brazenly attacked: Cavuscens, *Pela sobrevivência dos povos indígenas,* 55.

74 Another FUNAI functionary: Ibid., 55.

74 After that, company employees: Ibid., 55.

74 The huts' charred remains: Ibid., 55, 57.

75 "Quintino Mafra claimed . . .": Adelson Perreira Brás (riverboat pilot), interview, August 24, 2002.

75 Witnesses watched in horror: João Pacheco de Oliveira, "Sobre índios, macacos, peixes: narrativas e memórias de intolerância na Amazônia contemporânea," *Etnográfica* 5, no. 2 (2000): 290–91.

75 Yanomami communities with little: Geoffrey O'Connor, *Amazon Journal: Dispatches from a Vanishing Frontier* (New York: Dutton, 1997), 1–3.

76 He barely escaped: Perreira Brás, interview.

76 The process of physically demarcating: Possuelo, interview.

76 More recently, Possuelo had: Possuelo, interview.

76 A naturally peaceable people: Hemming, *Die If You Must,* 527.

77 The Indians of the Javari: Ibid., 554.

77 Many of the laborers: Ibid., 128.

78 Tapping rubber was hazardous: Rios, interview.

81 Until recently, elaborate legends: Juan Carlos Galeano, *Folktales of the Amazon*, trans. Rebecca Morgan and Kenneth Watson (Westport, Conn.: Libraries Unlimited, 2009), 19–29.

81 Shocking reports were coming in from around: Bradley Brooks, Associated Press, "Amazon River Dolphins Being Slaughtered for Bait," *U.S. News & World Report*, July 12, 2010, http://www.usnews.com/science/articles/2010/07/12/amazon-river-dolphins-being-slaughtered-for-bait.html.

83 howler monkeys were indeed known: Lamb and Córdova-Rios, *Kidnapped in the Amazon Jungle*, 61.

7. A GOVERNMENT OF ONE
Page

88 Reports of vampire attacks: James Owen, "Vampire Bats Attacking Cattle As Rain Forest Falls," *National Geographic News*, August 20, 2007, http://news.nationalgeographic.com/news/pf/49980020.html.

89 But what most people got instead: Nicolas Kozloff, *No Rain in the Amazon: How South America's Climate Change Affects the Entire Planet* (New York: Palgrave MacMillan, 2010), 60–63; Andrés Schipani and John Vidal, "Malaria Moves in Behind the Loggers," *Guardian*, October 23, 2007, http://www.guardian.co.uk/world/2007/oct/30/environment.climatechange.

89 Wildfires never before seen: W. F. Laurance et al., "The Future of the Brazilian Amazon," *Science* 291 (January 2001): 438–39.

89 Western Brazil and the airspace: Stephen Buckley, "Brazil Fears Fallout of Drug Crackdown," *Washington Post*, October 1, 2002.

89 Officials had just inaugurated: "Brazil Spies on Illegal Loggers," BBC, July 26, 2002, http://news.bbc.co.uk/2/hi/americas/2151222.stm.

91 He didn't know his exact age: Ivan Arapá (Matis Indian scout), discussion with author, Javari Valley, June 18, 2002.

93 As many as two-thirds: Arisi, "Matis e Korubo," 1–54.

98 Not even the Indians: USAID, *Report: 17th Annual Meeting of the Environment Program* (Belén, Pará, Brazil: USAID, October 2009), 10, http://brazil.usaid.gov/files/Report_Env_17th_USAID_2009.pdf.

99 There were rumors that: Amorim, "Povos indígenas isolados," 31; Possuelo, interview.

99 He'd previously tasked: da Rocha Freire, "Sagas sertanistas," 252.

100 Of all the tribes: Cavuscens, *Pela sobrevivência dos povos indígenas*, 44.

100 The Kanamari had managed: Luiz Antonio Costa, "As faces do jaguar: Parentesco, história e mitologia entre os Kanamari da Amazônia Ocidental" (Ph.D. diss., Museu Nacional da Universidade Federal do Rio de Janeiro, 2007), 63-64, http://www.slideshare.net/anandex/as-faces-do-jaguar-parentesco-histria-e-mitologia-entre-os-kanamari-da-amaznia-ocidental.

100 They drifted to the Itaquaí: Ibid., 113–15; Darcy Ribeiro, *Os índios e a civilização: A integração das populações indígenas no Brasil moderno* (São Paulo: Companhia de Letras, 1996), 44. The year 1910 marked the beginning of the end for the Rubber Boom in the Amazon. Prices began to fall precipitously, as plantation rubber produced in European colonies in South Asia flooded global markets. The domestication of rubber, initiated with the theft of *Hevea brasiliensis* seeds from Brazil in 1876, began to yield cheap, high-quality latex by 1909. In 1906, wild rubber from the Amazon and Africa accounted for 99 percent of global output. By 1920, it had dropped to just 10 percent, with plantation rubber from Southern Asia making up nearly 90 percent. See Goodman, *The Devil and Mr. Casement*, 153, 266; Stanfield, *Red Rubber, Bleeding Trees*, 164.

100 Other Kanamari found: Costa, "As faces do jaguar," 57.

102 To begin with: James Owen, "Fighting for the Survival of Uncontacted Tribes," *NatGeo News Watch,* April 29, 2010, http://blogs.nationalgeographic.com/blogs/news/chiefeditor/2010/04/fighting-for-the-survival-of-uncontacted-tribes.html; Fiona Watson et al., *Disinherited: Indians of Brazil* (London: Survival International, 2000), 9–10, 12.

102 But even after decades: Possuelo, interview.

102 But one thing was certain: Norman Lewis, "Genocide," *Sunday Times Magazine* (London), February 23, 1969, 44; Glenn H. Shepard Jr. (anthropologist and ethnographer, Emilio Goeldi Musuem, Belém, Brazil), phone interview, September 8, 2010.

8. BETWEEN TWO WORLDS

Page

107 I thought it might: Costa, "As faces do jaguar," 42.

108 In any case: Ibid., 119–20; Lagrou, "Kaxinawá."

108 In remote places: Possuelo, interview.

109 It was critical: Possuelo, interview.

111 The other arm bore: Stanfield, *Red Rubber, Bleeding Trees*, 56; Lagrou, "Kaxinawá," 3.

113 He had been coached: Possuelo, interview.

113 Such thinking stood: Hemming, *Die If You Must,* 79–80.

114 In naming the expedition: Possuelo, interview.

120 For a Kanamari Indian: Costa, "As faces do jaguar," 23.

122 He'd fared especially poorly: Possuelo, interview.

123 In an attempt to prove: Costa, "As faces do jaguar," 128–29; Sebastião Kurha, aka "Wura" (Kanamari elder), in discussion with Possuelo and author, Pedras, Brazil, June 28, 2002.

124 Contacted Indians: Possuelo, interview.

125 We were in the center: "Earth at Night" (map), *National Geographic* 206, no. 5 (November 2004).

126 Untold thousands: Possuelo, interview.

128 Ayahuasca was the most renowned: Wade Davis, *One River: Explorations and Discoveries in the Amazon Rain Forest* (New York: Touchstone, 1996), 153.

9. THE POINT OF NO RETURN
Page

136 After all, the Kanamari: Costa, "As faces do jaguar," 121n.

136 Their forebears had endured: Javier Ruedas, "Variability in Marubo Politics," *Tipití: Journal of the Society for Anthropology of Lowland South America* 2, no. 1 (June 2004): 23.

136 But over the ensuing years: Javier Ruedas (social anthropologist and University of New Orleans research associate), phone interview, July 30, 2010.

The tribal amalgamation among the Marubo described by Ruedas is echoed in the tale of another indigenous group that called itself the Huni Kui, possibly Kaxinawá or Amahuaca Indians. Chief Shumu recounts: "At our villages on the River Honowa-ia where we lived, our people were attacked by the rubber cutters. Many were killed and the children carried away. We had to leave again and hide in the forest. The Ishabo and Shabo people came here earlier into the depths of the forest. We found them and they let us join with them. Now we are one, the Donowan (Boa People)." Lamb and Córdova-Rios, *Kidnapped in the Amazon Jungle,* 104.

Critics raised doubts about the veracity of the tale related by Lamb and Córdova-Rios, particularly the identity of the tribesmen said to have kidnapped Córdova-Rios, among whom he lived for several years following his abduction. For discussion, see F. Bruce Lamb, "*Wizard of the Upper Amazon* as Ethnography," *Current Anthropology* 22, no. 5 (October 1981): 577–80, http://www.jstor.org/stable/2742293.

A similar story pertains to the Nahua tribe. "One possibility is that the

X-nahua essentially came into being as a coherent group in the late 19th and early 20th century [sic] as an amalgamation of survivors from a number of Panoan groups decimated by the violence and slaving activities of the Rubber Boom." Lev Michael, "How 'We' Became 'White People': A Tale of Indigenous Onomastic Strategies," *Greater Blogazonia*, November 8, 2007, http://anthroling.wordpress.com/2007/11/08/how-we-became-white-people-a-tale-of-indigenous-onomastic-strategies/.

136 Only in the 1960s: Ruedas, "Variability in Marubo Politics," 34.

136 In all, there were now: Ibid., 39–40.

147 They were as time-tested: Sale, *The Conquest of Paradise*, 314.

147 We were also here: Ibid., 126.

147 The point, from Possuelo's perspective: da Rocha Freire, "Sagas sertanistas," 144.

10. A FOREST DARK

Page

152 The simple contrivance: Terrance N. D'Altroy, *The Incas* (Oxford: Blackwell Publishing, 2002), 225.

156 *"When we speak . . ."*: Memorandum by Sydney Possuelo (translated by the author), "Frentes de atração: A última fronteira," FUNAI archives, August 27, 1981.

157 The *jaracuçu* is a near relative: Ted R. Kahn (herpetologist, expert in neotropical reptiles and amphibians), phone interview, December 11, 2010.

158 Researchers have uncovered: "Good Eyesight? Thank Snakes," *ABC News*, August 30, 2006, http://abcnews.go.com/Technology/DyeHard/story?id=2371692&page=1.

158 He was leading an exploratory team: Figueiredo, interview; Possuelo, interview.

160 The Mayá were never: Amorim, "Povos indígenas isolados," 12; Hemming, *Die If You Must*, 546.

11. THE HEADWATERS

Page

171 But in the end: Watson et al., *Disinherited: Indians of Brazil*, 3.

171 Even Possuelo's GPS: Possuelo, interview.

171 It also left Possuelo: Reel, *The Last of the Tribe*, 149.

176 Still, tropical expeditions: Anthony Smith, *Explorers of the Amazon* (Chicago: University of Chicago Press, 1990), 104–5.

12. LESSONS IN BIOLOGY

Page

180 The ants have evolved: Mark W. Moffet, *Adventures Among Ants: A Global Safari with a Cast of Trillions* (Berkeley: University of California Press, 2010), 121–22.

180 The ants get secure shelter: Ibid., 121.

181 It was entitled: Carl Stephenson, "Leiningen Versus the Ants," *Twenty-one Great Stories,* eds. Abraham H. Lass and Norma L. Tasman (New York: Mentor, 1969).

182 One night during his pursuit: Possuelo, interview.

182 Scattered bands: Luiz Filipe de Figueiredo, *Índios isolados: atração e sobrevivência eis a questão* (Cuiabá, Brazil: 2a Superintendecia da FUNAI, 1987), 15–16.

183 But others suspected: Hemming, *Die If You Must,* 278.

183 They fled but found themselves increasingly squeezed: Memorandum by Sydney Possuelo, "Sugestões para contacto com grupo arredio Parakanã," FUNAI archives, 1983.

183 Over the decades: Hemming, *Die If You Must,* 112–13.

185 The Javari remains: Arisi, "Matis e Korubo," 48.

186 Anthropologists subjected traditional societies: Possuelo, interview.

186 There was such a juiced-up: "Amazonian Amphibian Diversity Traced to Andes," *Science Daily,* March 10, 2009, http://www.sciencedaily.com/releases/2009/03/090309205313.htm.

187 Every acre of western Amazonian rainforest: Manuela Carneiro da Cunha and Mauro Barbosa de Almeida, eds., *Enciclopédia da floresta: O Alto Juruá: Práticas e conhecimentos das populações* (São Paulo: Companhia das Letras, 2002), 73.

187 By comparison, a typical forest: "Ecuador: A World Apart," *Ecuaworld,* http://www.ecuaworld.com/discover/oriente.htm.

187 We weren't all that far: Ibid.

187 A researcher he'd known: Possuelo, interview.

188 The fungal mycelia: Adrian Forsyth and Ken Miyata, *Tropical Nature: Life and Death in the Rain Forests of Central and South America* (New York: Touchstone, 1995), 18–19.

189 The *tucandeira,* or bullet ant: Ibid., 116–17.

189 In preliterate societies: David Abram, *The Spell of the Sensuous: Perception and Language in a More-Than-Human World* (New York: Vintage, 1996), 181.

190 Nearly all the Matis elders and shamans perished: Arisi, "Matis e Korubo," 54.

191 Most notable perhaps: Darrell Addison Posey, "Biodiversity, Genetic Resources, and Indigenous Peoples in Amazonia: (Re)Discovering the Wealth of Traditional Resources of Native Amazonians" (paper, Amazonia 2000 conference, Institute of Latin American Studies, University of London, 1998), 9.

191 Researchers at Merck: Loren McIntyre and W. Jesco von Puttkamer (photographer), "Last Days of Eden: Rondônia's Urueu-Wau-Wau Indians," *National Geographic* 174, no. 6 (December 1988): 807.

192 After being contacted by the drugmaker: Posey, "Biodiversity, Genetic Resources, and Indigenous Peoples in Amazonia," 9.

192 In the end: Graham Dutfield (professor of international governance, expert in intellectual property rights, University of Leeds School of Law), phone interview, September 6, 2010.

192 One-quarter of all prescription drugs: Gellerman, "REDD Path to a Green Planet"; Mark J. Plotkin, *Tales of a Shaman's Apprentice: An Ethnobotanist Searches for New Medicines in the Amazon Rain Forest* (New York: Penguin, 1993), 6–7.

192 Scientists have no doubt: Graham Dutfield, "Why Traditional Knowledge Is Important in Drug Discovery," *Future Medicinal Chemistry* 2, no. 9 (September 2010): 1409.

13. A Guerrilla Army
Page

197 The Matis had long since: Arisi, "Matis e Korubo," 61.

199 After all, tribal hunters: Abram, *The Spell of the Sensuous*, 140–41; Lamb and Córdova-Rios, *Kidnapped in the Amazon Jungle*, 48.

202 Despite the fact: Scott Wallace, "Hunting Down the Sons of Reagan," *Independent*, May 13, 1987.

14. In the Footsteps of Rondon
Page

206 It was hard to believe: Nigel J. H. Smith, "Aquatic Turtles of Amazonia: An Endangered Resource," *Biological Conservation* 16 (1979): 165–76, http://www.clas.ufl.edu/users/nsmith/pub/Aquatic%20turtles%20of%20Amazonia%20Biological%20Conservation%201979%20Nigel%20Smith.pdf.

206 The eggs would serve: Possuelo, interview.

207 By the time Cândido Rondon: Hemming, *Die If You Must*, 5–12.

207 As Rondon conceived it: da Rocha Freire, "Sagas sertanistas," 326.

208 Early contact teams: Domville-Fife, *Among Wild Tribes of the Amazons*, 79.

208 But once tribes were subdued: Norman Lewis, "Genocide," 41; Hemming, *Die If You Must,* 229–31.

208 They failed miserably: Hemming, *Die If You Must,* 118, 129.

208 Nevertheless, the principles: Dee Brown, *Bury My Heart at Wounded Knee: An Indian History of the American West* (New York: Bantam, 1971).

208 Instead, they got: Ibid., 162–64, 258.

208 Their extermination campaigns: Ibid., 254.

208 As the twentieth century progressed: Watson et al., *Disinherited,* 3.

209 Nearly 400,000 Indians: Hemming, *Die If You Must,* 636–38.

209 Indian lands and indigenous reserves: Wallace, "Last of the Amazon," 68.

209 In remote, mist-shrouded redoubts: Possuelo, interview. At the time of the expedition in 2002, the Department of Isolated Indians had confirmed the existence of 17 uncontacted tribes within the boundaries of Brazil. There were unconfirmed reports—"reference points," as they are called within the department—of as many as another 42 tribes that awaited investigation. By December 2010, *sertanistas* had confirmed the presence of 26 uncontacted tribes in Brazil, the country with the most such groups anywhere in the Amazon and, hence, in the world. Peru, with 14–15 indigenous peoples "living in voluntary isolation," hosts the second-largest number of isolated tribes.

With loggers and oil exploration crews penetrating deeper into the Peruvian jungle, uncontacted tribes from Peru are reported to be fleeing across the border into Brazil, triggering tensions among indigenous communities. The rainforests of both Ecuador and Bolivia also harbor smaller numbers of uncontacted Indians. Reports from Ecuador tell of sporadic, bloody clashes between illegal loggers and isolated tribesmen in and around the Yasuní National Park. Scattered bands of nomads may still wander the forests of Colombia and Venezuela. Outside of the Amazon Basin, there is one isolated group, called the Ayoreo, whose people inhabit the scrub forests of the Paraguayan Chaco. The Ayoreo are under pressure from ranchers bulldozing their forests. For the most complete list of such groups, see Brackelaire, "Situación de los últimos pueblos."

The London-based Survival International is waging a concerted campaign in support of uncontacted tribes: http://www.survivalinternational.org/uncontactedtribes/.

210 It was not out of the ordinary: Hemming, *Die If You Must,* 294.

210 Two of Possuelo's men: Memorandum by Sydney Possuelo, "Resumo Histórico do Povo Arara," FUNAI archives, October 1980.

211 They took what they could: Richard Hering and Stuart Tanner, *Plunder for Profit: The UK and Brazilian Mahogany Trade* (London: Friends of the Earth, 1998), 46, http://www.foe.co.uk/resource/reports/plunder_for_profit.pdf.

211 Those who hadn't suffered: "Os Arara saem da mata."

211 Victims and nonvictims alike: Anthropologist Wade Davis notes that the entire discipline of anthropology was borne of a nineteenth-century model of evolution that envisioned societies positioned along an ascending continuum from primitive hunter-gatherers to advanced, modern-day civilization. Every culture, it was presumed, would progress through the same stages, in like sequence. See Wade Davis, *The Wayfinders: Why Ancient Wisdom Matters in the Modern World* (Toronto: Anansi Press, 2009), 64.

211 We peer into the shadows: Charles C. Mann, *1491: New Revelations of the Americas Before Columbus* (New York: Knopf, 2005), 304.

211 Like the communities: da Rocha Freire, "Sagas sertanistas," 216.

211 To stay a step ahead: Hering and Tanner, *Plunder for Profit,* 45–46.

212 Possuelo's strategy borrowed: Ribeiro, *Os Índios e a civilização,* 184–87. Note: Born in Germany as Curt Unkel, Nimuendajú took as his official last name the honorific conferred on him by Guaraní Indians, meaning "he who lives among us," when they adopted him into their tribe (Hemming, *Die If You Must,* 64).

212 For starters: Possuelo, interview.

212 Sixty years earlier: Ribeiro, *Os Índios e a Civilização,* 187–88.

212 But once the Arara: "Arara" (action bulletin), *Survival International,* June 2004, http://assets.survivalinternational.org/static/files/related_material/45_22_160_arara_bulletin_june_04_pdf.pdf.

213 Possuelo was disgusted: Possuelo, interview.

213 Old-school SPI agents: Hemming, *Die If You Must,* 103.

213 But the precipitous decline: Figueiredo, interview.

213 In 1987: Hemming, *Die If You Must,* 290.

213 *"We can never forget . . ."*: Memorandum (translated by the author), "Primer encontro de sertanistas, documento final," FUNAI archives.

213 Then-president of FUNAI: FUNAI Presidential Decree No. 1901/87, July 6, 1987.

215 Shadowy criminal enterprises: Wallace, "Last of the Amazon," 49.

216 Between 1982 and 1996: American Indian Program, Cornell University, *Brazil: Hot Spots* (American Indian Program, Cornell University: Akwe:kon Press, December 31, 1996).

216 The environmental group Greenpeace: José Leland Barroso (chief inspector, IBAMA), in discussions with author, Iriri River, Brazil, March 10, 2002; "Our Role in Stopping the Illegal Brazilian Mahogany Trade," *Greenpeace News and Blogs,* October 15, 2003, http://www.greenpeace.org/usa/en/news-and-blogs/news/our-role-in-stopping-the-illeg/. I accompanied Leland Barroso on a major operation to seize illegally cut mahogany on the Iriri River in March 2002. The bust was made possible by equipment and information about the ill-gotten timber that Greenpeace shared with Leland and his environmental police agents in the Brazilian Institute of the Environment and Renewable Natural Resources, IBAMA.

216 But to the southwest: Txai Terri Valle de Aquino and Marcelo Piedrafita Iglesias, "Entrevista com o sertanista Meirelles (parte VIII)," Papo de Índio, *Página 20,* July 21, 2008, http://www.landcoalition.org/cpl-blog/wp-content/uploads/08_papo_meirelles_viii.pdf.

216 Asháninka communities inside Brazil: José Pimenta, "Asháninka: Encroachment by Loggers," Povos Indígenas No Brazil, last updated 2005, accessed November 17, 2010, http://pib.socioambiental.org/en/povo/ashaninka/152.

217 These spontaneous clearings: Forsyth and Miyata, *Tropical Nature,* 36–38.

15. THE MEANING OF CONTACT

Page

224 Some captains of industry: Reel, *The Last of the Tribe,* 148, 214.

224 Even many sympathetic: Glenn Shepard Jr., *Informe 1: Los grupos indígenas aislados del río Las Piedras* (report presented to Mobil Exploration Peru, Lima, 1996), 3–4.

224 In Brazil, the term *índios isolados*: Brackelaire, "Situación de los últimos pueblos," 10.

224 The isolation, even from: Glenn Shepard Jr., interview.

224 This was not, in other words: Bob Connolly and Robin Anderson, *First Contact: New Guinea's Highlanders Encounter the Outside World* (New York: Penguin, 1988), 68–70.

225 Nor was it even like: Euclides da Cunha, *The Amazon: Land Without History,* ed. Lúcia Sá, trans. Ronald Sousa (New York: Oxford University Press, 2006), 48–49. Chronicler and essayist Euclides da Cunha (1866–1909) wrote from the Amazon during the peak years of rubber extraction. His account of Fitzcarrald's massacre of Mashco warriors on the Madre de Dios River warrants repeating here:

"[T]he Mashco's only response was to ask about the arrows Fitzcarrald brought with him. And Fitzcarrald, smiling, handed him a Winchester cartridge.

"The savage looked it over for a long while, absorbed with the smallness of the projectile. He tried in vain to wound himself, pushing the bullet hard against his chest. Not achieving what he desired, he took up one of his own arrows and plunged it dramatically into his other arm. He then smiled, indifferent to the pain, contemplating with pride his own blood as it squirted out . . . and without saying a word turned around and, leaving the astonished explorer standing there, went back to his encampment with an illusion of superiority that would soon be dashed. In fact, a half an hour later, around one hundred Mashcos, the naive and recalcitrant chief among them, lay slaughtered on the river's edge."

225 Some indigenous languages even: *Pirinop: My First Contact,* directed by Mari Corrêa and Karané Ikpeng (Olinda: Vídeo nas Aldeis, 2007), DVD.

225 Amid the war cries: Ribeiro, *Os Índios e a civilização,* 185–86.

225 The allure of our magical objects: Memorandum by Possuelo, "Frentes de atração: A última fronteira," FUNAI archives, August 27, 1981.

226 The Huitoto Indians: Stanfield, *Red Rubber, Bleeding Trees,* 44.

226 But most of the isolated tribes: Watson et al., *Disinherited: Indians of Brazil,* 21.

226 The absence of peaceful contact: Wallace, "Napoleon in Exile," 98; Sale, *The Conquest of Paradise,* 159.

226 Within sixty years of Columbus's landfall: Sale, *The Conquest of Paradise,* 160–61.

226 In the years 1980–84: Memorandum by Carolina M. Bori to Dante Martins de Oliveira, "Grupos indígenas arredios do Vale do Javari," Brazilian Society for the Progress of Science, FUNAI archives, October 2, 1986. At the time, Carolina M. Bori was president of the Brazilian Society for the Progress of Science; Dante Martins de Oliveira was the minister of agrarian reform and development.

227 The Txikão were a warrior: Orlando Villas Boas and Claudio Villas Boas, archival footage in *Pirinop: My First Contact,* directed by Mari Corrêa and Karané Ikpeng.

227 The Txikão had long been locked: Ibid.; Possuelo, interview.

227 The Villas Boas brothers had attempted: Hemming, *Die If You Must,* 163–64.

227 It was not unheard of: Hemming, *Die If You Must,* 135–36.

228 At the roar: Orlando Villas Boas and Claudio Villas Boas, quoted in *Pirinop: My First Contact.*

228 But they were bewildered: Ibid.

228 American missionaries in Ecuador: Davis, *The Wayfinders,* 89–90.

228 The other half remain: Brackelaire, "Situación de los últimos pueblos," 6.

228 Only days after dropping their gifts: Villas Boas and Villas Boas, quoted in *Piriop: My First Contact.*

229 It was one night many years later: Ivan Arapá, interview.

229 Such was certainly: Lewis, "Genocide," 53.

230 The bodies were buried: Hemming, *Die If You Must,* 227.

231 The Kayapó raided settlers: Apoena Meirelles, interview.

231 In taking goods: Arisi, "Matis e Korubo," 82.

231 Across the border in Peru: Shepard, interview.

231 When New Guinean highlanders: Connolly and Anderson, *First Contact,* 47.

231 During the Arara contact: Possuelo, interview.

232 Did the bearer of a SAM-7: Wellington Figueiredo posed a similar question in our discussions: "Why did humans reach a point somewhere in the past where some opted for development and others did not? Maybe the latter chose a path that would look more deeply into themselves, to understand and respect the natural world."

235 Jaguars were central: Arisi, "Matis e Korubo," 95; Neil L. Whitehead, *Dark Shamans: Kanaima and the Poetics of Violent Death* (Durham, N.C.: Duke University Press, 2002), 66.

237 Isolated tribes under pressure: Reel, *The Last of the Tribe,* 123–24.

237 To guard against nasty foot injuries: Possuelo, interview.

16. OUR GUNS, OUR GERMS, AND OUR STEEL
Page

241 When it came to the business: Possuelo, interview.

242 For Possuelo, every gift: Possuelo, "Frentes de atração."

242 The anger would hint: de Figueiredo, "Índios isolados," 27.

242 Indians might take knives: Ibid.

242 The Parintintin routinely: Ribeiro, *Os Índios e a civilização,* 188.

242 Besides smashing gifts: de Figueiredo, "Índios isolados," 28.

246 Apprenticing themselves: Abram, *The Spell of the Sensuous,* 140–41; Costa, "As faces do jaguar," 126. In Costa's account of the Kanamari encounter with the *flecheiros,*

the same event described to us by Wura on the Itaquaí River, the Arrow People told their Kanamari guests that they had masked the screams of a white woman they assaulted by imitating the cries of capuchin monkeys.

250 Michigan native Napoleon Chagnon: Wallace, "Napoleon in Exile."

251 He plied reluctant: Ibid.

251 The genealogies formed: Ibid.

251 So docile were the Tasaday: Kenneth MacLeish and John Launois (photographer), "The Tasadays: Stone Age Cavemen of Mindinao," *National Geographic* 142, no. 2 (August 1972): 218–49; John Nance, *The Gentle Tasaday* (New York: Harcourt Brace Jovanovich, 1975), 75.

251 The Tasaday seemed to offer reassurance: "If our ancient ancestors were like the Tasadays, we come of far better stock that I had thought," concluded *National Geographic* writer Kenneth MacLeish. But doubters claimed the entire affair smacked of an elaborate hoax perpetrated by Manuel Elizalde, adviser on national minorities to President Ferdinand Marcos. Those who spent extended periods with the two dozen Tasaday and visited their cave dwellings were convinced that they were an authentic primitive society. The naked foragers first encountered by researchers now live as settled agriculturalists, beyond the forests that once harbored them.

251 Chagnon's critics charged: R. Brian Ferguson, *Yanomami Warfare: A Political History* (Santa Fe: School of American Research Press, 1995), 288–89.

252 In northeastern Australia, the introduction: Lauriston Sharp, "Steel Axes for Stone-Age Australians," in *Conformity and Conflict: Readings in Cultural Anthropology*, eds. James P. Spradley and David W. McCurdy (Boston: Little, Brown, 1974), 423–24.

17. THE DAY OF THE *MALOCA*

Page

254 "This is universal language . . .": Not all intruders would understand the meaning of such a signal, Apoena Meirelles told me: "Indians have always known they're numerically inferior to us, with inferior weapons, so they would always choose when to attack in order to win. The worst part of making contact would be if they left an arrow on the path, or if they blocked a path. This meant, 'Don't come any farther.' For those who didn't understand, like rubber tappers, the Indians would set up ambushes. People would die because they didn't understand their 'language.' The Indians would see them as invaders."

257 It was a point Possuelo: Possuelo, "Frentes de atração."

257 When Francisco Pizarro and the Spaniards: MacQuarrie, *The Last Days of the Incas*, 142–43.

257 As recently as the 1930s: Connolly and Anderson, *First Contact*, 36.

257 The handful of Mashcos: Shepard, interview.

257 As if the fear were embedded: Lewis, "Genocide," 51; Watson et al., *Disinherited*, 22.

259 By the time Possuelo: Possuelo, interview.

262 Applied to the tip: Alain Gheerbrant, *The Amazon: Past, Present, and Future*, trans. I. Mark Paris (New York: Harry N. Abrams, 1992), 28.

262 When it enters the bloodstream: Stanley Feldman, *Poison Arrows: The Amazing Story of How Prozac and Anesthetics Were Developed from Deadly Jungle Poison Darts* (London: Metro Publishing, 2005), 25; Davis, *One River*, 213–14.

262 But beyond the fearsome: Wade Davis (ethnobotanist and anthropologist), interview.

264 No one knows for sure: John J. Shea (professor of archaeology, State University of New York at Stony Brook), phone interview, March 30, 2010.

264 Scholars have long theorized: Lord Raglan, *How Came Civilization?* (London: Methuen & Co., 1939), 83.

264 Projectile-point technology was particularly: Shea, interview. Shea, a paleoanthropologist who specializes in the archaeology of human origins, points out that far from being a crude, primitive technology, the bow and arrow represented a "quantum leap" in human development that allowed Homo sapiens to prey on a much wider range of species.

264 But gunmen who pursued: Lamb and Córdova-Rios, *Kidnapped in the Amazon Jungle*, 140–41.

269 Early explorers had made: Plotkin, *Tales of a Shaman's Apprentice*, 138.

18. REPROVISIONED
Page

282 Nonetheless, it had: Scott Paul (Greenpeace Amazon campaigner), interview, Washington, D.C., January 29, 2002.

19. JUNGLE SHIPYARDS
Page

296 It wasn't like other places: Hemming, *Die If You Must*, 532–33.

296 It wasn't as though: Watson et al., *Disinherited*, 27–30. The razed forests and manhunts in Rondônia and Maranhão bear some resemblance to the scorched-earth campaign waged by the Guatemalan army in that country's western highlands in the 1980s, though for a different purpose. The army's counterinsurgency effort

spared no means to wrest political control over Mayan Indians from leftist rebels. Hundreds of native villages were torched, tens of thousands massacred. Communities that eluded capture were deemed "illegal" by military commanders, and treated accordingly. They lived in a state of constant flight, hounded by infantry sweeps and shelled by army howitzers. Just as logging roads have become the primary instrument of penetration and theft of Indian lands in the Amazon, the Guatemalan military saw road construction as a crucial component of domination and conquest. At the roadhead looking out on the Quiché Mountains, where "illegal villages" were still at large, one army commander told me: "Where the road ends is where the subversion begins." See Scott Wallace, "Support Won with Terror," *Guardian*, July 13, 1989.

296 The allure of: Possuelo, interview.

298 What if paradise: da Rocha Freire, "Sagas sertanistas," 310.

298 What if, as some critics: Alvaro Caldas Magalhães (owner, Casa Caldas Indústria e Comércio), interview, Benjamin Constant, Brazil, September 9, 2002.

299 The Arara or the Parintintin: Hemming, *Die If You Must*, 68, 291–92.

299 The survivors were soon corralled: Watson et al., *Disinherited*, 45–47.

299 In the wake of contact: Ibid., 282–83.

299 For a number of *sertanistas*: Figueiredo, interview, Brasília, December 10, 2009.

299 Contact left *sertanistas*: Ibid.

301 Figueiredo himself came to believe: Ibid.

21. EAST WITH THE RIVER
Page

316 But the thoroughfares: Possuelo, interview.

322 Every tributary offers: Ibid.

325 One of the world's largest: UNCTAD and the BioTrade Facilitation Programme, *Arapaima Gigas: Market Study* (Geneva: United Nations Conference on Trade and Development, 2006), http://www.biotrade.org/docs/biotradebrief-arapaimagigas.pdf.

326 Pirarucu had already vanished: Ibid.

22. BORDERLANDS
Page

335 In some Yanomami: Wallace, "Napoleon in Exile."

25. THE GOLD DREDGE

Page

378 A seemingly pathological lust: O'Connor, *Amazon Journal,* 57–59; Wright, *Stolen Continents,* 52; Sale, *The Conquest of Paradise,* 233.

378 So destructive were: Leland Barroso, interview, Manaus, Brazil, September 16, 2002.

382 The grieving nurse: Perpétua Borges Rosada, in discussion with author, Gorotire, Kayapó Indigenous Reserve, Brazil, July 16, 1992.

382 The Kayapó of Gorotire: Dr. Terence Turner (social anthropologist and Kayapó expert), discussion with author, Gorotire, Kayapó Indigenous Reserve, Brazil, July 15–16, 1992.

383 Pirate operators nearly always: Possuelo, interview.

385 The usually ebullient Amarildo: Amarildo Costas (backwoodsman), interview with author, aboard the *Kukahá,* Jutaí River, Brazil, August 2002.

26. CIVILIZATION AND OUR DISCONTENTS

Page

391 the Possuelo-led *sertanistas*: Memorandum, "Primer encontro de sertanistas, documento final," FUNAI archives, 5.

392 The dredge was rumored: Dr. Alysson Lima e Silva (delegate, Municipal Police, Jutaí), in discussion with Possuelo and author, Jutaí, Brazil, August 28, 2002.

393 That was quite a claim: Asclepíades de Souza (mayor of Jutaí Municipality), interview with author, Jutaí, Brazil, August 28, 2002.

393 Without a single boat: Silva, interview.

393 The municipality had never been able: de Souza, interview.

393 One of his companies: Lourvival Sant'Anna, "Ecos de um outro tempo," *Estado de São Paulo,* November 25, 2007, http://estado.com.br/amazonia/reservas_ecos_de_um_outro_tempo.htm.

398 The Amazon River: Goulding, Barthem, and Ferreira, *The Smithsonian Atlas of the Amazon,* 32–33.

398 Friar Gaspar de Carvajal: *The Discovery of the Amazon According to the Account of Friar Gaspar de Carvajal and Other Documents,* ed. José Toribio Medina, trans. Bertram T. Lee (New York: American Geographical Society, 1934), 200–203, 212–13; Gheerbrant, *The Amazon,* 24–26.

398 Recent years have seen: Dr. Michael Heckenberger (professor of archaeology and anthropology, University of Florida), phone interview, January 9, 2003.

399 Only the tremendous roar: Gheerbrant, *The Amazon*, 27–28.

403 After decades of despotic: Hemming, *Die If You Must*, 534.

404 With the temptation: Sergeant Fradique Queirós, in discussion with Possuelo and author, Anzol Inspection Station, Brazilian Federal Police, Amazon River (Solimões), Brazil, September 2, 2002.

405 Twelve million wild birds: Charles Bergman, "Wildlife Trafficking," *Smithsonian*, December 2009, http://www.smithsonianmag.com/people-places/Wildlife-Trafficking.html.

407 Colombia's three-way war: Simon Romero, "Wider Drug War Threatens Colombian Indians," *New York Times*, April 21, 2009, http://www.nytimes.com/2009/04/22/world/americas/22colombia.html?scp=1&sq=embera%20indians&st=cse.

407 As the war spread: Rick Kearns, "Colombian Indigenous Still in Danger of Extinction," *Indian Country Today*, October 31, 2010, http://www.indiancountry today.com/home/content/Colombian-indigenous-still-in-danger-of-extinction-106308458.html.

27. MEET THE HEAD-BASHERS

Page

412 There had also been the mixing: Arisi, "Matis e Korubo," 76–77.

412 The Matis always served: Ibid., 119.

412 Since the death of Sobral: Possuelo, interview.

413 Maya had led her band: Possuelo, interview.

414 Some warriors objected: Paul Raffaele, "Out of Time," *Smithsonian*, April 2005.

415 Like the rest of her people: Arisi, "Matis e Korubo," 80.

415 In at least one instance: Ibid., 80.

415 Some twenty-six whites: Ibid.

415 Three more had: Ibid., 80–81.

416 Possuelo and his team: Possuelo, interview.

418 The men had blithely: da Rocha Freire, "Sagas sertanistas," 137.

418 When the Korubo had appeared: Arisi, "Matis e Korubo," 87–88.

EPILOGUE

Page

425 Press reports had quoted: Leonêncio Nossa, *Homens Invisíveis* (Rio de Janeiro: Editora Record, 2007), 257.

425 Possuelo held nothing back: Ibid., 258.

425 Possuelo said Gomes's stance: Andrew Downie, "Champion for Brazil's Indigenous Gets Fired," *Christian Science Monitor,* January 26, 2006, http://www.csmonitor.com/2006/0126/p04s01-woam.html.

425 "I have never been . . .": Claudio Angelo, "Prime Directive for the Last Americans," *Scientific American,* April 15, 2007, http://www.scientificamerican.com/article.cfm?id=prime-directive-for-the-l&ref=rss, accessed May 20, 2009.

426 The number of uncontacted tribes: Elias Biggio (chief, Department of Isolated Indians, FUNAI), interview at his office in Brasília, December 9, 2009; e-mail.

426 A killer drought: Wallace, "Last of the Amazon," *National Geographic* 211, no. 1 (January 2007, 49).

426 Scientists called it: Simon L. Lewis et al., "The 2010 Amazon Drought," *Science* 331 (February 4, 2011): 554.

426 For the first time: Damian Carrington, "Mass Tree Deaths Prompt Fears of Amazon 'Climate Tipping Point,'" *Guardian,* February 3, 2011, http://www.guardian.co.uk/environment/2011/feb/03/tree-deaths-amazon-climate.

427 Eager to generate employment: Bryan Walsh, "Drilling for Oil Way, Way Offshore," *Time,* August 18, 2008, http://www.time.com/time/health/article/0,8599,1833379,00.html.

427 One official in the state oil: John Vidal, "Amazon's Uncontacted Tribe: How Media Coverage Can Trigger Action," *Guardian,* February 4, 2011, http://www.guardian.co.uk/environment/blog/2011/feb/04/amazon-uncontacted-tribe-media-coverage, accessed February 7, 2011.

427 The presence of isolated Indians: José "Pepe" Alvarez (director, Peruvian Amazon Research Institute), interview, Lima, Peru, September 24, 2008.

427 Breathless headlines pronounced: Michael Hanlon, "Incredible Pictures of One of Earth's Last Remaining Uncontacted Tribes Firing Bows and Arrows," *Daily Mail,* May 30, 2008, http://www.dailymail.co.uk/sciencetech/article-1022822/Incredible-pictures-Earths-uncontacted-tribes-firing-bows-arrows.html, accessed May 31, 2008; "Hoax of Lost Amazon Tribe," *Yahoo!,* www.yahoo.com, accessed June 24, 2008.

428 In effect, the media outlets: Stephen Pritchard, "The Reader's Editor on . . . How a Tribal People's Charity Was Misrepresented," *Observer,* August 31, 2008, http://www.guardian.co.uk/commentisfree/2008/aug/31/voluntarysector.

428 Loggers had invaded reserves: Upper Amazon Conservancy, "Peru: Illegal Mahogany Logging Continues in Reserve for Uncontacted Tribes," July 2010, http://www.upperamazon.org/PDF/Murunahua_Report_July2010.pdf; Survival

International, "Chronology of Evidence of Uncontacted Indians Fleeing from Peru to Brazil," March 2009, http://assets.survivalinternational.org/static/files/logging_report_eng.pdf.

428 Perhaps only a media campaign: *Human Planet Explorer,* BBC One, February 4, 2011, http://www.bbc.co.uk/nature/humanplanetexplorer/environments/jungles.

428 Director James Cameron traveled: Alexei Barrionuevo, "Tribes of Amazon Find an Ally out of 'Avatar,'" *New York Times,* April 10, 2010, http://www.nytimes.com/2010/04/11/world/americas/11brazil.html, accessed February 3, 2011.

429 Peruvian authorities promised: Vidal, "Amazon's Uncontacted Tribe."

429 In the summer of 2011: Scott Wallace, "Concern for Uncontacted Tribes as Armed Gang Invades the Forest," NewsWatch, NationalGeographic.com, August 8, 2011, http://newswatch.nationalgeographic.com/2011/08/08/concern-for-uncontacted-tribes-as-armed-gang-invades-brazilian-forest.

429 On the eastern side: "Brazil Murder of Indigenous Child Provokes Reaction," GlobalVoices.com, January 10, 2012, http://globalvoicesonline.org/2012/01/10/brazil-murder-indigenous-child-awa-guaja/.

429 Meanwhile, the government: "Brazil Dam Company Wins Belo Monte Appeal," BBC, December 16, 2011, http://www.bbc.co.uk/news/world-latin-america-16228680.

429 Not only will the $17 billion project: Survival International, "Tribe Reveals New Evidence of Uncontacted Indians Threatened by Dam," December 17, 2010, http://www.survivalinternational.org/news/6790, accessed December 21, 2010.

429 At the end of 2010: Sydney Possuelo, "Carta abierta en defensa de los pueblos indígenas aislados," Brasília, December 15, 2010, e-mail.

POSTSCRIPT

Page

432 The photo graces the cover: Gérard Moss and Margi Moss, *Brasil das Águas* (São Paulo: Supernova Editora, 2005).

Select Glossary
and Pronunciation Guide

Acre (AH-cray)—small Amazonian state in far western Brazil

Amazon—used interchangeably for the world's mightiest river and for the enormous region drained by its thousands of tributaries

DPF—Department of Federal Police

Etno—"The Ethnic," largest of the expedition boats

flecheiros (flay-SHAY-roze)—Arrow People, uncontacted tribe native to the Javari Valley

furo—a shortcut through flooded forest at a river bend

FUNAI—National Indian Foundation, Brazil's Indian affairs agency

homen branco—white man

igarapé (ee-gar-a-PAY)—a creek, or blackwater stream

índios bravos—wild Indians

Itaquaí (ee-tok-why-EE) River—tributary of Javari River and one of the main arteries of penetration into the depths of the Javari Valley Indigenous Land

Ituí (ee-too-EE) River—tributary of the Itaquaí River

Javari (zhah-var-EE) Valley Indigenous Land—Indian reserve in western Brazil drained by multiple tributaries of the Javari River and home of the largest concentration of uncontacted indigenous communities in the world

Jutaí (zhoo-tie-EE) River—Amazon tributary, expedition's exit route from the Javari

Juruá (zhoo-roo-AH) River—large Amazon tributary south of the Javari reserve

Kanamari (can-ah-mar-EE)—indigenous tribe inhabiting the banks of the Itaquaí and Jutaí rivers

Kayapó (ky-a-POE)—powerful tribe of the central Amazon basin, settled in scores of villages in the headwaters and along the tributaries of the Xingu River

Kukahá (koo-ka-HAH)—expedition boat and indigenous name for the Purús River

macaxeira (mock-a-SHARE-a)—manioc, the major staple crop of the Amazon

maloca (ma-LOW-ca)—a communal dwelling of indigenous people, or a thatched-hutted indigenous settlement

Maranhão (ma-ran-yeow)—largely deforested state in the eastern Amazon

Marubo (ma-ROO-bow)—indigenous tribe native to the upper Ituí River

mateiro—backwoodsman

Matis (ma-TISSE)—indigenous tribe native to upper Ituí River, the largest single ethnic group represented on the expedition

Mato Grosso—central Amazonian state, known for large-scale rainforest clearing to make way for cattle ranches and soy plantations

Pará (pah-RAH)—eastern Amazonian state renowned for violence and deforestation

quebrada (kay-BRA-dah)—snapped branch left by natives to mark their path as they walk through the forest

reais (REE-ice)—plural of *real*, the Brazilian currency

ribeirinho (ree-bay-REEN-yo)—riverbank dweller, a white or mixed-blooded Brazilian raised in the rural Amazon region

Rondon (Rhone-DOAN), Cândido—Brazilian army colonel and founder in 1910 of the SPI, the Indian Protection Service

Rondônia—western Amazonian state named after Col. Cândido Rondon

sertanista—wilderness scout dedicated to finding and protecting Brazil's isolated tribes

Sobral—expedition boat named after Raimundo "Sobral" Magalhães, *sertanista* clubbed to death by Korubo Indians

Solimões (SOLE-ee-moise) River—Brazilian name for the Amazon River above Manaus

SPI—Indian Protection Service, founded by Rondon, Alípio Bandeira, and others in 1910, merged with Central Brazil Foundation in 1967 to create FUNAI

tracajá (tra-ca-ZHA)—yellow-spotted Amazon river turtle

tracuá (track-QUA)—aggressive carpenter ant

tucandeira (too-can-DARE-ah)—bullet ant with hind stinger

Txikão (TEESH-cow)—warrior tribe of the central Amazon, pacified by the Villas Boas

Waiká (why-KAH)—expedition boat and name of a subtribe of the Yanomami

Xingu (shin-GOO) River—major north-flowing tributary of the Amazon

Zo'ê (Zoe-A)—isolated tribe native to the eastern Amazonian state of Pará

Bibliography

Abram, David. *The Spell of the Sensuous: Perception and Language in a More-Than-Human World*. New York: Vintage, 1996.

"The Amazon Ambassador." *TIME for Kids*, October 26, 1998. http://www.time.com/time/reports/environment/heroes/tfk/0,2967,tfk_possuelo,00.html.

"Amazonian Amphibian Diversity Traced to Andes." *Science Daily*, March 10, 2009. http://www.sciencedaily.com/releases/2009/03/090309205313.htm.

American Indian Program, Cornell University. *Brazil: Hot Spots*. Article downloaded from the Internet; no longer available but author has printed copy. Ithaca, N.Y.: Akwe:kon Press, December 31, 1996.

Amorim, Fabricio. "Povos indígenas isolados da Terra Indígena Vale do Javari." Brasília: FUNAI (Coordenação Geral de Índios Isolados), 2008.

"Andes Formation Was a 'Species Pump' for South America." *Science Daily*, January 11, 2009. http://www.sciencedaily.com/releases/2009/01/090109083451.htm

Angelo, Claudio. "Prime Directive for the Last Americans." *Scientific American*, April 25, 2007. http://www.scientificamerican.com/article.cfm?id=prime-directive-for-the-l&ref=rss.

Anoby, Stan, and David J. Holbrook. *A Survey of the Languages of the Javari River Valley*. Dallas: SIL International, 2010. http://www.sil.org/silesr/abstract.asp?ref=2010-003.

Arisi, Barbara Maisonnave. "Matis e Korubo: Contato e índios isolados, relações entre povos no Vale do Javari, Amazônia." Master's thesis, Universidade Federal de Santa Catarina, 2007. http://tede.ufsc.br/teses/PASO0186.pdf.

Barrionuevo, Alexei. "Tribes of Amazon Find an Ally out of 'Avatar.'" *New York Times*, April 10, 2010. http://www.nytimes.com/2010/04/11/world/americas/11brazil.html.

Bergman, Charles. "Wildlife Trafficking." *Smithsonian*, December 2009. http://www.smithsonianmag.com/people-places/Wildlife-Trafficking.html.

Biocca, Ettore. *Yanoáma: The Story of Helena Valero, a Girl Kidnapped by Amazonian Indians*. New York: Kodansha America, 1996.

"Bolivian Natives Tortured." *New York Times,* July 13,1912. http://query.nytimes.com/mem/archive-free/pdf?res=9C00E1DF1630E233A25750C1A9619C946396D6CF.

Brackelaire, Vincent. "Situación de los últimos pueblos indígenas aislados en América latina (Bolivia, Brasil, Colombia, Ecuador, Paraguay, Perú, Venezuela): Diagnóstico regional para facilitar estrategias de protección" (unpublished report). Brasilia, 2006. http://www.ibcperu.org/doc/isis/687.pdf.

Bradley Brooks and Associated Press. "Amazon River Dolphins Being Slaughtered for Bait." *U.S. News & World Report,* July 12, 2010. http://www.usnews.com/science/articles/2010/07/12/amazon-river-dolphins-being-slaughtered-for-bait.html.

Brasil, Kátia. "Eleição colombiana motiva ação na fronteira, diz general brasileiro." *Folha.com,* May 22, 2002. http://www1.folha.uol.com.br/folha/mundo/ult94u41603.shtml.

"Brazil Spies on Illegal Loggers." *BBC.* July 26, 2002. http://news.bbc.co.uk/2/hi/americas/2151222.stm.

Brown, Dee. *Bury My Heart at Wounded Knee: An Indian History of the American West.* New York: Bantam, 1971.

Brown, Michael F., and Eduardo Fernandez. "Tribe and State in a Frontier Mosaic: The Asháninka of Eastern Peru." In *War in the Tribal Zone: Expanding States and Indigenous Warfare,* edited by R. Brian Ferguson and Neil L. Whitehead, 413–27. Santa Fe: School of American Research Press, 1992.

Buckley, Stephen. "Brazil Fears Fallout of Drug Crackdown." *Washington Post,* October 1, 2002.

Campbell, David G. *Land of Ghosts: The Braided Lives of People and the Forest in Far Western Amazonia.* Boston: Houghton Mifflin, 2005.

Carneiro da Cunha, Manuela, and Mauro Barbosa de Almeida, eds. *Enciclopédia da floresta: O Alto Juruá: Práticas e conhecimentos das populações.* São Paulo: Companhia das Letras, 2002.

Carrington, Damian. "Mass Tree Deaths Prompt Fears of Amazon 'Climate Tipping Point.'" *Guardian,* February 3, 2011. http://www.guardian.co.uk/environment/2011/feb/03/tree-deaths-amazon-climate.

Carvajal, Gaspar de. *The Discovery of the Amazon.* Translated by Bertram T. Lee. New York: American Geographical Society, 1934.

Cavuscens, Silvio. *Pela sobrevivência dos povos indígenas do Vale do Javari.* Manaus, Brazil: CEDI, 1986.

Chagnon, Napoleon A. *Yanomamö: The Fierce People,* 3rd ed. Fort Worth: Holt, Rinehart and Winston, 1983.

Connolly, Bob, and Robin Anderson. *First Contact: New Guinea's Highlanders Encounter the Outside World.* New York: Penguin, 1988.

Costa, Luiz Antonio. "As faces do jaguar: Parentesco, história e mitologia entre os Kanamari da Amazônia Ocidental." Ph.D. diss., Museu Nacional da Universidade Federal do Rio de Janeiro, 2007. http://www.slideshare.net/anandex/as-faces-do-jaguar-parentesco-histria-e-mitologia-entre-os-kanamari-da-amaznia-ocidental.

Cowell, Adrian. *The Tribe That Hides from Man.* New York: Stein & Day, 1974.

da Cunha, Euclides. *The Amazon: Land Without History.* Edited by Lúcia Sá. Translated by Ronald Sousa. New York: Oxford University Press, 2006.

D'Altroy, Terrance N. *The Incas.* Oxford: Blackwell Publishing, 2002.

da Rocha Freire, Carlos Augustino. "Sagas sertanistas: práticas e representações do campo indigenista no século xx." Ph.D. diss., Universidade Federal do Rio de Janeiro, 2005. http://teses.ufrj.br/PPGAS_D/CarlosAugustoDaRochaFreire.pdf.

Davis, Wade. *One River: Explorations and Discoveries in the Amazon Rain Forest.* New York: Touchstone, 1996.

——. *The Wayfinders: Why Ancient Wisdom Matters in the Modern World.* Toronto: Anansi Press, 2009.

de Aquino, Txai Terri Valle, and Marcelo Piedrafita Iglesias. "Entrevista com o sertanista Meirelles. Parts I–X. Papo de Índio, *Página 20,* May 5, 2008; May 12, 2008; May 19, 2008; May 26, 2008; June 16, 2008; June 23, 2008; July 7, 2008; July 21, 2008; July 28, 2008; August 4, 2008.

de Candolle, Alphonse. *Origin of Cultivated Plants.* 2nd ed. London: Kegan Paul, Trench & Co., 1884.

de Castro, Ferreira. *Jungle: A Tale of the Amazon Rubber-Tappers.* New York: Viking, 1935.

de Figueiredo, Luiz Filipe. *Índios isolados: atração e sobrevivência eis a questão.* Cuiabá, Brazil: 2a Superintendecia da FUNAI, 1987.

de Oliveira, João Pacheco. "Sobre índios, macacos, peixes: narrativas e memórias de intolerância na Amazônia contemporânea." *Etnográfica* 5, no. 2 (2000): 290–91.

Diacon, Todd. *Stringing Together a Nation: Cândido Mariano da Silva Rondon and the Construction of a Modern Brazil, 1906–1930.* Chapel Hill, N.C.: Duke University Press, 2004.

Diamond, Jared. *Guns, Germs, and Steel.* New York: W.W. Norton, 1997.

Domville-Fife, Charles W. *Among Wild Tribes of the Amazons.* Philadelphia: J. B. Lippincott, 1924.

Dowie, Mark. *Conservation Refugees: The Hundred-Year Conflict Between Global Conservation and Native Peoples.* Cambridge, Mass.: MIT Press, 2009.

Downie, Andrew. "Champion for Brazil's Indigenous Gets Fired." *Christian Science Monitor,* January 26, 2006. http://www.csmonitor.com/2006/0126/p04s01-woam.html.

Dutfield, Graham. "Why Traditional Knowledge Is Important in Drug Discovery." *Future Medicinal Chemistry* 2, no. 9 (September 2010): 1405–9.

"Earth at Night" (map). *National Geographic.* November 2004.

Erikson, Philippe. "Uma singular pluralidade." In *História dos índios no Brasil,* edited by Manuela Carneiro da Cunha, 239–52. São Paulo: FAPESP/SMC, 1992.

Faleiros, Gustavo. "Brazilian President's Promises Crumble Under the Weight of Belo Monte." *Guardian,* February 1, 2011. http://www.guardian.co.uk/environment/blog/2011/feb/01/brazil-dilma-rousseff-hydroelectric-dam.

Feldman, Stanley. *Poison Arrows: The Amazing Story of How Prozac and Anesthetics Were Developed from Deadly Jungle Poison Darts.* London: Metro Publishing, 2005.

Ferguson, R. Brian. *Yanomami Warfare: A Political History.* Santa Fe: School of American Research Press, 1995.

Forsyth, Adrian, and Ken Miyata. *Tropical Nature: Life and Death in the Rain Forests of Central and South America.* New York: Touchstone, 1995.

FUNAI. "Projecto índios isolados." Ministério da Justiça. Last updated 2007. Accessed July 7, 2009. http://www.mj.gov.br/data/Pages/MJD0E56FE7ITEMIDE686F24 4540E4961BC3786AD6E76BE6FPTBRNN.htm.

———. "Projecto Javari." Ministério da Justiça. Last updated 2007. Accessed July 7, 2009. http://www.mj.gov.br/data/Pages/MJD0E56FE7ITEMIDF544570BEB04 45988704857DFB7815A4PTBRIE.htm.

FUNAI archives. Brasília and Museu Nacional do Índio, Rio de Janeiro.

Galeano, Juan Carlos. *Folktales of the Amazon.* Translated by Rebecca Morgan and Kenneth Watson. Westport, Conn.: Libraries Unlimited, 2009.

Gellerman, Bruce. "REDD Path to a Green Planet." *Living on Earth,* September 11, 2009. http://www.loe.org/shows/segments.htm?programID=09-P13-00037 &segmentID=6.

Gheerbrant, Alain. *The Amazon: Past, Present, and Future.* Translated by I. Mark Paris. New York: Harry N. Abrams, 1992.

———. *Journey to the Far Amazon*. Translated by Edward Fitzgerald. New York: Simon & Schuster, 1954.

"Good Eyesight? Thank Snakes." *ABC News*. August 30, 2006. http://abcnews.go.com/Technology/DyeHard/story?id=2371692&page=1.

Goodman, Jordan. *The Devil and Mr. Casement: One Man's Battle for Human Rights in South America's Heart of Darkness*. New York: Farrar, Straus & Giroux, 2010.

Goulding, Michael, Ronaldo Barthem, and Efrem Jorge Gondim Ferreira. *The Smithsonian Atlas of the Amazon*. Washington: Smithsonian Books, 2003.

Grann, David. *The Lost City of Z: A Tale of Deadly Obsession in the Amazon*. New York: Doubleday, 2009.

Greaves, Russell D. "The Ethnoarcheology of Hunting and Collecting: Pumé Foragers of Venezuela." *Expeditions* 49 no. 1 (Spring 2007): 18–27.

Hanlon, Michael. "Incredible Pictures of One of the Earth's Last Remaining Uncontacted Tribes Firing Bows and Arrows." *Daily Mail*, May 30, 2008. http://www.dailymail.co.uk/sciencetech/article-1022822/Incredible-pictures-Earths-uncontacted-tribes-firing-bows-arrows.html.

Hecht, Susanna, and Alexander Cockburn. *The Fate of the Forest*. New York: Harper-Collins, 1990.

Hemming, John. *Amazon Frontier: The Defeat of the Brazilian Indians*. London: Macmillian, 1987.

———. *Die If You Must: Brazilian Indians in the Twentieth Century*. London: Macmillian, 2003.

———. "Last Explorer of the Amazon: Distinguished Historian John Hemming Profiles the Career of Brazilian Explorer Sydney Possuelo, Who Was Recently Awarded a Royal Geographical Society Gold Medal for His Work with the Indigenous Peoples of the Amazon." *Geographical* 77 (February 2005): 59–63.

———. *Tree of Rivers: The Story of the Amazon*. New York: Thames & Hudson, 2008.

Hering, Richard, and Stuart Tanner. *Plunder for Profit: The UK and Brazilian Mahogany Trade*. London: Friends of the Earth, 1998. http://www.foe.co.uk/resource/reports/plunder_for_profit.pdf.

"Hoax of Lost Amazon Tribe." *Yahoo!*, June 24, 2008.

Hochschild, Adam. *King Leopold's Ghost: A Story of Greed, Terror, and Heroism in Colonial Africa*. Boston: Houghton Mifflin, 1998.

Huertas Castillo, Beatriz. *Indigenous Peoples in Isolation in the Peruvian Amazon.* Copenhagen: International Work Group for Indigenous Affairs, 2004.

Human Planet Explorer, "Jungles—People of the Trees." BBC One. February 4, 2011. http://www.bbc.co.uk/nature/humanplanetexplorer/environments/jungles.

"Just Saying Yes." *Brazzil,* January 1997. http://www.brazzil.com/cvrjan97.htm.

Kearns, Rick. "Colombian Indigenous Still in Danger of Extinction." *Indian Country Today,* October 31, 2010. http://www.indiancountrytoday.com/home/content/Colombian-indigenous-still-in-danger-of-extinction-106308458.html.

Kelly, John D. "Seeing Red: Mao Fetishism, Pax Americana, and the Moral Economy of War." In *Anthropology and Global Counterinsurgency,* edited by John D. Kelly, Beatrice Jauregui, Sean T. Mitchell, and Jeremy Walton, 67–83. Chicago: University of Chicago Press, 2010.

King, J. C. H. *First Peoples, First Contacts: Native Peoples of North America.* Cambridge, Mass.: Harvard University Press, 1999.

Kozloff, Nicolas. *No Rain in the Amazon: How South America's Climate Change Affects the Entire Planet.* New York: Palgrave MacMillan, 2010.

Kricher, John. *A Neotropical Companion.* Princeton, N.J.: Princeton University Press, 1997.

Kroeber, Theodora. *Ishi in Two Worlds: A Biography of the Last Wild Indian in North America.* Berkeley: University of California Press, 1961.

Lagrou, Elsje Maria. "Kaxinawá." *Povos indígenas no Brasil.* Last updated November 2004. Accessed November 19, 2010. http://pib.socioambiental.org/en/povo/kaxinawa/print.

Lamb, F. Bruce. "Wizard of the Upper Amazon as Ethnography." *Current Anthropology* 22, no. 5 (October 1981): 577–80. http://www.jstor.org/stable/2742293.

Lamb, F. Bruce, and Manuel Córdova-Rios. *Kidnapped in the Amazon Jungle.* Berkeley: North Atlantic Books, 1994.

Laurance, W. F., et al. "The Future of the Brazilian Amazon." *Science* 291, no. 5503 (January 2001): 438–39.

Lévi-Strauss, Claude. *Tristes Tropiques: An Anthropological Study of Primitive Societies in Brazil.* Translated by John Russell. New York: Atheneum, 1972.

Lewis, Meriwether, and William Clark. *The Journals of Lewis and Clark.* Edited by Bernard DeVoto. Boston: Houghton Mifflin, 1953.

Lewis, Norman. "Genocide." *Sunday Times Magazine* (London), February 23, 1969.

Lewis, Simon L., et al. "The 2010 Amazon Drought." *Science* 331 (February 4, 2011): 554.

London, Mark, and Brian Kelly. *The Last Forest: The Amazon in the Age of Globalization.* New York: Random House, 2007.

Long, William R. Long. "A New Call for Indian Activists." *Los Angeles Times,* February 9, 1993. http://articles.latimes.com/1993-02-09/news/wr-1380_1_latin-america/7.

MacLeish, Kenneth, and John Launois (photographer). "The Tasadays: Stone Age Cavemen of Mindinao." *National Geographic* 142, no. 2 (August 1972): 218–49.

MacQuarrie, Kim. *The Last Days of the Incas.* New York: Simon & Schuster, 2007.

Mann, Charles C. *1491: New Revelations of the Americas Before Columbus.* New York: Knopf, 2005.

McIntyre, Loren, and W. Jesco von Puttkamer (photographer). "Last Days of Eden." *National Geographic* 174, no. 6 (December 1988): 800–817.

Michael, Lev. "How 'We' Became 'White People': A Tale of Indigenous Onomastic Strategies." *Greater Blogazonia,* November 8, 2007. http://anthroling.wordpress.com/2007/11/08/how-we-became-white-people-a-tale-of-indigenous-onomastic-strategies/.

Millard, Candice. *The River of Doubt: Theodore Roosevelt's Darkest Journey.* New York: Doubleday, 2005.

Millman, Lawrence. *An Evening Among Headhunters and Other Reports from Roads Less Traveled.* Cambridge, Mass: Lumen Editions, 1998.

Moffett, Mark W. *Adventures Among Ants: A Global Safari with a Cast of Trillions.* Berkeley: University of California Press, 2010.

Moss, Gérard, and Margi Moss. *Brasil das Águas.* São Paulo: Supernova Editora, 2005.

Nance, John. *The Gentle Tasaday.* New York: Harcourt Brace Jovanovich, 1975.

Neves, Eduardo. "Amazônia—Ano 1000." *National Geographic Brasil,* May 2010. http://viajeaqui.abril.com.br/national-geographic/edicao-122/antigas-civilizacoes-amazonia-552374.shtml.

Nossa, Leonêncio. "Expedição amazônica busca tribos desconhecidas." *O Estado de São Paulo,* June 10, 2002.

———. *Homens Invisíveis.* Rio de Janeiro: Editora Record, 2007.

O'Connor, Geoffrey. *Amazon Journal: Dispatches from a Vanishing Frontier.* New York: Dutton, 1997.

"Os Arara saem da mata." *Veja,* March 11, 1981.

"Our Role in Stopping the Illegal Brazilian Mahogany Trade." *Greenpeace News and Blogs,* October 15, 2003. http://www.greenpeace.org/usa/en/news-and-blogs/news/our-role-in-stopping-the-illeg/.

Owen, James. "Fighting for the Survival of Uncontacted Tribes." *NatGeo News Watch,* April 29, 2010. http://blogs.nationalgeographic.com/blogs/news/chiefeditor/2010/04/fighting-for-the-survival-of-uncontacted-tribes.html.

————. "Vampire Bats Attacking Cattle As Rain Forest Falls." *National Geographic News,* August 20, 2007. http://news.nationalgeographic.com/news/pf/49980020.html.

Pirinop: My First Contact. DVD. Directed by Mari Corrêa and Karané Ikpeng. Olinda, Brazil: Vídeo nas Aldeis, 2007.

Plotkin, Mark J. *Tales of a Shaman's Apprentice: An Ethnobotanist Searches for New Medicines in the Amazon Rain Forest.* New York: Penguin, 1993.

Popescu, Petru. *Amazon Beaming.* New York: Viking Press, 1991.

Posey, Darrell Addison. "Biodiversity, Genetic Resources, and Indigenous Peoples in Amazonia: (Re)Discovering the Wealth of Traditional Resources of Native Amazonians." Paper presented at Amazonia 2000 conference, Institute of Latin American Studies, University of London, 1998.

Possuelo, Sydney. "Carta abierta en defensa de los pueblos indígenas aislados." Brasília: December 15, 2010, e-mail.

————."Frentes de atração: A última fronteira." Brasília: FUNAI archives, August 27, 1981.

Possuelo, Sydney, et al. *Coodenadoria de índios isolados: Sistema de proteção ao índio isolado.* Brasília: FUNAI, 1987.

Pritchard, Stephen. "The Reader's Editor on . . . How a Tribal People's Charity Was Misrepresented," *Observer,* August 31, 2008. http://www.guardian.co.uk/commentisfree/2008/aug/31/voluntarysector.

Raffaele, Paul. "Out of Time." *Smithsonian,* April 2005. http://www.smithsonianmag.com/travel/Out_of_Time.html.

Raglan, Lord. *How Came Civilization?* London: Methuen & Co., 1939.

Ramos, Alcida Rita. *Indigenism: Ethnic Politics in Brazil.* Madison: University of Wisconsin Press, 1998.

Reel, Monte. *The Last of the Tribe: The Epic Quest to Save a Lone Man in the Amazon.* New York: Scribner, 2010.

Ribeiro, Darcy. *Maíra*. Translated by E. H. Goodland and Thomas Colchie. New York: Vintage, 1984.

———. *Os índios e a civilização: A integração das populações indígenas no Brasil moderno*. São Paulo: Companhia de Letras, 1996.

Rochas, Jan. "Orlando Villas Boas." Obituary. *Guardian*, December 14, 2002.

Rockafellar, Nancy. "The Story of Ishi: A Chronology." University of California, San Francisco. Last modified 2010. http://history.library.ucsf.edu/ishi.html.

Romero, Simon. "Wider Drug War Threatens Colombian Indians." *New York Times*, April 21, 2009. http://www.nytimes.com/2009/04/22/world/americas/22colombia .html?scp=1&sq=embera%20indians&st=cse.

Ruedas, Javier. "Variability in Marubo Politics." *Tipití: Journal of the Society for Anthropology of Lowland South America* 2, no. 1 (June 2004): 23–64.

Sale, Kirkpatrick. *The Conquest of Paradise*. New York: Knopf, 1990.

Sant'Anna, Lourvival. "Ecos de um outro tempo." *Estado de São Paulo*, November 25, 2007. http://estado.com.br/amazonia/reservas_ecos_de_um_outro_tempo.htm.

"Satellites Show Amazon Parks, Indigenous Reserves Stop Forest Clearing." *Science Daily*, January 27, 2006. http://www.sciencedaily.com/releases/2006/01/060 126200147.htm.

"Saw Wholesale Murder in the Amazon Rubber Fields." *New York Times*, August 4, 1912.

Schipani, Andrés, and John Vidal. "Malaria Moves In Behind the Loggers." *Guardian*, October 23, 2007. http://www.guardian.co.uk/world/2007/oct/30/ environment.climatechange.

Schneebaum, Tobias. *Keep the River on Your Right*. New York: Grove Press, 1969.

Scott, James C. *The Art of Not Being Governed: An Anarchist History of Upland Southeast Asia*. New Haven: Yale University Press, 2009.

The Search for the Kidnappers. DVD. Directed by Adrian Cowell. Birmingham, England: Central Independent Television, 1988.

Searle, Francis F. "Peruvian Explorations and Settlements on the Upper Amazons." *Report of the Thirty-ninth Meeting of the British Association for the Advancement of Science; Held at Exeter in August 1869*. London: John Murray, 1870.

Sharp, Lauriston. "Steel Axes for Stone-Age Australians." In *Conformity and Conflict: Readings in Cultural Anthropology*. Edited by James P. Spradley and David W. McCurdy, 413-427. Boston: Little, Brown and Company, 1974.

Shepard, Glenn, Jr. *Informe 1: Los grupos indígenas aislados del río Las Piedras.* Report presented to Mobil Exploration Peru, Lima, Peru, 1996.

Shepard, Glenn H., Jr., et al. "Trouble in Paradise: Indigenous Populations, Anthropological Policies, and Biodiversity Conservation in Manu National Park, Peru." *Journal of Sustainable Forestry* 29, no. 2 (2010): 252–301.

Singh, Raghubir. "The Last Andaman Islanders." *National Geographic* 148, no. 1 (July 1975): 66–91.

Smith, Anthony. *Explorers of the Amazon.* Chicago: University of Chicago Press, 1990.

Smith, Nigel J. H. "Aquatic Turtles of Amazonia: An Endangered Resource." *Biological Conservation* 16 (1979), http://www.clas.ufl.edu/users/nsmith/pub/Aquatic%20turtles%20of%20Amazonia%20Bological%20Conservation%201979%20Nigel%20Smith.pdf.

Söderström, Erling. "The White Triangle: Anti-Cocaine Operations in the Javari Forest." Korubo. Last updated 2001. Accessed July 21, 2009. http://www.korubo.com/AMAZONDOC/coca.htm.

Sponsel, Leslie E. "Ecological Anthropology." *In Encyclopedia of Earth,* edited by Cutler J. Cleveland. Washington, D.C.: Environmental Information Coalition, National Council for Science and the Environment. Last updated May 2007. Accessed February 5, 2011. http://www.eoearth.org/article/Ecological_anthropology.

Stanfield, Michael Edward. *Red Rubber, Bleeding Trees: Violence, Slavery, and Empire in Northwest Amazonia, 1850–1933.* Albuquerque: University of New Mexico Press, 1998.

Stannard, David E. *American Holocaust: The Conquest of the New World.* New York: Oxford University Press, 1992.

Stephenson, Carl. "Leiningen Versus the Ants. " In *Twenty-one Great Stories,* edited by Abraham H. Lass and Norma L. Tasman. New York: Mentor, 1969.

Steward, Julian H., ed. *Handbook of South American Indians.* Vol. 1, *The Tropical Forest Tribes.* Washington, D.C.: United States Government Printing Office, 1948.

Survival International. *Arara* (action bulletin). June 2004. http://assets.survivalinternational.org/static/files/related_material/45_22_160_arara_bulletin_june_04_pdf.pdf.

———. "Chronology of Evidence of Uncontacted Indians Fleeing from Peru to Brazil." March 2009. http://assets.survivalinternational.org/static/files/logging_report_eng.pdf.

———. "Tribe Reveals New Evidence of Uncontacted Indians Threatened by Dam." December 17, 2010.

The Tailenders. DVD. Directed by Adele Horne. Harriman, N.Y.: New Day Films, 2005.

Tierney, Patrick. *Darkness in El Dorado: How Scientists and Journalists Devastated the Amazon.* New York: W.W. Norton, 2000.

Turner, Terence. "The Yanomami and the Ethics of Anthropological Practice." *Anthropological Niche of Douglas W. Hume.* Updated November 12, 2010. Accessed February 5, 2011. http://www.nku.edu/~humed1/darkness_in_el_dorado/documents/0497.htm.

Turner, Terence, and Leslie E. Sponsel. "Imminent Anthropological Scandal." Memo to Louise Lamphere, president, American Anthropological Association, and Don Brenneis, president-elect, AAA. September 2000. Accessed February 5, 2011. http://www.nku.edu/%7Ehumed1/darkness_in_el_dorado/documents/0055.htm.

UNCTAD and the BioTrade Facilitation Programme. *Arapaima Gigas: Market Study.* Geneva: United Nations Conference on Trade and Development, 2006.

Up de Graff, Fritz W. *Head Hunters of the Amazon; Seven Years of Exploration and Adventure.* New York: Duffield & Co., 1923.

Upper Amazon Conservancy. "Peru: Illegal Mahogany Logging Continues in Reserve for Uncontacted Tribes." July 2010. http://www.upperamazon.org/PDF/Murunahua_Report_July2010.pdf.

USAID. *Report: 17th Annual Meeting of the Environment Program.* Belén, Pará Brazil: USAID, October 2009.

Vidal, John. "Amazon's Uncontacted Tribe: How Media Coverage Can Trigger Action." *Guardian,* February 4, 2011. http://www.guardian.co.uk/environment/blog/2011/feb/04/amazon-uncontacted-tribe-media-coverage.

von Puttkamer, W. Jesco. "Brazil's Kreen-Akarores: Requiem for a Tribe" and "Brazil's Txukahameis: Good-bye to the Stone Age." *National Geographic* 147, no. 2 (February 1975): 254–83.

Wallace, Scott. "Hunting Down the Sons of Reagan." *Independent,* May 13, 1987.

———. "Into the Amazon." *National Geographic* 204, no. 2 (August 2003): 2–23.

———. "Last of the Amazon." *National Geographic* 211, no. 1 (January 2007): 40–71.

———. "The Mega-Fauna Man." *National Geographic Adventure* 8, no. 10 (December 2006–January 2007): 66–72, 108.

———. "Napoleon in Exile." *National Geographic Adventure* 4, no. 3 (April 2002): 52–61, 98–100.

———. "The Real Miskito Coast," *Newsweek,* December 15, 1986.

————. "Support Won with Terror." *Guardian,* July 13, 1989.

Walsh, Bryan. "Drilling for Oil Way, Way Offshore." *Time,* August 18, 2008. http://www.time.com/time/health/article/0,8599,1833379,00.html.

Watson, Fiona, et al. *Disinherited: Indians of Brazil.* London: Survival International, 2000.

Wells, Spencer. *The Journey of Man: A Genetic Odyssey.* New York: Random House, 2003.

Whitehead, Neil L. *Dark Shamans: Kanaima and the Poetics of Violent Death.* Durham, N.C.: Duke University Press, 2002.

Wright, Ronald. *Stolen Continents: The "New World" Through Indian Eyes.* New York: Houghton Mifflin, 1992.

Index